Public Opinion and Constitutional Controversy

Public Opinion and Constitutional Controversy

Edited by

Nathaniel Persily
Jack Citrin
Patrick J. Egan

OXFORD
UNIVERSITY PRESS

2008

OXFORD
UNIVERSITY PRESS

Oxford University Press, Inc., publishes works that further
Oxford University's objective of excellence
in research, scholarship, and education.

Oxford   New York
Auckland   Cape Town   Dar es Salaam   Hong Kong   Karachi
Kuala Lumpur   Madrid   Melbourne   Mexico City   Nairobi
New Delhi   Shanghai   Taipei   Toronto

With offices in
Argentina   Austria   Brazil   Chile   Czech Republic   France   Greece
Guatemala   Hungary   Italy   Japan   Poland   Portugal   Singapore
South Korea   Switzerland   Thailand   Turkey   Ukraine   Vietnam

Published by Oxford University Press, Inc.
198 Madison Avenue, New York, New York 10016

www.oup.com

Oxford is a registered trademark of Oxford University Press

Library of Congress Cataloging-in-Publication Data
Public opinion and constitutional controversy / edited by Nathaniel Persily,
Jack Citrin, and Patrick J. Egan.
   p. cm.
ISBN: 978–0–19–532941–4
ISBN: 978–0–19–532942–1 (pbk.)
1. Constitutional law—United States—Public opinion.
2. Public opinion—United States.   I. Persily, Nathaniel.   II. Citrin, Jack. III. Egan, Patrick J.
KF4550.P82 2008
342.73—dc22 2007025711

9 8 7 6 5 4 3 2 1

Printed in the United States of America

For my mother, Nancy Alfred Persily—NP
For my wife, Bonnie, and my daughter, Sarah—JC
For my parents, Dennis and Jane Egan—PJE

Contents

Contributors

Ryan Brown was research assistant to Nathaniel Persily from 2006 to 2007.

Jack Citrin is Heller Professor of Political Science and Director of the Institute for Governmental Studies at U.C. Berkeley.

Shari Seidman Diamond is a Senior Research Fellow at the American Bar Foundation and the Howard J. Trienens Professor of Law and Professor of Psychology at Northwestern University School of Law.

Patrick J. Egan is Assistant Professor in the Wilf Family Department of Politics at New York University.

Alison Gash is a Ph.D. candidate in Political Science at U.C. Berkeley.

Angelo Gonzales is a Ph.D. candidate in Political Science at U.C. Berkeley.

Darshan Goux is a Ph.D. candidate in Political Science at U.C. Berkeley.

Joshua A. Green is a Ph.D. candidate in Political Science at U.C. Berkeley.

John Hanley is a Ph.D. candidate in Political Science at U.C. Berkeley.

Peter Hanson is a Ph.D. candidate in Political Science at U.C. Berkeley.

Matthew G. Jarvis is Assistant Professor of Political Science at California State University, Fullerton.

Son-Ho Kim is a Ph.D. candidate at the Annenberg School for Communication of the University of Pennsylvania.

Loan Le is a Ph.D. candidate in Political Science at U.C. Berkeley.

Amy E. Lerman will be Assistant Professor of Politics and Public Affairs at Princeton University (commencing fall 2008).

Samantha Luks, Ph.D., is Director of Special Projects for YouGov/Polimetrix, a survey research firm in Palo Alto, California.

Manoj Mate is a Ph.D. candidate in Political Science at U.C. Berkeley and a Mellon-Sawyer Predoctoral Fellow at the Center for the Study of Law and Society for 2007–08.

Serena Mayeri is Assistant Professor at University of Pennsylvania Law School.

Megan Mullin is Assistant Professor of Political Science at Temple University.

Michael Murakami is an American Political Science Association Congressional Fellow and a Ph.D. candidate in Political Science at U.C. Berkeley.

Janice Nadler is a Research Fellow at the American Bar Foundation and Professor at Northwestern University School of Law.

Matthew M. Patton is a Ph.D. candidate in Social Psychology at the University of Chicago and a Doctoral Fellow at the American Bar Foundation.

Nathaniel Persily is Professor of Law and Political Science at Columbia Law School.

Michael Salamone is a Ph.D. candidate in Political Science at U.C. Berkeley.

Kevin Wallsten will be Assistant Professor of Political Science of California State University, Long Beach (commencing fall 2008).

Matthew Wright is a Ph.D. candidate in Political Science at U.C. Berkeley.

Acknowledgments

When we began this project, we were surprised by the absence of a book that assembled in one place all the public opinion data on contemporary constitutional controversies. After almost two years of work on this book, we no longer are puzzled by that former vacuum in the scholarly literature. This book represents the culmination of heroic efforts by a number of people, without whom this book never would have gotten off the ground.

We first must thank the chapter authors for their diligence, patience, and ingenuity. They bore the brunt of the task of gathering and analyzing all of the survey data presented here. Most of the chapters in this book are the first of their kind, and all at least provide an updated account of the state of public opinion on their particular issue and the relationship between such opinion and prominent Court decisions.

The raw material of these chapters was further forged by our excellent editors, Amy Einsohn, David McBride, and Brian Desmond. Most of these chapters are unrecognizable from the first drafts, and the book is much improved because of our editors' skill and insight. We also thank Adrienne Donovan and Katherine Minette for inputting the thousands of edits made by the authors.

For much of the survey data analyzed here, we, like all public opinion analysts, owe a great debt to archives of surveys that together have made it possible to analyze trends in Americans' attitudes on politics and social issues. This book would not have been possible without the American National Election Studies, the General Social Survey of the National Opinion Research Center, and the collections of the Roper Center for Public

Opinion Research. Several of the chapters also benefited greatly from the efforts of librarian Bill Draper at the University of Pennsylvania Law School, who searched assiduously and effectively for all data sets available on some of these topics.

For support, both financial and moral, we thank the Institute of Governmental Studies (IGS) at U.C. Berkeley. IGS played a special role in the intellectual development of many of the authors and provided a haven for us to meet to discuss and debate these chapters. Liz Wiener at IGS was indispensable in providing so much of the administrative work that a volume such as this requires. In addition, Patrick Egan acknowledges the Center for the Study of Democratic Politics at Princeton University's Woodrow Wilson School, where he was a visiting scholar for the 2006–07 academic year.

We benefited greatly from comments received from a number of reviewers. We thank, in particular, Thomas Marshall, Lee Epstein, Barry Friedman, Robert Shapiro, Gordon Silverstein, and Robert Kagan.

Public Opinion and Constitutional Controversy

Introduction

Nathaniel Persily

More than a century and a half ago, Alexis de Tocqueville observed: "There is hardly a political question in the United States which does not sooner or later turn into a judicial one" (Tocqueville 1969). Were he writing today, de Tocqueville might be equally struck by issue evolution in the opposite direction, with judicial opinions serving as the progenitors of political conflict and constitutional controversies increasingly defining the political cleavages of the American public. Whether the conflict concerns racial integration or abortion, school prayer or gay rights, flag burning or the right to die, the most polarizing controversies of today's politics often find a home in the courtroom as well as in the legislative chamber or candidate debate.

This book examines these and other constitutional controversies by focusing on the opinions the American public has expressed in the last half century of polling on these issues. Others have assessed the magnitude and importance of these debates by focusing on elite behavior and organized political action, but we were struck by the absence of a book that presents in one place the reservoir of relevant public opinion data (Rosenberg 1991; Klarman 2005). Indeed, for all the talk about the centrality of these highly emotional issues to modern political discourse, voting behavior, and public policy debates, systematic analysis of opinion on the collection of topics explored here presents itself only sporadically in journal articles, in the postmortem discussion of a particular election, or in individual chapters in larger works (Page & Shapiro 1992; Mayer 1993).

More than a compendium of interesting data on high-profile social conflicts, this book makes two chief contributions to contemporary debates concerning the place of public opinion in the constitutional order. The first concerns the burgeoning literature on "popular constitutionalism" that attempts to shift attention away from courts' pronouncements on the Constitution and toward the behavior of elected officials and popular social movements (Balkin & Siegel 2006; Balkin 2005; Kramer 2004; Tushnet 1999; Post & Seigel 2000). The second revolves around age-old questions concerning the political effects of Supreme Court decisions and therefore the proper role the Court should play in American democracy (Rosen 2006; Rosenberg 1991; Klarman 2005; Ely 1980).

The data presented and analyzed here inform, but do not settle, the debates in these respective literatures. The chapters that follow present public opinion data to describe what the American people have believed about these issues over the past half century and to infer from this how, if at all, court decisions have influenced the public's views. For those who argue about the preferability of a more democratic constitutional discourse or about the Court's abuse of its monopoly on constitutional interpretation, understanding where the American people stand on these issues represents an indispensable first step toward making such normative arguments.

Popular Constitutionalism and Public Opinion

Although many strands of the jurisprudential worldview now called "popular constitutionalism" have emerged, they are united by a general argument that constitutional discourse ought not to be the exclusive province of judges and lawyers. The Framers contemplated a system of constitutional development, the argument goes, involving all branches of government, at the state and federal levels, as well as the active participation of "the people themselves" (Kramer 2004). Therefore, the Supreme Court ought not have the final word on constitutional questions but rather participate as one player in a long-term, multiroped interpretive tug-of-war between groups of elites in different branches of government and the people on the outside. Under this view, what the Constitution means could change with each generation, not due to evolution in authoritative pronouncements from the Supreme Court, but from successful organization and persuasion by political leaders and the mass public.

Popular constitutionalism is both a way around and a response to the so-called countermajoritarian difficulty presented by the position of the judicial branch in our constitutional system (Bickel 1986; Friedman 1998; Somin 2003; Mishler & Sheehan 1993). That "difficulty," if it is one, serves the purposes of several different kinds of arguments. On the one hand, advocates point to federal courts' countermajoritarian nature as their chief virtue: No other institution of government is designed to protect "discrete and insular minorities" or unpopular individuals exercising rights the Constitution protects. Whether the subject is the integration of schools, protecting the right of

Communists to speak, or securing the equal right to marry, courts are better positioned than the political branches to defend the rights of the unpopular. On the other hand, what makes countermajoritarianism difficult are the necessarily unpopular stances the courts take when striking down legislation majorities have supported. Therefore, each exercise of judicial review must be justified by some theory as to why unelected, life-tenured judges ought to interpret the Constitution in a way as to check majority will. The omnipresent fear that judges might behave like Platonic guardians—or worse, like Leviathans—often presents itself in arguments about judges imposing their own values on the Constitution or arrogantly predicting the trajectory of Americans' (or even other countries') understanding of constitutional values. More pragmatically, lacking the power of the purse and the sword, the judiciary's effectiveness ultimately depends on its legitimacy—the belief that its decisions are morally valid. To some extent, the degree of difficulty presented by the Court's countermajoritarian status can be assessed by how out of step its decisions are with public opinion on constitutional issues. After all, if the Court merely reflected public opinion in its decisions, then whatever other problems it might have, it could not be described as countermajoritarian. Although the distinctive feature of the judicial role and position is its supposed insulation from the pressures of public opinion, in several recent cases the courts and litigants have put forth public opinion polls as evidence supporting a particular constitutional interpretation.[1] When used in this way, appeals to majoritarian sentiment (whether measurable or not) often justify a mode of constitutional argument that views the Constitution as a "living document" and judges' role as helping the Constitution keep up with the times. Critics of this position reply that the Constitution should keep up with the times through the amendment process and that judges are particularly unqualified to assess and evaluate majoritarian sentiment.

Curiously absent from the literature on popular constitutionalism or the countermajoritarian difficulty is any evaluation of what "the people themselves" actually think about the issues the Supreme Court has considered. If one is to place faith in mass politics as an avenue for constitutional development, public opinion on constitutional controversies ought to figure prominently in assessments of why an elitist view of judge-driven constitutionalism is inappropriate. For the most part, popular constitutionalists look to legislation, executive enforcement, and official acts of obstruction, rather than mere popular beliefs that fail to mature into observable political action. Indeed, there are good arguments in favor of paying attention to formal political activity, rather than nascent political beliefs. Nevertheless, popular understanding of particular constitutional rights and powers would seem to be a critical part of the story of how the Constitution should evolve to meet the changing demands of each generation.

To ascertain popular attitudes about the most pressing, or at least notorious, constitutional controversies, each chapter in this book examines trends in aggregate opinion on a particular issue with attention to events, such as court decisions, that may have shifted the public in one direction or another. Most chapters also gauge the salience of such events, as well as elite attention to the issue, by charting media coverage of the issue over the relevant period as well. Although we tend to think of the issues covered in this book as hot-button and widely publicized, extensive media coverage of events such as court decisions is rare and seldom sustained (Schauer 2006).

The available trend data on the topics in the following chapters can be categorized into three groups: those where opinion has become more liberal or more conservative, those where it has stayed relatively constant, and those where it shows no consistent trajectory. Even where we do find opinion change over time, however, we do not presume that individual minds have changed or that particular events, such as court decisions, are responsible for the observed change. In many instances, cohort replacement explains much of the change over time in public opinion—newer cohorts with liberal beliefs replace older ones with more traditionalist attitudes on moral values questions.

Of the topics analyzed in this book, attitudes toward racial integration of schools, gay rights, gender equality, flag burning, and the right to die have become more liberal. A larger share of the American public today than at the time polling began expresses support for integration, protecting gay rights, providing equal rights to women, granting a right to assisted suicide, and opposing a constitutional amendment prohibiting flag burning. This is not to say that a majority now takes a liberal position but simply that the trajectory has been relatively consistent in a liberal direction. Nor does this mean that on the more extreme subsets of these topics—such as busing, gay marriage, or drafting women into the army—the trajectory is comparable to what it is on the more general topic.

For most of the topics in this book, it is fair to say that a majority of the American public adheres to the conservative position, but rarely can we point to a consistent trajectory in a conservative direction. Public opinion on the death penalty, for example, shows consistent majorities in favor, although the trajectory in recent years has reversed course somewhat from the steep pro-death penalty trajectory of the 1970s and 1980s. The opposite may be true for abortion, school prayer, and affirmative action: a previous liberalizing trend appears to have leveled off or reversed in the past few decades. Most other controversies exhibit little change in aggregate opinion or sporadic change with no consistent trajectory. On issues such as the rights of the accused, the proper balance between national security and civil liberties, federalism, or government takings of private property, longitudinal polling data are unavailable, and what we have suggests levels of opinion remaining unchanged or rising and falling based on certain circumstances.

Each chapter also sets forth the structure of opinion on the topic and analyzes how groups break down in their attitudes. In several chapters, the most interesting analyses concern "who" believes "what" rather than "how much" of the American public has sided with a particular position over time. This is especially true for the topics for which the sporadic nature of polling constrains authors' abilities to assess change over time. The chapters provide the summary statistics for typical demographic and ideological groupings, as well as multivariate analysis to gauge the independent effect of certain variables while controlling for all others. Several chapters present more detailed statistical techniques, such as a bloc recursive analysis, in order to isolate the direct and indirect effects of different variables or families of variables.

Although the pattern of group differences in opinion varies considerably from one topic to another, a few social and political characteristics jump out as frequent explanatory variables across an array of constitutional controversies. Age, education, religiosity, and ideology (self-placement on a liberal-conservative continuum) tend to be among the most powerful predictors of opinion, especially on "moral values" issues, such as abortion, school prayer, gay rights, and the right to die. In some instances, race, gender, or region (usually South versus non-South) also plays a role, although less often than one might think once those earlier controls are added. Of course, the authors' ability to break down opinion into its constituent parts is constrained by the presence or absence of other questions on the given surveys.

The particular mix and order of questions on a given survey, the timing and frequency of surveys, and the particular wording of the relevant questions present inescapable limitations on this book. At the same time, the chapters' exploration of these limitations represents an important goal of the study. For example, question wording often has a major influence on the distribution of expressed preferences. This fact is not cause for writing off public opinion polling as akin to astrology or for resigning ourselves to the canard that you can get a majority to agree with anything if you tailor the question to do so. The effect of different frames on responses tells us something about the ambivalence of the public on a given issue and the strategies that might shift opinion in one direction or another as people make trade-offs among their values. For example, as the chapter on gay rights indicates, whether one includes a civil union option in a question can dramatically alter the levels of support and opposition to laws prohibiting same-sex marriage. Similarly, with respect to abortion, affirmative action, or the right to die, survey questions concerning the circumstances under which the respondent would support a given right or policy provide a more refined measure of aggregate opinion on the issue than questions that force a yes or no response.

We do not pretend that the analysis of aggregate shifts in public opinion on constitutional controversies, the structure of opinion, or the effect of certain frames on response rates will settle the "popular constitutionalism" debate. Rather, we hope it informs the positions of advocates on both sides, who often make assumptions about what the general public, as opposed to judges and lawyers, believes about these issues. Understanding where the American public stands on these issues can allow one to evaluate the costs and benefits of a more pluralized and less court-focused approach to constitutional development.

The Effect of Court Decisions on Public Opinion

Understanding public opinion about constitutional controversies allows us not only to measure the gap between Court decisions and public attitudes on these various issues but also to assess the relationship between the two. Most of the literature on the connection between Court decisions and public opinion focuses on public opinion of the Supreme Court itself or how responsive the Court may be to public opinion change (Caldeira & Gibson 1992; Gibson, Caldeira, & Spence 2003a and 2003b; Murphy, Tanenhaus, & Kastner 1973; Murphy & Tanenhaus 1969; Murphy & Tanenhaus 1974; Murphy & Tanenhaus 1968b; Murphy & Tanenhaus 1981; Dahl 1957; Epstein & Kobylka 1992; Epstein et al. 2001). For the most part, those authors find that opinion of the Court itself shifts more with attitudes toward government in general and that the effect of public opinion on Court decisions exists as a complex process in which public moods get incorporated through the appointment of new justices or through responses by the other branches of government. Thomas Marshall's 1989 study, *Public Opinion and the Supreme Court*, stands alone, though, as the only work that has attempted to examine across many issue areas how Court decisions affect public opinion on the issues the Supreme Court has considered.

The chapters in this volume seek to identify which of several hypothetical relationships between court decisions and subsequent public opinion occurred. One possible outcome, of course, is stability or lack of aggregate change in opinion. Indeed, we find that in the vast majority of the cases reviewed here, Supreme Court decisions had no effect on the overall distribution of public opinion. However, in some instances, we find evidence of public opinion shifts in line with or contrary to a particular decision. We label these outcomes as legitimation and backlash, respectively. Finally, in other cases we notice a change in the structure of opinion following a court decision, with groups shuffling their positions without, however, producing a significant alteration of aggregate opinion. We describe this last outcome as polarization.

No single hypothesis provides a universally applicable explanation for how and when courts affect public opinion. Moreover, the same Court decision might lead to short-term backlash, medium-term polarization, and long-term legitimation. We recognize that the effect of a court decision—as mediated through other elite action and mass mobilization—may be felt more over the long term than in the few years following the decision. Controversial holdings—such as the one-person, one-vote rule, the requirement of *Miranda* warnings, or perhaps the striking down of bans on same-sex sex—may become accepted over the long run, while others, such as upholding a right to an abortion, may become more controversial over time and generate increased opposition a decade after the decision. As difficult as it is to assess causality for short-term effects—a serious problem all chapters here confront—it is even more so with respect to changes in public opinion over the long term. We do not argue that the public opinion effects of a court decision—as with any legislative or executive action—should be felt only in its immediate aftermath. Nor do we deny that the independent effect of a court decision is often impossible to disentangle from the range of coinciding events that may affect public opinion.

If we had to summarize the findings of the very different chapters that follow, we would say simply that court decisions are events like any other. They can elevate issues onto the national agenda through media coverage, elite discussion, and other behavior that follows in their wake. The nature of court decisions' effects on public opinion is usually a product of the way elites react to the decision and the messages they send to the mass public concerning the issue adjudicated. To be sure, the reaction of elites will be a function of the degree to which a court decision upsets the status quo, the preexisting salience of the issue, and perhaps the level of division on the Court. However, we cannot arrive at any global conclusion as to how court decisions in the abstract will shape public thinking about constitutional issues. The idiosyncratic nature of constitutional controversies, however, makes the endeavor of this book that much more interesting. Identifying which cases have led to which reactions is a first step toward developing any larger theory about how the Court as an institution should relate to the mass public.

The Null Hypothesis: The Irrelevance of Court Decisions to Public Opinion on Constitutional Issues

For the most part, the decisions of the Supreme Court and other courts go unnoticed by the American public.[2] We should not be surprised to discover that in the overwhelming majority of cases, therefore, public opinion does not shift at all in response to a decision. Most issues courts deal with, whether they revolve around torts, antitrust, federal statutes, or even important questions of constitutional law, are overly complex and/or below the radar of both the mainstream media and public attention. The public often does not have either the relevant information concerning the court's decision or the tools to understand it, and we should not expect public opinion to change on those issues.

Moreover, even with highly salient and understandable issues (e.g., abortion, gay marriage, the death penalty), there is no a priori reason to believe that a court decision will shift people's opinions, which up until the decision have often been based on strong moral or political convictions. For a court decision to have an effect, public attitudes must be movable. Some share of the public must have an open mind such that the persuasive or repulsive effect of the decision itself or elites' transmission of it will shift a noticeable number of people toward or away from the court's position. If the public has all the information it needs and attitudes are firmly fixed, even a court decision on a controversial issue should not produce a public policy effect.

Most of the chapters in this book find the type of non-effect described here. For example, we are unsurprised to find that the Court's federalism decisions had no observable effect on public opinion. They are simply too complex and obscure to have altered the flimsy beliefs that most people have on the relevant issues. The same is true of the Court's terrorism decisions: although terrorism and national security are obviously salient issues, the court decisions concerning them have not been, and the precise legal issues involved are too complex to garner widespread, understandable media coverage. Similarly, with affirmative action and gender discrimination, the court cases themselves have not registered any noticeable public opinion changes in their immediate aftermath. Even with respect to very salient abortion decisions after *Roe v. Wade*, we cannot find any immediate subsequent shift in public opinion.

It may be the case, of course, that with some of these decisions the indirect effects will be felt over the long term. For example, it may be too soon to tell what the effect of the Terri Schiavo case has been on public opinion with respect to the right to die. Early surveys suggest it may have led to a rise in support for physician-assisted suicide, but no consistent pattern has emerged. Similarly, with respect to the Court's decision in *Kelo v. New London*, which most point to as provoking a backlash on the issue of government takings of private property, relevant polling data prior to the decision are unavailable. It may be the case that the public has always been against such takings and that the high level of disapproval noted following the decision is not new.

The Legitimation Hypothesis: Supreme Court as Republican Schoolmaster

A second hypothesis, known in the political science literature as the legitimation hypothesis, suggests that in some cases public opinion will adjust to align with court decisions (Lerner 1967; Eisgruber 1992; Rostow 1952; McCloskey 1960). In other words, some share of the population takes its cues as to how to think about issues from the courts, which are relatively respected institutions as compared with the political branches. Once courts, especially the Supreme Court, weigh in on an issue, perhaps some share of the population will now say, in effect, "if they believe it, it must be right." Those who view courts as some sort of conscience for the American people expect or hope that judges will lead us to our better selves—to be a "republican schoolmaster," as some have termed the Supreme Court. Whether the Court is persuading the American people of the unfairness of segregation or marshaling its political and institutional capital to weigh in on who should win the 2000 election, the relative respect the public has for the Court may lead to a presumption in favor of the position it takes in cases.

Only under special conditions and among certain populations should we expect the Court to act as an opinion leader. In one respect, we should expect the Court to have the most influence on issues that are complex and technical and among populations with weak prior beliefs. When an issue is confusing or novel, the Court's decision is likely to be the only (or perhaps the most credible) signal that the average person receives. That being said, the person must actually *receive* the signal: for the decision to have any effect on public attitudes, the issue must be one where the media conveys the Court's signal to the population. Of course, these factors cut in opposing directions. On the one hand, we should expect the Court to have the greatest influence on low-salience issues about which most people have not yet developed opinions, while at the same time, for the Court to have any influence, the news of its decision must be salient enough for it to be transferred to the public. We also might add into this mix the importance of the clarity of the Court's signal: unanimous decisions might have a greater pro-decision effect than divided rulings because the information flow directed toward the otherwise unin-formed public would be more likely to be one-sided (Zaller 1992). The power and clarity of the Supreme Court's signal on an issue could be obscured by the expressed opinions of elites other than dissenting justices. Uniform approval of the Court's decision (as with any public policy) should have a greater pro-decision public opinion effect than a decision that creates a firestorm of disap-proval; that is, the elite filter for the Court's decisions can be more important for the impact of the Court's signal than either the reasoning of the opinion itself or the unanimity of agreement on the Court.

Given the many ingredients needed for the Court to behave as an opin-ion leader, perhaps we should not be surprised that very few previous studies have found court decisions that shift public opinion in the Court's direction. Experiments that prime a subset of respondents as to the Supreme Court's ruling on an issue yield conflicting results as to the persuasive effect of the sig-nal sent by the Court's imprimatur (Mondak 1994; Jaros & Roper 1980; Bass & Thomas 1984). Valerie Hoekstra also finds some support for the notion that in the community directly affected, a court decision can shift public opinion in a positive direction (Hoekstra 2000 & 2003). Marshall finds some evidence that the Court's decisions striking down bans on interracial marriage or restric-tive covenants were followed by favorable public opinion trends, but given the preexisting liberal trends on these issues, it is unclear if the Court's action accelerated those trends (Marshall 1989).

To make an inference that a Court decision (and elite transmission of it) had some persuasive effect on opinion, one must be able to compare the trajectory of opinion before and after the Court's decision. If the trajectory changes course or is steeper following a decision, then perhaps the court decision was influential. We were surprised to find very few instances of a short-term legitimating effect of court decisions. Rarely do we see a notice-able conversion of the public to the Court's position immediately following a particular case. More often what we see is legitimation over the longer term, sometimes produced by a "slingshot" effect—with opinion shifting immedi-ately away from the Court's decision but eventually moving in the Court's direction. Such was the case with many of the most controversial Warren Court precedents. For example, *Brown v. Board of Education* appears to have been followed by a small and temporary backlash in opinion on desegregation of schools, particularly in the South, which soon reversed course. The same appears true of the Court's decisions on school prayer and flag burning, although, unlike desegregation, strong majorities continue to support a position contrary to that of the Court. Although we do not have enough continuous data on the rights of the accused, it is clear that the public is now much more supportive of the Court's decision in *Miranda v. Arizona* than it was in the immediate aftermath of the decision.

Backlash

A third theory about the relationship between court decisions and public opinion ("backlash") has engendered little systematic exploration, even if popular and scholarly accounts often suggest that "activist" decisions lead the public to lash back at the Court. The psychological and political dynamic that produces backlash is a bit complicated. In the event the public has a low opinion of the Court to begin with and therefore has a presumption against its decisions, we would expect the opposite dynamic to that predicted by the legitimation hypothesis. Precisely because an unpopular institution (the Court) advocates a particular position, the public will then react as if to say "if they believe it, then it must be wrong." However, backlash usually has roots that grow from sources other than a broad dislike of the institution issuing the decision. A court decision on an issue could raise its salience in some respondents' minds, and they perceive a threat they did not perceive before. Or perhaps, in the wake of a court decision, elites and interest groups mobilize against its holding, discussion of the issue becomes more critical than when the issue was absent from the media radar screen, and a section of the public then develops an opinion contrary to the Court's resolution of the case. Moreover, insofar as the decision itself has tangible policy effects (e.g., busing or the settling of a presidential election) or the political branches respond with laws that have tangible policy effects, respondents may accordingly change their positions on the issue because of these newly observed and felt implications of the Court's decision.

Backlash should be more likely when the decision is salient enough to send a signal to an otherwise inattentive public and simple enough for the public to understand it and react unfavorably. Similar to the case of legitimation, we should expect those with little information or weak prior beliefs to be most likely to change their minds. In other words, the *swayable* public should be the most susceptible to the Court's legitimating or backlash-inducing decisions, as should be true for any government action.

As mentioned before, several prominent Warren Court cases produced a short-term backlash. More recently, the Court's decision protecting the right of gays to have sex led to a temporary antigay backlash, limited not only to opinion on sodomy laws but also to the issue of same-sex marriage. In other instances, the Court's decision may have accelerated a preexisting trajectory against the Court's position. For example, support for the death penalty climbed markedly in the years following the Court's 1972 decision in *Furman v. Georgia*, which cast doubt on the constitutionality of the death penalty. However, that pro-death penalty trajectory may have preceded the Court's decision, and it continued to climb even after the Court reversed course in *Gregg v. Georgia* (1976) four years later. Finally, the recent decision in *Kelo v. New London* (2005) provoked a measurable political backlash, at least among elites, on the issue of government takings of private property. However, as noted previously, the available public opinion data do not allow us to conclude that public opinion changed as a result: the public was probably never much in favor of such takings, so the high level of disapproval following that decision was probably consistent with the preexisting trend.

Polarization

Not only might public opinion move in the same or opposite direction as the Court's decision but also a decision could alter the structure or group breakdown of public opinion on an issue. Many people might change their minds on an issue following court intervention even though the aggregate shift in opinion might appear slight or nonexistent. In addition, a decision could solidify people's prior beliefs, causing them to feel more strongly about the issue.

For polarization to occur, we suspect elite signals must be quite clear, and the issue should be salient enough such that those signals will be sent and received. Unlike legitimation or backlash, though, we should expect a two-sided information flow to be more likely to cause polarization than would a situation in which elite signals all push in the same direction (Zaller 1992). We should expect the undecided and the uninformed to pick sides according to elite discussion of the decision, with people taking cues from their reference groups and from opinion leaders they trusted before the decision. What might have been a bell-shaped or even random distribution of opinion prior to a court decision, under certain conditions could turn into more of a bimodal distribution as people sort themselves according to elite framing of the issue. Such "sorting out" could occur on the basis of ideology, partisanship, religion, race, or any other group-defining characteristic.

The paradigmatic case of polarization is public opinion concerning abortion. The public appeared to become slightly more pro-choice in the immediate aftermath of *Roe v. Wade*, a trend that preexisted the decision but plateaued soon afterward. The aggregate shifts mask change in the structure of opinion on abortion, however. The chapter on abortion in this book confirms the findings of Charles Franklin and Liane Kosaki (1989), who noticed that *Roe* led to an increasing polarization among demographic groups regarding the legalization of non-health-related abortions. In particular, the gap in opinion on discretionary abortion grew in 1973 between whites and blacks and between Protestants and Catholics.

In other instances, we find politicization of conflict, as the Court's injection into a constitutional controversy leads to partisan or ideological divisions on issues that previously did not have that character. On flag burning, for example, Republicans and Democrats have slowly diverged in the years since the Court issued its opinion protecting flag burning as a right of free speech. We also find that on the issue of gay rights the Court's decision legalizing sodomy in *Lawrence v. Texas* (2003) has led to greater ideological polarization on that issue. If you know where people place themselves on a liberal-conservative continuum, you are better able now to predict their position, particularly on same-sex marriage, than you could before that decision.

Assessing causality in political phenomena is always fraught with danger, and perhaps especially so when trying to identify the causes of public opinion shifts. However, even when we cannot conclude that *x* court decision led to *y* public opinion effect, we can ascertain the gap between the Court and the American people on a given issue. Those gaps, as the research contained in the following chapters concludes, have often been formidable and, in some cases, continue to grow.

Although this book focuses on public opinion about constitutional issues and the effect of court decisions on such opinions, implicit in all of the analysis is a concern about how to assess whether the Court has gone too far. We therefore conclude this volume with a discussion of public opinion of the Court itself, paying particular attention to the controversy surrounding the 2000 presidential election. The story told in the last chapter, like that of the chapters dealing with particular issues, reveals the resiliency of the Court in American public opinion. Under conditions of the greatest stress—integrating schools, protecting criminals' rights, interjecting itself into all types of life-and-death questions, and even deciding a presidential election—the aggregate level of public confidence in the Court has remained largely unchanged.

Recognizing the Court's resiliency will not assuage the concerns of those who view one or another decision as "activist" or "illegitimate." Nor do we expect the data here to persuade people as to the underlying merits of a particular constitutional interpretation. Rather, the goal of the chapters that follow is to counter much of the misinformation that exists about what the American people believe about certain constitutional disputes and how the Court may have indirectly shaped their beliefs. Understanding the dynamics of public opinion on these intense moral and political debates represents a first step toward marshaling the evidence needed to form a more general theory about the proper roles of both the mass public and the insular Court in constitutional development.

Notes

1. See, e.g., *Atkins v. Virginia*, 536 U.S. 304 (2002) (striking down law permitting execution of mentally retarded defendants, based in part on polls suggesting the public was against such executions); *McConnell v. FEC*, 251 F. Supp. 2d 176, 512–15 (D.D.C.) (opinion of Kollar-Kotelly, J.), *aff'd in part*, 124 S. Ct. 619 (2003) (upholding most of the Bipartisan Campaign Reform Act based on polls showing public perception of corruption). Marshall (1989) notes that the Supreme Court referred to public opinion in 142 opinions between 1934 and 1985–86, although most references to polls occur in death penalty cases.

2. See, e.g., Murphy and Tanenhaus (1968b) (finding that only 12.8% of American adults are aware of the Court's existence, recognize its function, and believe it to be impartial and competent); Murphy and Tanenhaus (1990) (updating their previous work, in the context of the Bork nomination fight); Caldeira (1990) (citing a 1989 *Washington Post* poll in which fewer than 10% of respondents could name the Chief Justice of the U.S. Supreme Court, although more than a quarter of respondents could identify television's Judge Wapner).

References

Balkin, Jack. 2005. "How Social Movements Change (or Fail to Change) the Constitution: The Case of the New Departure." *Suffolk Law Review* 39: 27.

Balkin, Jack, and Reva Seigel. 2006. "Principles, Practices, and Social Movements." *University of Pennsylvania Law Review* 154: 927.

Bass, Larry R., and Dan Thomas. 1984. "The Supreme Court and Policy Legitimation: Experimental Tests." *American Political Quarterly* 12: 335.

Bickel, Alexander. 1986. *The Least Dangerous Branch: The Supreme Court at the Bar of Politics*. New Haven: Yale University Press.

Caldeira, Gregory A. 1990. "Courts and Public Opinion." In *The American Courts: A Critical Assessment*, edited by John B. Gates and Charles A. Johnson. Washington, DC: Congressional Quarterly Press.

Caldeira, Gregory A., and James L. Gibson. 1992. "The Etiology of Public Support for the Supreme Court." *American Political Science Review* 36: 635–60.

Dahl, Robert. 1957. "Decision Making in a Democracy: The Supreme Court as a National Policy Maker." *Journal of Public Law* 6: 279.

De Tocqueville, Alexis. 1969. *Democracy in America* (George Lawrence, trans., J. P. Mayer, ed.). Garden City, New York: Doubleday.

Eisgruber, Christopher. 1992. "Is the Supreme Court an Educative Institution?" *NYU Law Review* 67: 961.

Ely, John Hart. 1980. *Democracy and Distrust: A Theory of Judicial Review*. Cambridge: Harvard University Press.

Epstein, Lee, and Joseph F. Kobylka. 1992. *The Supreme Court and Legal Change: Abortion and the Death Penalty*. Chapel Hill: University of North Carolina Press.

Epstein, Lee, et al. 2001. "The Supreme Court as a Strategic National Policymaker." *Emory Law Journal* 50: 583.

Franklin, Charles H., and Liane C. Kosaki. 1989. "Republican Schoolmaster: The U.S. Supreme Court, Public Opinion and Abortion." *American Political Science Review* 83: 751.

Friedman, Barry. 1998. "The History of the Countermajoritarian Difficulty, Part One: The Road to Judicial Supremacy." *NYU Law Review* 73: 333.

Gibson, James L., Gregory A. Caldeira, and Lester Kenyatta Spence. 2003a. "Measuring Attitudes toward the United States Supreme Court." *American Political Science Review* 47: 354.

———. 2003b. "The Supreme Court and the U.S. Presidential Election of 2000: Wounds, Self-Inflicted, or Otherwise?" *British Journal of Political Science* 33: 535.

Hoekstra, Valerie. 2000. "The Supreme Court and Local Public Opinion." *American Political Science Review* 94: 89.

———. 2003. *Public Reaction to Supreme Court Decisions.* New York: Cambridge University Press.

Jaros, Dean, and Robert Roper. 1980. "The U.S. Supreme Court: Myth, Diffuse Support, Specific Support, and Legitimacy." *American Political Quarterly* 8: 85.

Klarman, Michael. 2005. "Brown and Lawrence (and Goodridge)." *Michigan Law Review* 104: 431–89.

Kramer, Larry. 2004. *The People Themselves: Popular Constitutionalism and Judicial Review.* New York: Oxford University Press.

Lerner, Ralph. 1967. "The Supreme Court as Republican Schoolmaster." *Supreme Court Review* 1967: 127.

Marshall, Thomas. 1989. *Public Opinion and the Supreme Court.* Boston: Unwin Hyman.

Mayer, William G. 1993. *The Changing American Mind: How and Why American Public Opinion Changed between 1960 and 1988.* Ann Arbor: University of Michigan Press.

McCloskey, Robert G. 1960. *The American Supreme Court.* Chicago: University of Chicago Press.

Mishler, William, and Reginald S. Sheehan. 1993. "The Supreme Court as a Countermajoritarian Institution? The Impact of Public Opinion on Supreme Court Decisions." *American Political Science Review* 87: 87.

Mondak, Jeffrey J. 1994. "Policy Legitimacy and the Supreme Court: The Sources and Contexts of Legitimation." *Political Research Quarterly* 47: 675.

Murphy, Walter, and Joseph Tanenhaus. 1968a. "Public Opinion and Supreme Court: The Goldwater Campaign." *Public Opinion Quarterly* 32: 31.

———. 1968b. "Public Opinion and the United States Supreme Court: Mapping of Some Prerequisites for Court Legitimation of Regime Changes." *Law & Society Review* 2: 357.

———. 1969. "Constitutional Courts and Political Representation." In *Modern American Democracy,* edited by M. Danielson and W. Murphy. New York: Holt, Rinehart and Winston.

———. 1974. "Explaining Diffuse Support for the United States Supreme Court: An Assessment of Four Models." *Notre Dame Law Review* 49: 1037.

———. 1981. "Patterns of Public Support for the Supreme Court: A Panel Study." *Journal of Politics* 43: 24.

———. 1990. "Publicity, Public Opinion and the Court." *Northwestern University Law Review* 84:985.

Murphy, Walter, Joseph Tanenhaus, and D. Kastner. 1973. *Public Evaluations of Constitutional Courts: Alternative Explanations.* Beverly Hills, Calif.: Sage.

Page, Benjamin I., and Robert Y. Shapiro. 1992. *The Rational Public: Fifty Years of Trends in Americans' Policy Preferences.* Chicago: University of Chicago Press.

Post, Robert C., and Reva B. Siegel. 2000. "Equal Protection by Law: Federal Antidiscrimination Legislation after Morrison and Kimel." *Yale Law Journal* 110: 441–526.

Rosen, Jeffrey. 2006. *The Most Democratic Branch: How the Courts Serve America.* New York: Oxford University Press.

Rosenberg, Gerald N. 1991. *The Hollow Hope: Can Courts Bring about Social Change?* Chicago: University of Chicago Press.

Rostow, Eugene V. 1952. "The Democratic Character of Judicial Review." *Harvard Law Review* 66: 193.

Schauer, Frederick. 2006. "Foreword: The Court's Agenda—and the Nation's." *Harvard Law Review* 120: 4.

Somin, Ilya. 2003. "Political Ignorance and the Countermajoritarian Difficulty: A New Perspective on the Central Obsession of Constitutional Theory." *Iowa Law Review* 89: 1287.

Tushnet, Mark. 1999. *Taking the Constitution Away from the Courts.* Princeton, N.J.: Princeton University Press.

Zaller, John. 1992. *The Nature and Origins of Mass Opinion.* New York: Cambridge University Press.

1

Desegregation

Michael Murakami

On June 28, 2007, the U.S. Supreme Court issued a split 5–4 decision striking down the integration plans of public school districts in Seattle and Louisville because of their explicit use of individual students' race as criteria. All of the opinions in *Parents involved in Community Schools v. Seattle School District No. 1* (2006) claimed the mantle of racial progress and equality under the law that was the spirit of perhaps *the* most famous Supreme Court ruling ever issued: *Brown v. Board of Education of Topeka, Kansas*. Writing for a four-justice plurality, Chief Justice John Roberts argued the school districts' efforts resembled segregation policies before the landmark ruling: "Before *Brown*, schoolchildren were told where they could and could not go to school based on the color of their skin." Justice Stephen Breyer's dissenting opinion countered that comparing the programs under review, which attempt to bridge the racial divide rather than exacerbate it, is a "cruel distortion of history." Responding to the Chief Justice's suggestion that "the way to stop discrimination on the basis of race is to stop discriminating on the basis of race," Justice Kennedy's dispositive, hair-splitting concurring opinion admonished that "Fifty years of experience since *Brown v. Board of Education*...should teach us that the problem before defies so easy a solution." This rhetorical melee shows that even generations later, *Brown* is a decision that cannot be ignored, not just because of its legal precedent, but because of its prominent place in American history, basic civics education, and the national conscience.

Although most cases before the Supreme Court pass unnoticed by even careful observers of current affairs, the unanimous decision delivered on May 17, 1954, immediately captured the attention of elected officials, legal commentators, and ordinary citizens alike. Everyone understood that the Court was committing the nation to a new and historic course when it declared "separate educational facilities are inherently unequal" and ruled segregation in the public schools unconstitutional.

Some scholars credit *Brown* with having planted the seeds of the civil rights movement (Wilkinson 1979; Dudziak 1988; Fiss 1991; Greenberg 1994; Douglas 1995; Horwitz 1998; Finkelman 2005). Others, although acknowledging that the case inspired the succeeding wave of civil rights activists, suggest the movement would have launched even in the absence of *Brown* (Patterson 2001). A smaller group of researchers, however, raise doubts about the Court's influence on policy and education. Wolters (1984) concluded desegregation was a failure in four of the five school systems from the original *Brown* case—a testament to the limits of the judiciary's influence absent the cooperation of Congress, the executive branch, and local officials. Rosenberg (1991, 1994) emphasized that the segregation ban did little to integrate schools or colleges, increase black political involvement, or improve race relations. He also asserted there was no evidence to suggest the case changed the attitudes of whites or blacks or that it raised the salience of civil rights issues among the general public. Klarman (2004, 2005) took the argument a step further, claiming that *Brown* was a temporary setback for civil rights because it mobilized the segregationists and reversed the trend of increasing black voter suffrage (see also McMillen 1971; Greenberg 1994).

Few of these scholars, however, were able to benefit from the comprehensive analysis of public opinion surveys on segregation in the schools and on racial issues more generally. One difficulty concerns the dearth of polling about race and education prior to and (to a lesser extent) following *Brown*: "there was a 'tendency' by pollsters to overlook the 'race problem' when civil rights issues have been 'out of the public eye'" (Rosenberg 1991, 127). By focusing on a question asked by the Gallup organization during the seven years immediately after *Brown*, this chapter demonstrates how public sentiment rose and fell in response to the rhetoric of public officials, the positions stated by opinion leaders, and dramatic showdowns at Southern public schools and colleges.

Public Opinion on Integration and Segregation before *Brown*

In June 1942, the National Opinion Research Center (NORC) conducted one of the earliest available polls on the subject of race relations.[1] It portrays a public wary of racial integration in many areas of social life, presenting a snapshot of public opinion about segregation before the issue rose to the top of the national political agenda. Respondents displayed a moderate level of support for the segregation of public transportation, with 51% agreeing that there should be "separate sections for Negroes in street cars and buses." At this early point of U.S. involvement in World War II, 51% of respondents opposed integration of the armed forces. Support for segregation was even higher when the domain in question was brought closer to home. Eighty-four percent of respondents supported residential segregation, believing there should be "separate sections in towns and cities for Negroes to live in," while more than 90% of whites, even outside the South, were opposed to interracial marriage (from Gallup 1972, in Klarman 2005, 7).

Perceptions of educational inequality, at least at the local level, were strikingly low. The vast majority of respondents thought Negroes who lived in their town should (89%) and did (85%) have the same chance as whites to get a good education. Seventy-five percent thought Negroes in their "part of the country" had the same chance as whites to get a good education, but 54% thought that opportunities were not equal in all parts of the country, and 77% recognized that in general Negroes were not as well educated as whites. Thus, although most respondents believed there was a racial disparity in educational results and even in opportunity, many did not see inequalities in their own town or region.

When asked why they thought Negroes were not as well educated as whites, respondents most commonly offered a "lack of ambition" as the explanation (34%), followed by unequal educational opportunities (11%), the prejudice of whites (13%), Negroes' socioeconomic status (13%), and Negroes' innate inability to learn (8%).[2] Respondents tended to attribute differences in educational attainment to blacks' failure to work hard rather than to the effects of either racism or biological inferiority. When asked, "Do you think white students and Negro students should go to the same schools or to separate schools?" 66% preferred separate schools, and only 30% opted for the same schools. The argument that education played a unique role in shaping an informed citizenry and individual life chances, and therefore that equal access to equal education was a fundamental right—a cornerstone of the *Brown* decision—had not yet permeated public sentiment: support for segregated schools was higher than for segregated transportation and armed forces.

After this 1942 NORC survey, little national polling on segregation or racial issues was taken until after the *Brown* decision. Nevertheless, many scholars have inferred that the public's mood had become more supportive of desegregation. The notable contribution of black soldiers during World War II began to soften opposition to desegregation of the military, and President Truman issued Executive Order 9981 in July 1948, officially desegregating the armed forces over objections from Southern Democrats in Congress. Many observers found it intolerable that black soldiers who had risked their lives to help defeat the Axis Powers had no voting rights or equal access to public services when they returned home to the Jim Crow South. More and more commentators noted the disparity between America's democratic ideals and America's realities, an incongruence that undermined America's position in the ideological war against Communism (Dudziak 1988; Klarman 2004). Against this backdrop came a series of small but real changes in segregationist policies: in the South, black voter registration increased from 3% in 1940 to 20% in 1950 (Garrow 1978); blacks began serving on Southern juries; many

Southern urban areas began to integrate their police forces; major and minor league baseball, as well as many intercollegiate athletic organizations, integrated white and black athletes, and many Southern states peacefully desegregated their graduate and professional schools (Klarman 2005). It is difficult to imagine this pattern of events—shaped in large part by elected officials—in the absence of growing public support for desegregation.

The Immediate Reaction to *Brown*

Just days after the unanimous decision in *Brown*, Gallup asked a national sample this question: "The U.S. Supreme Court has ruled that racial segregation in the public schools is illegal. This means that all children, no matter what their race, must be allowed to go to the same schools. Do you approve or disapprove of this decision?" Almost 58% of all respondents and 80% of non-Southerners agreed with the decision initially. But during the first seven months after the decision was announced, public approval slowly declined, bottoming out at 54% in December 1954.

Local and state public officials' immediate reaction to *Brown* reflected regional practices and values. Georgia Governor Herman Talmadge, one of the most frequent and unabashed critics of the decision, promised, "There never will be mixed schools while I am Governor." He lambasted the Court for "blatantly ignor[ing] all law and precedent and usurp[ing] from the Congress and the people the power to amend the Constitution and from the Congress the authority to make the laws of the land" and remarked that the decision "confirms the worst fears of the motives of the men who sit on its bench and raises a grave question as to the future of the nation" ("Southern Leaders Vary in Reaction to Ruling," May 18, 1954, Los Angeles Times). Eugene Cook, Georgia's attorney general and president of the National Association of Attorneys General, commented that "[t]his decision has provoked a social, economic, political, and legal revolution in at least 23 States," later adding that if it became necessary to maintain educational segregation, he would abolish the public schools and give white and Negro children funds to attend separate private schools ("Southern Leaders Vary"; "Dixie Maps Fight for Segregation," May 19, 1954, L.A. Times). Governors Hugh White of Mississippi and William Umstead of North Carolina immediately voiced their disapproval as well, while Governor Thomas B. Stanley of Virginia stated, "I shall use every legal means at my command to continue segregated schools in Virginia" ("Stanley Backs Segregation," June 26, 1954, *New York Times*). At the local level, there was a clear Southern "determination to preserve segregation despite any action by the Supreme Court" ("Southern Leaders Vary").

Senator James O. Eastland of Mississippi affirmed that the South "will not abide by nor obey this legislative decision by a political court" and that attempts at school desegregation would cause "great strife and turmoil." Fellow Senator John C. Stennis asserted that "schools will continue to be separate in Mississippi" ("Talmadge Stands on Segregation," June 7, 1954, *N.Y. Times*), while Representative John Bell Williams, also of Mississippi, feared that "Negro education and interracial comity suffered their most damaging setback since the War Between the States" ("Mississippi Representative Hopes for Calm, but Eastland Sees Strife," May 17, 1954, *N.Y. Times*).

Some local officials were much more cautious in their rhetoric, however. State Education Commissioner Arch Ford of Arkansas declared his state to have the best race relations in the South, expressing confidence that the state would find a satisfactory result, while Governor Phil M. Donnelly of Missouri said he trusted the citizens of his state to abide by the law and uphold the Constitution ("Arkansas," May 17, 1954, *N.Y. Times*). Politicians in Border States and in states where segregation was allowed but not mandatory offered some of the least inflammatory reactions. In Kansas, Governor Edward Arn declared matter-of-factly that the "long-litigated question has now been decided," and Assistant Attorney General Paul Wilson believed segregation in the Kansas schools could be "ended in two years without any great problem" ("Kansas," May 17, 1954, *N.Y. Times*). In Kentucky, Governor Lawrence W. Wetherby said state officials would comply with the law, while State Superintendent of Public Instruction Wendell P. Butler speculated the most difficult problem would be convincing white parents to approve of sending their children to classes taught by Negro teachers.

Outside the South, newspaper editorial boards led the charge in support of the groundbreaking decision. In an editorial days after the decision, the *New York Times* acknowledged the difficult path ahead, conceding "These matters cannot be hurried," but was generous with praise: "[w]hen some hostile propagandist rises in Moscow or Peking to accuse us of being a class society we can if we wish recite the courageous words of yesterday's opinion. The highest court in the land, the guardian of our national conscience, has reaffirmed its faith...in the equality of all men and all children before the law" ("All God's Chillun," May 18, 1954). The *Washington Post* predicted, "[t]he decision will prove—whatever transient difficulties it may create and whatever irritations it may arouse—a profoundly healthy and healing one." Other newspapers in nonsegregated regions praised the Court's decision, in keeping with the "heart of America," the "Conscience of the Nation," and the "Spirit of Democracy"; they touted its "inevitability" and expected "peaceful adjustment." Student newspapers in particular framed the decision as one that legitimized American democracy on the world stage and provided a victory in the Cold War. Non-Southern politicians were more reticent, not wishing to fan the flames raised by a decision clearly targeted at Southern policies.

Newspapers in the Deep South and in border states were decidedly less optimistic. The *New Orleans Times-Picayune* warned, "the decision will do no service either to education or racial accommodation.... The disappointment and frustration of the majority of Southerners at the revolutionary overturn of the practice and usage cannot immediately result in the improvement of race relations." Echoing these concerns, the *Louisville Courier Journal* called it a "mortal blow" to the Old South, and the *Atlanta Constitution* cautioned it was "no time for hasty action" (all reported in "Editorial Excerpts from the Nation's Press on Segregation Ruling," May 18, 1954, *N.Y. Times*). Even black newspapers in the South, most of which had conservative reputations, criticized the decision as undemocratic and confrontational (Rosenberg 1991).

After the optimistic and sometimes sanguine reviews during May and June, the national newspapers became more cautious. Promises of resistance by outspoken Southern politicians and predictions of tough times ahead implied that the implementation of *Brown* could prove difficult and costly. As the division between regional elites intensified, the tone of newspaper editorials and articles turned from enthusiasm to uncertainty.

The Ebb and Flow of Public Approval, 1954–1961

For seven years after *Brown*, Gallup continued to ask the same question about approval or disapproval of the decision, and public support rose and fell in response to statements by public officials, coverage by national newspapers, and dramatic, often confrontational, events (see Figure 1.1).

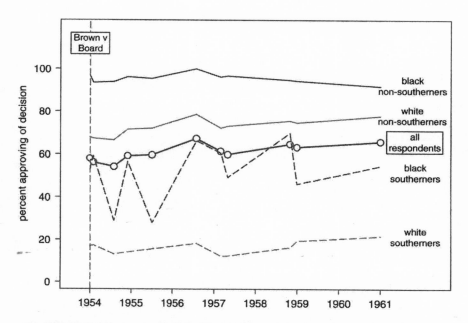

Figure 1.1. Public Approval of the Supreme Court's Decision in *Brown*, 1954–1961. Question wording: The U.S. Supreme Court has ruled that racial segregation in the public schools is illegal. This means that all children, no matter what their race, must be allowed to go to the same schools. Do you approve or disapprove of this decision? Source: Gallup.

The initial backlash against *Brown* was concentrated among Southern respondents (see Table 1.1). While support dropped in the nation as a whole by four percentage points between May and December 1954, the decline among all non-Southerners was a statistically insignificant one percentage point. During this seven-month period, the only subgroup among non-Southerners whose change in opinion reached statistical significance was those with at least a high school diploma; their seven-point drop in support may indicate these respondents, purportedly paying more attention to events and opinions outside their own backyard, were particularly concerned by the stiff opposition emerging in the South. Among Southerners, the softening of approval appeared most dramatic for blacks (a statistically significant decline of more than 22 points, although only 22 of the 1,352 people surveyed by Gallup were black Southerners). Perhaps some Southern blacks, responding to white pollsters during a period of charged relations, thought it best to keep their true opinions to themselves. Although levels of support for *Brown* among black Southerners were consistently lower than those for white and black non-Southerners, the small sample of black Southerners in the survey should caution against drawing any stark conclusions about shifts in their opinions over time.

Broad apprehension about racial tension was evident in three major national newspapers (see Figure 1.2), where the proportion of stories on segregation that contained the word "violence" soared from June 1954 (average of 0.01) to November 1954 (average of 0.13). At this time, the articles mostly warned of the potential for outbursts amid rising tensions—rather than reporting on actual conflicts. However, the start of the school year saw demonstrations in districts that had already begun desegregation efforts, including districts in Maryland, Delaware, and Washington, D.C. In Baltimore, a crowd attacked four pupils ("Baltimore Crowd Attacks Four Pupils," Oct. 2, 1954, N.Y. Times).

As the school year progressed, reports of boycotts decreased, and concerns over the potential for unrest waned. In December 1954, states affected by the ban on segregation began to file briefs for a hearing before the Supreme Court, scheduled for April 1955, which would establish specific guidelines for the transition to desegregation. By and large, the states argued for slow change, no national deadlines, and management of the transition by lower courts and local officials, a view the Eisenhower administration signaled it would support in its arguments as a friend of the court.

The one-year anniversary of *Brown* inspired a flood of assessments and retrospectives in the national newspapers, most of which highlighted the progress that had been made without incident in border states and in states where segregation had been tolerated though not mandated by state law. These newspapers sounded as optimistic as they had a year earlier. Two weeks later, on May 31, 1955, the Supreme Court issued its transitional guidelines (in *Brown II*): The district courts would enforce the desegregation of the schools as a local matter whose implementation would take into account local circumstances. Desegregation should continue with "all deliberate speed," but there would be no federal deadline. As fears lessened that the federal government

Table 1.1

Changes in Public Approval of the *Brown* Decision

			Change in Approval (in percentage points)				
		May '54	May '54 to Dec '54	Dec '54 to Dec '56	Dec '56 to Sept '57	Sept '57 to May '61	Entire Period
All Respondents		58%	−4*	+13***	−7***	+6***	+8***
Non-Southern							
Total		70	−1	+11***	−4**	+4**	+9***
Race	whites	68	−1	+12***	−6**	+5**	+10***
	blacks	97	−3	+6	−3	−5	−5
Party ID	Democrats	69	−1	+13***	−8**	+10***	+13***
	Independents	76	−7	+8*	−1	+2	+1
	Republicans	69	+0	+13***	−3	−3	+7**
Religion	Protestants	67	—	—	−4	+4*	+10***
	Catholics	71	—	—	−7**	+5	+10***
Education	less than HS	61	+3	+11***	−6*	+3	+12***
	HS	81	−7**	+10***	−4*	+3	+2
Age	under 35	74	−0	+6*	−2	+2	+6*
	35–45	72	−4	+16***	−9**	+6*	+9**
	over 45	64	+1	+11***	−4	+4*	+12***
Occupation	prof, bus	80	−6	+10**	−2	+3	+6*
	skilled	70	−1	+12**	−5	+4	+9***
	farmers	63	+1	+10**	−5	+6*	+12***
Southern							
Total		19	−4	+13***	−12***	+9***	+7**
Race:	whites	17	−4	+5*	−6*	+9***	+5*
	blacks	52	−22*	+37***	−18*	+6	+2
Party ID	Democrats	16	−6*	+11**	−9*	+11***	+8*
	Independents and Republicans	21	+4	+14*	−14**	+5	+9
Religion	Protestants	18	—	—	−11***	+9***	+7**
	Catholics	43	—	—	−10	+27*	+16
Education	less than HS	16	−5	+12***	−10**	+7**	+5
	HS	27	−5	+21***	−20**	+6	+2
Age	under 35	23	−5	+11*	−7	+10*	+8
	35–45	17	+1	+9	−9	+1	+2
	over 45	18	−5	+17***	−17***	+12***	+8*
Occupation	prof, bus	33	−12	+29***	−23**	+1	−5
	skilled	20	−1	+3	−10	+15**	+7
	farmers	13	−3	+20***	−13**	+6	+10**

*p<.05, **p<.01, ***p<.001

Source: Gallup. Question wording: See Figure 1.1.

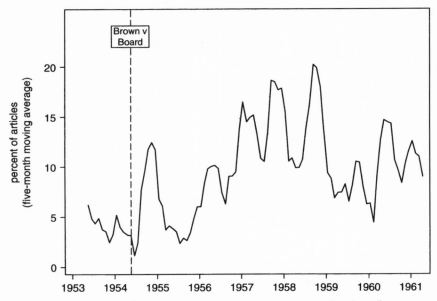

Figure 1.2. Percent of News Articles on Segregation Mentioning "Violence" (in *New York Times*, *Los Angeles Times*, and *Wall Street Journal*), 1953–1961. Sources: ProQuest Direct, Lexis-Nexis.

would force rapid change on the Old South, unease was replaced by relative calm, and the mentions of potential "violence" in media reports declined (see Figure 1.2).

Coinciding with the Court's willingness to yield to local governments on implementation, public approval of *Brown* soared (see Table 1.1, change in approval from December 1954 to December 1956). Approval of the decision increased about equally in the South and non-South, by 13 points and 11 points, respectively (the difference between the two is statistically insignificant). In the South, approval rose most dramatically among blacks—up 37 points, versus five points among Southern whites. The increase in approval for school integration was also greater among the highly educated than the less educated, among older respondents than younger ones, and among professionals and businessmen than other types of workers. But the principal trend dwarfs these nuances: in the non-South and South alike, every demographic and political group save one (Southerners age 35–45) experienced an increase in support that was both substantively and statistically significant over this two-year period.

After *Brown II*, Gallup included more questions about integration and segregation, and the responses largely confirm that both non-Southerners and Southerners supported the Court's decision in favor of local implementation.[3] When those who approved of *Brown* were asked, "Do you think integration—that is, bringing Negro and white children together in the schools—should be brought about gradually or do you think every means should be used to bring it about in the near future?" the vast majority of those with an opinion, 74% in both the South and non-South, preferred the gradual approach. Large majorities of white Southerners (86%), black Southerners (60%), and white non-Southerners (75%) supported this spirit of *Brown II*; only non-Southern blacks preferred immediate integration (59%).

Moreover, most respondents were optimistic about the immediate future of race relations in the South. When asked if they thought "the situation in the South between the races will get better or worse in the coming year?" only 37% of non-Southern whites and 11% of non-Southern blacks thought they would get worse. Southern blacks were hopeful as well, with only 15% believing the situation would deteriorate. Standing against this consensus, however, were Southern whites, 62% of whom expected the situation to deteriorate, with only 26% believing race relations would improve (the rest declined to respond or didn't know). Despite the decline in boycotts, increasingly friendly newspaper headlines, the Supreme Court's decision about local implementation, and growing national support for desegregation, Southern whites stood alone in predicting stormy days ahead.

Violent Resistance to Integration

For almost two years after *Brown*, there had been little violence and unrest in the South, largely because desegregation efforts had not yet begun in earnest. In February 1956, after a prolonged legal battle, a lower court ordered the University of Alabama to allow a black woman to attend classes, and the campus was engulfed by rioting and demonstrations. The university board of trustees decided to exclude the student from classes, ostensibly for her own safety. Across the country, editorial boards decried this first major instance of violent opposition to desegregation efforts. Walter Lippmann declared that "The Mob" had taken over the university and condemned the breakdown of law and order (in an editorial, Feb. 10, 1956, L.A. Times). Others criticized the governor for allowing the violence to get out of control and blamed national politicians for not speaking out more forcefully ("Violence in Alabama," Feb. 10, 1956, N.Y. Times). The conflict brought thousands to antisegregation rallies and even more into the folds of racist organizations ("10,000 in Alabama Hail Segregation," Wayne Phillips, Feb. 11, 1956, N.Y. Times).

Throughout 1956, Southern delegations in the U.S. House and Senate began in earnest to curb what they perceived as the Supreme Court's recent intrusions on states' rights on a variety of issues. The Ku Klux Klan resurfaced to hold rallies and recruit new members. In rural Tennessee, the integration of a local high school provoked mob violence, which spread to other towns, led to conflicts with state police and national guardsmen, and resulted in shootings, stabbings, and bombings. In November, the Supreme Court upheld a lower court ruling which declared that segregation on public buses in Alabama was unconstitutional (in a case brought after Rosa Parks was arrested earlier in December 1955). A few weeks later, Montgomery outlawed segregated seating on its buses, and the yearlong bus boycott ended in late December 1956. Within weeks, bombs exploded at four black churches, as well as at the homes of two ministers and three black families ("Bus Runs Halted in Alabama City after Six Bombings," Jan. 11, 1957, N.Y. Times).

One of the most wrenching and infamous showdowns of the civil rights era occurred in September 1957, when the local school board's plan to desegregate Little Rock Central High School escalated into a monthlong confrontation that led President Eisenhower to send federal troops to escort nine black children through the assembled mob and front doors of the school, where they suffered a year of harassment and abuse. Orval Faubus, the Democratic governor of Arkansas, was criticized in the national media for his failure to maintain order in implementing the school district's plan, but others saw the disorder as a sign that integration was being pushed on the South too fast: "The people of Little Rock were given less time to act....We do not think [the President's actions] quiet[ed] passions; it certainly runs the risk of increasing the desperate feeling of people who see themselves coerced by great power from afar. Federal troops can quell a riot. They can open the doors of a school building. They cannot make over the mores of a quarter of a nation" ("The Tragedy of Little Rock," Sept. 25, 1957, Wall Street Journal). The responses of Southern newspapers to the federal intervention ranged from acceptance to outrage. The *Arkansas Gazette* called it a "tragic day" caused by Governor Faubus's refusal to enforce the law, and the *Charlotte Observer* described the use of federal troops as a regrettable but necessary "last, bitter, desperate resort." The *Mobile Press* lamented that "[t]he big steamroller of totalitarian central government—heretofore considered something foreign to America—is now an established fact in our land," and the *Charleston News and Courier* asserted, "The President could wipe the State of Arkansas off the map. But he cannot solve the problem of race with either bombs or bayonets" (all excerpts from "Editorial Comment of Southern Newspapers on Use of Troops," Sept. 26, 1957, N.Y. Times).

The public, which had been increasingly supportive of desegregation, was divided on how best to handle the situation in Arkansas. When asked by Gallup, "Do you think the governor of Arkansas did the right thing or the wrong thing in placing national guardsmen around the school there?" 40% of respondents said he did the right thing, and 45% said he did the wrong thing. In the non-South, 54% of all respondents called it the wrong thing (including 52% of whites and 75% of blacks). In the South, 62% of all respondents and 67% of whites thought the governor did the right thing; only 33% of Southern blacks agreed. The regional split was even more pronounced when respondents were asked if they thought Arkansas should "wait until next year before trying to integrate the schools" or "admit the nine Negro children now." In the non-South, 61% of white respondents thought they should integrate immediately, and 24% thought they should wait a year. In the South, 11% of whites said they thought the children should be "admitted now," and 81% believed they should wait a year or said they were against integration entirely.

Despite enduring support for desegregation efforts outside the South, violence took its toll on public approval of *Brown*. In the South, approval dropped by 12 points (from December 1956 to September 1957), and declines occurred in all subgroups (see Table 1.1), with the decrease in support greater among blacks than whites, among Independents and Republicans than Democrats, among the highly educated than the less educated, and among older than younger respondents. In the rest of the country, the decline in approval was less pronounced, a drop of only four points. But public approval for *Brown*—both in the non-South and for the country as a whole—did not return to its previous high as long as Gallup continued to ask the question through May 1961.

Southerners Come to Terms with *Brown*

After the confrontation at Little Rock, the proportion of news stories about segregation mentioning "violence" fell dramatically (see Figure 1.2). News coverage of the issue returned to intermittent reports of progress on various desegregation efforts and to retrospectives, with a mix of positive and negative news. One article emphasized the progress made after the bus boycott with the headline "Year After Strike, Negroes Riding Buses in Amiable Voluntary Segregation" ("Pattern Shaped in Montgomery," Feb. 2, 1958, N.Y. Times), while another highlighted the latent tensions in Little Rock months after the national spotlight had shifted elsewhere ("Little Rock: More Tension Than Ever," Gertrude Samuels, March 23, 1958, N.Y. Times).

However, the start of a new school year brought new controversies and more negative media coverage (see Figure 1.2). In August, the Eighth Circuit Court of Appeals reversed a stay of integration for Little Rock High School set by a lower court, setting the stage for another showdown between state and federal authorities. Governor Faubus threatened to close the school if federal authorities forced integration, while the local school board asked the Supreme Court to delay integration at the site for two years. Segregationists hoped that changes in Court membership might produce a different result (four justices had been sworn in since *Brown*), but the Court unanimously ordered immediate integration in Little Rock. Most Northern and national newspapers applauded the courts for not having yielded to violence: the law had triumphed over the mob. Complaints that federal authorities were pushing too hard and too fast were replaced by the realization that integration was inevitable and that Governor Faubus and other Southern politicians were simply making the process more difficult. The *Hartford Courant* editorialized, "In Arkansas, in Virginia, and perhaps elsewhere the master-race politicians will close the schools rather than integrate them. That may lead to further years of litigation. But there can be only one end" (cited in "Editorial Comment on Decision by Supreme Court," Sept. 14, 1958, N.Y. Times).

That fall, Governor Faubus and Governor James Almond of Virginia closed some public schools to avoid the Court's latest desegregation order. When efforts to fund alternative private schools failed, both governors faced mounting pressure from constituents who thought that dismantling the school system was too high a price to pay. White residents of Norfolk, Virginia, sued the state government, arguing that closing public schools was unconstitutional. In a surprising turn of events, some Southern whites found themselves fighting for the implementation of *Brown*. By January 1959, Governor Almond acquiesced and approved an integration plan ("Virginia Viewed as Turning Point for Integration," Anthony Lewis, Feb. 1, 1959, N.Y. Times).

But in Little Rock, the schools remained closed for an entire year. When they reopened in August 1959 with a handful of black students—over Governor Faubus's objections—local residents offered scant resistance. The price of avoiding federal integration efforts had been painfully high: many of the city's residents had left, the city's growing industrial sector had ground to a halt, and families had to live apart because children were sent to attend schools elsewhere ("Act III Opens in Little Rock," editorial, Gertrude Samuels, Sept. 13, 1959, N.Y. Times). By this time, most local officials in the South believed that integration was inevitable and that they faced a simple choice: do it the easy way, or do it the hard way.

This sense of inevitability may help explain why, over the next few years, public approval of *Brown* rebounded, especially in the South. The rebound may also reflect the larger economic and cultural pressures that had been slowly liberalizing racial attitudes since the end of World War II, and some Americans may have been persuaded by the Supreme Court, whose language had helped shape the debate over school desegregation. Whatever the cause, between September 1957 and May 1961, approval grew by four percentage points among non-Southerners and by nine points among Southerners (see Table 1.1). In the South, approval rose faster among whites than among blacks and faster among respondents over age 45 than among younger respondents.

The Structure of Increasing Approval for *Brown*

Between May 1954 and May 1961, approval of *Brown* increased within almost every demographic and political segment of the population (see Table 1.1), although both the levels of approval and the rate of change varied among subgroups. For example, approval among non-Southern whites rose by 10 points (from 68% to 78%), while approval among Southern whites rose by only 5 points (from 17% to 22%). In non-Southern states, the largest increases in approval came from Democrats (13 points), respondents who had not completed high school (12 points), respondents over age 45 (12 points), and farmers and unskilled workers (12 points).

These differential growth rates in support among non-Southern respondents represent partial convergence: for race, party identification, education, age, and occupation, the groups with lower initial approval ratings registered the greatest increases in approval. In nonsegregated America, support for the Supreme Court's decision was reaching a more uniform level among subgroups over this seven-year period.

Some partial convergence was present among Southern respondents, although it was not as pervasive. In May 1954, approval among Southern whites was lower than among Southern blacks (17% versus 52%), and over the seven-year period, approval rose slightly more among Southern whites than among Southern blacks (5 points versus 2 points). Respondents with less than a high school diploma expressed lower levels of initial support than those holding at least a high school diploma (16% versus 27%) but also demonstrated larger increases over time (5 points versus 2), and those with low-status occupations displayed lower initial approval than those with high-status occupations (13% and 20% versus 33%), as well as greater increasing support (10 points and 7 versus 5). This pattern of larger gains in approval among groups initially the most critical, however, does not hold for partisanship, religion, or age. While partial convergence was smoothing out differences among religious, partisan, and generational subgroups in the non-South, in the South the subgroups least willing to initially embrace the decision continued their lower levels of support for *Brown* over time.

To examine whether partial convergence among racial, partisan, educational, age, and occupational groups in the non-South resulted in the diminishing importance of these categorizations for predicting approval, I performed two sets of analyses of multivariate probit models using respondents pooled from the two surveys taken in May 1954 and May 1961, with approval of *Brown* as the dependent variable. The first model includes dummy variables for being black (being white is the omitted reference category), identifying as a Republican or a Democrat (being an independent is the reference category), and being Protestant (Catholics, Jews, and others are the omitted category), as well as continuous variables for education and age (rescaled to range from 0 to 1). The first model "constrains" the effects of these demographic and social determinants to be consistent between these two surveys. The second model, which includes all of these variables plus interactions with a dummy variable for being a respondent in the second survey, allows their effects to vary between the two surveys. If all of the second-period interactions are insignificant, then the determinants of approval did not undergo statistically significant change over this seven-year period.

As the results of these analyses indicate (see Table 1.2), not all of the variables that demonstrate a clear bivariate relationship with approval exhibit a statistically significant association in this multivariate context. Outside the South, blacks were more supportive than whites, Protestants more supportive than those of other religious denominations, and the better educated more supportive than the less educated. However, there are few statistically significant partisan effects: by May 1961, non-Southern Democrats were more approving than Independents, and in

Table 1.2
Public Approval of *Brown* (pooled responses, May 1954 and May 1961)

Non-Southerners	Constrained			Unconstrained		
black	0.87	(0.14)	***	1.50	(0.34)	***
black x May '61	—	—		−0.83	(0.37)	*
Republican	−0.05	(0.07)		−0.08	(0.14)	
Republican x May '61	—	—		0.07	(0.16)	
Democrat	0.08	(0.07)		−0.18	(0.14)	
Democrat x May '61	—	—		0.36	(0.16)	*
Protestant	−0.22	(0.06)	***	−0.27	(0.10)	**
Protestant x May '61	—	—		0.08	(0.12)	
education	0.89	(0.11)	***	1.38	(0.22)	***
education x May '61	—	—		−0.73	(0.26)	**
age	−0.18	(0.12)		−0.27	(0.22)	
age x May '61	—	—		0.03	(0.27)	
May '61	—	—		0.11	(0.19)	
constant	0.69	(0.08)	***	0.13	(0.16)	***
N		3,144			3,144	
Pseudo R^2		.04			.05	

Southerners	Constrained			Unconstrained		
black	1.10	(0.13)	***	1.40	(0.36)	***
black x May '61	—	—		−0.37	(0.39)	
Republican	0.35	(0.15)	*	−0.13	(0.34)	
Republican x May '61	—	—		0.64	(0.38)	
Democrat	−0.03	(0.12)		−0.24	(0.28)	
Democrat x May '61	—	—		0.27	(0.31)	
Protestant	−0.86	(0.18)	***	−0.79	(0.33)	*
Protestant x May '61	—	—		−0.13	(0.39)	
education	0.80	(0.22)	***	1.85	(0.44)	***
education x May '61	—	—		−1.45	(0.51)	**
age	−0.02	(0.22)		−0.11	(0.51)	
age x May '61	—	—		0.13	(0.57)	
May '61	—	—		0.17	(0.47)	
constant	−0.26	(0.21)		−0.36	(0.40)	
N		991			991	
Pseudo R^2		.09			.01	

***$p<.001$, **$p<.01$, *$p<.05$
Cells contain probit regression coefficients with approval of the decision as the dichotomous dependent variable (standard errors are in parentheses).

Question wording: see Figure 1.1.

Source: Gallup.

the South, Republicans were generally more approving than Independents. But neither in the South nor outside the South can the effect of age be distinguished from statistical noise: that younger respondents were more supportive of the decision appears to be driven by their higher levels of education.

These analyses also demonstrate there were indeed changes in the determinants of approval between the two surveys. Among non-Southerners, blacks were more supportive of the decision than whites, but the period interaction yields a negative coefficient (−.83), indicating that this difference diminished over time. And although higher education is associated with a greater predicted probability of support, the period interaction also yields a negative coefficient, signifying that the association between educational attainment and approval of *Brown* weakened over time as well. This pattern is mirrored in the South, where the strong relationship between higher education and greater support again diminished between the first and last surveys. Not surprisingly, higher increases in the rate of approval among the less educated made education a less potent predictor over this period.

The Court and the Public's Agenda

There is limited evidence that the Supreme Court had a legitimizing effect on public opinion concerning school desegregation. In the short term, there appears to be a strong case for Southern-concentrated backlash, both immediately after the decision and in reaction to violent resistance to desegregation efforts in the years following. Ultimately, though, declining approval gave way to a slow national tide of racial tolerance that began long before and continued long after *Brown*.

However, the *Brown* decision did thrust the issue of segregation in the public schools to the fore of the national agenda. The number of articles on segregation published in the major national newspapers (the *New York Times*, the *Los Angeles Times*, and the *Wall Street Journal*) increased dramatically in the wake of *Brown*. Prior to May 1954, these three papers published an average of 35 articles per month that mentioned segregation, and coverage often dipped below 25 articles per month. After the decision, the average number of articles increased to 84 per month, and coverage never fell below 25 articles per month. Only in six of the 85 after-*Brown* months under study did coverage fall below 50 articles (see Figure 1.3).

This finding that *Brown* caused more discussion of racial segregation in the media, although buttressed by other scholars who find the Court successful as an agenda setter (Klarman 2005), runs counter to evidence presented by authors who, using other measures, suggest *Brown* failed to increase the salience of segregation in Southern newspapers (Carter 1957) or to increase the presence of stories on civil rights in national magazines like *Newsweek*, *Time*, *Reader's Digest*, and the *New York Times Magazine* until significantly after the decision (Rosenberg 1991). It may well be that Southern papers

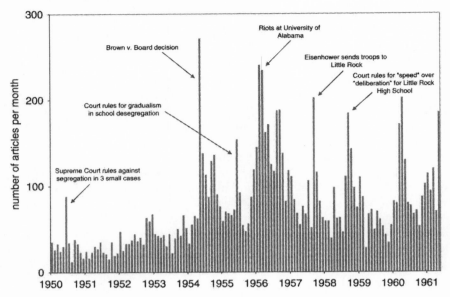

Figure 1.3. National Newspaper Coverage of Segregation (in *New York Times, Los Angeles Times*, and *Wall Street Journal*), 1950–1961. Sources: ProQuest Direct, Lexis-Nexis.

devoted less space to desegregation, and national magazines may have covered racial political issues less often, but *Brown* did have a significant impact on coverage in the country's most prominent national newspapers.

Public Opinion on Segregation and Busing, 1964–2004

Over the subsequent decades, support for integrated public schools continued to increase, receiving near unanimous support in 2004 (see Figure 1.4). The public policy debate has shifted from if and how to ban compulsory segregation programs in public schools to questions about implementing more proactive policies to achieve racial balance. Public opinion is divided on pragmatic issues such as the use of busing to integrate the schools, having the federal government ensure racial integration in public schools, and—among white parents—feelings about having one's own children attend a majority-black school (see Figure 1.4).

Why does racial equality in the abstract garner such widespread approval, yet policies that would implement equality struggle to find public support? Many argue the disparity is the result of latent racial resentment (Sears et al. 1979; Kinder & Sanders 1996; Sears et al. 1997; Bobo 2001), while others attribute it to a principled commitment to race neutrality and noninterventionist

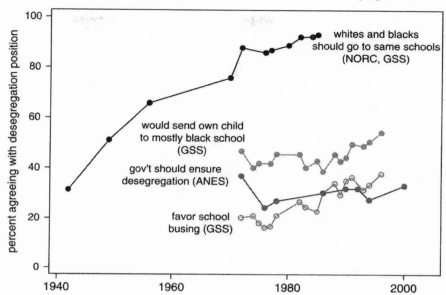

Figure 1.4. Public Opinion on School Integration and Busing, 1940–2000. Question wording: Do you think white students and (Negro/Black) students should go to the same schools or to separate schools?
[Asked only of white respondents] Would you yourself have any objection to sending your children to a school where a few of the children are (Negroes/Blacks/African-Americans)? Where half of the children are (Negroes/Blacks/African-Americans? Where more than half of the children are (Negroes/Blacks/African-Americans)?
In general, do you favor or oppose the busing of (Negro/Black/African-American) and white school children from one school district to another?
Some people say that the government in Washington should see to it that white and (colored/Negro/black) children go to the same schools. Others claim this is not the government's business. Do you think the government in Washington should see to it that white and colored/Negro/black children go to the same schools. Others claim this is not the government's business. Have you been concerned or interested enough about this question to favor one side over the other?
Sources: National Opinion Research Center (NORC), General Social Survey (GSS), American National Election Studies (ANES).

government (Sniderman & Carmines 1997; Thernstrom & Thernstrom 1997) or simple self-interest. Whatever the rationale, support for these measures was relatively low when questions about these programs were asked in 1972: 46% of whites did not object to sending their children to majority-black schools, 37% of all respondents thought the federal government should ensure that blacks and whites go to school together, and only 20% of all respondents supported busing.

During the next four years, support for all three of these measures suffered marked declines. This may represent backlash in public opinion to the renewed efforts to integrate public schools with forced busing programs. Such programs were one of the most widely advocated policies for bridging the persistent racial divide in the public schools, as residential segregation continued to result in white and black students separately attending local schools. Busing efforts began in earnest as early as 1969, were upheld by the Supreme Court in *Swann v. Charlotte-Mecklenburg Board of Education* in 1971, and were met with a hostile public reaction. In a Gallup poll taken in March 1970, only 14% of adults favored "the busing of negro and white children from one school district to another," and 81% were opposed. This hostility resulted in the ousting of local school boards (Rubin 1972) and the formation of extensive private school systems for white students in Northern and Southern communities alike (Farrell et al. 1977; Andrews 2002).

After this decline, however, support for policies to integrate schools—like support for integration in principle—began to increase, gradually but steadily (again, see Figure 1.4). From 1976 to 1996, willingness among whites to have a child in a majority-black school grew from 40% to 54%. Support for busing among all respondents more than doubled, from 16% in 1976 to almost 38% in 1996. But although support for federal government intervention to integrate the public schools gradually increased from its low of 24% in 1976, it failed to regain the level of support it had attained in 1972 (37%). In fact, by 1996 (the last year the General Social Survey asked this question), support for busing, a notably controversial practice when it was first introduced, actually exceeded support for federal action. Some say the public's enduring opposition to decisive government efforts to achieve school integration is a sign of latent racism, but others attribute it to conservative wariness of federal intervention in local matters.

This general trend of increasingly liberal attitudes concerning school integration tracks other measures that tapped opinion of segregation in other areas of social life and race relations more generally (see Figure 1.5). Respondents who believed there should be no laws barring interracial marriage increased from 61% of respondents in 1972 to 90% in 2002—a giant leap from 1954, when more than 90% of whites opposed interracial marriage. On the issue of residential integration, respondents who believed that blacks have the right to live in the same neighborhoods as whites increased from 57% in 1964 to 85% in 1976. Those who thought that home sellers should not be allowed to engage in racial discrimination climbed from 35% in 1973 to 68% in 2004. Those who believed that civil rights leaders were pushing "too slowly" or "about right" increased from 31% of all respondents in 1964 to 72% in 1992. The percentage of respondents who disagreed with the notion that blacks "shouldn't push themselves where they are not wanted" soared from 24% in 1972 to 64% in 2002.

These trends of increasing racial tolerance are well documented in the political science literature (for example, Schuman et al. 1985; Page & Shapiro

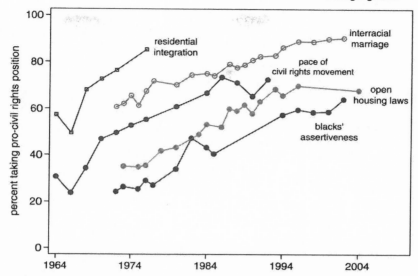

Figure 1.5. Public Opinion on Other Race Issues, 1964–2004. Question wording:
blacks' assertiveness: Here are some opinions other people have expressed in
connection with (Negro/Black)-white relations. Which statement on the card comes
closest to how you, yourself, feel? A. (Negroes/Blacks/African-Americans) shouldn't
push themselves where they're not wanted. (Source: General Social Survey)
open housing laws: Suppose there is a community-wide vote on the general
housing issue. There are two possible laws to vote on. A. One law says that a
homeowner can decide for himself whom to sell his house to, even if he prefers
not to sell to (Negroes/Blacks). B. The second law says that a homeowner cannot
refuse to sell to someone because of their race or color. Which law would you
vote for? (Source: General Social Survey)
interracial marriage: Do you think there should be laws against marriages between
(Negroes/Blacks/African-Americans) and whites? (Source: General Social Survey)
pace of civil rights movement: Some say that the civil rights people have been trying to
push too fast. Others feel they haven't pushed fast enough. How about you: Do you
think that civil rights leaders are trying to push too fast, are going too slowly, or are
they moving about the right speed? (Source: American National Election Studies)
residential integration: Which of these statements would you agree with: Some
people say that Negroes should be allowed to live in any part of town they want
to. How do you feel? Should Negroes be allowed to live in any part of town they
want to, or not? (Source: American National Election Studies)

1992; Mayer 1993; Thernstrom & Thernstrom 1997). Many scholars believe
that much of this increased support is illusory, as racial tolerance becomes
the new social norm and support of these programs is increasingly buttressed
by social desirability effects. But if at least a fraction of the increasing support
for racial integration is genuine, these trends provide a context for assessing the influence of the Supreme Court in this arena. Increasing support for

school desegregation might have taken place over time even in the absence of any Supreme Court ruling against segregation, because increasing tolerance in racial matters resembles an exogenous, long-term trend. Indeed, it appears that the justices knew that the public was becoming increasingly supportive of desegregation when they were writing the decision and that this knowledge emboldened them to act when they did (Klarman 2005). On the other hand, it is difficult to imagine profound social change in the absence of important milestones, which are both enabled by earlier social trends and instrumental in furthering them. Whether increasing support for school desegregation in the wake of *Brown* was the result, direct or indirect, of Supreme Court action or only part of a secular trend of liberalizing racial attitudes may never be known for certain, but *Brown* jump-started the process of change in policy, however bumpy and tortuous this proved to be in its immediate aftermath.

Conclusion

American public opinion on matters of race has been liberalizing dramatically since the 1940s. Many argue that this increasing tolerance was as much a cause of *Brown* as a consequence, and indeed it is quite difficult to differentiate any "legitimation" effect of the case from a default path. Yet, the fact that public support for the Supreme Court's ban on segregation in the public schools did not steadily increase or sharply decline during the 1950s is telling. The Court's written opinion did not change minds by its pure persuasive power; after all, few ordinary Americans ever read the opinion. Rather, the power of a case like *Brown* resides in its ability to mobilize the political class, to inspire public outcry, and to trigger dramatic events. The Court, of course, has no power to implement its decisions and has little or no control over mediating agents. The Supreme Court is effective in rallying public opinion to its cause only if it garners the widespread cooperation of the two other branches of the federal government, local and state officials, and decision makers in the mass media.

However, the Supreme Court is in a unique position to affect the nation's agenda: it cannot make politicians or publics agree, but it can try to make them pay attention. Southerners may not have agreed that "separate" was inherently unequal, but they could not ignore the ruling of the highest court in the land. This suggests that the Court's more potent decisions are the ones that elites cannot ignore and the ones that inspire the most activity among elites. But because these influential decisions arise out of controversy, justices must issue such opinions only on rare occasions, lest they risk the institution's legitimacy. Keenly aware that the Court could not routinely emit shock waves, the justices waited more than a decade, and only after public opinion had shifted in their direction, to strike down laws banning interracial marriage in *Loving v. Virginia* in 1967 (Klarman 2005). A case like *Brown*, which is powerful enough to shape public opinion by commanding sustained public attention, is, out of necessity, extremely rare.

Notes

1. This survey is purportedly a representative national sample, although almost no detailed information is available on the sampling methodology. The published data provide the responses by subgroups (e.g., by race, region) for only some questions.

2. These are responses to an open-ended question coded by the survey house.

3. Because the main question under study, concerning approval of the Supreme Court's decision to desegregate public schools, was asked before any other questions on desegregation, these additional questions are not contributing to any effect of question ordering on the time series analysis.

References

Andrews, Kenneth T. 2002. "Movement-countermovement Dynamics and the Emergence of New Institutions: The Case of 'White Flight' Schools in Mississippi." *Social Forces* 80: 911–36.

Bobo, Lawrence. 2001. "Racial Attitudes and Relations at the Close of the Twentieth Century." In *America Becoming: Racial Trends and Their Consequences, Vol. 1*, edited by Neil J. Smelser, William Julius Wilson, and Faith Mitchell, pp. 264–301. Washington, D.C.: National Academy Press.

Carter, R. E. Jr. 1957. "Segregation and the News: A Regional Content Study." *Journalism Quarterly* 34:3–18.

Douglas, Davison. 1995. *Reading, Writing, & Race: The Desegregation of the Charlotte Schools*. Chapel Hill: University of North Carolina Press.

Dudziak, Mary L. 1988. "Desegregation as a Cold War Imperative." *Stanford Law Review* 41.

Farrell, Claude H., David N. Hyman, and Loren A. Ihnen. 1977. "Forced Busing and the Demand for Private Schooling." *Journal of Legal Studies*, 6(2): 363–72.

Finkelman, Paul. 2005. "Civil Rights in Historical Context: In Defense of Brown." *Harvard Law Review* 118.

Fiss, Owen. 1991. "A Life Lived Twice." *Yale Law Journal* 100.

Gallup, George H. 1972. *The Gallup Poll: Public Opinion 1935–1971*. 1249–50. New York: Random House.

Garrow, David J. 1978. *Protest at Selma: Martin Luther King, Jr. and the Voting Rights Act of 1965*. New Haven: Yale University Press.

Greenberg, Jack. 1994. *Crusaders in the Courts: How a Dedicated Band of Lawyers Fought for the Civil Rights Revolution*. New York: Basic Books.

Horwitz, Morton J. 1998. *The Warren Court and the Pursuit of Justice*. New York: Hill and Wang.

Kinder, Donald, and Lynn Sanders. 1996. *Divided by Color: Racial Politics and Democratic Ideals*. Chicago: University of Chicago Press, pp. 92–127.

Klarman, Michael J. 2004. *From Jim Crow to Civil Rights: The Supreme Court and the Struggle for Racial Equality.* Oxford: Oxford University Press.

——. 2005. "Brown and Lawrence (and Goodridge)." Unpublished manuscript.

Mayer, William G. 1992. *The Changing American Mind: How and Why American Public Opinion Changed between 1960 and 1988.* Ann Arbor: University of Michigan Press.

McMillen, Neil R. 1971. *The Citizens' Council: Organized Resistance to the Second Reconstruction, 1954–64.* Urbana: University of Illinois Press.

Page, Benjamin I., and Robert Y. Shapiro. 1992. The Rational Public: Fifty Years of Trends in Americans' Policy Preferences. Chicago: University of Chicago Press.

Patterson, James T. 2001. *Brown v. Board of Education.* New York: Oxford University Press.

Rosenberg, Gerald N. 1991. *The Hollow Hope: Can Courts Bring About Social Change?* Chicago: University of Chicago Press.

——. 1994. "Brown Is Dead! Long Live Brown! The Endless Attempt to Canonize a Case." *Virginia Law Review* 80.

Rubin, Lillian B. 1972. *Busing and Backlash.* Berkeley: University of California Press.

Schuman, Howard, Charlotte Steeh, and Lawrence Bobo. 1985. *Racial Attitudes in America: Trends and Interpretations.* Cambridge: Harvard University Press.

Sears, David O., Carl P. Hensler, and Leslie K. Speer. 1979. "Whites' Opposition to 'Busing': Self-Interest or Symbolic Politics?" *American Political Science Review* 73(2): 369–84.

Sears, David O., Colette van Laar, Mary Carillo, and Richard Kosterman. 1997. "Is It Really Racism? The Origins of White Americans' Opposition to Race-Targeted Policies." *Public Opinion Quarterly* 61(1): 16–53.

Sniderman, Paul, and Edward Carmines. 1997. *Reaching beyond Race.* Cambridge: Harvard University Press, pp. 99–139.

Thernstrom, Stephan, and Abigail Thernstrom. 1997. *America in Black and White: One Nation, Indivisible.* New York: Simon and Schuster.

Wilkinson, Harvie J. 1979. *From Brown to Bakke: The Supreme Court and School Integration, 1954–1978.* Oxford: Oxford University Press.

Wolters, Raymond. 1984. *The Burden of Brown: Thirty Years of School Desegregation.* Knoxville: University of Tennessee Press.

2

The Rights of the Accused

Amy E. Lerman

In determining what protections to accord those accused of criminal activity, the Supreme Court has tried to balance the Constitution's protection of individual liberties and the state's need to ensure public safety. Ideally, criminal justice procedures would protect citizens from excessive intrusions by government and protect the falsely accused, while enabling the state to prosecute criminals and punish those who undermine the social order. In practice, we have seen a debate between proponents of a due process model, which emphasizes the protection of individual liberties against the abuse of government power, and proponents of a crime-control model, which gives priority to maintaining safety and security through the detention and prosecution of accused criminals (Packer 1964; Roach 1989).

This chapter examines changing public attitudes toward these competing priorities over the last half century in light of three major Supreme Court decisions (*Gideon v. Wainwright, Miranda v. Arizona*, and *Mapp v. Ohio*). Through these decisions, the Supreme Court bolstered the due process rights of the accused, even as the public by and large preferred to strengthen prosecutorial power. In the 1970s, for example, almost half of the public expressed a willingness to forgo certain constitutional rights in order to control crime.

Since then, polls indicate greater public acceptance of the Court's decisions in these landmark cases. However, the public continues to perceive a trade-off between protecting individual rights and aggressively fighting crime. When forced to choose, the majority continues to value public safety over the rights of the accused.

The analyses presented in this chapter suggest some important points about the power of the Court and its role in shaping the attitudes of the mass public. First, the relationship between Court decisions and public opinion must be understood in a broader political context that includes the interplay among political institutions with different incentives and constituencies. In the case of rights for criminal defendants, the ideological push of the Court was countered with a steady and strong push back from the executive, the legislature, law enforcement agencies, and the media. On this issue, it appears these competing forces may have ultimately held more sway over public opinion.

Second, trends in public opinion regarding the rights of the accused suggest that although the Court may have significant power to legitimize procedural rules, public support for specific limits on law enforcement and prosecutors does not always extend to the ideological justification for these limits. Although over time much of the public has come to support the rules of criminal procedure that were outlined by the Court in the 1960s, public opinion is still skeptical of the philosophical underpinnings of those rules.

The "Rights Revolution"

In the 1960s, in a trio of cases concerning the constitutionality of criminal procedures in state courts, the Supreme Court expanded legal protections granted to the accused. In *Mapp v. Ohio* (1961), the Court revisited an issue it had addressed in 1949 in *Wolf v. Colorado*: in a state criminal proceeding, did the due process clause of the Fourteenth Amendment disallow the admission of evidence obtained in violation of the Fourth Amendment's prohibition against unreasonable search and seizure? In *Wolf*, the Court found such evidence admissible; in *Mapp*, it concluded that such evidence was inadmissible—a principle that has come to be known as the exclusionary rule.

Two years later, in *Gideon v. Wainwright*, the Court revisited *Betts v. Brady* (1942), in which the Court held that the right to a lawyer was guaranteed in state criminal cases only when special circumstances would otherwise make a fair trial impossible, such as particularly complicated or capital cases. Justice Black delivered the majority opinion in *Gideon*, asserting that, contrary to *Betts*, the guarantee of counsel was a right deemed by the Court to be "fundamental and essential to a fair trial."

And in 1966, in *Miranda v. Arizona*, the Court addressed the question of whether constitutional rights could be assured in practice if the police were not required to inform the accused of those rights. The Court ruled that a confession would be admissible in court only if, prior to custodial interrogation, the police had made the detainee aware that he had a right to remain silent, that anything he said could be used against him at trial, that he had a right to speak with an attorney and to have an attorney present during questioning, and that if he could not afford to hire an attorney, the state was obligated to appoint one for him.

In these and several other cases, the Warren Court established precedents to protect the rights of those accused of crimes. In many ways, however, the

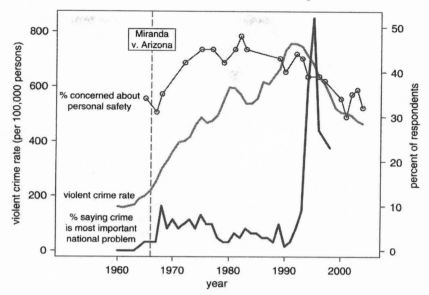

Figure 2.1. Crime rates and public concern about crime, 1960–2004.
concern about personal safety: the percentage of respondents answering yes to the
question: Is there any area near where you live—that is, within a mile—where you
would be afraid to walk alone at night? (Source: Bureau of Justice Statistics).
violent crime rate: violent crimes per 100,000 persons (Bureau of Justice Statistics).
crime as most important problem: the percentage of respondents mentioning crime
in response to the question: What do you think is the most important problem
facing this country today? Source: Gallup.

Court's decisions were out of step with public opinion and may even have
shifted public opinion against the Court's pro-rights position.

In part, this was because the Court's decisions were handed down at a time
when the public was becoming increasingly concerned about rising rates of
crime (see Figure 2.1). According to the Bureau of Justice Statistics, the rate of
violent crime doubled during the 1960s, from 161 crimes per 100,000 persons in
1960 to 329 per 100,000 in 1969. The rate of property crime also doubled, from
1,726 per 100,000 persons in 1960 to 3,351 per 100,000 in 1969. In Gallup surveys, the percentage of respondents who identified crime as the most important
problem facing the country rose from 1–2% in the mid-1960s to 5–10% in the
late 1960s and early 1970s, and concerns about personal safety also increased.

Vocal critics held the Supreme Court accountable for these rising rates of
crime: "the rate of crime did skyrocket in the midst of the Warren Court's hey-
day, a time when the accused and convicted seemed to win a victory every week,
and so it is not surprising that some should conclude that the Supreme Court
was at fault" (Caldeira 1986, 1216). As the Court continued to dramatically

alter the balance between protections for the accused and the state's prosecutorial powers, elected officials in both parties seized on the burgeoning dismay over the rising crime rate. "The political tide began to build against the due process revolution two years before *Miranda* when Barry Goldwater seized upon law and order as a campaign issue. Richard Nixon exploited fear of crime to win the presidency in 1968. He blamed crime on decisions like *Miranda*, which allegedly forced prosecutors to free guilty criminals" (Baker 1983). Nixon promised to appoint more conservative justices to the bench, judges who would end the coddling of criminals and return authority to police officers (Smith et al. 2003, 130), and some conservative legislators went so far as to call for Warren's impeachment (Friedman 1993, 302).

The U.S. Congress was likewise unwilling to endorse the Court's pro-rights mandates. Only two years after *Miranda*, Congress passed a law that substantially decreased the role of *Miranda* warnings in determining the admissibility of confessions.[1] The Supreme Court did not conclusively address this law until 2000, when in *Dickerson v. United States* it asserted that "*Miranda* [had] announced a constitutional rule that Congress may not supersede legislatively."[2]

The Supreme Court was also chastised by various state courts for overreaching and for trampling on state sovereignty through decisions that sought a "federalization of the criminal law" (Specter 1962; Canon 1973). In an article presenting the "Prosecutor's Stand," Fred Inbau concurred, arguing that "the Court has taken it upon itself, without constitutional authorization, to police the police... [going] beyond all reasonable bounds in imposing its own divided concepts of due process upon the states" (1962, 1414).

Many law enforcement officials also spoke out against the Court, criticizing its decisions for tying their hands (Canon 1973); as a veteran law enforcement official wrote, "We believe that court decisions have gone too far, that the courts are, in many cases, ignoring the public right to protection" (Leonard 1965). Other police officials found more to support in the Supreme Court's rulings, but even they warned that "law enforcement [must] not be deterred from its task of maintaining law and social order, by restrictions which may render it substantially less effective" (Broderick 1966).[3]

The general public may not have understood the finer points of constitutional law, but they heard and responded to media reports that were critical of the Court's decisions (MacKenzie 1968; Leo 1996; Leo & Thomas 1998, xvi) and to elite consternation over rates of rising crime and an increasingly activist Court (Baker 1983): "These dramatic decisions of the Warren Court proved to be quite controversial.... The Court was criticized, sometimes hysterically, on the grounds that it was perverting the meaning of the Constitution, tilting the scales too far in the criminal's direction" (Friedman 1993, 302).

Over the course of the 1970s, a liberal activist Court committed to the protection of individual rights became increasingly at odds with a public concerned about rising crime rates and social upheaval. Noting that public confidence in the Court dropped precipitously from 1966 to 1984 and "hit rock bottom in 1971," Gregory Caldeira presents some evidence to suggest that as the Court handed down more rulings in support of the rights of the accused, the public's confidence in the Court decreased (1986). Although admitting that the public may not have "sharply defined conceptions of the Court or its policies," Caldeira concludes that "the mass public as a whole responds in a systematic fashion to shifts in the public policies the judges enunciate. Clearly, the public has little sympathy for either the esoterica of criminal procedure or the people who most often utilize these safeguards and apparently translates these attitudes into lack of confidence in the Court" (1986, 1223).

The story that emerges, then, is more a tale of a public at odds with the Supreme Court than a public led by it. It is difficult to delineate the precise role the Court's decisions played in sparking the backlash of the late 1960s and early 1970s, and it is likely that public opinion was more directly shaped by the fear that social forces were moving the country toward greater unrest. However, the Court served as an attractive antagonist against which politicians, eager to exploit public concerns about crime, could define their own agendas.

Public Opinion on Due Process and Crime, 1964–1978

The first year in which surveys began to tap public sentiments related to the Court and the rights of the accused was 1964, and it was not until the 1970s that pollsters asked specific and repeated questions about this topic. In the absence of long-term, time-series data on public opinion toward Court cases affirming the rights of the accused, we must piece together data from a variety of different sources. That said, the available data tell a compelling story.

The 1960s witnessed a significant rise in public awareness of rights for the accused, and evidence suggests that ordinary citizens, to the extent that they are ever attentive to the activities of the Supreme Court, became increasingly aware that this issue was repeatedly before the Court. In 1964 (the year after *Gideon* and two years after *Mapp*) and again in 1966 (the year of *Miranda*), the American National Election Study (ANES) at the University of Michigan asked respondents whether they could name actions taken by the Supreme Court that they either liked or disliked.[4] In 1964, 83% of respondents named no positive action taken by the Court, and 91% named no negative action— results that doubtless reflected respondents' low levels of political information and awareness (Converse 1964; Zaller 1992). After all, the open-ended question required respondents to come up with a topic, not merely to respond to a question about a given issue. To answer, a respondent would have had to be aware of what the Supreme Court was doing, interested enough to have formed an opinion about it, and confident enough of that opinion to express it. Of those who did make a positive comment about the Court, the vast majority

(71%) cited civil rights as the area in which they viewed the Supreme Court most positively. Of those who responded with a negative comment, civil rights and school prayer were the two dominant concerns; protection of the rights of the accused came in third.

When the NES asked the same question just two years later, a similar percentage (17%) named something they liked about the Supreme Court. However, a full 38% expressed a specific dislike. This suggests both that the public had become more aware of the actions of the Court and that their increasing awareness was predominantly of actions the public disliked. Almost 20% of respondents who mentioned a specific dislike (or about 8% of the total respondents) cited protection of the rights of the accused as their complaint, noting their aversion to the Court's support for the right to counsel, a fair trial, and protection from forced confessions.

By 1970, the NES was directly registering the public's growing interest in the rights of the accused. When asked "How important would you say this issue of protecting the rights of the accused is to you: very important, somewhat important, not very important, not important," 67% of respondents replied "very important," and another 28% said "somewhat important." Black respondents evinced a more intense level of interest than whites: 75% of blacks, compared with 66% of whites, answered "very important."[5] However, the data show no significant relationship between party affiliation and interest in the issue, with 69% of Democrats, 68% of independents, and 64% of Republicans replying that the issue was very important to them.[6]

Over the course of the 1970s, the NES also recorded a shift in aggregate public opinion, as a larger proportion of respondents asserted the belief that "stop[ping] criminal activity" was more important than "protect[ing] the legal rights of the accused." In 1970, 37% of the public placed themselves at the due process end of the scale. By 1978, only 28% did so (see Figure 2.2).[7] Concurrently, respondents at the crime-control end of the scale rose from 47% in 1970 to 54% in 1978.

Like most national survey samples, the longitudinal NES study interviewed relatively few African Americans—roughly 200 each time the survey was administered—and inferences about differences between racial groups are therefore tentative. That said, the statistics suggest a somewhat surprising picture: in 1970, black and white Americans had significantly different responses to the NES question about the rights of the accused, but by 1978 the opinions of blacks had almost converged with those of whites (see Figure 2.3). In 1970, 30% of white respondents and 68% of black respondents expressed a due process position; by 1978, these percentages had fallen to 27% of whites and 32% of blacks—a difference that is statistically insignificant.

The NES also collected data on party affiliation, with respondents identifying themselves on a 7-point scale: strong Democrat, weak Democrat, independent who leans Democrat, "true" independent, independent who leans Republican, weak Republican, or strong Republican. In the data reported here,

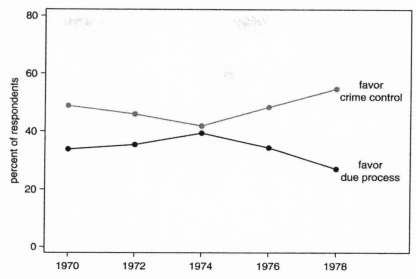

Figure 2.2. Public Attitudes toward Due Process and Crime Control, 1970–1978. Percentages indicate support for positions on a 7-point scale in response to the question, Some people are primarily concerned with doing everything possible to protect the legal rights of those accused of committing crimes. Others feel that it is more important to stop criminal activity even at the risk of reducing the rights of the accused. Where would you place yourself on this scale, or haven't you thought much about this? (7-point scale shown to respondent, with 1 = "protect rights of the accused" and 7 = "stop crime regardless of rights of the accused"). Source: American National Election Studies.

this scale is collapsed into three categories to compare the mean scores of "true" independents to the mean scores of those with Republican or Democratic leanings and identifications. Democratic respondents are subdivided into Northerners and Southerners. With black respondents excluded, the data show some partisan differences, but these are rather small. Moreover, all three partisan groups shifted their opinions uniformly over the decade. The difference-in-difference between Democrats and Republicans at the end of the decade, 0.4 (or 6% of the scale), is almost identical to that at the beginning.

The significant variation appears within the Democratic Party itself, between white Northern Democrats and white Southern Democrats. In 1970, the average self-rating for Northern Democrats was 4, slightly above the mean of the index, compared with 4.9 for Southern Democrats, a difference of about 13% of the total scale.[8] By the end of the decade, however, the difference between Northern and Southern white Democrats was no longer statistically significant.

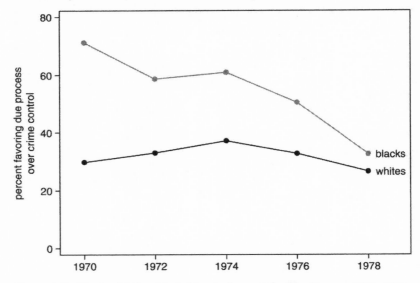

Figure 2.3. The Racial Gap Diminishes in Support for Due Process, 1970–1978. Percentages indicate proportion indicating support for "due process" position (5, 6, or 7) on a 7-point scale. See Figure 2.2 for question wording. Source: American National Election Studies.

Multivariate regression analyses confirm and extend our understanding of these NES data. In the multistage models shown in Table 2.1, support for crime control (as opposed to due process) in 1970 is regressed on four sets of variables. Model I uses only age, race, and sex as attitude predictors; model II adds social characteristics to these; model III adds several measures of political ideology (party identification, attitudes toward the war in Vietnam, attitude toward racial desegregation, support for small government); and model IV adds concerns about social unrest, measures of the perceived importance of the rights of the accused, whether crime is viewed as a major issue, and the degree to which a respondent has positive feelings toward marijuana users.

These regression analyses indicate that both race and age are significant predictors of attitudes on this issue. African Americans were significantly more likely to support the rights of the accused in 1970, and older respondents were somewhat less likely to take a pro-rights stance. However, the age effect disappears once one controls for the effects of political variables.

Somewhat surprisingly, neither gender nor most of the social characteristics included in model II appear significantly correlated with attitudes toward the rights of the accused. Exceptions to this are that people with more education were likely to be somewhat more supportive of due process, as were those residing outside the South. When education and Southern residence are accounted for, racial differences appear slightly larger.

Table 2.1

Predicting Support for Crime Control over Due Process

Variables	I	II	III	IV
Immutable demographic characteristics				
Age	.02***	.02***	.01	.00
	(.00)	(.00)	(.01)	(.01)
Black	−1.54***	−1.81***	−.98***	−.65*
	(.15)	(.19)	(.28)	(.28)
Female	.11	.15	−.08	−.02
	(.11)	(.12)	(.18)	(.18)
Social characteristics				
Education		−.01***	−.02***	−.01*
		(.00)	(.01)	(.01)
Income		.05*	.04	.03
		(.03)	(.05)	(.05)
South		.26*	−.08	−.16
		(.13)	(.20)	(.19
Nonurban		−.03	−.03	−.01
		(.04)	(.06)	(.06)
Children		−.12	−.30	−.33
		(.17)	(.23)	(.23)
Unemployment		−.20	.02	−.03
		(.35)	(.47)	(.45)
Political Orientation				
Democrat			−.48*	−.31
			(.21)	(.21)
Independent			.02	.22
			(.31)	(.30)
Support for Vietnam			.04	−.02
			(.04)	(.04)
Support for racial desegregation			.06	.00
			(.07)	(.07)
Support for small government			.43***	.35***
			(.08)	(.08)
Rights of the Accused				
Support using force to quell unrest				.32***
				(.06)
Rights of accused important issue				.46**
				(.15)
Crime major issue				.05
				(.19)
FT of marijuana users				−.01#
				(.00)

(continued)

Table 2.1

(continued)

Variables	I	II	III	IV
Constant	3.36***	4.04***	3.70***	.95
	(.17)	(.43)	(.76)	(.93)
N	1,424	1,208	556	532
Adj. R²	.10	.11	.18	.25
S.E.E.	2.089	2.061	2.001	1.90

Table entries are unstandardized regression coefficients with estimated standard errors in parentheses. ***$p<.001$; **$p<.01$; *$p<.05$; #$p<.10$.
Dependent variable measures proportion indicating support for "due process" position (5, 6, or 7) on a 7-point scale. See notes to Figure 2.2 for question wording.
Source: American National Election Studies.

Model III generally confirms the partisan trends already discussed, show-ing that Democrats were somewhat more rights-supportive than Republi-cans. These partisan differences were quite small, though, and they disappear altogether in model IV, when opinions on crime and social unrest are accounted for.

As model IV indicates, respondents who viewed the rights of the accused as an important issue were more inclined to favor crime prevention at the expense of individual rights. The NES survey also included several questions tapping respondents' relative social conservatism, including attitudes toward the war in Vietnam and toward racial integration, but there was no signifi-cant relation between respondents' attitudes on those issues and their position on crime control. In contrast, attitudes toward the rights of the accused were significantly related to feelings about urban and campus unrest: respondents who supported the use of force to quell these disturbances were more likely to support the crime-control model of criminal justice. Not surprisingly, respon-dents who felt more positively toward marijuana users were also slightly more inclined toward protecting the rights of the accused.

The 1978 NES did not ask all the same questions as the 1970 survey, but it did include enough of the same variables to allow us to run models I through III and compare the regressions. These regression analyses corroborate the trend noted earlier: that by 1978 there was no longer a significant difference between black and white respondents on the issue of the rights of the accused.

Public Opinion in the Rehnquist Era

Over the years, the public has continued to remain interested in issues sur-rounding the rights of the accused. As Julian Roberts points out, "Stories relating to criminal justice are never far from the front pages and from the collective consciousness" (1992). When asked to name any of the constitutional rights accorded to people accused of serious crimes, 78% of the public can name at least one (Center for Survey Research & Analysis 2000)—an impressively high percentage for a mostly uninformed public. Likewise, public interest in the rights of the accused has by no means waned. In 1996, 68% of the public felt that protecting the rights of the accused was very important to them, and another 20% said it was somewhat important to them (Texas A & M University, Sam Houston State University, and Public Policy Research Institute 1996).

As discussed in detail below, surveys also suggest that the public has gradually come to accept the once-controversial rulings of the Warren Court and that far fewer people now believe that the Court's decisions in cases like *Mapp, Gideon,* and *Miranda* were seriously flawed. Yet although the public may have become more comfortable with due process rules and procedures laid out by the Court in these cases, they remain as skeptical as ever of the underlying ideology. In general, the public remains apprehensive of expanding the rights of the accused and unwilling to support individual rights at the expense of fighting crime. When forced to choose, a large majority of the public continues to believe that being tough on criminals is more important than protecting individual rights.

Changing Attitudes toward Miranda

Leo and Thomas (1998) go so far as to call *Miranda* "the most controversial criminal procedure case that the Court had ever decided" and discuss its onerous struggle to acquire legitimacy, given that it was "truly without precedent in the United States." At the time of the 1966 decision, only 32% of the public believed that the restrictions on police power laid out by the Court were correct and fair. A majority, 56%, believed instead that the police should be allowed to be tougher with suspects (Opinion Research Corporation 1966).

Yet a great deal has changed since then, as the *Miranda* warning has become an integral, and even mundane, part of police work. "[T]he same law enforcement community that once regarded the 1966 *Miranda* decision as a death blow to criminal investigation has now come to see the explanation of rights as a routine part of the process—simply a piece of station house furniture, if not a civilizing influence on police work itself" (Simon 1991). As the Court noted in its opinion on *Dickerson v. United States,* "*Miranda* has become embedded in routine police practice to the point where the warnings have become part of our national culture" (2000).

Thus in 2000, when the Court reaffirmed *Miranda* in *Dickerson,* 86% of the public agreed with the decision to require "police to inform arrested suspects of their rights to remain silent and to have a lawyer present during any questioning" (Newsweek and Princeton Survey Research Associates). The data show no sizable differences in support for upholding *Miranda* by either race or partisan identification: a large majority of both blacks (89%) and whites

(86%) agreed with the Court's decision, as did a large majority of Democrats (90%), independents (86%), and Republicans (82%). There were likewise no significant differences between Southerners and those from other regions of the country.

Nor did perceptions of the Supreme Court itself appear to significantly influence agreement with the *Dickerson* ruling. When asked about the ideological leaning of the Supreme Court, about 17% of the public felt that the Court is generally liberal, 14% that the Court is generally conservative, and 62% that the Court makes decisions "more on a case-by-case basis" (Newsweek and Princeton Survey Research Associates 2000). Not surprisingly, this perception is affected by party identification, with more Republicans (30%) than Democrats (9%) holding the Court to be generally liberal in its decision making, and more Democrats (20%) than Republicans (10%) perceiving a conservative Court.

Yet these perceptions do not appear to influence support for the Court's decision in *Dickerson*. Republicans who thought that the Court was generally liberal were no less likely to support the *Dickerson* ruling than Republicans who thought the Court tends toward conservatism. Democrats who thought the Court was conservative supported the *Dickerson* ruling at roughly similar rates as those who perceived the Court to be generally liberal. The same holds for measures of general confidence in the Court. Those who purported to have a great deal of confidence in the Court were no more likely to support the decision to uphold *Miranda* rights than those who stated some or very little confidence in the Supreme Court as an institution (Newsweek and Princeton Survey Research Associates 2000).

Public Opinion and the Right to Counsel

The public remains well aware of a criminal defendant's right to a lawyer. In three surveys—a 1977 survey by the National Center for State Courts, a 1983 study by the Hearst Corporation, and a 2001 survey by Belden, Russonello, and Stewart for the National Legal Aid and Defender Association—between 93% and 97% of respondents identified the right to a lawyer as a constitutional guarantee, and 88% identified the right to a court-appointed lawyer if a defender could not afford one. Moreover, the vast majority of Americans (91%) consider the provision of legal assistance for indigent defendants to be an important component of the criminal justice system (Texas A&M University 1996); a full 96% deem the provision of a defense lawyer for those who cannot afford one to be a right that is either "essential" or "important but not essential" (Center for Survey Research and Analysis 2000). The right to counsel is also a right that few people would willingly give up: a 1994 Gallup/ America's Talking poll on patriotism found that only 14% of people would willingly give up the right to have a lawyer if they were arrested, even in an effort to reduce overall levels of crime.

Of the major Court decisions on the rights of the accused, *Gideon* was arguably received as the least controversial. Most states recognized the need for counsel in order to assure a fair trial (Beaney 1963, 1156), and as Anthony Lewis writes in *Gideon's Trumpet*, "To even the best-informed person unfamiliar with the law it seemed inconceivable, in the year 1962, that the Constitution would allow a man to be tried without a lawyer because he could not afford one" (1989). Although Lewis perhaps overstates the case when it comes to the general public, "for the most part, media and the legal community praised Gideon" (Rosen 1986).

Questions about the modern public's enthusiasm for *Gideon* arise when one reviews the states' unwillingness or inability to assure *effective* counsel for the indigent. In particular, many state legislatures have declined to adopt stringent oversight of state-provided counsel and have failed to provide the resources to public defenders that are available to privately hired counsel (Levine 1975; Lewis 2003). The public has not been aggressive in calling for greater support for state-appointed counsel. Indeed, despite almost unanimous support for the right to a lawyer, only 57% of respondents support guaranteeing indigent defendants a lawyer with a small caseload, and only 48% support guaranteeing indigent defendants a lawyer with equivalent experience to that of a private lawyer (Belden et al. 2001).

The public is equally divided over who should pay for court-appointed lawyers and how much money should be spent. When asked whether they favored or opposed using taxpayer funds to provide court-appointed lawyers to people accused of crimes, only 64% were in favor (Belden et al. 2001)—far below the 91% and 96% who voiced support for the right to a lawyer. When further asked whether in their state the government "should be spending more or spending less on legal defense for people who cannot afford a lawyer," 57% supported keeping spending at its current level, 14% supported a reduction, and 17% supported an increase (Belden et al. 2001).

Public Opinion and Police Tactics

In *Mapp*, the Supreme Court formally expanded the scope of the exclusionary rule by ruling that evidence obtained illegally is inadmissible in state courts. We have little survey data about public attitudes toward exclusionary standards in the years immediately following *Mapp*. More recently, the public has been divided over whether evidence obtained illegally should be admissible in a court of law, with a significant proportion opposed to exclusion of relevant evidence. In 1981, 56% of people supported the admissibility at trial of evidence that was obtained illegally "if police thought they were complying with the law when they seized the evidence." Only 30% of people favored excluding such evidence (Roper Organization). In 1989, 41% agreed with the statement "Prosecutors should have the right to use any evidence of wrongdoing they have against a person accused of a crime, even if it was obtained illegally"

(American Civil Liberties Union and Peter D. Hart Research Associates 1989). In 2000, 64% either strongly or somewhat agreed that "even if evidence is illegally obtained it should be allowed in court if it helps to prove that someone is guilty" (Center for Survey Research & Analysis).

Contemporary Attitudes toward the Ideology of Due Process

As the preceding discussion has suggested, the public has in many ways become more comfortable with the Supreme Court's rulings on criminal procedure. In 1970, 77% felt that the decisions of the Court had made it too easy for criminals to escape punishment (Time Magazine), but by 1991, 63% felt that the Supreme Court was doing too much to protect the rights of the accused (ABC News/Washington Post). While the phrasing is somewhat different between these two questions, the 14-point decrease suggests a change in public opinion in the direction of support for due process. However, it may also reflect a significant change in the character of the Court. In the post-Warren era, the Court has been less overtly supportive of the rights of the accused and has handed down a number of decisions on the side of crime control (Smith et al. 2003, 125–37).

Yet despite increasing support for the Court's decisions around criminal procedure and for many of the legal protocols these decisions enshrined, a sizable majority of the public continues to embrace an ideological position most closely aligned with a crime-control model. When we track public attitudes from 1970 through 2002, we find a decreasing percentage of the public supporting a due process position. In 1989, only 16% of the public were concerned that "the constitutional rights of some people accused of committing crimes [were] not being upheld," compared with 79% who were more worried that criminals were being "let off too easily" (Gallup Organization). Notably, by 2002 only 18% felt that "even if this means some guilty people are let go, it's important to protect the rights of the accused" (Farkas et al. 2002)—one measure of the considerable disconnect between the Warren Court's criminal justice philosophy and the ideological position of contemporary Americans.[9]

The data from 2002 show no significant difference between blacks' and whites' attitudes on this question. Apparently, high incarceration rates among African American men have not caused the racial gap in attitudes seen in the early 1970s to reemerge.[10] The data also show no significant partisan differences in expressions of support for due process, with Republicans, independents, and Democrats expressing support at aggregate levels of 17%, 20%, and 18%, respectively. Partisan differences appear only in support for crime control relative to the other options, and even here the gap is not particularly large. Republicans (34%) are slightly more likely to express support for crime control relative to due process or both than either independents (28%) or Democrats (27%).

An even clearer indication of the continuing ideological divide between the Warren Court and the modern public is that, when forced to make a choice, the public at large remains unwilling to support rights protections at the expense of public safety. In a 1998 survey, a national sample of adults was asked, if they "absolutely had to choose between each of the following values, which is more important to you, personally? Being tough on criminals, or protecting the rights of those accused of crime?" Here, a large majority (76%) felt that it was more important to be tough on criminals (Washington Post/Kaiser Family Foundation/Harvard Americans on Values Follow-up Survey).

Moreover, respondents who chose being tough on crime felt more strongly about their position than respondents who chose protecting rights. Of those who said that protecting the rights of the accused was more important to them, 40% said that it was much more important, and 37% that it was somewhat more important. By comparison, 66% of respondents who chose being tough on criminals said that this was much more important to them than protecting the rights of those accused of crimes, with an additional 25% calling it somewhat more important (Washington Post, Henry J. Kaiser Family Foundation, and Harvard University 1998).

The continuing hesitation of the public to afford the accused more rights may be due in part to a strong sense that those who are accused of crimes are usually guilty. Although the law assumes that anyone who has been accused of a crime is innocent until proven guilty (Goldstein 1971; Fleming 1974), only a minority of Americans believe that the system should be predicated on the assumption of innocence, and most believe that those who are accused of committing crimes are usually guilty. A majority of Americans (64% in 1993 and 57% in 1995) believe that "regardless of what the law says, a defendant in a criminal trial should be required to prove his or her innocence" (Cable News Network, USA Today, and Gallup Organization). Similarly, 54% of Americans believe those who are accused of crimes are either always or frequently guilty (National Legal Aid and Defender Association), and 63% believe that those who are arrested for crimes are always or frequently guilty (Belden et al. 2001). The belief that those who have been arrested are generally guilty appears significantly related to attitudes about what services the accused should be afforded. Those who agree that "most people who are arrested and charged with crimes are guilty" are also significantly more likely to voice opposition to increased government funding for court-appointed lawyers (Belden et al. 2001).

The public's hesitancy to support the rights of the accused may also be linked to a pervasive feeling that the criminal justice system is broken. Most Americans are reasonably confident that the criminal justice system "generally makes the right decision" about guilt and innocence; in 2001, 80% of Americans expressed either a great deal or some confidence in the system's ability to come to the right conclusion (CBS News). Yet only 23% of whites and 25% of blacks express confidence in the criminal justice system as a whole, and a significant proportion of the public doubts the ability of the criminal justice system to carry out its most fundamental responsibility: combating crime (Gallup

Organization 2000). When asked how often they think "people who commit crimes get away without being punished," 94% of the public responded that this occurs either often or sometimes (Center for Survey Research & Analysis 2000). Indeed, in a 1979 poll, more people named the excessive leniency of the judicial system as responsible for the increasing national crime rate (25%) than named unemployment (20%), lack of parental guidance or discipline (18%), the economic situation and inflation (13%), or drugs and alcohol (12%) (Gallup Organization). In a 1994 poll, 33% of people felt that the courts and the prison system were the institutions most culpable for increases in crime, more than home and schools (27%), pop culture and the media (14%), the government (12%), or the law enforcement system (8%) (Wirthlin Group).

The public clearly perceives a tension between the protection of individual rights and the ability of police and courts to effectively fight crime, and these concerns have serious implications for public attitudes toward the rights of the accused. In a 1989 poll, 78% of the public agreed that "protecting the constitutional rights of accused criminals makes law enforcement very difficult" (American Civil Liberties Union and Peter D. Hart Research Associates), and in a 1993 poll, 70% indicated their belief that "the criminal justice system makes it too hard for the police and prosecutors to convict people accused of crimes" (Cable News Network, USA Today, and Gallup Organization). As long as the public perceives a trade-off between individual rights and the maintenance of safety and security, the majority are likely to continue supporting crime control over a due process model of criminal justice.

Conclusion

In a recent debate over the addition of a crime victim's amendment to the Constitution, Senator Patrick Leahy (D-Vermont) wrote: "The few and limited rights of the accused in the Constitution are there precisely because it will often be unpopular to enforce them—so that even when we are afraid of a rising tide of crime, we will be protected against our own impulses to take shortcuts that could sacrifice a fair trial of the accused and increase the risk of wrongful conviction" (2003).

To illustrate the historical disparity between the decisions of the Supreme Court and public attitudes toward the rights of the accused, this chapter has addressed changes in aggregate public opinion, as well as its composition, following the years in which the Court handed down a series of significant rulings (*Gideon v. Wainwright*; *Miranda v. Arizona*; and *Mapp v. Ohio*). The scarcity of polling data prior to these major Supreme Court decisions makes it difficult to establish whether the Court's decision directly affected the attitudes of the public toward the rights of the accused. What empirical evidence we have, however, suggests that the attitudes of the general public were out of sync with the Court in the years following its decisions and that the public in the aggregate became even less rights-oriented over the following decade.

The 1970s public does not appear to have divided along party lines in its support of crime control. Although there is evidence of a slight difference between Republican and Democratic evaluations of the importance of crime control relative to the protection of individual rights, this difference is substantively small. There is also evidence of decreasing divisions between the attitudes of black and white Americans. Whereas in 1970 African Americans were somewhat more likely to support a due process vision over one guided by crime control, this gap almost completely disappeared by 1978. Over the course of the decade, African American attitudes appear to have moved steadily toward that of whites and away from the position of the Court.

In the decades since, the public appears to have become more comfortable with the procedures and protocols established by the Supreme Court's due process decisions. In particular, the public has come to view the outcomes of *Gideon* and *Miranda* as broadly legitimate. Yet this by no means suggests that the public has come to embrace the philosophical position of the Court on constitutional protections for the accused. When the rights of those accused of crimes are considered in light of competing concerns, such as the desire to prosecute crime and to ensure that those who are guilty are found guilty, the modern public appears still more closely aligned with an ideological position emphasizing crime control.

Appendix: Data and Methods

The following surveys are analyzed and presented in the text:

Surveys by the American National Election Studies. Multiple years. Conducted through face-to-face interviews with a nationally representative sample of adults.

Surveys by the Gallup Organization. Multiple years. Conducted through telephone interviews with a nationally representative samples of adults.

Surveys by the General Social Survey. Conducted by the National Opinion Research Center (NORC) at the University of Chicago, multiple years. Conducted through national area probability sample of about 1,500 adults prior to 1994 and 3,000 adults thereafter. Data include black oversamples.

Survey by National Constitution Center. Conducted by Public Agenda Foundation, July 10–July 24, 2002. Based on telephone interviews with a national adult sample of 1,520. Fieldwork by Robinson and Muenster Associates, Inc.

Survey by Newsweek and Princeton Survey Research Associates, June 29–June 30, 2000. Based on telephone interviews with a national adult sample of 752.

The following survey results are reported in the text and were obtained from searches of the Gallup Brain online database provided by the Gallup Organization, Princeton, N.J.:

Survey by Gallup Organization, June 8–June 11, 1989. Based on telephone interviews with a national adult sample of 1,235.

Survey by Gallup Organization, October 1979. Based on telephone interviews with a national adult sample of 1,541.

The following survey results are reported in the text and were obtained from searches of the iPOLL Databank and other resources provided by the Roper Center for Public Opinion Research, University of Connecticut:

Survey by ABC News/Washington Post, July 1, 1991. Based on telephone interviews with a national adult sample of 553. Interviewing was conducted by ICR Survey Research Group.

Survey by American Civil Liberties Union and Peter D. Hart Research Associates, February 21–February 25, 1989. Conducted by Peter D. Hart Research Associates and based on telephone interviews with a national adult sample of 1,003.

Survey by Cable News Network, USA Today, and Gallup Organization, February 8–February 9, 1993. Based on telephone interviews with a national adult sample of 840. The sample included 503 whites and 315 blacks. The national results are weighted to the correct proportion in the population. The questions in this survey replicate the questions asked of the jurors in the jury selection for the Rodney King case in federal court.

Survey by Cable News Network, USA Today, and Gallup Organization, March 17–March 19, 1995. Conducted by Gallup Organization and based on telephone interviews with a national adult sample of 1,220. The survey included 1,000 national adults and an oversample of 220 blacks. The results reported were asked of the national adult and black oversample and are weighted to be representative of the national adult population.

Survey by CBS News, June 9, 2001. Based on telephone interviews with a national adult sample of 565. The respondents were first interviewed May 1–12, 2001, and were reinterviewed June 9, 2001.

Survey by CBS News, September 5–September 6, 1995. Based on telephone interviews with a national adult sample of 1,069. The sample included an oversample of blacks. Results were weighted to be representative of a national adult population.

Survey by CBS News, July 5, 1994. Based on telephone interviews with a national adult sample of 601.

Survey by Center for Survey Research & Analysis, University of Connecticut, February 17–March 7, 2000. Based on telephone interviews with a national adult sample of 1,011.

Survey by TIME Magazine. Conducted by Louis Harris and Associates, 1970.

Survey by Hearst Corporation and Research & Forecasts, August 20–August 25, 1983. Conducted by Research & Forecasts, August 20–August 25, 1983, and based on telephone interviews with a national adult sample of 983.

Survey by National Center for State Courts and Yankelovich Clancy Shulman, October 1–December 31, 1977. Based on personal interviews with a national adult sample of 1,931. The study also had three other samples of influentials: 317 lawyers, 194 state and local judges, and 278 community leaders.

Survey by Newsweek and Princeton Survey Research Associates, June 29–June 30, 2000. Based on telephone interviews with a national adult sample of 752.

Survey by Newsweek and Gallup Organization, November, 1970. Conducted by Gallup Organization and based on personal interviews with a national adult sample of 519.

Survey by Opinion Research Corporation, December 1966. Based on personal interviews with a national adult sample of 946.

Survey by Roper Organization, September 19–September 26, 1981. Based on personal interviews with a national adult sample of 2,000.

Survey by Texas A & M University, Sam Houston State University, and Public Policy Research Institute, Texas A&M University, May 16–June 1, 1996. Conducted by Public Policy Research Institute, Texas A&M University, and based on telephone interviews with a national adult sample of 1,085.

Survey by Washington Post, Henry J. Kaiser Family Foundation, Harvard University, August 10–August 27, 1998. Conducted by Washington Post and based on telephone interviews with a national adult sample of 1,200. Interviewing was conducted by Chilton Research.

Survey by Washington Post, January 1978. Based on telephone interviews with a national adult sample of 1,519. Interviewing was conducted by George Fine Research, Inc.

Survey by Wirthlin Group, September 6–September 9, 1994. Based on telephone interviews with a national adult sample of 1,019.

Notes

1. Under U.S. Code 3501, reading a *Miranda* warning to a suspect was treated as one of several criteria to be weighed in judging the admissibility of a confession, and a confession was admissible even if one of the factors had been overlooked. This effectively moved the admissibility standard back toward the voluntariness test, where it had been prior to the *Miranda* ruling.

2. Some argue that in deciding *Miranda* the Court invited Congress to legislate its own safeguards so long as they were as effective as *Miranda* in preventing self-incrimination; see Hendrie (1997) and Cassell (2001). It is unlikely, however, that 3501 is what the justices had in mind, to the extent that the statutory law as written undermines *Miranda*'s specific safeguards.

3. Of course, there was also dissension among elites, and many in the legal community directly challenged these criticisms of the Court; see Kamisar (1962).

4. Question: "We are all pretty busy these days and can't be expected to keep up on everything. Have you had time to pay any attention to what the Supreme Court of the United States has been doing in the past few years? Is there anything in particular that it has done that you have liked or disliked? What is that? Anything else?"

5. The chi-square for these group differences is 8.654 and is significant at the $p<.05$ level. However, as the sample size of African American respondents is small, this finding is suggestive rather than conclusive.

6. There likewise appears to be no difference relative to employment status, income, or education. All demographic variables were assessed in simple crosstabs, as well as in a logistic regression.

7. The exact question was "Some people are primarily concerned with doing everything possible to protect the legal rights of those accused of committing crimes. Others feel that it is more important to stop criminal activity even at the risk of reducing the rights of the accused" (for the response scale, see Figure 2.2). It is worth noting an asymmetry in the phrasing: expressing greater support for stopping criminal activity required a trade-off between crime control and the reduction of rights for the accused, but expressing greater support for the protection of individual rights did not require the respondent to explicitly risk an increase in criminal activity. This framing, if it had any affect, likely influenced respondents to place themselves lower on the scale, in the direction of support for rights protections.

8. This difference is significant at the $p<.001$ level, with an F statistic of 21.539.

9. There is some evidence that a larger proportion of the public has come to support *both* due process and crime control. Compared with 18% of the public in 1978 who held a position somewhere in the middle of the ideological spectrum, in 2002 50% of the public felt that "it's just as important to protect the rights of the accused as it is to put guilty people in jail" (Farkas et al. 2002).

10. The African American samples in these surveys are again too small for conclusive analyses.

_____

References

Baker, L. 1983. *Miranda: The Crime, the Law, the Politics.* New York: Atheneum.

Balkin, S. 1979. "Victimization Rates, Safety and Fear of Crime." *Social Problems* 26: 343–58.

Beaney, W. M. 1963. "The Right to Counsel: Past, Present and Future." *Virginia Law Review* 49(6): 1150–59.

Belden, Russonello, and Stewart Research and Communications. 2001. *Developing a National Message for Indigent Defense: Analysis of a National Survey.* Washington, D.C.: Open Society Institute and National Legal Aid and Defender Association.

Broderick, V. L. 1966. "The Supreme Court and the Police: A Police Viewpoint." *Journal of Criminal Law, Criminology and Police Science* 57(3): 271–82.

Caldeira, G. 1986. "Neither the Purse nor the Sword: Dynamics of Public Confidence in the Supreme Court." *American Political Science Review* 80(4): 1209–26.

Canon, B. C. 1973. "Reactions of State Supreme Courts to a U.S. Supreme Court Civil Liberties Decision." *Law and Society Review* 8(1): 109–34.

Cassell, P. G. 2001. "The Paths Not Taken: The Supreme Court's Failures in Dickerson." *Michigan Law Review* (Symposium: Miranda after Dickerson: The Future of Confession Law) 99(5): 898–940.

Converse, P. 1964. "The Nature of Belief Systems in Mass Publics." In *Ideology and Discontent,* edited by David Apter. New York: Free Press.

Farkas, S., J. Johnson, and A. Duffett. 2002. *Knowing It by Heart: Americans Consider the Constitution and Its Meaning.* Philadelphia: Public Agenda Foundation for the National Constitution Center.

Fleming, M. 1974. *The Price of Perfect Justice: The Adverse Consequences of Current Legal Doctrine on the American Courtroom.* New York: Basic Books.

Friedman, L. M. 1993. *Crime and Punishment in American History.* New York: Basic Books.

"Gideon's Promise Unfulfilled: The Need for Litigated Reform of Indigent Defense." 2000. *Harvard Law Review Note* 113(8): 2062–79.

Goldstein, A. S. 1971. "The State and the Accused: Balance of Advantage." In *Crime, Law and Society,* edited by Abraham S. Goldstein and Joseph Goldstein. New York: Free Press.

Hendrie, E. M. 1997. "Beyond 'Miranda.'" *FBI Law Enforcement Bulletin.*

Inbau, F. 1962. "Public Safety v. Individual Civil Liberties: The Prosecutor's Stand." *Journal of Criminal Law and Criminology* 89(4): 1413–20.

Kamisar, Y. 1962. "Public Safety v. Individual Liberties: Some 'Facts' and 'Theories.'" *Journal of Criminal Law* 53(2): 171–93.

Leahy, P. 2003. "Statement of Senator Patrick Leahy Markup of S.J. Res. 1 (Victims Rights Constitutional Amendment"

Leo, R. A. 1996. "The Impact of 'Miranda' Revisited." *Journal of Criminal Law and Criminology* 86(3): 621–92.

Leo, R. A., and G. C. Thomas III. 1998. *The Miranda Debate: Law, Justice and Policing.* Boston: Northeastern University Press.

Leonard, D. S. 1965. "The Changing Face of Criminal Law." *Journal of Criminal Law, Criminology and Police Science* 56(4): 517–22.

Levine, J. P. 1975. "The Impact of 'Gideon': The Performance of Public and Private Criminal Defense Lawyers." *Polity* 8(2): 215–40.

Lewis, A. 1989. *Gideon's Trumpet.* New York: Knopf.

Lewis, A. 2003. "The Silencing of Gideon's Trumpet." *New York Times Magazine,* April 23.

MacKenzie, J. P. 1968. "The Warren Court and the Press." *Michigan Law Review* 67(2): 303–16.

Packer, H. 1964. "Two Models of the Criminal Process." *University of Pennsylvania Law Review* 113(1).

Roach, K. 1989. "Four Models of the Criminal Justice Process." *Journal of Criminal Law and Criminology* 89(2): 671.

Roberts, J. V. 1992. "Public Opinion, Crime and Criminal Justice." *Crime and Justice* 16: 99–180.

Rosen, C. J. 1986. "'Miranda': Crime, Law and Politics." *Journal of Criminal Law and Criminology* 77(1): 248–51.

Simon, D. 1991. "Homicide: A Year on the Killing Streets." In *The Miranda Debate,* edited by Richard A. Leo and George C. Thomas III. Boston: Northeastern University Press.

Smith, C. E., C. DeJong, and J. D. Burrow. 2003. *The Supreme Court, Crime, and the Ideal of Equal Justice.* New York: Peter Lang.

Specter, A. 1962. "Mapp v. Ohio: Pandora's Problems for the Prosecutor." *University of Pennsylvania Law Review* 111(1): 4–45.

Zaller, J. 1992. *The Nature and Origins of Mass Opinion.* Cambridge: Cambridge University Press.

3

School Prayer

Alison Gash and Angelo Gonzales

The practice of prayer in American public schools is as old as American public education itself. Although the earliest systematic surveys of the practice were not performed until the middle of the twentieth century, they show that twenty-four states either allowed or required a prayer as part of the school day. Moreover, according to a 1961 survey of public school superintendents, 42% of schools conducted Bible reading, about half of the school systems included schools that permitted homeroom devotionals, and 76% distributed materials to their teachers to help them teach about religion (Fenwick 1989, 135). Beginning in the early 1960s, however, school prayer became a matter of national debate after two landmark Supreme Court decisions each held that prayer in public schools violated the Establishment Clause of the First Amendment. In *Engel v. Vitale* (1962), the Supreme Court ruled unconstitutional the following prayer that students in the New York State public schools recited at the beginning of each day: "Almighty God, we acknowledge our dependence upon Thee, and we beg Thy blessings upon us, our parents, our teachers and our Country." One year later, in *Abington School District v. Schempp* (1963), the Court struck down a Pennsylvania statute that required Bible reading, as well as a Baltimore ordinance that required the recitation of the Lord's Prayer in public schools. In all these cases, the fact that students could be excused from these religious exercises with the permission of their parents was insufficient to cure the statutes' constitutional defects.[1]

The decisions sent shock waves across the country. They clearly ran counter to the preference of an overwhelming majority of the American public. Tracking the trend in public opinion after the initial shock shows that over time public support for the right to conduct prayers in the public schools has declined somewhat, but a majority of Americans still disapprove of the Court's decisions. Even so, members of Congress have been unable to muster enough votes for a proposed constitutional amendment that would overturn the Court's rulings. In part, this may be due to the lower salience of the issue as people acquiesced, however grudgingly, to the new regime. As for the underpinnings of opposition to the Court's position on school prayer, religious affiliation rather than allegiance to a political party is a crucial factor, but education, age, and ethnic background also matter. Religiosity remains an important strand in the nation's political culture, and this helps explain the public's resistance to the Supreme Court's interpretation of the Establishment Clause in the school prayer cases.

The Controversy over School Prayer

For much of the public, the Court's rulings unexpectedly undermined local authorities' ability to craft school policies. Many also felt that the rulings disregarded the fundamental freedom of religious expression. Within days after the Court announced its decision in *Engel*, members of Congress from both sides of the aisle drafted proposals to overturn the ruling and to reprimand the Court. In all, fifty-six constitutional amendments were introduced (Flemming, Bohte, & Wood 1997, 1246). Senator Herman Talmadge (D-GA) characterized the decision as "unconscionable...an outrageous edict"; another member of Congress stated that it was "a deliberately and carefully planned conspiracy to substitute materialism for spiritual values and thus to communize America" (Alley 1994, 109). Congressman Frank Becker (R-NY), a leading opponent of the Court's ruling, asserted that it was "the most tragic decision in the history of the U.S." (Alley 1994, 109). House members voted unanimously to place "In God We Trust" behind the Speaker's desk, and one member circulated a bill to purchase a Bible for each Supreme Court justice (Beaney & Beiser 1964, 478). After *Schempp*, members of Congress introduced almost 150 constitutional amendments, spurred by a deluge of angry constituent letters (Beaney & Beiser 1964, 492).

Many state and local government officials were equally distraught over the decisions. In several states, school prayers had been required by statutes that had now been declared unconstitutional. In the absence of any institutional mechanism for assuring compliance—except through monitoring by local residents—states could delay implementation of the Court's decisions: "With the prospect of no rewards and few punishments, local elements were especially free to exercise their own discretion" (Dolbeare & Hammond, 1971, 136). For example, Alabama Governor George Wallace expressed his opposition to *Engel* by threatening to pray in a classroom, and mandatory daily Bible reading in Alabama's public schools ended only in 1971, after a ruling by a federal district court (Sorauf 1976, 295). Other governors concurred: One month after *Engel*, a governors' conference in Pennsylvania voted unanimously to support a constitutional amendment to overturn the decision; only Nelson Rockefeller of New York abstained (Beaney & Beiser 1964, 481). Throughout the nation, local city councils pledged to continue school prayers (Sorauf 1976, 295).

Schempp provoked more widespread backlash than *Engel* because it covered a larger category of prayers. Whereas *Engel* allowed policymakers to construe the ruling as applying solely to New York—or to a school prayer policy similar to New York's—*Schempp* declared unconstitutional an extensive set of policies and statutes. In a defiant response, the Kentucky state superintendent of public instruction encouraged schools to "continue to read and pray until somebody stops you." In Rhode Island, the state commissioner of education swore that he did "not now or in the future intend to prostitute the office of the Commissioner of Education, to further the cause of the irreligious, the atheistic, the unreligious, or the agnostic" (Beaney & Beiser 1964, 487). Creative state legislatures introduced alternative mechanisms for promoting "spirituality," such as reciting the lyrics to "America" during class, singing hymns in music appreciation class, studying the Bible for literary purposes, or starting the school day with a moment of meditation (Beaney & Beiser 1964, 487, 489). In fall 1963, among the ten states where Bible readings were still performed in the schools, three states—Arkansas, Alabama, and Delaware—required religious instruction in their public schools (Beaney & Beiser 1964, 490).

Unswayed by the vehement public dissent, the Court continued to declare religious instruction in public schools to be unconstitutional. In *Wallace v. Jaffree*, 472 U.S. 38 (1985), the Court expanded the scope of its precedents and overturned an Alabama law requiring that each school day begin with a moment of silence or meditation. The majority held that the Alabama statute failed to demonstrate any secular purpose for requiring a moment of silence and that the record offered "unrebutted" evidence that the Alabama legislature's sole intent was to return prayer to the public schools.

The contentiousness of the debate over school prayer arguably reflects the intensity of media coverage of the issue. To investigate this possibility, we tracked *New York Times* coverage of school prayer from 1962 to 2004 (see Figure 3.1). In general, coverage is sparse, spiking only in years when a ruling on school prayer was announced by the Supreme Court (1962–1963) or when the U.S. Congress voted on a proposed constitutional amendment (1964, 1982, 1984, and 1994). Between 1965 and 1982, the *New York Times* published an average of eight articles per year on school prayer (range: 1 to 19 articles). Heightened attention in 1982 and 1984 reflects congressional debates on a constitutional amendment, increased Christian Right activity on the issue, and statements by President Reagan in support of voluntary prayer in the schools. Although coverage rises again in 1994, it does not reach the levels seen in the aftermath of *Engel* and *Schempp* or surrounding the frenzy of legislative activity in the early 1980s.

Even as coverage in the *New York Times* clusters around major events and dips to low or moderate levels in the intervening years, the public's support for school prayer and its disapproval of the Court's decisions have remained relatively consistent and high, and fluctuations in media attention have had little or

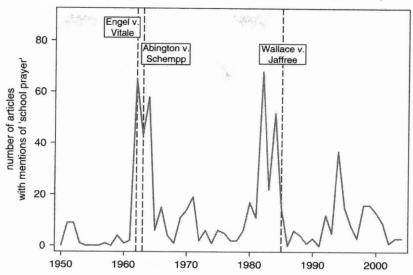

Figure 3.1. Coverage of School Prayer in the *New York Times*, 1950–2004. Source: ProQuest Direct.

no impact. That a majority of the public has remained so consistently against the Supreme Court's school prayer decisions for more than forty years, in the absence of consistent media coverage, is a notable finding, indicating that the opposition to these decisions has been fueled by something other than agenda setting by the media elite. As noted by Marshall (1989) and others, on the issue of prayer in public schools, the Supreme Court has indeed remained countermajoritarian.

Review of the Literature

Research on the response to the Supreme Court's school prayer decisions has focused on the responses of elite actors (e.g., Kurland 1962; Beaney & Beiser 1964) and interest groups (Sorauf 1976) and on local officials' decision to comply with or resist the rulings (e.g., Muir 1967; Johnson 1967; Dolbeare & Hammond 1971). Only a handful of studies examine the nature and structure of public opinion regarding school prayer, and most of those analyses treat school prayer as one of many policy domains through which to measure citizens' reactions to Court decisions (Murphy & Tanenhaus 1968; Tanenhaus & Murphy 1981; Barnum 1985; Marshall 1989; Flemming, Bohte, & Wood 1997; Hoekstra 2000; Alvarez, Brehn, & Wilson 2003). Flemming, Bohte, and Wood (1997) analyze the effect of Supreme Court decisions on public, elite, and media attentiveness to various issues, and they posit that significant Supreme Court decisions yield "large and enduring shifts in system-wide attention" (1224).

Analyzing media coverage on church-state issues, school desegregation, and freedom of speech, they find that four major decisions—on school prayer, desegregation, flag burning, and religious instruction in public schools—produced long-term shifts in issue attention. Specifically, the Court's decisions in *Engel* and in *McCollum v. Board of Education* (1948), which struck down a program to release students for religious instruction in public school, produced "immediate and enduring" increases in media attention and political response to church-state issues (1246).

Hoekstra (2000) uses panel data to identify factors that affect public opinion regarding Supreme Court cases (two establishment clause cases and two economic regulation cases) in the communities from which the cases emerged. She names two factors: the amount of information available about the decision and the extent to which individuals believe the decision and issue to be consequential. Media coverage influences an individual's awareness of Court decisions, as do geographic proximity to the affected area, education, gender, attentiveness to media, and frequency of political discussions. In analyzing variation in public opinion, Alvarez, Brehm, and Wilson (2003) find that individuals who score high on measures of traditional morality are more likely to support school prayer, and individuals with higher levels of "political informedness" have more stable opinions (20).

A few quantitative studies focus more exclusively on school prayer. Elifson and Hadaway (1985) use General Social Survey (GSS) and National Election Studies (NES) data from 1974, 1980, and 1982 to examine the demographic and social characteristics of individuals who support and oppose school prayer. They find that those supporting school prayer tend to be older, less educated, and politically and socially conservative; they also find that religious orthodoxy and religious salience are key predictors of support for school prayer. Wilcox (1993) analyzed the structure of attitudes regarding school prayer and other establishment clause issues through a 1987 phone survey of 1,708 respondents. The survey measured general attitudes toward the separation of church and state, as well as specific opinions on school prayer and creationism. Wilcox finds that while Americans endorse the separation of church and state in principle, they also support specific church-state ties.

Methods and Data

Our analysis relies on data collected by a number of studies and survey houses over the past forty years and most heavily on the cumulative files of the General Social Survey (GSS) and the American National Election Studies (ANES). Change in question wording over time complicates the study of opinion trends on school prayer because respondents are clearly influenced by the way questions are phrased. To contend with this challenge, we have identified three types of question wording among all the surveys and have analyzed each type separately (see Table 3.1). The first type of question asks individuals whether

Table 3.1
Three types of school prayer questions

Type	Survey Houses	Distinguishing Features	Typical Question Wording
1a	Gallup, Roper, USA Today, GSS (1991 only), Time-CNN	Support for public school prayer OR opposition to public school prayer	• Do you feel that individual school prayer should be allowed in the classroom? (USA Today 1985) • Do you favor or oppose allowing school children to say prayers in public schools? (Time/CNN 1991) • This card lists various proposals being discussed in this country today. Would you tell me whether you generally favor or generally oppose each of these proposals...prayer in public schools? (Gallup 1984)
1b	ANES (1964–1984), Student-Parent Socialization Panel, NBC/Wall Street Journal	Support for public school prayer OR opposition to religion in public schools	Some people think it is all right for the public schools to start each day with a prayer. Others feel that religion does not belong in the public schools but should be taken care of by the family and the church. Have you been interested enough in this to favor one side over the other? (IF YES) Which do you think—schools should be allowed to start each day with a prayer or religion does not belong in the schools? (ANES)
2	GSS, Gallup, Harris, NBC/Wall Street Journal	Approval of the Supreme Court's school prayer decisions OR disapproval of the Supreme Court's school prayer decisions	The United States Supreme Court has ruled that no state or local government may require the reading of the Lord's Prayer or Bible verses in public schools. What are your views on this—do you approve or disapprove of the court ruling? (GSS)
3	Gallup, Harris, NBC/WSJ, Roper	Support for a constitutional amendment OR opposition to a constitutional amendment	Please tell me whether you favor or oppose a constitutional amendment to allow voluntary prayer in public schools. (Gallup)

they support prayer in public schools. One variation of this question (type 1a) simply asks respondents whether they support or oppose school prayer. Some variations of this type (type 1b) put the choice to survey respondents more starkly, requiring them to say whether they support school prayer or are opposed to religion in public schools altogether. The second type of question asks respondents whether they agree or disagree with the Supreme Court's decisions regarding school prayer. A third type asks respondents whether they support the adoption of a constitutional amendment permitting prayer in public schools.

Aggregate Trends in Public Opinion

Over the course of more than four decades of public opinion research, Americans have supported prayer in public schools by large majorities. But by any measure, support for school prayer has declined somewhat over this time. Figure 3.2 plots responses collected by nine survey houses to the three types of questions assessing support for school prayer.[2] Included on these graphs are trend lines plotted with the "lowess" technique, which "smoothes" out random variation to better depict how the trend has changed over time (for a description, see Cleveland 1993; Fox 1997). The left panel of Figure 3.2, which plots responses to questions of type 1, shows that approval of school prayer dropped from the 1960s to the early 1980s and has remained relatively stable since then. As the broad span of data points suggests, however, question wording and survey methodology can have a dramatic effect on results, leading to differences that exceed 30 percentage points between surveys conducted within a relatively brief span of time. We plot two additional trends in the right-hand panel of Figure 3.2. At the bottom of this graph is the trend in disapproval of the Supreme Court's rulings on school prayer (question type 2). At the top of the graph is a trend indicating the proportion of Americans favoring the adoption of a constitutional amendment to permit prayer in public schools (question type 3). Both trends follow the same general pattern, with pro-school prayer opinion declining somewhat between the 1960s and 1980s but remaining strong and relatively stable since then. Throughout the entire period, though, rates of support for school prayer and support for a constitutional amendment exceeded rates of disapproval of the Supreme Court's decisions.

We can gain further insight about nuances of opinion on school prayer by examining how survey responses changed after the ANES altered its standard school prayer question beginning in 1986. Before then, the ANES used question version 1b: the survey forced respondents to choose whether they thought that "[public] schools should be allowed to start each day with a prayer" or that "religion does not belong in the schools." As shown in Figure 3.3, support for school prayer by this measure fell by some 30 percentage points between 1964 and 1984. But when the survey question was reworded in 1986, respondents were given the choice between silent prayer, general prayer, Christian prayer,

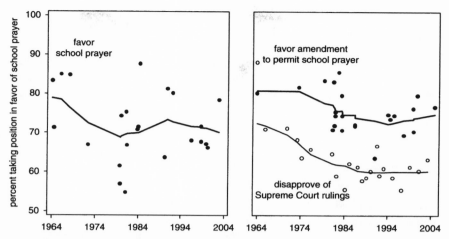

Figure 3.2. Support for School Prayer, 1964–2005. Question wording and sources: see text.

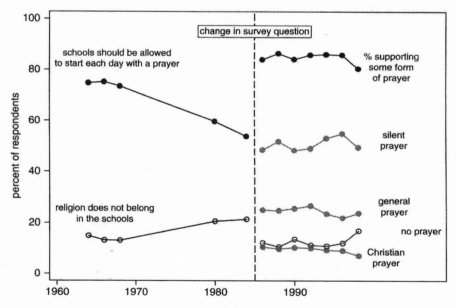

Figure 3.3. Support for School Prayer, 1964–1998. Question wording: see text.
Source: American National Election Studies.

and no prayer whatsoever. As shown on the right-hand side of the graph, this question revealed that the combined support for allowing some form of prayer was actually more than 80%—with half of respondents typically expressing a preference for silent prayer. Opinion remained at similar levels over the next twelve years.[3] In sum, even as more Americans came to believe that "religion does not belong in the public schools," most continued to approve of allowing schools to provide time for students to engage in voluntary silent prayer.

The Structure of Public Opinion on the Supreme Court's School Prayer Ban

The GSS has asked respondents their opinion regarding the Supreme Court's ban on prayer in public schools since 1974. We use these data to examine the structure of public opinion on the school prayer ban in three ways. In Figure 3.4, we plot trends in disapproval of the Court's rulings with regard to four relevant characteristics: race, birth cohort, religious denomination, and party identification. In Table 3.2, we employ multivariate analysis to better assess the extent to which the structure of opinion has changed over time.

Finally, in Table 3.3, we use a multistage estimation technique to closely examine the structure of opinion in 2004, the latest year for which GSS data

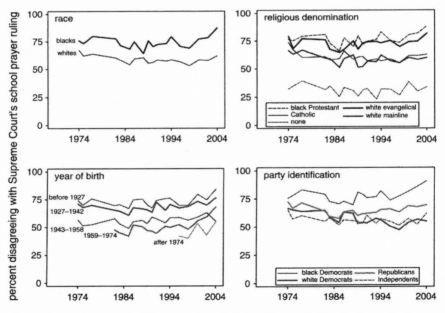

Figure 3.4. Disapproval of Supreme Court's School Prayer Rulings by Race, Birth Cohort, Religious Denomination, and Party Identification, 1974–2004. Question wording: See Table 3.2. Source: General Social Survey.

Table 3.2

The Structure of Opinion of the Supreme Court's Decisions on School Prayer, 1974–2004

	1974	1986	1996	2004
Sex, age, race, religion				
Female	.04	−.17	.00	.10
	(.12)	(.12)	(.07)	(.10)
Age	.01**	.01**	.01**	.01
	(.00)	(.00)	(.00)	(.00)
Attendance at religious services	.05*	.07**	.04**	.08***
	(.02)	(.02)	(.02)	(.02)
Black Protestant§	.78**	.54	.71***	1.23***
	(.30)	(.28)	(.16)	(.28)
Catholic§	.85***	.35	.42***	.26
	(.26)	(.25)	(.12)	(.16)
White evangelical Protestant§	1.06***	.30	.63***	.78***
	(.27)	(.25)	(.13)	(.18)
White mainline Protestant§	.67**	.20	.25	.34*
	(.24)	(.24)	(.13)	(.16)
Jewish§	−.44	−.64	−.46	−.15
	(.42)	(.37)	(.28)	(.44)
Other religion§	.33		−.02	.47*
	(.90)		(.19)	(.22)
Long-term social characteristics				
College graduate	−.28	−.51**	−.64***	−.58***
	(.16)	(.16)	(.08)	(.12)
Number of children	.06	−.01	.07**	.01
	(.03)	(.03)	(.02)	(.04)
Family income ($10,000s)	−.01	−.05	−.02	−.03
	(.02)	(.03)	(.01)	(.01)
Values & political orientation				
Political ideology	.03	.16***	.09***	.05
(liberal to conservative)	(.04)	(.04)	(.02)	(.04)
Party identification	−.06	−.19	.22*	.25
(Democrat to Republican)	(.15)	(.16)	(.10)	(.15)
Intercept	−1.21**	−1.16**	−1.01***	−.54
	(.38)	(.38)	(.23)	(.35)
Pseudo R-squared	.12	.15	.15	.16
N	616	610	1,512	747

Note: All cell entries are probit coefficients with their estimated standard errors in parentheses. All estimations include regional dummy variables (not shown).

Source: General Social Survey.

§Omitted (base) category for race/religion variable is "no religion." "Other religion" was dropped from 1986 estimation because it perfectly predicted the dependent variable.

Effects are significantly different from zero at *p < .05, **p < .01, ***p < .001 (two-tailed test).

Question wording: "The United States Supreme Court has ruled that no state or local government may require the reading of the Lord's Prayer or Bible verses in public schools. What are your views on this—do you approve or disapprove of the Court's ruling?"

are available. To illustrate the current structure of attitudes, Table 3.3 presents the results of a multivariate analysis conducted with 2004 GSS data. We specify four models, each representing a group, or "block," of variables that we might expect to have an effect on an individual's opinion of school prayer at a different stage of the causal process. As do other authors in this book, we theorize that the blocks can be situated in the following causal order: demographic characteristics such as sex, age, religious denomination, and religiosity (block I), long-term social characteristics (II), and political values and orientation (III).[4] Our final estimation (model IV) includes "dummy variables" for each of the nine geographic regions into which the GSS categorizes its respondents.[5] The cells in the last column of the table are "first differences" derived from Model IV—that is, the effect of a shift from the minimum to the maximum value of each independent variable on the probability of disapproving of the Court's rulings, holding all other variables constant at their means.

Race and Religion

Our analysis of how public opinion regarding the Supreme Court's school prayer ban differs along racial and religious lines incorporates the fact that

Table 3.3
Structure of Disapproval of the Supreme Court's Decisions on School Prayer, 2004

	I	II	III	IV	
				Probit	Min/Max
Sex, age, race, religion					
Female	.09	.04	.08	.10	.04
	(.10)	(.10)	(.10)	(.10)	
Age	.01*	.01	.01	.01	.17
	(.00)	(.00)	(.00)	(.00)	
Attendance of religious services	.07***	.09***	.08***	.08***	.22
	(.02)	(.02)	(.02)	(.02)	
Black Protestant[§]	1.31***	1.22***	1.31***	1.23***	.32
	(.26)	(.26)	(.27)	(.28)	
Catholic[§]	.35*	.29	.29	.26	.09
	(.15)	(.16)	(.16)	(.16)	
White evangelical Protestant[§]	.97***	.87***	.81***	.78***	.25
	(.17)	(.17)	(.18)	(.18)	
White mainline Protestant[§]	.38*	.43**	.37*	.34*	.12
	(.17)	(.16)	(16)	(.16)	
Jewish[§]	−.39	−.06	−.04	−.15	−.05
	(.42)	(.43)	(.43)	(.44)	
Other religion[§]	.53	.48*	.46*	.47*	.15
	(.21)	(.22)	(.22)	(.22)	

Table 3.3
(continued)

	I	II	III	IV	
				Probit	Min/Max
Long-term Social Characteristics					
College graduate		−.51***	−.52***	−.58***	−.22
		(.12)	(.12)	(.12)	
Number of children		.02	.02	.01	.04
		(.03)	(.03)	(.04)	
Family income ($10,000s)		−.03*	−.03*	−.03	−.12
		(.01)	(.01)	(.01)	
Values & Political Orientation					
Political ideology			.05	.05	.08
(liberal to conservative)			(.04)	(.04)	
Party identification			.24	.25	.09
(Democrat to Republican)			(.14)	(.15)	
Intercept	−.71***	−.45***	−.75***	−.54	
	(.17)	(.18)	(.22)	(.35)	
Regional Dummy Variables	No	No	No	Yes	
Pseudo R-squared	.10	.13	.14	.16	
Percent correctly predicted	68.3	70.7	71.1	72.2	
Log likelihood statistic	−442.52	−426.95	−420.71	−414.10	
N	747	747	747	747	

Note: All cell entries, except those in the rightmost column, are probit coefficients. Cell entries in the last column are first differences derived from the probit analysis in Model IV. Each of these entries is an estimate of the change in probability of disapproving of the Supreme Court's school prayer decisions from the minimum to the maximum value of each independent variable, holding all other variables constant at their means. Values in parentheses are standard errors.
§Omitted (base) category for race/religion variable is "no religion."
Effects are significantly different from zero at *$p < .05$, **$p < .01$, ***$p < .001$ (two-tailed test).
Question Wording: see Table 3.2.
Source: General Social Survey.

the political effects of these two variables are often intertwined, as has long been recognized by sociologists of religion (see Steensland et al. 2000). On the whole, African Americans, the more religiously observant, and those who adhere to an evangelical Christian religious tradition have been more likely to disapprove of the ban than whites, the nonreligious, and Jews. As we will show, these patterns largely persist when we control for other potential confounding factors.

The top left panel of Figure 3.4 indicates that blacks have consistently been less supportive of the school prayer ban than whites—and that this racial divide appears to have increased in recent years. In 2004, the gap between blacks and whites exceeded 25 percentage points. The top right panel of Figure 3.4 presents how disapproval of the Court's school prayer ban varies by religious denomination. The figure shows that majorities in all four denominational groups on which we have enough data to track year-to-year change disapprove of the Court's rulings.[6] But it also indicates that a significant gap in disapproval exists between Christians who tend to adhere to an evangelical tradition (white evangelical Protestants and black Protestants) and those who do not (Roman Catholics and white mainline Protestants). Although these differences have been present for most of the thirty-year span of the GSS data, the gap has been particularly large and persistent since the early 1990s. This gap between evangelicals and nonevangelicals is now nearly 20 percentage points in size.

These racial and religious differences generally hold over time when we control for other mediating variables in Table 3.2. White evangelicals and black Protestants are consistently more likely to disagree with the Court's school prayer ban than are white mainline Protestants, Catholics, or Jews—even after we control for the direct effects of long-term social characteristics and political values and orientation. Table 3.3 shows that in 2004, the effects of religious affiliation were strong before controlling for any mediating variables (in Model I) and remained so even after controlling for variables that we might expect to intervene in their effects on attitudes toward the school prayer rulings, such as education, ideology, party affiliation, and region (Model IV). In fact, by the measure of "first differences," the effects of religious denomination for black Protestants (who are 32 percentage points more likely to disagree with the Court's ban than are those who have no religious affiliation) and white evangelical Protestants (25 percentage points more likely) are larger than for any of the other variables in our models.

Attendance at religious services—which we consider a proxy variable for the importance of religion to GSS respondents—has also been a consistent and important predictor of disapproval of the school prayer ban. This variable was a statistically significant predictor of attitudes on the ban throughout the range of our analysis in Table 3.2. In 2004, the most religiously observant were 22 percentage points more likely to disapprove of the Court's ban than the least observant, holding other variables constant at their means (as shown in Table 3.3). Figure 3.5—which plots the relationship between religious observance and attitudes on school prayer by religious denomination—shows that this direct relationship holds for all religious groups except Jews. It is particularly strong for those who do not consider themselves as belonging to any religious denomination.

Age and Birth Cohort

The lower left panel of Figure 3.4 shows that later birth cohorts are more supportive of the Supreme Court's decisions and that this difference is probably due to differences between successive generations (rather than to age per se). Within each cohort, the trend line of opinion has been relatively flat. These

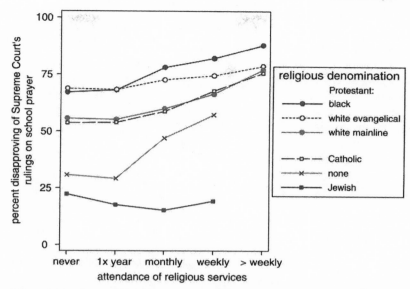

Figure 3.5. Disapproval of Supreme Court's School Prayer Rulings by Religious Denomination and Attendance of Religious Services, 1974–2004. Question wording: See Table 3.2. Source: General Social Survey.

results, combined with the overall picture of opinion change discussed in the previous section, suggest that the slight decline in opposition to the Court's decisions shown in Figure 3.2 reflects generational replacement (i.e., different opinions predominate among the different generations) rather than life cycle effects (i.e., changes that every individual experiences as part of aging) or period effects (i.e., changes that result from societal forces, such as secularization). If either of the latter factors were operating to a significant degree, we would see changes in attitudes within cohorts. Instead, cohorts show remarkable persistence in their opinions about school prayer, which leads us to conclude that the most likely explanation for the change in disapproval over time is gradual replacement of individuals who belong to earlier, more disapproving cohorts.

In Table 3.2, we see that the effect of birth cohort (measured cross-sectionally as the effect of age) is generally consistent across the thirty years of the GSS.[7] The only year in which the effect of age is not statistically significant is 2004. The analysis in Table 3.3 helps explain why this is the case. We can interpret the fact that age is statistically significant in Model I but fails to achieve significance in models incorporating variables later in the causal chain as indicating that, in 2004, the effect of age operated through these later variables, such as college education (in 2004, college-educated respondents tended to be younger than the non-college educated).

Sex

We note here briefly that—unlike the case of many of the other issues discussed in this book—women tend to take a more socially conservative position than men. For example, in 2004, 67% of women expressed disapproval of the Court's school prayer ban, and only 60% of men did. But this difference fails to attain statistical significance in our multivariate analyses in Tables 3.2 and 3.3. This is in large part due to the fact that women are more likely than men to consider themselves part of a religious denomination and more frequently attend religious services.[8]

Long-Term Social Characteristics

Among social characteristics, educational attainment has the most dramatic effect on opinions about school prayer. In 2004, only 43% of college-educated GSS respondents expressed disapproval of the Court's decisions, compared with 72% of those with less than a college degree. In each GSS survey we analyzed in Table 3.2 except that conducted in 1974, college education remained a statistically significant predictor of attitudes after controlling for other factors. As shown in the last column of Table 3.3, in 2004 those with a college degree were 22 percentage points more likely to approve of the Court's school prayer rulings than those without a degree, holding all other variables constant at their means.

Household income has also been a relatively consistent predictor of support for the Court's school prayer rulings. We estimate in Table 3.3 that the difference in approval in 2004 between the wealthiest and poorest respondents who were otherwise similar was 12 percentage points. This distinction, however, fails to achieve statistical significance in any of the full models we estimate in Table 3.2.

We might expect that the presence of children in the home would affect attitudes on school prayer, but our estimates in Tables 3.2 and 3.3 indicate that this characteristic has had varying—and relatively small—effects. We conclude that this variable is not a noteworthy predictor of attitudes.

Values and Political Orientation

We might imagine school prayer as an issue that divides Americans along ideological and partisan lines. To some extent this is true: as shown in the lower right panel of Figure 3.4, Americans have become increasingly polarized by party affiliation regarding school prayer over the past thirty years. This is particularly the case when we compare white Democrats to white Republicans, where a 14-percentage point gap now exists on attitudes regarding school prayer. At the same time, school prayer remains an issue that splits Democrats by race. As white Democrats have become more approving of the school prayer ban, black Democrats have become less so, and the gap in approval of the Supreme Court's school prayer ban between black and white Democrats now exceeds 35 percentage points.

However, neither partisan nor ideological distinctions hold up as consistent, significant predictors of school prayer attitudes in the multivariate analyses presented in Tables 3.2 and 3.3. These findings indicate that these distinctions are explained somewhat by the religious, educational, and income differences among Americans, which are correlated with party and ideology.

Conclusion

In the aggregate, public opinion has remained solidly against the Court's landmark decisions declaring school prayer unconstitutional. The public has been and continues to be highly supportive of a constitutional amendment overturning these decisions. Although results vary according to survey house and question wording, public sentiment has changed only modestly over the years, even though the percentage of Americans who express no religious preference has noticeably increased. *Engel*, *Schempp*, and their progeny illustrate the limited persuasive power of the Supreme Court when entrenched attitudes and cherished identities are involved. Our analysis of various subgroups confirms several expected findings—that the more educated are more likely to approve of the Court's decisions and that those who attend religious services are more likely to disapprove. But we also discovered unanticipated results: race plays an important role in predicting disapproval starting in the early 1990s; African Americans—particularly African American Protestants—are much more likely than secular whites to disapprove of the Supreme Court's decisions. Additionally, much of the modest decline in support for school prayer is probably due to generational replacement, with later cohorts generally more supportive of the Court's decisions. Moreover, the cohort effect is probably mediated by educational attainment, as later cohorts tend to be more educated than their parents and grandparents. Still, there is some evidence of a new rise in support for school prayer after 1996. What this review of public opinion suggests is that, failing a significant change in the religiosity and values of large segments of American society, the public will continue to support efforts to cross the line in the sand drawn by the Supreme Court in its school prayer decisions.

Notes

1. The City of Baltimore allowed students to be excused from recitation of the Lord's Prayer only after the plaintiffs filed their complaint.

2. We recognize the problems caused by combining surveys that have different questions, methodologies, and biases. However, the consistency of the trends across question wordings gives us confidence that our general finding—high support for

school prayer that has declined somewhat over time—is robust to these measurement challenges.

3. Unfortunately, the ANES has not asked this question since 1998.

4. A full list of these variables and a discussion about how they were coded are available from the authors upon request.

5. Estimates of the effects of residence by region are not shown in the table; none of the coefficients was significantly different from zero at $p<.05$.

6. Two other categories of the denomination variable—Jewish and those specifying "other religion"—typically do not have enough observations in each year of the GSS to make valid year-to-year comparisons.

7. Year of birth is, of course, collinear with age in the cross-sectional analyses that appear in Tables 3.2 and 3.3. For easier interpretation, we estimated these models using age rather than year of birth.

8. In 2004, 11% of women told the GSS they did not belong to any religious denomination, compared with 17% of men. Nearly a third of women—31%—said they attended religious services once per week or more, but only 23% of men did.

References

Alley, Robert S. 1994. *School Prayer: The Court, the Congress and the First Amendment.* Buffalo, N.Y.: Prometheus Books.

Alvarez, R. Michael, John Brehm, and Catherine Wilson. 2003. "Uncertainty and American Public Opinion." In *Uncertainty in American Politics*, edited by Barry C. Burden. Cambridge: Cambridge University Press.

Barnum, David G. 1985. "The Supreme Court and Public Opinion: Judicial Decision Making in the Post-New Deal Period." *Journal of Politics* 47: 652–66.

Beaney, William M., and Edward N. Beiser. 1964. "Prayer and Politics: The Impact of *Engel* and *Schempp* on the Political Process." *Journal of Public Law* 13: 475.

Cleveland, William S. 1993. *Visualizing Data.* Summit, N.J.: Hobart Press.

Davis, James A., Tom W. Smith, and Peter V. Marsden. 2005. GENERAL SOCIAL SURVEYS, 1972–2004 [CUMULATIVE FILE] [Computer file]. ICPSR04295-v1. Chicago, IL: National Opinion Research Center [producer], 2005. Storrs, CT: Roper Center for Public Opinion Research, University of Connecticut/Ann Arbor, MI: Inter-university Consortium for Political and Social Research [distributors], 2005–09–02.

Dolbeare, Kenneth M., and Phillip E. Hammond. 1971. *The School Prayer Decisions: From Court Policy to Local Practice.* Chicago: University of Chicago Press.

Elifson, Kirk W., and C. Kirk Hadaway. 1985. "Prayer in Public Schools: When Church and State Collide." *Public Opinion Quarterly* 49: 317–29.

Fenwick, Lynda Beck. 1989. *Should the Children Pray? A Historical, Judicial, and Political Examination of Public School Prayer.* Waco, Texas: Baylor University Press.

Flemming, Roy B., John Bohte, and B. Dan Wood. 1997. "One Voice among Many: The Supreme Court's Influence on Attentiveness to Issues in the United States 1947–1972." *American Journal of Political Science* 41: 1224–50.

Fox, John. 1997. *Applied Regression Analysis, Linear Models, and Related Methods.* Thousand Oaks, CA: Sage.

Hoekstra, Victoria. 2000. "The Supreme Court and Local Public Opinion." *American Political Science Review* 94: 89–100.

Jennings, M. Kent, Gregory B. Markus, Richard G. Niemi, and Laura Stoker. 2005. YOUTH-PARENT SOCIALIZATION PANEL STUDY, 1965–1997: FOUR WAVES COMBINED [Computer file]. ICPSR04037-v1. Ann Arbor, MI: University of Michigan, Center for Political Studies/Survey Research Center [producer], 2004. Ann Arbor, MI: Inter-university Consortium for Political and Social Research [distributor], 2005–11–04.

Johnson, Richard M. 1967. *The Dynamics of Compliance: Supreme Court Decision-Making from a New Perspective.* Evanston, Ill.: Northwestern University Press.

Kurland, Phillip B. 1962. "The Regents' Prayer Case: 'Full of Sound and Fury, Signifying…'" *Supreme Court Review* 1962: 1–33.

Marshall, Thomas R. 1989. *Public Opinion and the Supreme Court.* Boston: Unwin Wyman.

Muir, William K., Jr. 1967. *Prayer in the Public Schools: Law and Attitude Change.* Chicago: University of Chicago Press.

Murphy, Walter F., and Joseph Tanenhaus. 1968. "Public Opinion and the United States Supreme Court: Mapping of Some Prerequisites for Court Legitimation of Regime Changes." *Law & Society Review* 2 (3): 357–84.

The National Election Studies (http://www.electionstudies.org/). 2004. THE 2004 NATIONAL ELECTION STUDY [dataset]. Ann Arbor, MI: University of Michigan, Center for Political Studies [producer and distributor].

Sorauf, Frank. 1976. *The Wall of Separation.* Princeton, N.J.: Princeton University Press.

Steensland, Brian, Jerry Z. Park, Mark D. Regnerus, Lynn D. Robinson, W. Bradford Wilcox, and Robert D. Woodberry. 2000. "The Measure of American Religion: Toward Improving the State of the Art." *Social Forces* 79: 291–318.

Tanenhaus, Joseph, and Walter F. Murphy, 1981. "Patterns of Public Support for the Supreme Court: A Panel Study." *Journal of Politics* 43 (1): 24–39.

Wilcox, Clyde. 1993. "The Dimensionality of Public Attitudes toward Church-State Establishment Issues." *Journal for the Scientific Study of Religion* 32: 169–76.

4

Abortion

Samantha Luks and Michael Salamone

Galvanized public opinion on abortion in the United States is for the most part a modern phenomenon. States began to proscribe abortion throughout the nineteenth century in a movement led mainly by medical and religious elites, but historical records suggest that the public in general did not hold strong opinions on the issue (Sauer 1974). Throughout the 1950s, however, the public became more accepting of abortion for reasons other than to save the pregnant woman's life. An organized movement to legalize abortion coalesced in the 1960s, roughly concurrent with the start of a dramatic upturn in public approval for legalized abortion. This increased acceptance, it is worth noting, predated *Roe v. Wade* (1973), and it prevailed across such demographic categories as religious affiliation and educational attainment (Granberg & Granberg 1980). By the early 1970s, several states had liberalized their abortion laws.

But it was not until the Supreme Court announced its opinion in *Roe v. Wade*—and overturned as unconstitutional all existing state laws outlawing abortion—that abortion became a salient national issue. Since then, a majority of Americans have continued to favor retaining the right to an abortion, as well as imposing various restrictions on that right (Shaw 2003; Fiorina, Abrams, & Pope 2005; Cook, Jelen, & Wilcox 1992; Craig & O'Brien 1993). Over time, the public has also become more polarized on the issue (Blake 1977; Barnum 1985; Franklin & Kosaki 1989). In the decades since *Roe,* the Supreme Court has issued a series of abortion-related decisions, but these have not had a significant effect on public opinion.

Previous Studies of Public Opinion on Abortion

The surge in public approval of legalized abortion that began in the mid-1960s continued for several years after *Roe v. Wade* was decided. The sustained increase in support, however, resulted from momentum rather than a response to the Court's decision (Blake 1977; Franklin & Kosaki 1989). The upward trend flattened by the late 1970s, and public opinion even began to reverse direction modestly (Ebaugh & Haney 1980; Granberg & Granberg 1980).

Throughout the 1980s and 1990s, there were small, largely unexplained fluctuations in public sentiment (Jelen & Wilcox 2003). Wlezien and Goggin (1993) suggest that abortion policy preferences did not change during this time period but rather that the public was responding to a perceived threat of imminent restrictions on access to abortion. Such fluctuations aside, throughout the 1990s a majority of Americans supported legal abortion during the first three months of pregnancy; an equally large majority opposed abortion after the first trimester (Shaw 2003). The current dominant position favors legal abortion but also approves of restrictions that limit the practice (Shaw 2003; Fiorina et al. 2005; Cook, Jelen, & Wilcox 1992; Craig & O'Brien 1993).

Of the few studies that examine the direct effect of judicial decisions on public attitudes toward abortion, Franklin and Kosaki's (1989) work on the topic is particularly influential. In response to arguments that an aggregate shift in public opinion could not be attributed to *Roe* (Blake 1977; Uslaner & Weber 1979), Franklin and Kosaki offer a "structural response hypothesis," which asserts that the principal effect of *Roe* was to polarize public opinion: The decision did not change aggregate opinion, but it enhanced support for abortion among those already in favor of legalization, and it diminished support among those (including Catholics and blacks) already opposed to legalization.

Johnson and Martin (1998) accept Franklin and Kosaki's findings but amend those findings to account for the lack of public reaction to the Supreme Court's later decision in *Webster v. Reproductive Health Services* (1989). Johnson and Martin's "conditional response hypothesis" posits that when the Court first rules on an issue, the public responds with polarization, but when the Court revisits an issue, it has no effect on public opinion.

In another analysis of the *Webster* decision, Grosskopf and Mondak (1998) examine how the decision affected the public's confidence in the Court itself. They found no measurable increase in confidence in the Court among those who supported the decision. But confidence fell sharply among those who disagreed with the decision, resulting in an overall drop in support for the institution. Controversial rulings on issues like abortion, they conclude, endanger the Court's political capital.

Whereas these studies focus on the Court's ability to influence public sentiment, others have described the Supreme Court as generally acting like a majoritarian institution, with the public ultimately leading the way (e.g., Dahl 1957; Marshall 1989; Mishler & Sheehan 1993; Rosen 2006). Barnum (1985), however, demonstrates that on controversial issues the Court often follows the trajectory of changing public attitudes, even if the new position has yet to earn majority support. In the case of abortion, he points out, approval of elective abortion for unmarried women was already trending sharply upward at the time of the *Roe* decision, though a slight majority still disapproved.

Because the Court intervened on abortion before there existed nationwide majority support, a debate has spawned over the efficacy of the decision. Some scholars and advocates—including Ruth Bader Ginsburg (1992) before she joined the Court—have argued that *Roe* undercut a growing pro-choice political movement and created a backlash that impeded the liberalization of abortion policy in the long run. Others observe that, even though a couple of states (chiefly Washington and New York) had repealed their abortion laws prior to *Roe*, even more states preserved or strengthened their restrictive abortion laws. Moreover, the Court's decision may have forced a shift in antiabortion arguments *away* from across-the-board prohibitions and *toward* permissible restrictions (Nossiff 1994). Rosenberg's oft-cited "hollow hope" argument (1991) is that the instances in which courts can serve as an effective vehicle for social change are rare, due in part to courts' limited enforcement powers. But he contends that abortion is a policy domain in which the Supreme Court made change possible. The Court had no power to compel hospitals to perform abortions (and many refused to in the years immediately following the decision). But *Roe* meant that abortion clinics were now free to open to respond to demand for the procedure—and many did, even in the face of local opposition to the practice in conservative regions of the United States.

Research on the Structure of Opinion on Abortion

Numerous scholars have investigated how abortion attitudes vary across the population, particularly with regard to gender, race, and religion. Most studies of men's and women's attitudes toward abortion conclude there is no noticeable gender gap (Strickler & Danigelis 2002; Craig & O'Brien 1993). Cook, Jelen, and Wilcox (1992) found that men were more likely to have liberal views of abortion, and Legge (1983) found that women were more likely to be either strongly pro-choice or pro-life, while men had more moderate views. Strickler and Danigelis (2002) show that belief in feminist values is not necessarily accompanied by a liberal attitude toward abortion. Thus, even as feminism becomes increasingly accepted by mainstream society, that trend does not in itself affect attitudes toward abortion.

In addition, several studies of the structure of opinion on abortion have compared the attitudes of whites and blacks. Scott and Schuman (1988) found that blacks are less likely than whites to have a strong opinion on the issue. Combs and Welch (1982) concluded that blacks were more likely than whites to oppose abortion rights, and Hall and Ferree (1986) determined that this racial divide persisted into the 1980s. Using new data, however, Wilcox (1990) found that attitudes were converging and that controlling for a modified measure of religiosity weakened the independent effect of race in Hall and Ferree's study. Strickler and Danigelis (2002) also found that, after controlling for other influences, the racial divide had reversed itself—with blacks being more supportive of legal abortion than whites—by the mid-1990s.

Although the effects of gender and race have been shown to be inconsistent, many studies have shown that religion is a very important factor in determining attitudes on abortion. The split between Catholics and Protestants has been widely studied (e.g., Blake 1977; Cook, Jelen, & Wilcox 1993c; Franklin & Kosaki 1989; Granberg & Granberg 1980; Legge 1983). Franklin and Kosaki (1989) found that white Protestants were more likely to support and Catholics more likely to oppose abortion before *Roe* and that the gap between the two groups increased after *Roe*. Legge (1983) found that mainstream Protestants and Jews were more pro-choice in their attitudes than their Catholic and evangelical counterparts. But other studies indicate that it is religiosity, rather than affiliation with any particular religion, that explains attitudes. Singh and Leahy (1978) found that higher levels of education and lower levels of religiosity are two significant factors in determining pro-choice attitudes. Craig and O'Brien (1993) found that both Protestants and Catholics who consider religion an important part of their lives were less supportive of abortion than those who did not consider themselves to be religious. Strickler and Danigelis (2002) observed a possible decline in opposition to abortion among Catholics in the late 1980s and early 1990s; however, they suggest that the growing strength and rhetoric of the Christian Right has led to a correlation between views on abortion and views on political liberalism.

Some researchers have also looked at how abortion opinion and policy differ state by state. Wetstein and Albritton (1995) argue that public opinion within individual states affects not only state abortion policies but also the rates at which abortion services are utilized. But Cook, Jelen, and Wilcox (1993a) argue that, after controlling for education, sex, income, party, ideology, religion, and religiosity, state differences disappear. In other words, the state and regional differences in attitudes and policies result from forces other than local culture.

Among studies of how attitudes toward abortion affect voting, Smith (1994) and Abramowitz (1995) both conclude that pro-choice voters were more likely than pro-life voters to cast their ballot for president based on the candidate's position on abortion. Looking at gubernatorial elections in the state of Louisiana, Howell and Sims (1993) argue that the side that is perceived to be most threatened is most likely to take the issue into account. Moreover, Adams (1997) contends that opinion on abortion is an example of "issue evolution," as a polarization along party lines among elites on the issue in the late 1970s was followed by a similar polarization in mass opinion by the late 1980s.

Other studies have paid close attention to the opinions and rhetoric of activists on both sides of the debate. Luker (1984) found large differences in the worldviews of pro-life and pro-choice activist women. Pro-life women shared more traditionalist views of gender and sexuality and saw abortion as a threat to that structure and to the value of their role as women and home-makers. Pro-choice women, on the other hand, had a more egalitarian view of gender and a less restrictive view of sexuality, and they saw the criminaliza-tion of abortion as a threat to their ability to pursue careers outside home. Cook, Jelen, and Wilcox (1992) found similar patterns among pro-life and pro-choice women who were not activists, although with more overlap on measures of education and traditionalism between the two groups.

Given the salience of the abortion controversy, some portray the issue as part of a greater "culture war" within the United States. At one extreme, Hunter (1994) argues that abortion is a central issue in a divide that may threaten American democracy. Others have presented evidence that abortion is one of very few issues polarizing Americans (DiMaggio, Evans, & Bryson 1996; Evans 2003; Klitsch 1990). Yet others believe that there is a broad consensus among Americans that abortion should be legal and restricted (Fiorina, Abrams, & Pope 2005; Cook, Jelen, & Wilcox 1992; Witwer 1989). Specifically, Fiorina and his colleagues argue that the attitudes of the general public are far more nuanced and less extreme than those held by elites. Other studies suggest that the public is not simply moderate but ambivalent about abortion—that indi-viduals simultaneously hold conflicting beliefs on the topic (Craig, Kane, & Martinez 2002; Alvarez & Brehm 1995).

News Coverage of Abortion and the Supreme Court

Media coverage of abortion has varied considerably over the past thirty years, and the Supreme Court has often been the reason for the fluctua-tion. Figure 4.1 plots the number of stories mentioning the word "abortion" published in the *New York Times* since 1960.[1]

It also plots the proportion of these stories mentioning the Supreme Court. As shown on the graph, coverage of the abortion issue jumped dramati-cally in the *Times* from the mid-1960s to the early 1970s—but not, apparently, because of *Roe*. Handed down on the same day that former President Lyndon Johnson died, the ruling was a relatively low-salience event at its time, espe-cially given its eventual importance. The total number of stories in the *Times* that mentioned abortion was actually higher in the year preceding the deci-sion.[2] Coverage climbed slowly upward from the mid-1970s through the late 1980s, when *Webster v. Reproductive Health Services*—a case many thought might lead to the overturning of *Roe*—led to a dramatic increase in cover-age in 1989. Coverage leapt again with *Planned Parenthood v. Casey* (1992), a case in which the Court stepped back from *Webster* and reaffirmed the central holding of *Roe*. The *Times'* attention to abortion continued to remain higher in the 1990s than in the two previous decades until dropping sharply in 2001, as public attention turned to international rather than domestic policy issues in the wake of the September 11 attacks. Although coverage of abortion has

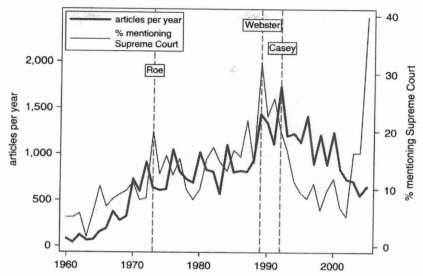

Figure 4.1. Coverage of Abortion in the *New York Times*, 1960–2005.
Source: ProQuest Direct, Lexis-Nexis.

declined in recent years, the issue is increasingly associated with the Supreme
Court: in 2005—the year of John Roberts, Harriet Myers, and Samuel Alito's
nominations—an unprecedentedly high proportion of stories mentioning
abortion also mention the Court.

Trends in Opinion

The earliest measures of public opinion on abortion come from the Gallup
Poll, which asked respondents their opinion on whether abortion should be
legal in three circumstances—risk to the pregnant woman's health, risk of
birth defects, and financial hardship—in 1962, 1965, and 1969. As shown on
the left-hand side of Figure 4.2, Gallup found majority support for legal abortion in the first two cases but very little support in the third. Also shown in
Figure 4.2 is the best source of over-time trends in public opinion on abortion: data from the National Opinion Research Center (NORC) at the University of Chicago, which has posed consistently worded questions about
abortion to survey respondents since 1965. Since 1972, these questions have
been fielded as part of the General Social Survey (GSS), which is administered
by the NORC.[3] The NORC/GSS data are also shown in Figure 4.2. As was the
case in the Gallup surveys, NORC/GSS respondents are asked whether abortion should be legally permitted in several different cases, which allows them
to select any one or any combination of circumstances. Notably, about 15% of

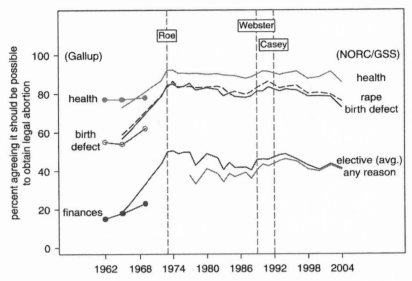

Figure 4.2. Public Opinion on Conditions Under Which Abortion
Should Be Legal, 1962–2004. Question wording: (source: Gallup) Do you
think abortion operations should or should not be legal in the following
cases...(health)...where the health of the mother is in danger? (birth
defect)...where the child may be born deformed? (finances)...where the family
does not have enough money to support another child?
(source: NORC/GSS) Please tell me whether or not you think it should be possible
for a pregnant woman to obtain a legal abortion...(health) If the woman's
own health is seriously endangered by the pregnancy? (birth defect) If there is
a strong chance of serious defect in the baby? (rape) If she became pregnant
as a result of rape? (elective) average of: If she is married and does not want
any more children? If the family has a very low income and cannot afford any
more children? If she is not married and does not want to marry the man? (any
reason) The woman wants it for any reason? (asked since 1977).

respondents who say that a woman should be able to have an abortion for "any
reason" nonetheless reject at least one of the specific reasons.

These trends show that the public distinguishes between abortions that are
performed for reasons such as the woman's health, rape, and birth defects and
those performed for what many scholars called "elective" reasons (Franklin &
Kosaki 1989).[4] The series shows that support for legal abortion for all reasons
rose quite sharply in the seven-year period between 1965 and 1972. Although
opinion about health-related abortions has been fairly stable since then, opinion
about non-health-related abortions has fluctuated: support for elective abortion was at its highest in the years right after *Roe v. Wade*; it gradually declined
during the 1980s, rebounded during the early 1990s, and has gradually declined
since then. Support for health-related abortions also reached a low in 2004, but
it is too soon to know if this change is the start of a greater decline.

Effects of Question Wording on Survey Responses

As might be expected, even minor changes in survey questions about abortion alter the picture of public opinion about this issue. A typical survey question on abortion offers respondents pro-choice and pro-life options, as well as one or more intermediate positions. But cues within the response options will attract or deter respondents. The question wordings of five widely publicized series of questions are shown in Table 4.1, along with the proportion of respondents choosing each of the positions in the most recent administration

Table 4.1

The Effects of Question Wording on Responses to Surveys Regarding Abortion

Survey house, survey question, and date of survey	Percentage of "pro-life" respondents	Percentage of "intermediate" respondents	Percentage of "pro-choice" respondents
CNN/USA Today/Gallup: "Do you think abortions should be legal under any circumstances, legal only under certain circumstances, or illegal in all circumstances?" (May 2006)	15%	53%	30%
American National Election Studies (ANES): "There has been some discussion about abortion during recent years. Which one of the opinions on this page best agrees with your view? You can just tell me the number of the opinion you choose. 1. By law, abortion should never be permitted. 2. The law should permit abortion only in case of rape, incest, or when the woman's life is in danger. 3. The law should permit abortion for reasons other than rape, incest, or danger to the woman's life, but only after the need for the abortion has been clearly established. 4. By law, a woman should always be able to obtain an abortion as a matter of personal choice." (Fall 2004)	14%	32% (option 2) 17% (option 3) total: 49%	36%

(continued)

Table 4.1

(continued)

Survey house, survey question, and date of survey	Percentage of "pro-life" respondents	Percentage of "intermediate" respondents	Percentage of "pro-choice" respondents
Time/CNN: "Which of these positions best represents your views about abortion? A woman should be able to get an abortion if she decides she wants one no matter what the reason. Abortion should only be legal in certain circumstances, such as when a woman's health is endangered or when the pregnancy results from rape or incest. Abortion should be illegal in all circumstances." (October 2004)	9%	45%	44%
CBS News/New York Times: "Which of these comes closest to your view? Abortion should be generally available to those who want it. OR, Abortion should be available, but under stricter limits than it is now. OR, Abortion should not be permitted." (March 2007)	23%	41%	34%
NBC/Wall Street Journal: "Which of the following best represents your views about abortion? The choice on abortion should be left up to the woman and her doctor. Abortion should be legal only in cases in which pregnancy results from rape or incest or when the life of the woman is at risk. OR, Abortion should be illegal in all circumstances." (May 2005)	14%	29%	55%

Questions are listed in order of those eliciting the greatest proportion of "intermediate" responses. "Not sure" responses are not shown but are included in calculations of percentages.

Sources: Roper Archive, American National Election Studies.

of the question as of this writing. (The question wording effects shown in the table are broadly similar to those seen across the entire time series.)

There are several distinctive qualities to each survey question. For one, the CNN/USA Today/Gallup ("Gallup") series is the only one that gives no specific circumstances for abortion or comparisons with current abortion law, and so its intermediate category ("legal only under certain circumstances") could mean anything from only to save the life of the woman to only performed before the third trimester. By comparison, the Time/CNN ("Time"), ANES, and NBC items give examples of rape, incest, and health risk to the woman for an intermediate category, and the CBS item specifies stricter limits to abortion than exist now.

In three of the question series, the most restrictive option is "illegal in all circumstances." The CBS item, in contrast, does not use the word "illegal"; instead, the most restrictive option is that abortion "should not be permitted." It is conceivable that the absence of a reference to illegality may make respondents more likely to select this option, as the mention of legality may also evoke opinions about government intervention.[5]

There are also important differences among the most permissive options of each survey question. The NBC question specifies that the abortion decision is made by a woman *and her doctor*, which may make that response more attractive to respondents. At the other end of the spectrum, the Gallup question gives the option of "legal in any circumstances"—an option that potentially goes well beyond what any of the mainstream abortion rights groups advocate.

The effects of question wording can be seen in the marginals from Table 4.1. Among the various wordings for the pro-choice responses, the inclusion of "doctor" in the NBC item boosts acceptance by 11 to 25 percentage points compared with the other questions, and the majority of respondents for the NBC polls have picked this option since the question was first asked in the early 1990s.[6]

Among the response rates for the middle position, the Gallup item garners the most support, and the NBC item the least. This result at least partially reflects the wording of the other options, in that the intermediate position was least popular among NBC respondents, who gravitated toward the pro-choice response. Gallup respondents were, on the other hand, considerably more likely to pick the intermediate response than they were the most pro-choice response. With two intermediate options, the ANES item boosts the proportion of respondents who are neither firmly pro-choice nor pro-life. Finally, the pro-life response from the CBS polls (which uses the phrase "should not be permitted") is considerably more popular than the pro-life responses that mention "illegality."

Despite the differences that result from question wording effects, over-time change among the five polls is similar to that seen in Figure 4.2: pro-choice sentiment was at its highest between 1990 and 1995, and recent years have seen a slight uptick in pro-life beliefs.

The Effect of the Supreme Court on Attitudes about Abortion

Roe v. Wade

Before the *Roe* decision, there were significant differences in attitudes about abortion among demographic groups, with education, race, and religion the most significant predictors of opinion (Franklin & Kosaki 1989). The *Roe* decision did not affect the overall level of public support for abortion, but it did affect the opinion of certain population subgroups: women, nonwhites, and Catholics became less supportive of legalized abortion for non-health-related reasons, although in the public overall there was a general increase in approval for health-related abortions. The greatest shifts in opinion were structural rather than directional, and as Franklin and Kosaki conclude, "the impact of the Court decision was, instead, to crystallize issue preferences further and to lead to greater homogeneity of with-in group preferences" (p. 762).

Pollsters have found strong support for the notion of upholding *Roe v. Wade*, even though (as shown in Table 4.1) support for the rights actually set forth in the *Roe* ruling is much lower. The nuances of public opinion regarding *Roe* can be seen in Figure 4.3, which shows how Gallup has measured attitudes about the ruling since 1974. In the first fifteen years following *Roe*, Gallup assessed support for the decision with a question that spelled out its implications but did not mention its name (see Figure 4.3 for question wording). This question found a public divided about the ruling, with those favoring it slightly outnumbering those who opposed it. Gallup changed its standard question in 1988. The new question explicitly named *Roe* and asked respondents not if they favored the ruling but if they wanted to overturn it. The result was a sharp, sustained increase in the proportion of respondents supporting the ruling. Over the past twenty years, nearly two thirds of Americans have typically voiced support for *Roe* by this measure. Resistance to a proposed constitutional amendment that would overturn *Roe* and ban abortion in all circumstances other than to save the life of the woman is similarly strong: in Gallup surveys in 1996, 2003, and 2005, six in ten respondents typically opposed the idea.

Webster v. Reproductive Health Services

Sixteen years after *Roe*, the Supreme Court's opinion in the *Webster* case moved away from the trimester framework and toward an approach focused on fetal viability. But the Court did not use *Webster* as an opportunity to overturn *Roe*'s general protection of abortion rights. Anticipating the possibility that *Webster* might overturn *Roe*, several media organizations fielded detailed survey questions about abortion attitudes. One of the best series was done by the CBS/New York Times polls in 1989, which fielded one survey in April (a few

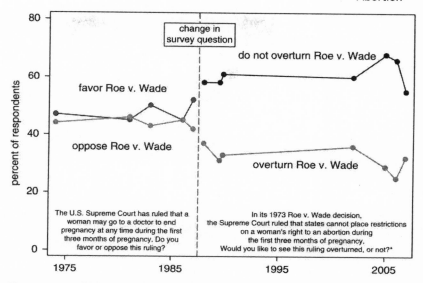

Figure 4.3. Public Opinion Regarding *Roe v. Wade*, 1974–2006. Source: Gallup. *Represents a typical question asked by Gallup since 1988. In this period, Gallup has used additional similar questions that also explicitly mention *Roe v. Wade*.

months before the July 1989 ruling) and two shortly afterward. The surveys found that responses to the question "Should abortion be legal as it is now, or legal only in such cases as rape, incest, or to save the life of the mother, or should it not be permitted at all?" changed hardly at all after *Webster*. Roughly half of the respondents wanted abortion to remain legal "as it is now," and roughly 10% preferred that it not be legal at all. *Webster* appears to have had little effect on public opinion about abortion.[7]

The April 1989 survey also included a number of revealing questions about the beliefs underlying Americans' attitudes about legalized abortion (see Table 4.2). For example, 59% of pro-life respondents—compared with 32% of pro-choice respondents—believed that making abortion illegal would reduce the number of abortions. And 37% of pro-life respondents—compared with 11% of pro-choice respondents—believed that "many" women use abortion as their primary method of birth control. About a quarter of both groups named unwanted pregnancy as the main reason women have abortions, but the remaining pro-life respondents more often mentioned negative personality traits ("selfishness," "don't want responsibility," "convenience"), and the remaining pro-choice respondents more often mentioned "economics" and being "too young/unprepared" for motherhood. Only 2% of respondents, regardless of attitudes about abortion, mentioned rape or life-threatening medical conditions as "the main reason" women seek abortions.

Table 4.2

Beliefs about Abortion by Preferences about Abortion's Legality, April 1989

	Preferences about legality of abortion			
	Legal as now	Save mother, rape, or incest	Not legal at all	All respondents
Would illegal abortion reduce number of abortions?				
Yes	32.1%	50.1	59.0	41.6
No	66.2	46.6	38.2	56.0
Depends	1.7	3.3	2.9	2.4
N	665	509	116	1,290
Belief about how many use abortion as primary method of birth control				
Many	11.1%	28.9	37.4	20.5
Some	41.4	44.9	50.5	43.6
Hardly any	46.0	25.6	12.1	34.9
None	1.6	0.6	0.0	1.1
N	602	475	98	1,175
Belief about main reason for abortion				
Unwanted pregnancy	24.9%	25.7	23.4	25.1
Economics	26.9	14.2	9.3	20.2
Too young/unprepared	12.1	7.9	8.6	10.1
Don't want responsibility	7.3	12.4	11.8	9.8
Trouble with mate/personal trouble	7.3	5.7	1.8	6.1
Selfishness/other personal	3.7	5.8	14.8	5.5
Birth control	2.4	7.1	4.0	4.5
Not married	4.1	3.7	5.6	4.1
Convenience	2.3	4.7	10.9	4.0
Rape	0.8	1.2	4.0	1.3
Life threatening to mother	1.0	1.0	0.0	0.9
Other	7.3	10.6	6.0	8.5
N	548	441	97	1,086

Source: CBS/New York Times polls.

Question wording:

Legality of abortion. Should abortion be legal as it is now, or legal only in such cases as rape, incest, or to save the life of the mother, or should it not be permitted at all?

Reduction in abortions. If the Supreme Court makes abortion illegal, do you think it would reduce the number of abortions significantly, or would it not reduce the number of abortions significantly?

Abortion as birth control. How many women do you think now use abortion repeatedly, as their primary means of birth control—many women, some women, or hardly any women?

Main reason for abortion. What do you think is the main reason women have abortions?

Casey v. Planned Parenthood

The July 1992 *Casey* decision had greater consequences for abortion law than the *Webster* decision, in that it reaffirmed the central holding of *Roe* while establishing fetal viability as the benchmark for abortion rights. Yet little polling was done in the wake of *Casey*. Our best measure of the public's reaction to Casey is a survey fielded by Gallup immediately after the decision.[8] Question wording and the frequencies of responses for the Gallup survey

Table 4.3
Public Opinion Regarding the Supreme Court's Ruling in *Planned Parenthood v. Casey*, June 1992

	Opinion about *Casey* Decision					
	Went too far	Not far enough	About right	Don't know/ refused	Percent "about right" of those with opinion	N
Total	31.3%	14.8	37.3	16.5	44.7	589
Sex						
Male	33.8	14.4	38.2	13.6	44.2	288
Female	29.0	15.2	36.5	19.3	45.2	301
Age						
18–29	25.9	13.9	51.7	8.5	56.5	133
30–44	34.1	11.8	37.2	17.0	44.7	177
45–64	24.6	20.7	35.8	18.9	44.1	145
65 and older	38.3	14.4	25.4	21.9	32.5	124
Education						
Less than high school	33.8	15.9	27.0	23.4	35.2	97
High school graduate	24.3	15.8	47.8	12.1	54.4	200
Some college	30.6	13.8	35.0	20.7	44.1	144
College graduate+	39.3	14.9	34.1	11.7	38.6	137
Race						
White	30.7	14.9	37.2	17.3	44.9	502
Black	36.2	14.9	41.5	7.4	44.8	64
Other	17.5	23.3	46.4	12.8	53.3	11
Party identification						
Republican	26.5	12.6	45.9	15.0	54.0	219
Democrat	36.2	15.9	32.2	15.8	38.2	287
Independent	22.2	20.4	36.9	20.4	46.4	66

Registered voters only.

Question wording: As you may know, in its decision today, the Supreme Court approved some abortion restrictions in a Pennsylvania law but said states cannot make abortion illegal in most cases. All in all, do you think this decision went too far in restricting access to abortions, not far enough in restricting access to abortions, or was it about right? Source: Gallup Poll.

questions are shown in Table 4.3. Because people on both sides of the abortion debate were dissatisfied with the *Casey* decision (and for entirely opposite reasons), Gallup asked respondents not if they approved or disapproved of the ruling but whether it went "too far" or "not far enough." The survey found that younger voters and Republicans were most likely to approve of the decision, and college graduates, Democrats, and seniors were more likely to say it went "too far."

The Gallup poll also asked respondents how they felt about the restrictions upheld by the Court: the requirement that doctors tell a woman seeking an abortion about alternatives to abortion, the imposition of a twenty-four-hour waiting period before obtaining an abortion, and the parental consent requirements for a woman under age eighteen. Overall, respondents who thought the Court was "about right" in *Casey* were the most likely to approve of each of the three restrictions. Respondents who felt that the Court "did not go far enough" expressed lower rates of approval for the restrictions, presumably because they felt that the restrictions were not restrictive enough (see Table 4.4).[9] Since 1992, support for these restrictions has been fairly consistent. Typically, more than 85% of Americans approve of a requirement that doctors provide information about abortion alternatives to those seeking abortions, and between 70 and 80% of Americans approve of a twenty-four-hour waiting period and parental consent laws.

The Structure of Attitudes about Abortion

To examine longitudinal trends among different demographic groups, we turn to the GSS time series data. As mentioned earlier, the GSS asks respondents whether "it should be possible for a pregnant woman to obtain a legal abortion" in seven specific circumstances. We took three of those circumstances to represent abortion for health-related reasons (there is a strong chance the baby has a serious defect; a woman's health is seriously endangered by the pregnancy; the pregnancy was the result of rape) and three to represent abortion for elective reasons (a married woman does not want any more children; a low-income family cannot afford any more children; an unmarried woman does not want to marry the man).[10] We examined the longitudinal trends in attitudes toward health-related and elective abortion by age, cohort, race, sex, education, religion, marital status, presence of children in the household, party identification, and ideology. The results are summarized next.

Age and Cohort
It is useful to distinguish life cycle, or aging, effects (the effects of growing older) from generational, or cohort, effects (the effects of membership in a historical generation).[11] For example, respondents old enough to have teenage

Table 4.4
Opinion on Abortion Restrictions, by Reactions to *Casey* Decision, June 1992

Proposed abortion restriction	Opinion about *Casey* ruling				
	Went too far	Not far enough	About right	Don't know/ refused	All respondents
Inform about alternatives to abortion					
Favor	67.3%	82.9	90.6	83.4	81.0
Oppose	30.2	14.7	7.8	6.3	15.6
DK/Refused	2.6	2.4	1.6	10.2	3.5
	100	100	100	100	
24-hour waiting period					
Favor	55.2	77.1	86.6	73.6	73.2
Oppose	43.1	22.4	10.4	15.2	23.2
DK/Refused	1.7	0.6	3.0	11.2	3.6
	100	100	100	100	
Parental consent if under 18					
Favor	57.5	66.1	86.9	65.5	71.1
Oppose	39.1	32.5	11.5	23.3	25.2
DK/Refused	3.4	1.3	1.6	11.2	3.7
	100	100	100	100	

Registered voters only. $N = 589$.

Question wording: I'm going to read off three abortion restrictions upheld by the Court today. As I read each one, tell me if you would favor or oppose this restriction in your state…
…a law requiring doctors to inform patients about alternatives to abortion before performing the procedure;
…a law requiring women seeking abortions to wait 24 hours before having the procedure done;
…a law requiring women under 18 to get parental consent for any abortion.
Source: Gallup Poll.

children may feel differently about abortion than younger respondents (a life cycle effect), and the attitudes of respondents who came into young adulthood during or immediately after *Roe* might have been shaped by that decision more than members of later generations (a cohort effect).

In general, the generation born between 1945 and 1963 (known as the "baby boomers") has been the most supportive of abortion rights, and the oldest generation has been the least supportive (see Figure 4.4).[12] The youngest generation was relatively more pro-choice during the 1990s but never as supportive of elective abortion as the baby boomers. By 2000, the opinion of the

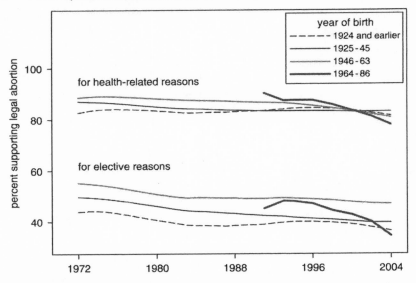

Figure 4.4. Support for Legal Abortion by Birth Cohort, 1972–2004. Question wording: see text. Source: General Social Survey.

youngest generation on elective abortion was more similar to that of the two oldest generations than it was to the chronologically closer baby boomers. On the topic of health-related abortions, most generational differences in attitude disappeared by the late 1990s.

   To distinguish the effects of age from those of cohort, along with other demographic and political variables, we estimated regression models for both health-related and elective abortion.[13] With controls in place, the youngest respondents (regardless of cohort) and the members of the youngest cohort were the least likely to favor elective abortion. Age and cohort had no significant effect on attitudes toward health-related abortion.

Race
In a well-publicized speech in 1977, Jesse Jackson equated abortion with "black genocide." In subsequent research, blacks have been found to be less supportive of abortion rights than whites (Scott & Schuman 1988). However, even before this speech, blacks were substantially less likely to support health-related or elective abortion than whites. Through 1990, black respondents were the least supportive of health-related abortions by a considerable margin, and a similar gap in opinion on elective abortion persists through 1985. In more recent years, the gap between blacks and whites on abortion attitudes has narrowed. Additionally, with controls in place, both blacks and other nonwhites remain significantly less supportive than whites of both health-related and elective abortion.

Gender

Overall, men are more supportive than women of legalized abortion, which is remarkable because women are more likely than men to be Democrats. Specifically, men are marginally, but consistently, more supportive of elective abortion, although gender differences are not significant with other demographic and political controls in place.

Education

In general, higher educational attainment is associated with greater support for both elective and health-related abortion rights. On heath-related abortion, the attitudinal difference between the least-educated and most-educated groups is fairly moderate over time. Differences in attitudes toward elective abortion are far more pronounced, and in the multivariate analysis, educational differences are highly significant. Educational differences become even more striking when studied in conjunction with gender effects (see Figure 4.5). Among men and women who have not completed high school, women have been consistently more pro-life in their attitudes about elective abortion. In contrast, men and women who are college graduates share similar attitudes, although starting in the late 1990s, female college graduates became marginally more pro-choice than male college graduates.

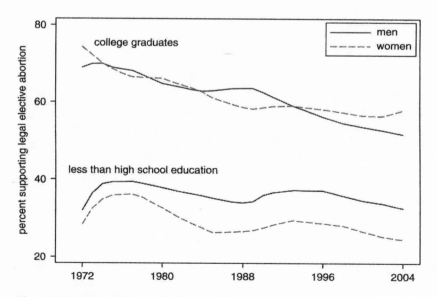

Figure 4.5. Support for Legal Elective Abortion by Education and Sex, 1972–2004. Question wording: see text. Source: General Social Survey.

Religion
As mentioned earlier, Catholics and Protestants have long differed on abortion. Through the mid-1980s, Protestants were significantly more likely to hold pro-choice views on both elective and health-related abortion. Afterward, however, this gap on elective abortion disappeared, mostly because of shifts in opinion among Protestants. Throughout the entire time series, both non-Christians and those who had no religious preference were much more likely to believe that elective abortion should be permitted. Religious differences were also highly significant at the multivariate level.

Marital and parental status
In general, individuals who are divorced, separated, or unmarried are the most likely to support abortion rights, and widowed individuals are least likely to support abortion rights—but the opinions of the widowed in part reflect age and cohort effects. Adults who have children are also consistently less supportive of abortion than childless adults. All of these differences are also significant in the multivariate analyses.

Party identification and ideology
On both health-related and elective abortion, the differences between Democrats and Republicans were relatively small in the 1970s (see Figure 4.6).

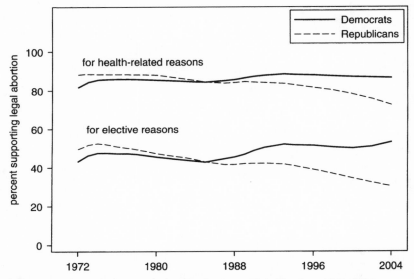

Figure 4.6. Support for Legal Abortion by Party Identification, 1972–2004. Question wording: see text. Source: General Social Survey.

If anything, Republicans were more supportive than Democrats of health-related abortions (as noted by Adams 1997). After 1985, attitudes diverged, with Republicans (and to a lesser extent, Independents) becoming increasingly opposed to abortion, while Democrats became somewhat more supportive of abortion. By 2004, the gap between Democrats and Republicans on elective abortion had increased to 25 percentage points. Similarly, the relationship between ideology and attitudes about abortion has polarized since the early 1970s. Between 1974 and 2004, the gap between liberals and conservatives in attitudes about elective abortion nearly tripled in size. Differences in attitudes about abortion by party and ideology are also highly significant in the multivariate analysis.

Confidence in the Court and Current Abortion Controversies

As we have seen, the Court's opinions in cases on abortion subsequent to *Roe* have not significantly affected public opinion on abortion. An additional consideration is whether these decisions have affected the public's confidence in the Court as an institution. Starting in 1973, the GSS asked respondents if they had a great deal of confidence, only some confidence, or hardly any confidence in the *people running* the U.S. Supreme Court. The Court has fared well in comparison with the legislative and executive branches of government. On a 0 to 100 scale, public confidence in the Court has ranged between 53 and 63 over time, whereas confidence in the other two branches has been as low as 30 and is seldom above 50.

To examine the bivariate relationship between opinion about abortion and confidence in the Court, we divided respondents into three categories: those who opposed the legalization of all elective abortions ("pro-life"), those who approved of the legalization of all elective abortions ("pro-choice"), and those who approved of only some circumstances for elective abortion ("intermediate").[14] Since 1973, pro-choice respondents have tended to have the most confidence in the Court, and pro-life respondents have had the least (see Figure 4.7). In all groups, confidence generally increased during the 1980s, fell in the early 1990s, and rebounded in the late 1990s—shifts in confidence that correspond to similar shifts in trust in government during this time period (Luks & Citrin 2001). However, the gap in confidence may be closing. Starting in 2000, the pro-choice and intermediate groups began to lose confidence in the Court, while the pro-life group gained confidence in the Court. By 2004, the pro-life and pro-choice confidence levels were nearly equal.

The public also appears to believe that decisions about abortion are among the most important decisions made by the Court. In a poll conducted by the

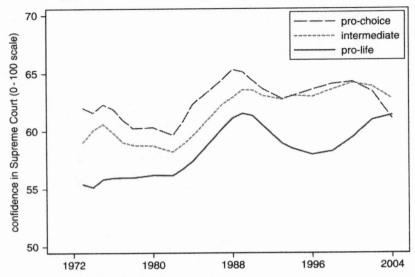

Figure 4.7. Confidence in the Supreme Court by Position on Abortion, 1972–2004. Question wording: see text. Source: General Social Survey.

Pew Research Center in July 2005, respondents were asked whether Court decisions on given topics were very important, fairly important, or not at all important to them (see Table 4.5). Abortion was the issue that was rated "very important" by the largest number of people (63%). Additionally, according to a December 2005 poll conducted by CBS/New York Times, 37% of Americans believe it is very important for the U.S. Senate to know a Supreme Court nominee's stance on abortion before he or she is confirmed, and an additional 34% say it is somewhat important.

Table 4.5.
Importance of Court Decisions on Various Issues, July 2005

Issue	Percent saying "Very Important"
Abortion	62.7
Rights of people held as suspects in terrorism cases	61.5
Religious displays on government property	54.9
Awards in personal injury lawsuits	48.7
Affirmative action	43.4
Gay rights	37.2

Question wording: "Are court decisions on [issue] very important, fairly important, not too important, or not at all important to you?"
Source: Pew Research Center.

The most recent abortion-related issue to make its way to the Supreme Court concerned a federal ban on dilation and extraction (D&X), a procedure popularly referred to as "partial birth" or "late-term" abortion. The U.S. Congress passed, and President Bush signed, the Partial-Birth Abortion Ban Act in 2003, and the Court upheld the ban in *Gonzales v. Carhart* in 2007. Despite an earlier decision (*Stenberg v. Carhart* 2000) striking down a similar state ban, the Court upheld the federal law while deferring to congressional findings that the procedure is not necessary to protect the health of the pregnant woman.

Prior to the opinion, when asked whether "partial-birth abortion" should be banned, a fairly large majority of the public said yes in polls conducted in 2003 and 2006 (see Table 4.6).[15] But when an ABC News Poll asked if an exception should be made to protect the health of the woman, more than half of the people who initially believed the procedure should be illegal changed their minds. An NBC poll conducted in November 2003 showed considerably more support for keeping partial birth abortion legal (only 47% of respondents believed it should be banned). However, the question mentioned that President Bush and the Republican-led U.S. Congress had approved the partial birth abortion ban, which undoubtedly stimulated respondents' partisan attitudes.

Conclusion

Although commentators may consider abortion to be the paradigmatic constitutional controversy, the survey data point to a public and constitutional jurisprudence largely in sync with one another. Solid majorities want the Court to uphold *Roe v. Wade* and are in favor of abortion rights in the abstract. However, equally substantial majorities favor procedural and other restrictions, including waiting periods, parental consent, spousal notification, and bans on "partial-birth" abortion. The sometimes dramatic effect of question wording and the tendency of a plurality to cluster toward a middle position when one is offered suggest that large sections of the public have ambivalent or nuanced opinions on this issue.

Since the 1970s, the issue clearly has become more politicized, and differences between partisans have intensified. Overall, African Americans, people who are more religious, people with less education, and married people are more likely to be pro-life, and pro-choice opinions are more common among whites, the better educated, the less religious, and the unmarried. However, even though abortion rulings have almost certainly shaped the political climate surrounding abortion, since *Roe* no decision of the Supreme Court seems to have directly affected the trajectory or structure of public opinion on abortion rights.

Table 4.6
Opinion about "Partial Birth"/ "Late Term" Abortion, 1996–2006
All cell entries represent percentages.

	Banned	Not Banned	Unsure
"Do you think partial-birth abortions—an abortion procedure conducted late in pregnancy—should be banned or not?" (Fox News)			
Feb–06	61	28	11
Jul–98	54	28	18
May–96	46	37	17

	Favor	Oppose	Unsure
"As you may know, President Bush and the U.S. Congress recently approved a new law that prohibits a procedure commonly known as a 'partial-birth abortion.' Do you favor or oppose this new law?" (NBC/WSJ)			
Nov–03	47	40	13

	Illegal	Legal	Unsure
"Now I would like to ask your opinion about a specific abortion procedure known as 'late-term' abortion or 'partial-birth' abortion, which is sometimes performed on women during the last few months of pregnancy. Do you think that the government should make this procedure illegal, or do you think that this procedure should be legal?" (CNN/USA Today/Gallup)			
Oct–03	68	25	7

Table 4.6
(*continued*)

	Illegal	Legal	Depends	(vol.) No opinion
"Do you think the late-term abortion procedure known as dilation and extraction, or partial-birth abortion, should be legal or illegal?" (ABC News)				
Jul–03	62	20	12	5

	Illegal	Answered "legal" to first question	Answered "legal" to follow-up question	Depends	(vol.) No opinion
(If illegal, depends, or no opinion) "What if it would prevent a serious threat to the woman's health? In that case, do you think the late-term abortion procedure known as dilation and extraction, or partial-birth abortion, should be legal or illegal?"					
Jul–03	33	20	41	3	3

Notes

1. As an elite media source, the *New York Times* might be considered unrepresentative of coverage by mainstream media. But an analysis we undertook of coverage in *Newsweek* magazine—considered by scholars to reflect mainstream media attention (Kellstedt 2000)—discovered broadly similar trends to those of the *Times*. Unfortunately, electronic archives for *Newsweek* date only to 1975, making an analysis of its coverage before *Roe* prohibitive.

2. It should be noted that very few of the stories that mentioned abortion in 1972 dealt with the upcoming *Roe v. Wade* decision; as can be seen in Figure 4.1, more than 90% of the stories that mentioned abortion that year make no mention of the Supreme Court.

3. The 1965 data are reported by Granberg and Granberg 1980 (Table 4.1).

4. An exploratory factor analysis of these items confirms this interpretation.

5. Similar effects have been found with other types of survey questions. For instance, survey respondents are significantly more likely to agree that something should "not be allowed" than that something should "be forbidden" (Schuman & Presser 1981).

6. A similar item was used by the CBS/New York Times poll for a limited period of time: "If a woman wants to have an abortion and her doctor agrees to it, should she be allowed to have an abortion or not?" This question also enjoyed a relatively high level of support from the public, with approval generally above 60%.

7. The lack of opinion change on abortion accompanying *Webster* appears to hold among almost all demographic groups. In multivariate analysis not presented here, we found no statistically significant relationships between opinion on the *Webster* decision and opinion on elective abortion with regard to respondents' gender, education, race, party identification, religious affiliation, or income. One exception is that we found a strong relationship between religiosity, opinion on the *Webster* decision, and attitudes toward elective abortion.

8. The Gallup survey is not ideal: it consisted of only 589 interviews conducted in a single day, and the survey was limited to registered voters. (Surveys that have data collection periods that span one or two days tend to overrepresent the easy-to-reach and those with work schedules compatible with the data collection period.) The only other survey about *Casey* we located was conducted by Harris Interactive in July 1992, and it contained fewer detailed questions than the Gallup survey did.

9. Although the number of respondents who felt that *Casey* did not go far enough is quite small (87), the differences between this group and the those who felt that *Casey* was about right are statistically significant for approval of a twenty-four-hour waiting period and parental consent.

10. The seventh circumstance (when a woman wants an abortion for any reason) is omitted from this analysis because it was not asked until 1977. The distribution of this response is not substantially different than those for the other reasons for elective abortion.

11. Examples of generational effects include reactions to the Vietnam War (Jennings & Niemi 1981) and to women's suffrage (Wolfinger & Rosenstone 1980).

12. The figures in this section use a lowess smoothing technique (Cleveland 1979) to reveal over-time trends that may be obscured by random variation between surveys.

13. The predictors in this model were age, birth cohort, year of survey, race, sex, education, religion, marital status, whether respondent has children, party identification, and ideology. Age and cohort were collapsed into categories to reduce multicollinearity in the model.

14. Health-related abortion was not included for this analysis because there is relatively little variation in opinion about its legality.

15. None of the major survey organizations used an alternate term for this type of abortion procedure, so we were unable to test for question wording effects.

References

Abramowitz, Alan I. 1995. "It's Abortion, Stupid: Policy Voting in the 1992 Presidential Election." *Journal of Politics* 57(1): 176–86.

Adams, Greg D. 1997. "Abortion: Evidence of an Issue Evolution." *American Journal of Political Science* 41(3): 718–37.

Alvarez, R. Michael, and John Brehm. 1995. "American Ambivalence toward Abortion Policy: Development of a Heteroskedastic Probit Model of Competing Values." *American Journal of Political Science* 39(4): 1055–82.

Barnum, David G. 1985. "The Supreme Court and Public Opinion: Judicial Decision Making in the Post-New Deal Period." *Journal of Politics* 47(2): 652–66.

Blake, Judith. 1977. "The Supreme Court's Abortion Decisions and Public Opinion in the United States." *Population and Development Review* 3(1/2): 45–62.

Cleveland, William S. 1979. "Robust Locally Weighted Regression and Smoothing Scatterplots." *Journal of the American Statistical Association* 74: 829–836.

Combs, Michael W., and Susan Welch. 1982. "Blacks, Whites, and Attitudes toward Abortion." *Public Opinion Quarterly* 46(4): 510–20.

Cook, Elizabeth Adell, Ted G. Jelen, and Clyde Wilcox. 1992. *Between Two Absolutes: Public Opinion and the Politics of Abortion*. Boulder, Colo.: Westview.

———. 1993a. "State Political Cultures and Public Opinion about Abortion." *Political Research Quarterly* 46(4): 771–81.

———. 1993b. "Measuring Public Attitudes on Abortion: Methodological and Substantive Considerations." *Family Planning Perspectives* 25(3): 118–21, 145.

———. 1993c. "Catholicism and Abortion Attitudes in the American States: A Contextual Analysis." *Journal for the Scientific Study of Religion* 32(3): 223–30.

Craig, Barbara Hinkson, and David M. O'Brien. 1993. *Abortion and American Politics*. Chatham, N.J.: Chatham House Publishers.

Craig, Stephen C., James G. Kane, and Michael D. Martinez. 2002. "Sometimes You Feel Like a Nut, Sometimes You Don't: Citizens' Ambivalence about Abortion." *Political Psychology* 23(2): 285–301.

Dahl, Robert. 1957. "Decisionmaking in a Democracy: The Supreme Court as a National Policymaker." *Journal of Public Law* 6: 279–95.

DiMaggio, Paul, John Evans, and Bethany Bryson. 1996. "Have Americans' Social Attitudes Become More Polarized?" *American Journal of Sociology* 102(3): 690–755.

Ebaugh, Helen Rose Fuchs, and C. Allen Haney. 1980. "Shifts in Abortion Attitudes: 1972–1978." *Journal of Marriage and the Family* 42(3): 491–99.

Evans, John H. 2003. "Have Americans' Attitudes Become More Polarized?—An Update." *Social Science Quarterly* 84(1): 71–90.

Fiorina, Morris P., Samuel J. Abrams, and Jeremy C. Pope. 2005. *The Culture War? The Myth of a Polarized America*. New York: Pearson Longman.

Franklin, Charles H., and Liane C. Kosaki. 1989. "Republican Schoolmaster: The U.S. Supreme Court, Public Opinion, and Abortion." *American Political Science Review* 83(3): 751–71.

Ginsburg, Ruth Bader. 1992. "Speaking in a Judicial Voice." *New York University Law Review* 67(6): 1185–1209.

Granberg, Donald, and Beth Wellman Granberg. 1980. "Abortion Attitudes, 1965–1980: Trends and Determinants." *Family Planning Perspectives* 12(5): 250–61.

Grosskopf, Anke, and Jeffery J. Mondak. 1998. "Do Attitudes toward Specific Supreme Court Decisions Matter? The Impact of *Webster* and *Texas v. Johnson* on Public Confidence in the Supreme Court." *Political Research Quarterly* 51(3): 633–54.

Hall, Elaine J., and Myra Marx Ferree. 1986. "Race Differences in Abortion Attitudes." *Public Opinion Quarterly* 50(2): 193–207.

Howell, Susan, and Robert Sims. 1993. "Abortion Attitudes and the Louisiana Governor's Election." *American Politics Quarterly* 21: 54–64.

Hunter, James Davidson. 1994. *Before the Shooting Begins: Searching for Democracy in America's Culture War*. New York: Free Press.

Jelen, Ted G., and Clyde Wilcox. 2003. "Causes and Consequences of Public Attitudes toward Abortion: A Review and Research Agenda." *Political Research Quarterly* 56(4): 489–500.

Jennings, M. Kent, and Richard G. Niemi. *Generations and Politics: A Panel Study of Young Adults and Their Parents*. Princeton, N.J.: Princeton University Press, 1981.

Johnson, Timothy R., and Andrew D. Martin. 1998. "The Public's Conditional Response to Supreme Court Decisions." *American Political Science Review* 92(2): 299–309.

Kellstedt, Paul M. 2000. "Media Framing and the Dynamics of Racial Policy Preferences." *American Journal of Political Science* 44: 245–60.

Klitsch, M. 1990. "Americans Become More Committed to Both Sides of Debate over Abortion during the Past Decade." *Family Planning Perspectives* 22(1): 40.

Legge, Jerome S., Jr. 1983. "The Determinants of Attitudes toward Abortion in the American Electorate." *Western Political Quarterly* 36(3): 479–90.

Luker, Kristin. 1984. *Abortion and the Politics of Motherhood*. Berkeley: University of California Press.

Luks, Samantha, and Jack Citrin. 2001. "Political Trust Revisited: Déjà Vu All Over Again?" In *What Is It About Government that Americans Dislike?* edited by John R. Hibbing and Elizabeth Theiss-Morse. Cambridge University Press.

Marshall, Thomas. 1989. *Public Opinion and the Supreme Court*. New York: Longman.

Mishler, William, and Reginald S. Sheehan. 1993. "The Supreme Court as a Countermajoritarian Institution? The Impact of Public Opinion on Supreme Court Decisions." *American Political Science Review* 87(1): 87–101.

Nossiff, Rosemary. 1994. "Why Justice Ginsburg Is Wrong about States Expanding Abortion Rights." *PS: Political Science and Politics* 27(2): 227–31.

Rosen, Jeffrey. 2006. *The Most Democratic Branch*. New York: Oxford University Press.

Rosen, R. A. Hudson, et al. 1974. "Health Professionals' Attitudes toward Abortion." *Public Opinion Quarterly* 38(2): 159–73.

Rosenberg, Gerald N. 1991. *The Hollow Hope: Can Courts Bring about Social Change?* Chicago: University of Chicago Press.

Sauer, R. 1974. "Attitudes to Abortion in America, 1800–1973." *Population Studies* 28(1): 53–67.

Schuman, H., and S. Presser. 1981. *Questions and Answers in Attitude Surveys: Experiments on Question Form, Wording, and Context*. New York: Academic Press.

Scott, Jaqueline, and Howard Schuman. 1988. "Attitude Strength and Social Action in the Abortion Dispute." *American Sociological Review* 53(5): 785–93.

Shaw, Greg M. 2003. "The Polls—Trends: Abortion." *Public Opinion Quarterly* 67: 407–429.

Singh, B. Krishna, and Peter J. Leahy. 1978. "Contextual and Ideological Dimensions of Attitudes toward Discretionary Abortion." *Demography* 15(3): 381–88.

Smith, Kevin B. 1994. "Abortion Attitudes and Vote Choice in the 1984 and 1988 Presidential Elections." *American Politics Quarterly* 22(3): 354–69.

Strickler, Jennifer, and Nicholas L. Danigelis. 2002. "Changing Frameworks in Attitudes toward Abortion." *Sociological Forum* 17(2): 187–201.

Uslaner, Eric M., and Ronald E. Weber. 1979. "Public Support for Pro-Choice Abortion Policies in the Nation and States: Changes and Stability after the *Roe* and *Doe* Decisions." *Michigan Law Review* 77(7): 1772–89.

Wetstein, Matthew E., and Robert B. Albritton. 1995. "Effects of Public Opinion on Abortion Policies and Use in the American States." *Publius* 25(4): 91–105.

Wilcox, Clyde. 1990. "Race Differences in Abortion Attitudes: Some Additional Evidence." *Public Opinion Quarterly* 54(2): 248–55.

Witwer, M. 1989. "Many Americans Oppose Government Intervention in Both Abortion Rights, but Endorse Some Restrictions." *Family Planning Perspectives* 21(5): 229–30.

Wlezien, Christopher B., and Malcolm L. Gloggin. 1993. "The Courts, Interest Groups, and Public Opinion about Abortion." *Political Behavior* 15(4): 381–405.

Wolfinger, Raymond E., and Stephen J. Rosenstone. 1980. *Who Votes?* New Haven: Yale University Press.

5

The Death Penalty

John Hanley

In a controversial footnote to the Supreme Court's 2002 decision in *Atkins v. Virginia*, Justice John Paul Stevens invoked public opinion polls, among other evidence, to reach the conclusion that a societal consensus existed against executing mentally retarded prisoners. The dissenting judges and many outsiders objected that the meaning of a constitutional provision ought not depend on a counting of noses or general feelings about emotionally loaded questions. Nevertheless, public opinion—reflected in referendums, filtered through legislative acts, or indicated in polls—has helped to guide the Court's determinations of what constitutes "cruel and unusual punishment" for more than thirty years. The case of mental retardation stands out, however, as an exception to a pattern of broad public support for the death penalty first manifested in the early 1970s.

Well before the Supreme Court's first intervention on the issue of whether the death penalty constitutes an unconstitutional "cruel and unusual punishment," first the Founders and then legislators throughout the nineteenth and twentieth centuries grappled with the question. The persistent contention over the morality of the death penalty makes it difficult to isolate the effect, if any, of Court decisions on preexisting public opinion. Johnson and Martin (1998) have shown changes in the structure of public opinion coincident with Supreme Court decisions, but they also indicate that these effects are dwarfed by the movement of aggregate opinion over long stretches of time. Still, by setting boundaries on the policies enacted by states, and thus influencing the implementation of capital punishment, the Supreme Court shapes the public's experience and thus, indirectly, its appraisals of the policy.

This chapter first examines the nature of public opinion on capital punishment before the Supreme Court's decision in *Furman v. Georgia* (1972), the case in which the corpus of state death penalty statutes was overturned. It then analyzes the rise in death penalty support into the 1980s and its brief decline in the 1990s. A separate section discusses opinion about specific applications of the death penalty. The chapter concludes with a look at the Court's use of public opinion poll data in *Atkins* and other death penalty cases.

A Historical Overview

By prohibiting "cruel and unusual punishment," the Founders consciously imposed a restriction on government power. Early concern for the death penalty is reflected in work by Louis Masur (1989, 94–96). He shows that concern for public morals and angry responses to botched executions were major factors in the move away from public executions, a reform that originated in Pennsylvania in 1834 and spread rapidly to neighboring states. More generally, nineteenth-century Americans did not unanimously favor capital punishment. In 1846, Michigan banned capital punishment for all crimes except treason, a ban that has stood to the present day. Epstein and Kobylka (1992) show that acts to abolish the death penalty—some later reversed, others sustained—were passed by state legislatures or the public on fifteen occasions throughout the century following Michigan's action. States that have retained the death penalty have consistently adopted new methods of execution believed to be more humane.

In the last hundred years, Americans have directly expressed their views on capital punishment through referendums and public opinion polls. Progressive Era referendums in Ohio, Oregon, and Arizona reveal electorates closely divided on the abolition of the death penalty, with Oregon voters going so far as to affirm the death penalty in 1912, reject it in 1914 by a very narrow margin, and then vote for its restoration in 1920. In April 1931, Michigan residents voted to uphold the state's near-ban on capital punishment by 57% to 43%. These results do not speak to public opinion nationwide, but they do suggest that the level of support for executions varied and that in states where the death penalty was (at least temporarily) abolished by legislation, legislators' preferences were not radically different from those of their constituents.

The earliest national polls on the death penalty were conducted in 1936 and 1937, after the execution of Bruno Hauptmann for the kidnapping and murder of the infant Charles A. Lindbergh Jr.—then billed as the "crime of the century." These data are valuable but pose special challenges, owing to the fact that polling in that era had not yet developed techniques for drawing a representative sample from the national population. A 1936 Gallup Poll that reported 61% support for the death penalty (Table 5.1) probably overestimated the level of support in the American population because of the underrepresentation of women, blacks, and Southerners in the sample. Members of the underrepresented groups, however,

Table 5.1
Selected Pre-1947 Gallup Polls on Capital Punishment

Poll Date	Position on capital punishment			Question wording
	Pro	Anti	Other	
July 1936	62	33	5	Are you in favor of the death penalty for murder?
November 1936	61	39		Are you in favor of the death penalty for murder?
November 1937	60	33	7	Are you in favor of the death penalty for murder?
December 1937	65	35		Do you favor or oppose capital punishment for murder?
May 1947	43	47	9	Which do you think is the better sentence for a person found guilty of murder in the U.S.—a long prison term or death?
November 1953	68	25	7	Are you in favor of the death penalty for persons convicted of murder?
March 1956	53	34	13	Are you in favor of the death penalty for persons convicted of murder?
March 1960	51	36	13	Are you in favor of the death penalty for persons convicted of murder?
February 1965	45	43	12	Are you in favor of the death penalty for persons convicted of murder?

Note: Early polls are unrepresentative samples of American opinion. See text for explanation and examples of corrected estimates.

Source: Roper Archive.

tended to be more opposed to the death penalty. For example, support among women polled was 50%, versus 65% among men; women made up less than 30% of Gallup's sample. Only thirty-two respondents of 2,200 were not white—twelve, or 38%, were in favor.

Despite these shortcomings, the 61% statistic has been cited in numerous works. Using a cell-weighting procedure similar to that used by Berinsky (2006) to correct for the unequal sampling of women, Southerners, and blacks, we arrive at a more modest 55–56% estimate for both of the late 1930s polls. These polls included few other demographic variables, but unweighted analysis of the 1936 survey indicates that aggregate support was nearly identical between those who had "been to college" and those who had not (60% versus 61%), between urban and rural dwellers (60% versus 64%), between Southerners and non-Southerners (61% versus 61%), and between Roosevelt and Landon voters (61% versus 62%).

In a separate Gallup study prepared to coincide with the 1936 presidential election, a much larger sample was generated, permitting between-state analyses of opinion. The 1936 state-by-state results indicate that support for the death penalty was lowest, for the most part, in states where capital punishment was fully or nearly abolished. All seven of the states without capital punishment were among the nine lowest in death penalty support.[1]

In 1947, Gallup asked a related, but not directly comparable, question: whether a "long prison term" or death was the better sentence for a person found guilty of murder. Given this choice, 43% said prison, and 47% selected death. When Gallup resumed asking whether a respondent "favored" the death penalty, in January 1953, some five months before execution of Julius and Ethel Rosenberg, 72% of respondents favored the death penalty for treason. In this survey, opinion was rather uniform among different demographic groups: support was only 6 points lower among women than among men and 3 points higher for Republicans than for Democrats. Support was higher among respondents with some college education or a college degree than those without. In November 1953, Gallup reported that 68% of respondents favored the death penalty for murder (including 4% who gave a "qualified yes").

Four years later, death penalty support had declined. In a 1957 Gallup poll, 47% of the public surveyed stood in support, 34% were opposed, and 18% had no definite opinion. The death penalty was supported by 53% of men and 42% of women, a larger gap than four years previously, and by 49% of Republicans and 47% of Democrats. Three polls in the early 1960s showed little change: in a poll conducted by the National Opinion Research Center eleven months after the Kennedy assassination, 51% of the public supported the statement that "having the death penalty for the worst crimes is a good idea." The alternative position offered by the poll—that one was "against the death penalty"—was chosen by 43% of the public.

A Gallup Poll conducted in May 1966 showed, for the first time since the advent of polling, a slight plurality *against* capital punishment. In this poll, only 42% of respondents supported the death penalty; low levels of support were observed among all subgroups, with majority support found only among Westerners (50%) and Republicans (51%). Other organizations also reported lower support. The California (later Field) Poll registered a 5-point drop in support from 1963 to 1965, and a July 1966 Harris Poll showed only 38% in favor, with 47% opposed (Erskine 1970). Within a year and a half, however, the majority again approved of the death penalty, with 53% of the public in favor and only 39% opposed. Four more Gallup polls conducted between 1967 and the Supreme Court's 1972 decision in *Furman v. Georgia* reported levels of support between 49% and 54%.

In addition to polling data, evidence comes from the results of various state referendums that predated *Furman*. In 1964, when death penalty support had fallen nationwide, more than 60% of Oregon voters cast ballots to abolish the death penalty. But in three referendums later in the decade, resounding majorities confirmed the practice. In 1966, Colorado voters rejected a referendum to abolish the death penalty by a two-to-one margin. Two years later, more than 60% of Massachusetts voters responded affirmatively to the nonbinding question "Shall Massachusetts retain capital punishment?"[2] In 1970, Illinois voters rejected abolition by 64% to 36%.[3] Combined, these three affirmative referendums reflected the opinion of almost 10% of the American population.

Thus, support for the death penalty had already bottomed out several years before *Furman* and was possibly increasing even before the Court called into question state death penalty statutes nationwide. Three months before the announcement of the *Furman* decision, a Gallup poll showed half of respondents supported the death penalty, with 42% opposed and 9% expressing no opinion. The General Social Survey, conducted from February to April 1972, found 53% in support and 39% opposed. Four months after the June 29 announcement of the *Furman* decision, a Gallup poll indicated 57% supporting the death penalty, with 32% opposed.

Interpreting the meaning of public opinion polls immediately before and after the *Furman* decision is complicated by the fact that the decision occurred during a presidential election campaign. Both the Nixon and McGovern campaigns focused heavily on crime. While Republicans accused the Democratic candidate of moral degeneracy, famously tagging McGovern as the candidate of "acid, abortion, and amnesty,"[4] McGovern pointed to the nation's rising crime rates as a failure of the Nixon administration (*New York Times*, 1972). Inferences about how *Furman* influenced public opinion are also complicated by the February 1972 California Supreme Court decision in *California v. Anderson*, which found the death penalty unconstitutional under California's state constitution. Public anger at this decision instigated a successful ballot initiative, Proposition 17, which explicitly enshrined capital punishment in the state constitution. This constellation of events and the data available make it difficult to conclude that *Furman* itself created a backlash.

Some tentative points can be made about public sentiment before *Furman*. First, if we employ cell weighting for the 1930s polls and consider the fraction of the population favoring the death penalty (that is, not removing "no opinion" respondents from our denominator), support is lower than modern levels and fairly stable, with the exception of the Rosenberg-era result, in which 68% of the public favored capital punishment for murder. Second, state referendums in the late 1960s show considerably more support for the death penalty than contemporaneous public opinion polls, indicating that more politically engaged citizens were more favorable to the policy than the rest of the public.

After *Furman*, support for the death penalty continued to climb throughout the 1970s and early 1980s. By the mid-1980s, a sea change in national public opinion had occurred. Whereas support for the death penalty had fallen as low as 42% in 1966, by the mid-1980s and early 1990s about three of every four Americans favored it. In a September 1994 Gallup poll, support touched 80%, a level that reflected a sharp increase in support among

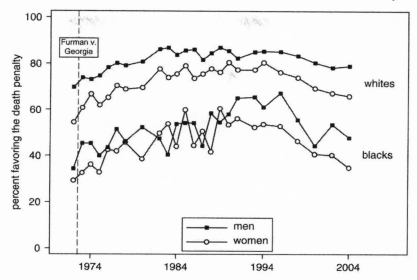

Figure 5.1. Support for the Death Penalty by Race and Sex, 1972–2004. Question wording: Do you favor or oppose the death penalty for persons convicted of murder? Source: General Social Survey.

many subgroups. Men and women, Democrats and Republicans, whites and blacks—all were more likely to support the death penalty in the 1990s than in the 1970s (see Figure 5.1). Even events that could be hypothesized to reduce death penalty support among specific groups (for instance the *McCleskey v. Kemp* (1987) case, which exposed evidence of bias against blacks in the imposition of death sentences) did not derail this trend.

Support for capital punishment receded slightly in the mid- and late 1990s, wavering between 65% and 75%. Though the amount of drop-off varied slightly among different groups, the overall downward trend occurred across the board, just as the post-1970 rise had been. The evidence from a variety of polls conducted between 1995 and 2006 suggests that the slide in support slowed after 2000, with the current level of support for the death penalty settling in at around 70% of the public (Figure 5.2).

Explanations for Over-Time Variation in Opinion

Scholarly writing about the death penalty in America has touched on the highs and lows of public opinion without much speculation about what moved the level of support. For instance, the 1966 poll result showing a plurality of Americans opposing capital punishment has been frequently cited in death

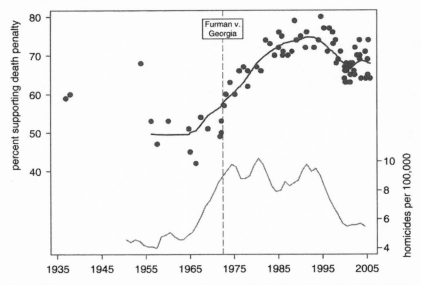

Figure 5.2. National Murder Rate and Support for the Death Penalty, 1935–2005. Question wording varies. Source: Roper Archive.

penalty scholarship, but still unknown are the reasons for such low support, or why support increased sharply from the 1966 to 1967 polls.

As mentioned earlier, individual states have at various times imposed and abolished capital punishment. Up until *Furman*, there had also been considerable variation among the states in the definition of a capital crime and in the procedures for imposing and carrying out the death penalty. For example, until 1963, death was the *mandatory* punishment for first-degree murder in the state of New York. In both Massachusetts and Connecticut, discretionary sentencing in first-degree murder cases began only in 1951 (Lee & Mooney 1999). In most other states, sentencing was discretionary, but kidnapping and rape were often capital crimes.[5] The Court's decision in *Furman*, and subsequent clarifications such as those provided by *Gregg v. Georgia* (1976, approving a set of state death penalty procedures) and in *Coker v. Georgia* (1977, forbidding capital punishment for the rape of an adult woman), however, sharply reduced the variance in state death penalty statutes.

Attempts to link state policy to state public opinion, however, raise complex causal questions: does more aggressive application of the death penalty provoke public opposition to capital punishment, or does it reflect the public's preferences and in this way solidify prior opinion? Erikson's (1976) analysis finds a strong positive relationship between state policy and public opinion, but Brace and colleagues (2002), looking at GSS data for 1974–1998, find a negative relationship between public support for the death penalty and the number of inmates on death row (controlled for state population) in a respondent's state.

In one of the nation's most notable death penalty cases, the result appears to have been stronger support for capital punishment, offset by a temporary change in the correlates of opinion, with the level of formal education becoming more negatively associated with death penalty support. In 1960, California's death penalty became the focus of national and international attention when an execution date was scheduled for Caryl Chessman, who had been sentenced to die in 1948 under the state's antikidnapping law for a series of robbery-rape attacks in Southern California.[6] In more than a decade on death row, Chessman had educated himself and written several books about his experiences, leading to an uncommon public familiarity with (and sympathy for) his life. As Epstein and Kobylka (1992) note, many commentators have identified the Chessman case as the catalyst for elite mobilization against the death penalty. Pro-Chessman rallies were attended by Marlon Brando and Shirley MacLaine, whom the media presented as emblems of a new brand of socially conscious Hollywood celebrity (Schumach 1960). So intense was international opposition to the Chessman execution that the U.S. State Department, worried about demonstrations during President Eisenhower's upcoming visit to South America, pressured California Governor Pat Brown to grant the prisoner a stay (Davies 1960). Brown then called the state legislature into special session to abolish the state's death penalty, but the legislators had read the mood of their constituents and refused. According to a 1960 California Poll, 55% of Californians believed that the death penalty "should be kept as punishment for serious crimes" (up from 46% in 1956). Between the 1956 and 1960 polls, the percentage of Californians opposed to the death penalty had also increased, as the proportion of the population with no opinion on the matter declined sharply. A national Gallup Poll conducted in March 1960 also showed polarization, with 46% in favor of capital punishment for murder, and 53% opposed—an increase of 6 percentage points in death penalty support from a 1957 Gallup poll.

The results of the March 1960 national poll parallel elite criticism of the death penalty, with education having a statistically negative relationship to support in a multivariate model. Following Johnson and Martin (1998), I conducted a test to determine whether individual covariates, such as race or education, became more powerful predictors of a respondent's death penalty support after the Chessman controversy. Because the 1957 Gallup Poll did not include demographic questions regarding religious affiliation or religiosity, I could not use those covariates. Nonetheless, comparing constrained and unconstrained models for the two Gallup polls, the comparison test indicates a strong likelihood that the structure of overall opinion was different in 1960 than it was in 1957 (see Table 5.2).

The public response to the Chessman case also illustrates the connection between the salience of the death penalty and the polarization of opinion between high- and low-education respondents. Despite a controversial sentence and prolonged opposition from elites within the state and from outside groups, aggregate support for the death penalty rose in California in the months preceding the execution.

Table 5.2
Change in the Structure of Support for Capital Punishment During Caryl
Chessman Controversy, 1957 and 1960

	Constrained Model	Unconstrained Model
Education	−.01	.04
	(.02)	(.03)
Education × 1960		−.09**
		(.03)
Male	.27***	.28***
	(.04)	(.07)
Male × 1960		−.01
		(.08)
White	.39***	.16
	(.06)	(.13)
White × 1960		.32*
		(.15)
Party identification	.04+	.02
	(.02)	(.04)
Party identification × 1960		.04
		(.05)
Age 30 and under	.08	.12
	(.05)	(.09)
Age 30 and under × 1960		−.05
		(.11)
Intercept	−.55***	−.43**
	(.07)	(.13)
1960 dummy	.16***	.01
	(.04)	(.15)
N	4,362	4,362
Pseudo R-squared	.02	.02
Chi-square statistic	104.68	117.13
Log likelihood	−2969.98	−2963.75
Likelihood test	12.45	
Significance	<.05	

Coefficients significantly different from zero at $^+p<.10$, $^*p<.05$, $^{**}p<.01$, $^{***}p<.001$ (two-tailed test). Standard errors in parentheses.

Source: Gallup.

Question wording: "Are you in favor of the death penalty for persons convicted of murder?"

After the execution, national approval of the death penalty dropped, falling to its lowest point in the 1966 Gallup poll before rebounding in the late 1960s and early 1970s. Page and Shapiro (1992) situate the decline in support between the 1953 and 1966 Gallup results as part of a "general libertarian movement of opinion." Bohm (1992) mentions several broad trends that may explain some of the change in death penalty support in the 1960s: the increased salience of crime, the social turmoil and resulting backlash, tensions in race relations, and economic conditions. (Analysis of Gallup polls, however, suggests that racial tension may account for earlier *declines* in death penalty support among Southern whites, because unusually low support rates in some states coincided with capital trials for the murders of civil rights leaders and activists.)

Legislative action to abolish or restrict capital punishment both in the United States and abroad in the mid-1960s was consistent with reduced public support and may have contributed to this trend. In 1965, capital punishment was abolished in West Virginia and Iowa and restricted to the very point of abolition in Vermont and New York, as well as in Great Britain.[7] Additionally, Deputy Attorney General Ramsey Clark, on behalf of the Department of Justice, appealed to Congress to abolish the federal death penalty. But only a month later, the U.S. Congress enacted the death penalty for the crime of assassinating the president of the United States or any person in the line of succession to the presidency.

The 1966 Gallup poll is also notable because it indicates the opening of a gap in opinion between younger and older Americans. In polls conducted in 1960 and 1965, support levels were very close for the under-30 and over-30 groups, but the 1966 and 1967 surveys showed a gap of 4.5 percentage points, with the younger group less supportive of the death penalty. By the time of the Court's decision in *Furman*, the gap had widened to approximately 10 points in the Gallup Poll.[8] (See Figure 5.3.) This gap between younger and older adults closed in the mid-1980s.

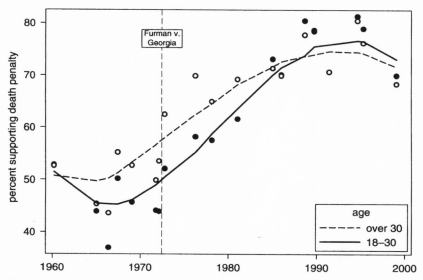

Figure 5.3. Support for the Death Penalty by Age, 1960–2000. Question wording: Are you in favor of the death penalty for persons convicted of murder? Source: Gallup.

Perhaps the most startling relationship between aggregate death penalty support and a hypothesized independent variable, however, relates support to increases in crime in the middle and late 1960s. Research has shown that support for harsher punishment is not related to individual crime victimization but rather to broader concerns about aggregate levels of crime in the nation as a whole. Fox, Radelet, and Bonsteel (1990) speculate on two reasons for the rise in support for capital punishment in wake of *Furman*: increased media attention to crime and public misperception of sentencing alternatives (i.e., that high-publicity parole hearings cause the public to falsely frame the question as capital punishment versus the possibility of letting killers go free, thus ignoring the option of life without parole).

As shown in Figure 5.2, a dramatic increase in violent crime preceded the *Furman* decision: from 1965 to 1972, the nation's murder rate jumped from 5.1 murders per 100,000 residents to 9 murders per 100,000; this increase represented an additional 8,700 murders per year. Even those Americans who paid little attention to crime statistics could not ignore the many high-profile crimes that touched both well-known public figures and ordinary Americans: the assassinations of Martin Luther King Jr. and Robert Kennedy; the mass shooting by Charles Whitman in Austin, Texas, in 1966; the murders committed by Charles Manson and his followers in 1969 and 1970; and the Zodiac killings in the San Francisco Bay Area in 1968 and 1969. The rising crime rate was also made salient by political campaigns: for example, in 1968, Richard Nixon ran on a theme of "law and order."

A spate of airplane hijackings was another factor that is likely to have contributed to public concern about brazen criminal activity. Between 1968 and 1972, 137 aircraft were hijacked by passengers boarding in the United States, with many planes diverted to Cuba (Holden 1986). Though almost all of these hijackings were resolved without loss of life, such episodes of high drama made for an anxious public. In his initial public response to the Court's decision in *Furman*, Nixon stated that although he personally felt that capital punishment was "inhumane," he believed that it was necessary and valuable in serving to deter kidnapping and hijacking. Several of the post-*Furman* death penalty statutes enacted by states, imitating federal law and solicitous of "aggravating factors," made hijacking a capital crime or made murder a capital crime when committed in the act of hijacking an airplane.[9]

Though Ellsworth and Gross (1994) observe, looking at the 1980s and early 1990s, no discernible relationship between fluctuations in the murder rate and the overall level of support for the death penalty, they speculate that the relationship is mediated by public perception of crime rates. As various studies have shown, public perception held that crime was increasing through the 1980s, even though this was not the case. A highly publicized decline in crime in the middle and late 1990s, particularly in urban environments such as New York City, was accompanied by a noticeable drop in death penalty support. Ellsworth and Gross note that over the course of the 1980s, deterrence declined as a respondent's justification for the death penalty, and retribution increased markedly.

To understand the extent to which the Court's decision in *Furman* affected public opinion about the death penalty, we must also look at the underpinnings of public opinion and the factors driving changes in opinion. Johnson and Martin (1998) argue that *Furman* led to a change in the structure of public opinion on the death penalty because it was the first time the Court had ruled on the issue. They find that later rulings on capital punishment (*Gregg v. Georgia* (1976) and *McClesky v. Kemp* (1987)) failed to have the same effect because the Court had already visited the topic.

Other commentators have described the change in public opinion after *Furman* as an instance of a "frustration-aggression" response (Zimring & Hawkins 1986). However, this hypothesis does not explain why many Americans seemed to move away from agreement with a court decision that seemed to validate their own anti–death penalty preferences. And although public support for capital punishment increased sharply after *Furman*, as we have seen, growth in support for capital punishment predated *Furman*, and a slower but unambiguous increase persisted through the late 1980s.

Perhaps the best example of a strong shift in public opinion in opposition to *Furman* took place in the South. In the post–World War II era, executions had declined more slowly in the South than in other regions. After *Furman*—a case that had originated in Georgia—Southern legislatures were among the most aggressive in restoring death penalty statutes. The comparatively low levels of support among Southerners—even considering only white Southerners—stand in relief to the popularity of capital punishment among elected officeholders. White Southerners' comparatively high levels of support for the death penalty persisted, despite the opposition to capital punishment among elites. Most notably, in the wake of *Furman*, the gap in support between Southern white men and women narrowed from almost 30 percentage points in 1972 to 16 points in 1978. Some have speculated that the stronger support for the death penalty in the South after *Furman* was a reaction against an already unpopular Supreme Court. However, it is quite conceivable that the dramatic change in Southern women's opinion after 1972 was caused by the increased salience of the death penalty and the subsequent transmission of political beliefs within households. Jennings and Stoker (2001), using panel data, find that on political topics broadly "58% of the wives admitted to moving in the husband's direction while only 14% said their husbands swung toward their way."

The Death Penalty and the American Public Today

Today, the determinants of death penalty support reflect many of the prevailing cleavages in American society. Table 5.3 indicates the proportion of various demographic groups who supported the death penalty for convicted murderers in 2004. Table 5.4 presents a probit analysis that assesses the extent to which any group differences remain significant once we control for other individual characteristics. We focus here on differences with regard to race, sex, religion, education, and political orientation.

Table 5.3
Support for Death Penalty by Demographic Group, 2004

Category		Percent
Region	Northeast	62%
	Midwest	67%
	South	68%
	West	75%
Sex	Male	76%
	Female	61%
Race	White	72%
	Black	39%
	Other	67%
Marital status	Married	72%
	Widowed	64%
	Divorced	69%
	Separated	52%
	Never married	62%
Number of children	Zero	64%
	One	75%
	Two	68%
	Three	69%
	Four or more	68%
Ideology	Extremely liberal	38%
	Liberal	47%
	Slightly liberal	66%
	Moderate	69%
	Slightly conservative	75%
	Conservative	75%
	Extremely conservative	78%
Religion	Protestant	73%
	Catholic	67%
	Jewish	71%
	None	58%
Church attendance	Never	72%
	Less than once/year	68%
	Once a year	70%
	Several times a year	70%
	Once a month	78%
	2–3 times a month	59%
	Nearly every week	69%
	Every week	64%
	More than once a week	62%
Party	Strong Democrat	50%
	Not strong Democrat	63%
	Independent, near Democrat	64%
	Independent	67%

Table 5.3
(continued)

Category		Percent
	Independent, near Republican	69%
	Not strong Republican	78%
	Strong Republican	87%
Education (degree)	Less than high school	60%
	High school	72%
	Junior college	71%
	Bachelor	68%
	Graduate	62%
Age	18–25	64%
	26–35	67%
	36–45	67%
	46–55	70%
	56–65	70%

Source: General Social Survey.

Question wording: see Figure 5.1.

Table 5.4
The Structure of Support for the Death Penalty, 2004

	Probit Coefficient	Standard Error	z
Male	.35	.08	4.29***
Age thirty or younger	−.06	.10	−.67
Catholic	−.06	.09	−.65
Postsecondary education	−.26	.11	−2.34*
Party identification	.10	.02	4.25***
Ideology	.10	.03	3.06**
White	.41	.10	3.95***
South	.19	.12	1.65
Midwest	.14	.12	1.12
West	.40	.13	3.07**
Church attendance	−.03	.02	−2.22*
(Constant)	−.56	.16	−3.44**
N	1,210		
Pseudo R-squared	.09		
Log likelihood statistic	−688.21		

Source: General Social Survey.

Question wording: See Figure 5.1.

Table 5.3 quantifies the divisions by race and sex regarding support for the death penalty that were seen earlier in Figure 5.1. In 2004, 72% of whites but only 39% of blacks approved of the death penalty. Furthermore, the large, statistically significant coefficient associated with whites in Table 5.4 indicates that this difference remains even after controlling for other individual characteristics. As shown in Figure 5.1, this racial gap has remained consistently large over the past thirty years. The same is true for differences by sex, where 76% of men, but only 61% of women, say they favor the death penalty—another distinction that remains strong in our multivariate analysis. The data shown in Figure 5.1 indicate that white men are consistently more supportive of the death penalty than white women. In addition, since 1990 black men have been more supportive of the death penalty than black women, after a period of fluctuation in the late 1970s and 1980s.

We now turn to differences along religious lines, keeping in mind the doctrinal opposition of some religious groups (and in particular, Roman Catholic doctrine) to the death penalty. Table 5.3 indicates that, among those indicating a religious preference, Catholics were the least supportive denomination of the death penalty in 2004: 67% approved of it. In Figure 5.4, we plot support for the death penalty over the past four decades among adherents of five major religious traditions in the United States: Protestants (divided into white evangelical, white mainline, and African American categories), Roman Catholics, and Jews. As seen in the figure, Catholics have been consistently less supportive of the death penalty than white Protestants since the 1980s, and Jews, ideologically the most liberal of these religious groups, have become distinctively more opposed to capital punishment over the past quarter century. In the model shown in Table 5.4, church attendance and dummy variables for being Catholic did not have a statistically significant effect on death penalty opinion in 2004 after controlling for party identification and political ideology.

The relationship between educational attainment and death penalty support is complex. Support is lowest among the least educated and the most educated: Adults who did not finish high school and those who have completed some postgraduate work are less likely to support capital punishment than those in other educational attainment groups. (In analysis not shown here, we find that this pattern is not because blacks have lower educational attainment than whites.) Adults with some college education were once less supportive of capital punishment than high school graduates, but in recent iterations of the GSS, support among these two groups has been nearly identical. College graduates have consistently shown lower levels of support than high school graduates, but this difference has waxed and waned over time. In the GSS series, death penalty support among college graduates peaked in 1984; support among high school graduates and adults with "some college" peaked in 1994.

Since the 1960s, support for capital punishment has been higher among conservatives and Republicans than among liberals and Democrats. Over time, this divergence of opinion has become more pronounced, even when the movement of Southerners to the Republican Party is disregarded. In iterations

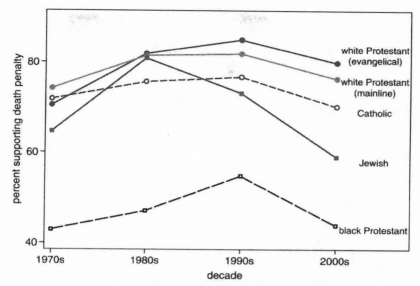

Figure 5.4. Support for the Death Penalty by Religious Denomination, 1970–2000. Question wording: Do you favor or oppose the death penalty for persons convicted of murder? Source: General Social Survey.

of the GSS in the 1970s and early 1980s, the difference between Democrats and Republicans outside the South was at most 15 percentage points, but in the mid-1990s and again since 2002, this gap has approached or exceeded 20 points. As shown in Table 5.3, the difference between the most intense partisans in 2004 was nearly 40 points. A divide of similar size occurs between extreme liberals and extreme conservatives. These differences are statistically significant after we control for other variables in Table 5.4.

Opinion on the Death Penalty versus Life without Parole

Critics of capital punishment have often suggested life imprisonment without eligibility for parole as an alternative sentence that would protect society from murderers while allowing for the possibility that a wrongful conviction may, due to new evidence, be overturned. Some also argue that life imprisonment is less expensive for taxpayers, because capital punishment entails years of costly legal appeals.

Several authors have proposed that a component of death penalty support is the absence or misunderstanding of the sentence of life without parole. A number of high-profile murderers, such as David Berkowitz and Charles Manson, are eligible for parole, and publicity surrounding these hearings undoubtedly leads some Americans to question the ability of the penal system to protect citizens. Until recently, sentencing a convicted murderer to life without parole was not an option in many states, including Texas, which as of 2007 had the second highest execution rate per capita of any state (Death Penalty Information Center, 2007).

Though some scholars (Bowers, Vandiver, & Dugan 1994; Kirchmeier 2002) cite support in polls for life without parole and "life without parole and restitution to the victim's family," we must be cautious about the claim (sometimes explicitly normative) that such options increase the public's willingness to abandon capital punishment. For instance, Bowers, Vandiver, and Dugan present the following poll question:

Which is closer to your opinion?
 • As an alternative to the death penalty, I would be willing to support
   a plan that sentenced a convicted murderer to prison for life, with no
   possibility of parole and have him work in a prison industry where his
   earnings would go into a victim's fund
 • I would not support any alternatives to the death penalty—I support the
   death penalty for people convicted of murder
 • Not sure, don't know, no answer

Forty-nine percent of respondents in this sample chose the life without parole with restitution option, and 42% opted for the death penalty. Asking respondents whether they would support a given punishment as "an alternative to the death penalty," however, is not equivalent to explicitly asking them whether they would be willing to abolish capital punishment and substitute other punishments. And we do not know whether the preference for alternative sentencing schemes persists when a respondent is given specific circumstances, such as the murder of a small child or a police officer. To conclude from a generic question about "life without parole" that "death penalty support drops when people are given other punishment options" (Kirchmeier 2002) improperly conflates preference and acceptance.

Polling organizations have put these kinds of questions to Americans since 1984. A typical phrasing of this question (and less leading than the one just described) is "What do you think should be the penalty for murder—the death penalty, or life imprisonment with absolutely no possibility for parole?" Survey questions like these typically find support for the death penalty to be a substantial 20 percentage points lower than those asking simply whether respondents support or oppose the death penalty (see Figure 5.5). The proportion of respondents who prefer the death penalty in this context has varied in rough correlation with the proportion of the public that supports the death penalty generally.

A May 2005 Washington Post/ABC News poll shows that within the population of death penalty supporters, Republicans and men who support the death penalty are more likely to name the death penalty as their *preferred*

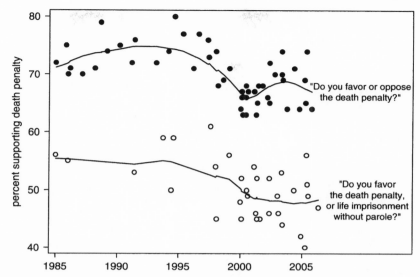

Figure 5.5. Support for Death Penalty Whether Offered the Option of Life Imprisonment without Parole, 1984–2006. Question wording varies. Text in graph represents typical question wording. Source: Roper Archive.

sanction for murder than are Democratic and female death penalty supporters. Although the gap between men and women on this preference question has not changed between 1985 and 2005, the difference between Republicans and Democrats has widened. Among white Democrats who support the death penalty, 72% prefer the death penalty for those convicted of murder; the comparable figure for white Republicans is 85%, for men 79%, and for women 70%. Unfortunately, only a handful of polls have asked the same respondents about both their opinions on the death penalty and their preferred punishment for murder—more common has been the use of split samples. Depending on the survey, people who describe themselves as opposed to the death penalty sometimes support the death penalty in a particular case. For example, in a May 2001 CBS News poll, 48 of 257 self-professed death penalty opponents supported the death penalty for Timothy McVeigh, and 35 of these said that they *preferred* the death penalty for McVeigh.

In sum, although abstract questions about "preferred" punishments may lead to moderate opinions, salient crimes leave many Americans unwilling to *abandon* capital punishment. Approval may have risen for the life without parole option, but the proportion of respondents preferring that option has stalled since 2000. It also remains to be seen whether support in principle for life without parole will persist or falter when a highly publicized crime is unusually heinous.

Opinion Concerning Specific Applications of the Death Penalty

Execution of the Mentally Retarded

In a six–three decision in *Atkins v. Virginia*, announced on June 20, 2002, the Supreme Court struck down the death penalty for offenders who are mentally retarded. Aside from eliciting some sharp comments about the use of public opinion poll data in making a determination that society stood against the death penalty in these circumstances, the conclusion of the justices was relatively uncontroversial. President Bush had opposed a bill to forbid the execution of retarded offenders when he was governor of Texas,[10] but in reaction to the case White House Press Secretary Ari Fleischer spoke only of the president's opinion that mentally retarded individuals "should not" be executed.

As shown in Table 5.5, poll numbers for executing retarded offenders have borne scant resemblance to the levels of support shown for the death penalty generally. A battery of questions in a Gallup Poll one month before the Court's decision in *Atkins* showed only 13% of the public approved of imposing the death penalty in cases involving the mentally retarded, compared with 68% approval for capital punishment for women offenders, 19% for offenders who were mentally ill, and 26% for juvenile offenders. In the same poll, 72% of respondents favored the death penalty for murder, with 25% opposed.

With the exception of a 2003 Quinnipiac Poll question asking whether a respondent agreed with the Court's decision, there have been no questions asked of a national sample about the death penalty and retarded persons since the decision in *Atkins*. Other detailed surveys have shown that even staunch death penalty proponents often make a special exception for the mentally retarded. For example, in a 1989 Field Poll, 4% of Californians who strongly supported the death penalty said that they would "always vote to impose it, in every single case, no matter what the evidence showed." But two questions later in the survey, only half of these strong death penalty supporters said that it was "all right" to execute a mentally retarded person. In the same survey, a bare majority supported the death penalty for juveniles, and 80% agreed with the statement that "the insanity plea is a loophole that allows too many guilty people to go free."

The Death Penalty for Juvenile Offenders

In the three decades since *Gregg v. Georgia*, the Supreme Court has confronted the issue of capital punishment and juvenile offenders on several occasions. In 1988, the Court in *Thompson v. Oklahoma* struck down death sentences for offenses committed before an individual's sixteenth birthday.[11] A year later, in *Stanford v. Kentucky*, the Court affirmed a death sentence for a murder committed when the offender was 17 years, 4 months old.[12] In 2005, however, in *Roper v. Simmons*, the Court revisited *Stanford* and rejected capital

Table 5.5
Polls on Whether to Impose the Death Penalty on Mentally Retarded
Offenders, 1988–2003

Poll Date	Organization (Client)	Opinion on Death Penalty		
		Support	Oppose	Uncertain, Refused, etc.
6/3/1988	Harris (for NAACP Legal Defense Fund)	21	71	7
6/28/1989	Time/CNN/Yankelovich	27	61	12
2/28/1993	Greenberg/Lake (for Death Penalty Information Center)	32	56	11
7/27/1995	PSRA/Newsweek	9	83	8
6/6/2001	Fox	19	67	14
5/6/2002	Gallup	13	82	5
2/26/2003	Quinnipiac	29	66	5

Question wording:

Harris (1988): Some people think that persons convicted of murder who have a mental age of less than 18 (or the 'retarded') should not be executed. Other people think that 'retarded' persons should be subject to the death penalty like anyone else. Which is closer to the way you feel, that 'retarded' persons should not be executed, or that 'retarded' persons should be subject to the death penalty like anyone else?

Time (1989): Do you favor or oppose the death penalty for mentally retarded individuals convicted of serious crimes, such as murder?

Greenberg/Lake (1993): Some people feel that there is nothing wrong with imposing the death penalty on persons who are mentally retarded, depending on the circumstances. Others feel that the death penalty should never be imposed on persons who are mentally retarded under any circumstances. Which of these views comes closest to your own?

PSRA/Newsweek (1995): (Please tell me whether you would generally favor or oppose the death penalty for murder in each of the following circumstances.) If the convicted person was...mentally retarded, would you favor or oppose the death penalty?

Fox (2001): Do you favor or oppose the death penalty for a person convicted of premeditated murder, if that person is shown to be mentally retarded?

Gallup (2002): Do you favor or oppose the death penalty for the mentally retarded?

Quinnipiac (2003): In general do you agree or disagree with the decision that banned the death penalty for the mentally retarded?

Source: Roper Archive.

punishment for offenders under 18 years old.[13] Criticism of the Court's decision was muted. The White House press secretary offered no objection to the decision and expressed support for the existing exclusion of juvenile offenders in federal death penalty statutes. Media coverage of the decision was limited, overshadowed by attention to the concurrent controversy over Terri Schiavo. Thus, a debate that had lasted for decades over the death penalty for young offenders was resolved quietly. There exists seventy years of polling on the subject of the death penalty for young people. In the December 1936 Gallup Poll, respondents who said they favored the death penalty for murderers were asked if they were "in favor of it for persons under 21." Only 30% of the sample thus expressed support in this instance. Similar questions have been asked many times since, but different surveys set different age cutoffs: the Pew and Field studies ask about offenders under the age of eighteen, while the 1957 and 1994 Gallup polls refer to "teenagers"—ostensibly including eighteen and nineteen-year-olds—and the 1936 and 1965 Gallup Polls ask about offenders under age twenty-one (see Table 5.6).

Table 5.6
Poll Questions About the Death Penalty and Juveniles

Month and Year	Poll (Organization)	Question	Support	Oppose
December 1936	Gallup	Are you in favor of the death penalty for persons under 21 (for murder)?	30	70
November 1953	Gallup (AIPO)	Are you in favor of the death penalty for persons under 21 who are convicted of murder?	27	64
August 1957	Gallup (AIPO)	When a teenager commits a murder, and is found guilty by a jury, do you think he should get the death penalty or should he be spared because of his youth?	16	71
January 1965	Gallup (AIPO)	Are you in favor of the death penalty for persons under 21?	21	75
December 1989	Field (California only)	Some people feel that there is nothing wrong with imposing the death penalty on juveniles under the age of 18, depending on the circumstances. Others feel that the death penalty should never be imposed on juveniles under any circumstance. Do you think it is, or is not, all right to impose the death penalty on juveniles under the age of 18?	52	42
March 1991	Great American TV Poll (Princeton Survey Research Associates)	If a teenager commits a crime that could carry the death penalty for an adult, do you think he or she should receive a death sentence, or not?	64	33

Table 5.6

(continued)

Month and Year	Poll (Organization)	Question	Support	Oppose
September 1994	Gallup/CNN/USA Today	When a teenager commits a murder and is found guilty by a jury, do you think he should get the death penalty or should he be spared because of his youth?	60	30
July 1995	PSRA/Newsweek	(Please tell me whether you would generally favor or oppose the death penalty for murder in each of the following circumstances.) If the convicted person was…a young teenager at the time of the crime, would you favor or oppose the death penalty?	47	44
April 1999	Fox/Opinion Dynamics	Do you think teens who kill other teens should face the possibility of the death penalty?	75	16
May 2001	PSRA/Newsweek	In states that have a death penalty, do you think it should or should not apply to those convicted of murder who are… juveniles younger than 18 years of age?	38	55
May 2001	National Gun Policy Survey (NORC, JHU Center for Gun Policy)	Do you favor or oppose the death penalty for persons convicted of murder who were under the age of 18 when they committed the crime?	34	55
May 2002	Gallup	Do you favor or oppose the death penalty for… juveniles?	26	69
June 2003	Pew Religion and Public Life	All in all, do you strongly favor, favor, oppose or strongly oppose…the death penalty for persons convicted of murder when they were under the age of 18?	35	58

(continued)

Table 5.6

(*continued*)

Month and Year	Poll (Organization)	Question	Support	Oppose
December 2003	ABC	Do you support or oppose the death penalty for people who are convicted of murder that they committed when they were juveniles—that is, when they were younger than age 18?	49	49
July 2005	Pew Religion and Public Life	All in all, do you strongly favor, favor, oppose, or strongly oppose...the death penalty for persons convicted of murder when they were under the age of 18?	37	54

Source: Roper Archive.

Question wordings also invoke different ideas and considerations. The wording of some questions also confounds different themes. For example, the 1957 and 1994 Gallup polls ask whether a juvenile should be "spared because of his youth," implying that the death penalty is already in force. Because a person may oppose the death penalty and yet disagree with the proposition of leniency for youth, the question may provoke responses driven by equity rather than an opinion regarding capital punishment.

In addition, the pre-*Furman* surveys concern age at the time of execution, but more recent surveys focus on age at the time a murder was committed. This change reflects the fact that in the modern era, the appeals process has effectively ended the execution of convicts in their teens or early twenties. Between 1950 and 1959, for example, at least seventy-one individuals age twenty-one or younger were executed.[14] In contrast, since executions resumed in 1977, the youngest person to have been executed was a twenty-two-year-old who had abandoned the appeals process (Espy & Smykla 2004; Fink 1997). Thus, the older surveys were inquiring about the appropriateness of the government taking a person's life at an early age, and in the later surveys, the issue is the culpability of an individual for crimes committed before age eighteen.

If we put aside these differences in question wording, we see a striking growth in support for subjecting young offenders to death penalty. In 1965, only 21% of the public favored the death penalty for offenders under twenty-one years old. But by the early 1990s, only about a third of respondents *opposed* the death penalty for teenagers (see Table 5.6). Among supporters of the death penalty, those who favored the death penalty for a teenager convicted of murder rose from 33% in 1957 to 71% in 1994.

Since the early 1990s, support for the death penalty for young offenders appears to have slackened. In a Fox News/Opinion Dynamics poll conducted the two days after the shootings at Columbine High School in 1999, the "possibility" of capital punishment for juvenile murderers was supported by 74% of respondents. But on surveys conducted since 2000 at less emotionally charged times, support for the juvenile death penalty has ranged from 26% to 38% of respondents. Only in December 2003, during the trial of Lee Malvo for his role in the Beltway sniper attacks, did support for the juvenile death penalty temporarily surge to 49%. These results suggest that before the Court's decision in *Roper v. Simmons*, the public was hesitant to impose the death sentence for murders committed while an offender was a juvenile. Absent an event like Columbine or the Malvo trial, support for the juvenile death penalty was about half the level of support for the death penalty generally.

Analysis of Pew surveys conducted in 2003 and July 2005 does not indicate that the Court's decision in *Roper* had much of an effect on public attitudes toward capital punishment for juvenile offenders. The following question was asked both before the decision and four months after: "Do you strongly favor, favor, oppose, or strongly oppose the death penalty for persons convicted of murder when they were under the age of 18?" Overall, from 2003 to 2005, support for this application of the death penalty remained almost unchanged, inching up from 35% to 36%, even as support for the death penalty in general rose from 64% to 68%. In recent years, there does not appear to have been any change in the structure of opinion about the death penalty for juveniles.

The Illinois Moratorium and Execution of the Innocent

In January 2001, Governor George Ryan of Illinois, citing the exoneration of several of the state's death row inmates, declared a moratorium on executions in Illinois. In February 2001, Gallup asked respondents whether they favored extending the Illinois moratorium across the country, and 57% of the public favored a nationwide moratorium. It is worth noting, however, that respondents were not given any definition of "moratorium,"[15] which may explain an unusual result: only two in three death penalty opponents said they favored the moratorium. Within the half-sample asked whether death or life imprisonment without parole is a "better penalty" for murder, 57% of those who chose the death penalty favored a nationwide moratorium; among those who preferred life without parole, 67% favored a nationwide moratorium. The following month, the matter was again posed in different ways to separate half-samples: one group was told that Illinois had "instituted a moratorium, or temporary halt...until it can be better determined if the death penalty is being administered accurately and fairly in that state" and asked whether they supported or opposed a national moratorium. The other half was asked to agree with either a similar statement expressing concern for accuracy and fairness, or a statement opposing a moratorium because "sufficient safeguards... already exist in the criminal justice system to prevent the execution of innocent people."[16] Respondents informed of the Illinois example and not provided the opposing language favored a moratorium 53% to 40%, while 55% of respondents in the other half-sample opposed a moratorium.

The moratorium issue was engaged again by a pair of polls in early 2003. In a Time/CNN/Harris Interactive poll in January, 60% of respondents favored a "temporary moratorium or halt...to allow government to reduce the chances that an innocent person will be put to death." In an NBC News/Wall Street Journal poll taken in the same month, the option of a nationwide moratorium only "until death penalty procedures are officially reviewed" received only 34% support.

An obstacle to pro-moratorium opinion is the apparent public tolerance of false convictions in capital cases and of the possibility that some convicts have been or will be executed for crimes they did not commit. In a 1995 Gallup/CNN/USA Today poll, 74% of death penalty supporters said that they would maintain their support even if it were true that 1% of death row inmates were innocent. In 2000, during the presidential campaign of George W. Bush and controversies about his oversight of clemency appeals from death row inmates while governor of Texas, a number of polls asked questions about the likelihood of mistaken executions. A June 2000 Gallup poll found 60% support for capital punishment among those who believed that an innocent person had been executed in the United States in the previous five years. In a separate, national half-sample, the death penalty was supported by 63% of those who believed that at least one innocent person had been executed during Bush's governorship. In this poll, questions about the likelihood of the execution of innocent people were posed after the respondent had already stated a position on capital punishment (we might expect lower support when the possibility of execution of the innocent is made immediately salient).

In a 2003 Harris poll, respondents who said that innocent people are sometimes convicted of murder were asked: "If you believe that quite a substantial number of innocent people are convicted of murder, would you then believe in or oppose the death penalty for murder?" Fifty-one percent said that in this instance they would oppose capital punishment. But we must note that a number of topics are conflated here: Not all murder convictions are capital convictions, the question posits "quite a substantial number" of erroneous convictions, and respondents are given the somewhat imbalanced choice between "believe in" and "oppose." This one poll aside, the possibility of erroneous convictions does not appear to undermine the public's support for the death penalty.

The Supreme Court and Public Opinion Data

As a subject before the Supreme Court, capital punishment is unique in that the Eighth Amendment, in prohibiting "cruel and unusual punishment," suggests that the standard may shift with changing values and practices. The modern formulation of the Court's standard came in *Trop v. Dulles* (1958), which established that "The [Eighth] Amendment must draw its meaning from the evolving standards of decency that mark the progress of a maturing society."[17]

This broad mandate notwithstanding, many eyebrows were raised at the Court's decision in *Atkins*, when Justice Stevens referenced an amicus brief from the American Association on Mental Retardation that cited a series of state and national public opinion polls showing broad opposition to the execution of mentally retarded persons.[18] In a sharply critical dissent, Justice Scalia singled out Stevens's footnote (which also touched on opposition from religious and professional organizations to executing retarded persons) for the "Prize for the Court's Most Feeble Effort to fabricate 'national consensus' (sic)."[19] Chief Justice Rehnquist was more thorough in questioning the legitimacy of opinion polls, pointing out that such polls offered the Court no assurance of proper sampling techniques, fair question wording, or even correct analysis.

Invocation of polling data in death penalty cases, however, did not begin with *Atkins* but has appeared since the 1960s. In his dissent in *Furman*, Chief Justice Burger used the results of the 1966 and 1969 Gallup Polls to argue that the state legislatures still had an accurate sense of community standards. "Without assessing the reliability of such polls," the Chief Justice wrote, "it need only be noted that the reported results have shown nothing approximating the universal condemnation of capital punishment that might lead us to suspect that the legislatures in general have lost touch with current social values."[20] Wading into the matter of public opinion—and fully acknowledging that stated opinions did not indicate by themselves the unconstitutionality of capital punishment—Justice Brennan argued that "the likelihood is great" that the death penalty support shown in polls and referendums was contingent on the infrequency with which the penalty was carried out.[21] Justice Thurgood Marshall, in forming his famous hypothesis that an informed citizenry would reject capital punishment, kept a safe distance from poll results, writing that "While a public opinion poll obviously is of some assistance in indicating public acceptance or rejection of a specific penalty, its utility cannot be very great."[22]

In the Court's decision in *Gregg*, Justice Stewart observed in a footnote that a December 1972 Gallup Poll and a 1973 Harris Poll both showed majority support for capital punishment. However, the majority opinion in *Gregg* did not affirm the use of polling data for the purposes of gauging "evolving standards of decency" as dictated by *Trop*. Rather, the Court's opinion states that "the assessment of contemporary values concerning the infliction of a challenged sanction is relevant to the application of the Eighth Amendment" and that "this assessment does not call for a subjective judgment. It requires, rather, that we look to objective indicia that reflect the public attitude toward a given sanction."[23] The justices left open the question of what constituted "objective indicia," aside from declaring that court decisions did not meet this standard, and that legislatures were the organs, in Burger's words from four years earlier, "constituted to respond to the will and consequently the moral values of the people."[24] The decision in *Gregg* cited the actions of thirty-five state legislatures, juries across the country, and the voters of the state of California as an "indication of society's endorsement of the death penalty for murder."[25]

Later, in *Thompson v. Oklahoma*, Justice O'Connor expanded on the comments made by Stewart, using the resurgence of the death penalty in the 1970s and 1980s to warn that findings that a punishment is opposed by a "national consensus" can be premature. Unlike Stewart or Burger, however, O'Connor relied exclusively on state enactments as evidence of standards in operation, and she stopped short of the plurality's finding that capital punishment was unconstitutional for murders committed when an offender was younger than sixteen. Noting that executions had declined in the 1950s and 1960s and that several states had abolished the death penalty, abolitionists had proclaimed the emergence of a consensus. But, writes O'Connor, "We now know that any inference of a societal consensus rejecting the death penalty would have been mistaken."[26] O'Connor's approach, in *Thompson* as well as subsequent death penalty cases, steered a course between the legislature-friendly approach of the Court's conservatives and the more aggressive anti–death penalty tack taken by the Court's liberals.

Nonetheless, even those who express doubts about the reliability of polling cannot dispute that on the key issue in *Atkins*, the execution of mentally retarded offenders, public opinion is unmistakably clear. Rehnquist's primary objection, though, was not so much to the methodology of specific polls as to the Court's "blind face credence" in the results of polls whose methodologies are not readily available for examination. And, of course, Rehnquist opposed the use of opinion polls to settle the question of national standards and stated that these should not "be accorded any weight on the Eighth Amendment scale when the elected representatives of a State's populace have not deemed them persuasive enough to prompt legislative action."[27] Yet there has never been a single poll showing a plurality in favor of executing the mentally retarded, although majorities have assented to imposing the death penalty for rape, child molestation, a plot to assassinate the president, and spying for a foreign nation.[28]

Of some comfort to death penalty proponents, the Court's use of public opinion data in *Atkins* marks perhaps the only occasion where the results indicate strong opposition to capital punishment. No public opinion polls were cited by the majority in *Roper v. Simmons*, which struck down the death penalty for murder committed before an offender's eighteenth birthday. Indeed, the results of public opinion polls would have contradicted the Court's finding that a national consensus had emerged rejecting death sentences for juvenile offenders.

Conclusion: Nearing Another Crossroads?

More than thirty years after the Supreme Court's decision striking down the corpus of state death penalty statutes in *Furman v. Georgia*, public support for capital punishment is robust. In November 2006, 56% of Wisconsin voters supported an advisory referendum that asked the state legislature to reverse a ban on capital punishment enacted in 1853. A few states have also established criteria under which sex crimes against children can be punished by death; the constitutionality of such penalties has not been decided by the Court.[29] Yet pro-death penalty sentiment is far from uniform across the United States: a poll of New York State voters in March 2005 found a narrow plurality opposed to reinstituting the state's death penalty (Siena Research Institute 2005).[30]

History's general lesson is that opinion concerning capital punishment is far from fixed. As an example, though large majorities of the public continue to approve of the death penalty even when the likelihood of false convictions is posed in survey questions, it is conceivable that renewed elite opposition, spurred by revelations of false convictions, could change the distribution of preferences. In this regard, it would be valuable to track reactions to the increased use of DNA testing.

In the 1970s, the Supreme Court appears to have had an impact on opinion, bolstering anti–death penalty sentiment among more-educated Americans, but the Court's indirect contribution to state policies may have also buttressed support for the death penalty. Complete control of policy in this area by the states during the 1950s and 1960s cannot be divorced from the public's uncertain feelings toward the death penalty itself. By establishing minimum procedural standards for state death penalties and imposing certain restrictions on the use of the death penalty, the Supreme Court has in some ways shielded the death penalty from controversy. With *Atkins v. Virginia* and *Roper v. Simmons*, the raw material for developing anti–death penalty sentiment is further diminished. Although public opinion does not appear to have changed appreciably in reaction to the Court's decisions in *Atkins* or *Roper*, these decisions affect the handling of capital cases across the nation, and thus the Court may exert a subtle influence on public opinion about the application of the death penalty.

Notes

1. "Majority Favors Death Penalty for Murder, Survey Finds." Institute of Public Opinion. 1937. *Washington Post*, January 3, 19. These results were brought back to scholarly attention by Erikson (1976).

2. The vote was 1,159,348 for; 730,649 against; 458,008 left blank.

3. *Gregg v. Georgia*, n. 25.

4. The description of McGovern comes from Senate Minority Leader Hugh Scott (R-PA).

5. At the beginning of 1972, twenty-nine states authorized the death penalty for kidnapping, and sixteen states authorized it for rape.

6. Chessman disguised his car as a police vehicle and preyed on couples parked in "lovers' lanes," robbing them and sexually assaulting the female member of the couple. No murders were committed. Chessman was executed at San Quentin State Prison on May 2, 1960.

7. Murder of a police officer remained a capital offense in New York and Vermont. The same was true for a second murder, unrelated to a first, for which a person had received a life sentence (Vermont) or murder committed by an inmate in prison for murder (New York). Britain retained the death penalty for several years for such crimes as treason, piracy, and arson in a naval dockyard.

8. The generational gap found in the Gallup Poll is corroborated by the General Social Survey, where in 1973 support for the death penalty was at 50% among respondents age 18–30, compared with 68% among older respondents.

9. For examples, see Georgia Code 16–5-44, Mississippi Code of 1972, 97–25–55, Code of Alabama 13A-5–40.

10. Bush had defended existing procedures, which prohibited the execution of the mentally incompetent, and allowed jurors in capital cases to consider mental retardation as a mitigating factor in sentencing. See Langford, Terry. "Senator's Bill Excludes Retarded Killers from Death Sentence," Associated Press State and Local Wire, April 14, 1999. Lexis-Nexis.

11. 487 U.S. 815.

12. 492 U.S. 361.

13. 543 U.S. 551.

14. Of the 724 executions in this period, the offender's age at the time of execution is known in 648 cases (90% of the cases). See Espy and Smykla (2004).

15. A. The question wording was as follows: "As you may know, Illinois has instituted a moratorium on the use of the death penalty until it can be better determined if the death penalty is being administered accurately and fairly in that state. Would you say you favor or oppose such a moratorium on the death penalty in all other states with the death penalty?"

16. Questions: (1) "As you may know, Illinois has instituted a moratorium, or temporary halt, on the use of the death penalty until it can be better determined if the death penalty is being administered accurately and fairly in that state. Would you say you favor or oppose such a moratorium on the death penalty in all other states with the death penalty?" (2) "Which comes closer to your view? There should be a moratorium, or temporary halt, on the death penalty until it can be better determined if the death penalty is being administered accurately and fairly in this country. There should not be a moratorium, or temporary halt, on the death penalty because there are already sufficient safeguards in the current justice system to prevent the execution of innocent people."

17. 356 U.S. 86, at 101.

18. 536 U.S. 304, at 316 n. 21. The brief had originally been filed in the case of *McCarver v. North Carolina*, which was granted certiorari by the Supreme Court. The case was rendered moot when North Carolina enacted legislation forbidding the execution of mentally retarded prisoners in August 2001. The AAMR is now known as the American Association on Intellectual and Developmental Disabilities.

19. 536 U.S. 304, at 347.

20. 408 U.S. 238, at 385.

21. 408 U.S. 238, at 299.

22. 408 U.S. 238, at 361.

23. 428 U.S. 153, at 173.

24. Ibid., at 176.

25. Ibid., at 179.

26. 487 U.S. 815, at 855.

27. 536 U.S. 304, at 326.

28. For molestation, see Time/CNN/Yankelovich June 1997; for rape and attempted assassination, Gallup September 1988; for spying, Harris January 1986.

29. For a newspaper article on this subject, see Liptak 2006. National polls on the death penalty for sexual abuse of children have been few: in a 1985 poll by the *Los Angeles Times*, only 10% of those surveyed chose death from a list of alternatives as the "appropriate punishment"; in 1991, a Star-Tribune poll found 47% of respondents in favor of the death penalty for sexual abuse of a child (compared with 72% in favor for murder and 24% for rape of an adult). A 1997 Time/CNN/Yankelovich Partners poll put support for capital punishment in this instance at 65% (versus 75% in favor for murder and 47% for rape).

30. Many will recall the 1994 New York gubernatorial race in which Mario Cuomo, the three-term incumbent governor and a death penalty opponent, was defeated by George E. Pataki, who vowed to restore capital punishment in the state. Though the death penalty issue was widely seen as crucial in the outcome, a New York Times/WCBS poll taken September 29–October 2, 1994 found 47% of likely voters supported the death penalty, with 36% supporting a maximum sentence of life without parole, and 6% supporting a parole option. The only Democratic candidate for state attorney general that year to support the death penalty, Eliot Spitzer, spent $2.5 million of his own money, only to finish last in a four-way primary. See Kevin Sack. "Deep Discontent with Cuomo Strengthens Pataki, Poll Shows," *New York Times*, Oct. 5, 1994; Ian Fisher. "Clamor over Death Penalty Dominates Debate on Crime," *New York Times*, Oct. 9, 1994.

References

Berinsky, Adam J. 2006. "American Public Opinion in the 1930s and 1940s: The Analysis of Quota-Controlled Sample Survey Data." *Public Opinion Quarterly* 70: 499–529.

Bohm, Robert M. 1992. "Toward an Understanding of Death Penalty Opinion Change in the United States: The Pivotal Years, 1966 and 1967." *Humanity and Society* 16: 524–42.

Bowers, William, Margaret Vandiver, and Patricia Dugan. 1994. "A New Look at Public Opinion on Capital Punishment: What Citizens and Legislators Prefer." *American Journal of Criminal Law* 22: 77–150.

Brace, Paul, Kellie Sims-Butler, Kevin Arceneaux, and Martin Johnson. 2002. "Public Opinion in the American States: New Perspectives Using National Survey Data." *American Journal of Political Science* 46: 173–89.

Davies, Lawrence E. 1960. "U.S. Intervention in Chessman Case a Factor in Stay." *New York Times*, February 20.

Death Penalty Information Center. 2007. "State Execution Rates." http://www. deathpenaltyinfo.org/article.php?scid=8&did=477. Accessed April 2007.

Ellsworth, Phoebe C., and Samuel R. Gross. 1994. "Hardening of the Attitudes: Americans' Views on the Death Penalty." *Journal of Social Issues* 50: 19–52.

Epstein, Lee, and Joseph F. Kobylka. 1992. *The Supreme Court and Legal Change: Abortion and the Death Penalty*. Chapel Hill: University of North Carolina Press.

Erikson, Robert S. 1976. "The Relationship between Public Opinion and State Policy: A New Look Based on Some Forgotten Data." *American Journal of Political Science* 20: 25–36.

Erskine, Hazel. 1970. "The Polls: Capital Punishment." *Public Opinion Quarterly* 34: 290–307.

Espy, M. Watt, and John Ortiz Smykla. 2004. EXECUTIONS IN THE UNITED STATES, 1608–2002: THE ESPY FILE [Computer file]. 4th ICPSR ed. Compiled by M. Watt Espy and John Ortiz Smykla, University of Alabama. Ann Arbor, MI: Inter-university Consortium for Political and Social Research [producer and distributor].

Fink, Jerry. 1997. "Judge OKs Execution Bid." *Tulsa World*, February 14.

Fox, James Alan, Michael L. Radelet, and Julie L. Bonsteel. 1990. "Death Penalty Opinion in the Post-*Furman* Years." *New York Review of Law and Social Change* 18: 499–528.

Holden, Robert T. 1986. "The Contagiousness of Aircraft Hijacking." *American Journal of Sociology* 91: 874–904.

Jennings, M. Kent, and Laura Stoker. 2001. "Political Similarity and Influence between Husbands and Wives." Institute of Governmental Studies Working Paper 2001–14.

Johnson, Timothy R., and Andrew D. Martin. 1998. "The Public's Conditional Response to Supreme Court Decisions." *American Political Science Review* 92: 299–309.

Kirchmeier, Jeffrey L. 2002. "Another Place beyond Here: The Death Penalty Moratorium Movement in the United States." *University of Colorado Law Review* 73: 1–116.

Lee, Mei-Hsien, and Christopher Z. Mooney. 1999. "The Temporal Diffusion of Morality Policy: The Case of Death Penalty Legislation in the American States." *Policy Studies Journal* 27: 675–80.

Liptak, Adam. 2006. "Death Penalty in Some Cases of Child Sex Is Widening." *New York Times*, June 10.

Masur, Louis P. 1989. *Rites of Execution: Capital Punishment and the Transformation of American Culture, 1776–1865*. New York: Oxford University Press.

New York Times. 1972. "McGovern Asserts Nixon Is Neglecting Domestic Ills." September 7.

——. 1965. "U.S. Aide Asks End of Death Penalty." July 23.

Page, Benjamin I. and Robert Y. Shapiro. 1992. *The Rational Public: Fifty Years of Trends in Americans' Policy Preferences*. Chicago: University of Chicago Press.

Schumach, Murray. 1960. "'Thinking' Actors in Vogue on Coast." *New York Times*, May 5.

Siena Research Institute. 2005. "Death Penalty: NY Split; Favor Life without Parole." News release.

Zimring, Frank E., and Gerald Hawkins. 1986. *Capital Punishment and the American Agenda*. Cambridge: Cambridge University Press.

6

Gender Equality

Serena Mayeri, Ryan Brown, Nathaniel Persily,
and Son Ho Kim

Over the past forty-five years, a series of Supreme Court decisions and legislative enactments have dramatically changed the legal landscape in the area of gender equality. Legislation—most prominently the Equal Pay Act of 1963, Title VII of the Civil Rights Act of 1964, and Title IX of the Education Amendments of 1972—gave women legal rights to be free of sex discrimination in education and employment that are enforceable in court. In the early 1970s, the Court began incrementally to reverse its long-standing presumption that legal classifications based on sex were constitutional. Measuring the effects of these court decisions on public opinion is virtually impossible. Polling organizations have not consistently asked questions about Americans' attitudes toward specific legal and constitutional questions related to sex discrimination and gender equality. Even if they had, it seems unlikely that the incremental, low-profile court decisions of the 1970s, 1980s, and 1990s would have been salient enough to register significant blips in public opinion.

With the important exception of *Roe v. Wade*'s legalization of abortion (dealt with in another chapter of this book), no individual court decisions stand out as beacons of women's constitutional equality. Feminist hopes for a "women's *Brown v. Board of Education*" foundered in the mid-1960s, when factually compelling cases challenging the exclusion of women from jury service in the Deep South failed to reach the Supreme Court (Mayeri 2004). Instead, the Court developed its constitutional sex equality jurisprudence in fits and starts, beginning in 1971 with a cryptic decision in *Reed v. Reed*, which invalidated an Idaho state law preferring male over female estate administrators but did not articulate a new framework for deciding constitutional sex discrimination cases. In *Frontiero v. Richardson* (1973), a plurality of four justices voted to apply the highest standard of review, "strict scrutiny," to sex-based classifications, but without a majority to endorse that standard, constitutional doctrine remained in flux. The Court eventually settled on "intermediate scrutiny," a standard of review somewhere between the strict scrutiny accorded racial classifications and the lenient "reasonableness" requirement traditionally applied to laws that distinguished between individuals on the basis of sex (*Craig v. Boren* (1976)).

Applying heightened scrutiny to sex-based classifications proved a mixed blessing from feminists' perspective. On the one hand, the justices invalidated many laws that differentiated between men and women for the purpose of allocating government benefits or responsibilities, declaring in *Stanton v. Stanton* (1975), "No longer is the female destined solely for the home and the rearing of the family, and only the male for the marketplace and the world of ideas." Accordingly, policies that assumed men's breadwinner status and women's economic dependency solely on the basis of sex met their demise as violations of the Fifth and Fourteenth Amendments. In some cases, the justices proved more inclined to justify sex-based policies arguably designed to combat generalized societal discrimination against women than they were to uphold affirmative action programs for racial minorities (*Kahn v. Shevin* (1974); *Schlesinger v. Ballard* (1975); *Califano v. Webster* (1977)). By the late 1990s, the Court had invalidated sex-based peremptory challenges in jury selection (*J.E.B. v. Alabama* ex rel. T.B. (1994) and ruled that the publicly funded Virginia Military Institute, long a male bastion, was constitutionally compelled to admit women (*United States v. Virginia* (1996)).

On the other hand, the Court's commitment to sex equality under the Constitution had its limits. The Court declined to accept women's rights advocates' invitation to require that women be subjected to the military draft on the same basis as men (*Rostker v. Goldberg* (1981)), to define discrimination against pregnant women as constitutionally prohibited sex discrimination (*Geduldig v. Aiello* (1974)), to mandate federal funding of abortions for poor women (*Harris v. McRae* (1980)), and to rethink statutory rape laws that applied sex-specific penalties (*Michael M. v. Superior Court* (1981)). Nor was the Court willing to question the constitutionality of awarding preferences to veterans in civil service employment, despite their extremely disproportionate impact on women's job opportunities (*Personnel Administrator v. Feeney* (1979)).

In some of these instances, Congress, the courts, and the executive branch—prodded by women's rights advocates—compensated for the shortcomings of constitutional jurisprudence and provided women with additional legal protections. Title VII of the Civil Rights Act of 1964 prohibited employment discrimination on the basis of sex, and pressure from women's organizations in the late 1960s and early 1970s convinced the initially reluctant EEOC to enforce the sex discrimination provision. Persistent advocacy produced other legal innovations that gave teeth to antidiscrimination legislation, including affirmative action in job training and hiring, the redefinition of sex discrimination to include sexual harassment, and new legislation to fill gaps in the 1964 Act, such as Title IX of the Education Amendments of 1972, the Pregnancy Discrimination Act of 1978, and the Family and Medical Leave Act of 1993.

Despite these important legal developments, to which the courts were significant though hardly exclusive contributors, for the most part individual court decisions tended not to attract public attention and scrutiny comparable to many of the controversies considered in this book.[1] The language of the Court's decisions reflected the women's movement's impact on societal attitudes toward gender roles—compare Justice John Marshall Harlan's declaration in *Hoyt v. Florida* (1961) that "woman is still regarded as the center of home and family life" with Justice William J. Brennan Jr.'s invocation a dozen years later of the nation's "long and unfortunate history of sex discrimination.... rationalized by an attitude of 'romantic paternalism' which, in practical effect, put women, not on a pedestal, but in a cage" (*Frontiero v. Richardson* (1973)). But direct reciprocal effects of court decisions on public opinion remain elusive.

To be sure, social movements and the general public engaged in heated debates over the proper roles of men and women in politics, the workplace, and the family in general, and over women's status under the Constitution in particular. To the extent that these constitutional controversies had a symbolic center, though, it was not individual court cases but rather the Equal Rights Amendment (ERA). The federal ERA, passed by Congress in 1972 and ratified by thirty-five states, ultimately fell short of the three-fourths majority required to amend the constitution before the ratification deadline in June 1982. The ERA is one of the few legal gender equality issues about which there is significant polling data across time. However, even if we had more polling data on attitudes toward legal and constitutional issues other than the ERA, the potential for measuring the effects of court decisions on public opinion would probably be limited by the complexity, obscurity, and specificity of many of the sex equality questions that came before the courts during this period.[2]

These two factors—the limitations of the polling data and the absence of identifiably pivotal court cases—lead us to take a different approach here than in the other chapters in this book. Instead of examining the short- and long-term effects of individual court decisions on public opinion, we instead analyze data and review existing literature on long-term trends in attitudes toward three topics: gender roles in the abstract (as measured consistently by the GSS over three decades), the proposed Equal Rights Amendment to the federal Constitution, and the potential inclusion of women in the military draft. We chose to focus on these areas for three primary reasons. First, and most basically, the ERA and the military draft are rare instances in which polling organizations have asked about a specific constitutional controversy across a substantial time period. Second, juxtaposing these topics provides a rare opportunity to compare long-term trends in attitudes toward gender roles stated in abstract terms with opinions about concrete policy questions. Third, the availability of long-term data in each of these areas enables us to trace shifts in the structure of public opinion on gender equality issues.

We begin with a look at public opinion polling that examines attitudes concerning gender roles. We find, as have others, that between the early 1970s and the early 2000s, public opinion moved steadily in a more egalitarian direction without any dramatic shifts correlated to particular events. We then examine the data and literature concerning public opinion toward the proposed Equal Rights Amendment to the federal Constitution. At the national level, we can discern a similar liberalizing effect over time, though state-level data tell a more complicated story, reflecting how important the structure of opinion can be to the outcome of an attempt at constitutional amendment. Finally, we examine public opinion toward women and the draft. Although military conscription ended in 1973, young men are still required to register with the selective service, and the Supreme Court declared single-sex registration constitutional in *Rostker v. Goldberg* (1981). Despite egalitarian movement on other topics, opinion on the male-only draft has remained virtually stable: over the past thirty-five years, Americans have remained evenly split on whether women should be drafted alongside men.

Survey Data on Attitudes toward Gender Roles

As public opinion analyst Hazel Erskine observed in her 1971 survey, "The Polls: Woman's Role," polling organizations canvassed attitudes toward women's roles rather extensively during the 1940s, virtually abandoned the project in the 1950s, and gradually resumed their study of gender-related attitudes in the mid-1960s. Over time, both the wording and content of questions about gender roles changed, in an attempt to reflect social, economic, political, and cultural developments. As Erskine put it, "What pollsters do and what they say are...signs of the times" (1971, 276).

The career of the question "Do you approve of a married woman earning money in business or industry if she has a husband capable of supporting her?" illustrates the magnitude of transformation in attitudes. Gallup and later the General Social Survey (GSS) have posed this question to Americans for more than sixty years (see Figure 6.1). In the mid-1930s, about 20% of respondents answered yes, with women only slightly more likely than men to approve.[3]

This percentage had barely budged by 1945, but by 1969 the question garnered 55% approval (Erskine 1971, 283).[4] As shown in Figure 6.1, later polls found a continued rise in approval of married women's work, reaching a sustained level of above 80% in the 1990s. Of course, now that a majority of married women work outside the home, the answers to this question tell us much less than they once did. For instance, it is one thing for a married woman to "earn money," quite another to have a career comparable to her husband's, and yet another for her to work when her children are very young. There is also

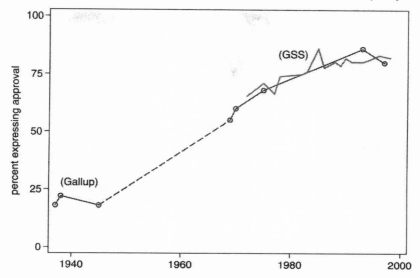

Figure 6.1. Approval of Married Women's Work outside the Home, 1938–2000.
Question wording: Do you approve of a married woman earning money in
business or industry if she has a husband capable of supporting her?
Source: Gallup, General Social Survey.

reason to believe that seemingly minor variations in question wording may
affect responses dramatically. Mansbridge observes that, in 1981, 84% of the
American public agreed that "There is no reason why women with young children shouldn't work outside the home if they choose to." But when given the
statement "a woman with young children should not work outside the home
unless financially necessary," 76% concurred (Mansbridge 1986, 23). Mansbridge cites a number of similar inconsistencies that suggest Americans' views
in this area were ambivalent and highly responsive to changes in phrasing.

As many scholars have recognized, though the GSS items are a unique
source of data, they are less than ideal measures of gender-related attitudes.
Mason and Lu point out that "not only do [the GSS questions] ignore many
aspects of women's familial roles and power; they ignore men's roles as husbands and fathers completely." Referring to "working mothers" in contrast to
"women who do not work" implies that homemaking and family caregiving
are not work, and fails to distinguish between women who perform house-
work and child care duties themselves and those who hire others to perform
some or all of these tasks (Mason & Lu 1988, 43). The GSS items also assume a
traditional nuclear family structure, headed by a husband and wife, although
this arrangement—never universal—has become less common in the last
thirty years. Even when questions are asked consistently and with consistent
wording, attitudes toward gender roles can be oversimplified by the typical
answer structure ("agree," "disagree," or "don't know").

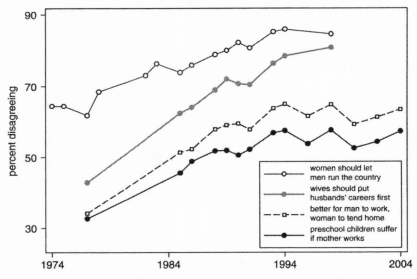

Figure 6.2. Attitudes on Women's Roles, 1974–2004. Question wording: Now I'm going to read several more statements. As I read each one, please tell me whether you strongly agree, agree, disagree, or strongly disagree with it. Women should take care of running their homes and leave running the country up to men. It is more important for a wife to help her husband's career than to have one herself. It is much better for everyone involved if the man is the achiever outside the home and the woman takes care of the home and family. A preschool child is likely to suffer if his or her mother works. Source: General Social Survey.

Moreover, as Sapiro and Conover (2001) point out, equality has both an empirical and a normative dimension—perceptions of the degree to which equality has been achieved are distinct from prescriptive views of how much and what kind of equality are desirable as a matter of principle. In addition, approval of a general statement about gender equality may not be indicative of actual policy preferences. An individual's attitudes about gender equality may differ considerably across the domains of family, work, and politics. Finally, Sapiro and Conover argue, equality itself is a vague and slippery concept, and perceptions of and attitudes toward the relative power and influence of men and women may be more revealing indicators of gender-role preferences.

Despite their shortcomings, the GSS items are among the few for which we have consistent question wording across the past three decades.[5] Using various combinations of GSS items, scholars have found long-term liberalization of gender-related attitudes overall. This trend can be illustrated by looking at answers to four gender roles questions asked in various combinations by the GSS from 1974 to through 2004 (see Figure 6.2). The topics of the questions range from women's roles in the political arena to their responsibilities as mothers and wives.

Brewster and Padavic (2000) observe that the rate of change differs on these items: the egalitarian response to the question of whether women should

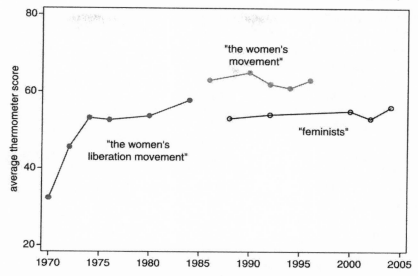

Figure 6.3. "Feeling Thermometer" Scores Assigned to Those Advocating for Women's Rights, 1970–2004. Source: American National Election Studies.

"leave running the country to men" rose steadily from 1974 through 1998 (the last time it was included on the GSS). But responses to questions about whether mothers with young children should work outside the home appear to have stabilized since the mid-1990s at levels just above majority support.

Similarly, after enjoying a rise in popularity in the 1970s, support for the women's movement has leveled off in recent years. The American National Election Studies (ANES) has assessed popular sentiment toward women's rights advocates with its "feeling thermometer" series since 1970. Feeling thermometer questions ask survey participants to assign a rating of zero (very cold) to 100 (very warm) to several groups, individuals, and institutions. As shown in Figure 6.3, the ANES has changed its terminology for this measure three times. From 1970 through 1984, it asked respondents to rate the "women's liberation movement." The question referred to the "women's movement" beginning in 1986 and employed this language through 1996. In 1988, the ANES also began asking respondents' views on "feminists"—a term it continues to use in the most recent studies available. Figure 6.3 illustrates how these changes in terminology are consequential: respondents appear to feel warmer about those in the women's movement when "liberation" is not the movement's explicit goal, and Americans feel substantially cooler toward "feminists" than they do about the "women's movement."

Notwithstanding these limitations, the GSS items suggest Americans' gradual rejection of traditional, sharply differentiated gender roles. Is this transformation due to actual attitude change, generational replacement, or both? To explore this question, we compare change within and between birth cohorts over time. Egalitarian attitudes have been negatively correlated with age at least since the early 1970s, but the respective roles of intracohort change and cohort succession have shifted over time. It appears that a shift in the average position toward gender equality within age groups played an important role in the late 1960s, the 1970s, and the early 1980s but that the changing relative sizes of each age group accounted for an increasing proportion of the attitudinal change in the late 1980s and 1990s. A 1976 study found little evidence that attitudinal change in the late 1960s and early 1970s was due to cohort succession (Mason et al. 1976). Mason and Lu again assessed the relative contributions of intracohort change and cohort succession in 1988, finding that intracohort change still accounted for more of the attitudinal change between 1977 and 1985 than did cohort succession.

The increasing role of cohort replacement between 1977 and 1985, though, led Mason and Lu to forecast that cohort replacement would play a more central role in the future liberalization of attitudes. Indeed, a follow-up study by Brewster and Padavic confirmed Mason and Lu's prediction, finding that intracohort change accounted for about 70% of overall change between 1977 and 1985 but only about 50% of change between 1986 and 1998. As Mason and Lu foresaw, this shift from intracohort change to cohort replacement as the dominant basis of attitudinal shifts also heralded a slowdown in attitudinal change (Brewster & Padavic 2000). Still, despite this slowdown, Brewster and Padavic note that remaining cohort differences may portend some further liberalization of gender-related attitudes because of continued shifting of cohort sizes.

In 1982, for example, 70% of respondents disagreed with the statement "Women should take care of running their homes and leave running the country to men." At that time, 41% of all the respondents were born between 1940 and 1959. By 1998, 82% of all respondents disagreed with the statement, and the cohort born between 1960 and 1979 had become the dominant group (41%). The shifting cohort sizes have helped move the sample toward a more feminist viewpoint on gender role questions, but the impact of intracohort attitude change cannot be discounted.

Here we analyze responses to the "leave running the country to men" item by birth cohort in order to determine whether intracohort change is causing the shifting aggregate views (see Figure 6.4). For each cohort, the figure plots the mean responses for each year of the GSS, as well as a linear trend line. In a case where there was no intracohort change, the trend line for each cohort would be horizontal because members of each cohort would retain the same average attitudes toward the question over time. Figure 6.4 shows that this is not the case, as each of the four birth cohorts (those born between 1883 and 1919, 1920 and 1939, 1940 and 1959, and 1960 and 1979) shows steadily liberalizing views on this question about gender roles.

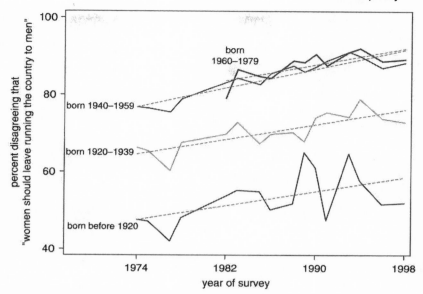

Figure 6.4. Rejection of Traditional Gender Roles by Birth Cohort, 1974–1998.
Question wording: Do you agree or disagree with this statement? Women should
take care of running their homes and leave running the country up to men.
Source: General Social Survey.

The Structure of Opinion Regarding Gender Roles

The story of slow liberalization in attitudes toward gender roles masks great
diversity among demographic and ideological groups. In this section, we
examine the data and literature concerning the attitudes of various segments of the population toward abstract questions about gender roles. We
look at the responses between 2000 and 2004 to the GSS question "Please
tell me whether you strongly agree, agree, disagree, or strongly disagree.... It
is much better for everyone involved if the man is the achiever outside the
home and the woman takes care of the home and family." Our analysis of
these recent data confirms what others have found: statistically significant
relationships between gender-related attitudes and age, gender, education,
religiosity, and ideology.[6]

We present the data in two formats. Cross-tabulations for this question
among various demographic groups in 2004 are shown in Appendix A. To
permit analysis of the separate effects of variables holding others constant,
Table 6.1 presents logistic regressions for four separate blocks of variables
in the order of their effects on attitudes toward women's roles: immutable
demographic characteristics (age, gender, race) (in Model I); childhood characteristics (region of residence at age sixteen and the respondent's mother's
employment and education) (Model II), long-term social characteristics

(education, number of children, and marital status) (Model III), and religious and political orientation (frequency of attendance of religious services, partisanship, and ideology) (Model IV). All models also include "dummy variables" for each of the years of the survey administration to control for any over-time variation.

Table 6.1
Predictors of Attitudes on Women's Roles, 2000–2004

Variables	I	II	III	IV
Immutable demographic characteristics				
Female	.05***	.07***	.07***	.08**
Black	−.02	.03	.05	.04
Age	−.59***	−.49***	−.46***	−.45***
Childhood Characteristics				
Lived in South at Age 16		−.10***	−.09***	−.06**
Working Mother		.08**	.08***	.07***
Mother's Education		.18***	.05	.05
Long-Term Social Characteristics				
Education[1]			.58***	.65***
Number of Children			−.15**	−.10
Married			−.01	.02
Political and Religious Orientation				
Party identification[2]				−.09**
Ideology[3]				−.15***
Attendance of religious services[4]				−.15***
Year of Survey				
2002	.01	.01	.01	.02
2004	.02	.02	.01	.02
Log Likelihood	−1825.11	−1790.75	−1749.72	−1697.89
Pseudo-R^2	.07	.09	.11	.13
N	2,950	2,950	2,950	2,950

Cell entries are first differences derived from a logit analysis. They are estimates of the change in probability of disagreeing with the gender inequality statement, given a shift from the minimum to the maximum value of each independent variable, holding all other variables constant at their means. Cell entries in bold are a variable's total effect—that is, the effect of a variable on disagreement with the gender inequality statement before the consideration of mediating effects of intervening variables. Logit coefficients are significantly different from zero at *$p<.05$, **$p<.01$, ***$p<.001$.
1 Highest grade level completed by respondent.
2 Three-point scale from Democrat (0) to Republican (1).
3 Three-point scale from liberal (0) to conservative (1).
4 Scale from never attend (0) to attend more than once per week (1).

Question wording: It is much better for everyone involved if the man is the achiever outside the home and the woman takes care of the home and family. Dependent variable is scored 0 = agree, 1 = disagree.
Source: General Social Survey.

Demographic Characteristics

Age is a consistent, strong predictor of attitudes on women's roles. A total of 72% of the youngest respondents (age 18 to 29) but only 56% of the oldest respondents (age 50 and over) rejected the traditional gender role divisions proposed in the GSS question. The effect of age remains significant in the models even after controlling for intervening variables.

In contrast, the cross-tabulations of the data do not reveal major differences between men and women: only a difference of about 2 percentage points on average, with women more likely to express the more egalitarian view. However, this difference grows to 8 percentage points when we hold all other variables constant at their means in Table 6.1, Model IV. Other scholars have reported similar findings. Brewster and Padavic (2000) found that sex differences among recent cohorts are more pronounced than among earlier cohorts and that the gap between men's and women's attitudes on some measures widened between the mid-1970s and the late 1990s. These differences are most pronounced, others argue, when it comes to men's assessments of the effect of maternal employment on children (Bolzendahl & Myers 2004; Ciabattari 2001; Mason & Lu 1988).

Of course, different factors may lead to a liberalization in views among men as opposed to women. For example, Bennett and Bennett (1992) observed that married women tended to have more traditional attitudes than single women, whereas marriage had the opposite effect on men. Divorce has also been found to have different results on men's and women's gender role attitudes, with divorce having a feminist effect on women only (Bolzendahl & Myers 2004). Similarly, parenthood produces differential effects: one study found that between 1987 and 1998, women with children had more liberal attitudes toward women's and mothers' employment, but men with children were more traditional than childless men (Bolzendahl & Myers 2004).

Employed women and their spouses are significantly more likely to endorse pro-equality statements than homemakers and their husbands (Wilkie 1993; Mason & Lu 1988). In general, men in two-income households were more receptive to gender role equity, though there was a time lag between changes in life circumstances and changes in attitudes (Wilkie 1993). Wilkie found two exceptions, however: men with lower incomes were more likely to disapprove of married women earning money, and married men were more likely than single men to agree with the statement "It is much better for everyone involved if the man is the achiever outside the home and the woman takes care of the home and family."

We found small, statistically insignificant differences in gender role attitudes between blacks and whites, with blacks tending to express more egalitarian attitudes than whites. In our multivariate analyses, the effect of race is small and never significantly different from zero. Others who have studied similar questions have found complicated relationships between race and gender attitudes. Kane (2000) contends that looking more broadly at beliefs—both descriptive and normative—about gender equality reveals that African American men and women tend to be more critical than whites of the gender status quo. She also notes that support for government action to remedy inequality is more robust among African Americans: with a few exceptions, the evidence "suggests that African Americans are more aware of the extent of gender inequality and more likely to attribute such inequality to structural origins." Kane has suggested, however, that when attitudes toward leadership within the family are examined separately from attitudes toward women's roles in the spheres of employment and politics, African Americans are more traditional than whites.

Kane (2000, 1992) has also found that the differences between men and women in their gender-role attitudes tend to be smaller among African Americans than among whites. Ciabattari (2001) suggests that African American men express less concern than do white men about the negative effects of maternal employment on children. Another study found that although racial differences were negligible with respect to questions concerning family responsibilities, with regard to gender roles in the political sphere, African American men were more conservative than white men, but African American women were more feminist than white women (Bolzendahl & Myers 2004, 779). The sources of these racial differences are unclear. One study concluded that racial and ethnic variation reflects socioeconomic and family structure characteristics rather than cultural differences (Wilkie 1993).

Long-Term Social Characteristics

Education is a strong predictor of egalitarian attitudes with regard to gender roles. Only 25% of college graduates agree with the statement that men should be the outside achiever and women should take care of the family, whereas 41% of non-college graduates agree with that statement. Our multivariate analysis found the difference in attitudes between those with the highest and lowest levels of education (65 percentage points in Model IV) to be greater than a similarly measured effect associated with any other variable in our models. This finding is consistent with other research, although some argue that the effect of education is weaker among more recent cohorts (Brewster & Padavic 2000).

The GSS questions concerning "man as achiever outside the home" and women as "tak[ing] care of home and family" also allow us to examine the effects of marital status and family size. Seventy-four percent of those who have never married give an egalitarian response on the GSS question, compared with 59% of those who are married. Given that unmarried people tend to be younger and that the more educated tend to delay marriage, this variable is not statistically significant in the multivariate analysis. In contrast, the number of children in a household is statistically significant, at least before controlling for political and religious orientation. The larger one's family is, the more likely one is to express a traditionalist response to the question about women's roles.

Childhood Characteristics

Our analysis suggests that a mother's employment status has a significant effect on her children's gender role attitudes. Of those respondents whose mother worked outside the home, 68% express an egalitarian response on the GSS question, compared with 55% of those whose mother did not work outside the home. The mother's educational attainment also exerts an egalitarian effect, although the independent effect of that variable drops out once the respondent's own level of education is added to the regressions. In other words, educated respondents tend to have educated mothers, but an individual's own educational level is a more powerful predictor of his or her own attitudes toward the role of women. In addition, the long-term effect of being raised in the South is to bolster support for traditional attitudes toward gender roles. Even after controlling for intervening variables, those raised in the South are 6 percentage points more likely to believe that men should be the outside achievers and women should take care of the family (Model IV).

Religious and Political Orientation

Religiosity has a traditionalizing effect on attitudes related to gender roles, and its effects are more pronounced in recent cohorts (Brewster & Padavic 2000). The GSS data support the conclusion that respondents who attend religious services more frequently are less egalitarian than those who attend less often: 47% of those who attend at least once a week register an egalitarian response to the GSS question, compared with 72% of those who attend less than once a month. Holding other variables constant, the most religiously observant are 15 percentage points more likely to hold traditional views about gender roles than the least observant (Model IV). Other studies have found that conservative Protestants have the most traditional views, Jews are the most supportive of gender egalitarianism, and Catholics and mainline Protestants fall somewhere in the middle (Bolzendahl & Myers 2004, citing Greeley 1989, Hoffman & Miller 1997, 1998).

On the issue of gender roles, the ideological divide between liberals and conservatives (23 percentage points) is much more pronounced than the partisan divide between Democrats and Republicans (9 percentage points). This pattern persists after we control for other variables (Model IV): holding other variables constant at their mean values, the gap between liberals and conservatives is 15 percentage points, and the gap between partisans is only 9 points.

Public Opinion on the Equal Rights Amendment

For those interested in the effect of social movements on public opinion in an area of constitutional significance, the history of the proposed Equal Rights Amendment—which stipulated that "Equality of rights under the law shall

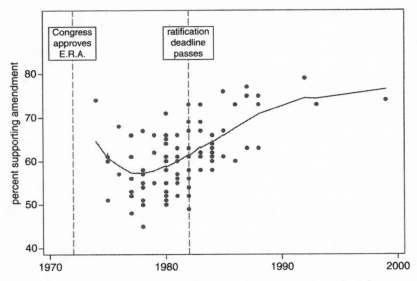

Figure 6.5. Support for the Equal Rights Amendment, 1974–1999. Question wording varies. Source: Roper Archive.

not be denied or abridged by the United States or by any State on account of sex"—provides a unique case study. The ERA is the only gender-related constitutional question (besides abortion) for which we have consistent, long-term public opinion data. Mansbridge (1986) and Bolce and colleagues (1987) provide comprehensive treatments of the issues relevant to public opinion and the ERA, and we summarize their findings here, paying particular attention to the importance of the underlying structure of opinion in understanding the outcome of this constitutional controversy.

First, these studies suggest that national-level opinion data on the ERA concealed important regional and state-level trends. The national trend showed a small, gradual increase in support over time after an initial dip in the late 1970s, with a consistent majority in favor of the amendment between 1974 and 1982 (see Figure 6.5). But this picture masked important shifts in the structure of opinion and obscured divergences at the state level between ratified and unratified states.

Bolce and his colleagues (1987), for example, found that even as the national endorsement rate rose, support for the ERA declined by almost a third between 1976 and 1980 in the unratified states. Mansbridge (1986) also found that state-level opinion was "a poor guide" to whether individual states would ratify the amendment. In New York, New Jersey, Iowa, Florida, and Maine, for instance, polls showed a majority in favor of the ERA, but the amendment was defeated in statewide referendums. One reason for these misleading results is that the national survey measures of bare support and opposition to the amendment obscured significant differences in the quality of that support and opposition: opponents' views were more strongly held than proponents' (Bolce et al. 1987).

At a superficial level, there appears to be some disagreement among scholars about the effect of the ratification debate—and, in particular, the impact of Phyllis Schlafly's STOP ERA movement and other New Right activities—on public opinion about the ERA. Upon closer inspection, however, different analysts' conclusions depend almost entirely upon whether they are examining data at the national level or at the state level. For instance, Mansbridge (1986, 16) writes, "The bitterly fought ratification campaign did not, on the best available evidence, have any effect, either positive or negative, on public support for the ERA *in the nation as a whole*." She notes that with one exception, "no survey organization ever found any clear trend in public support for the ERA over this period." Daniels and colleagues (1982) concluded, also based on national survey data, that the "ERA won—at least in the opinion polls." But as Mansbridge (1986, 18) argues, "even the stable picture painted by most national survey organizations masked a growing gap between the ratified and unratified states."

Scholars examining *state*-level opinion generally agree that 1977 was a turning point in attitudes toward the ERA. Mansbridge (1986, 18) dates the effective blockage of ERA ratification in the states to 1977 and notes a "significant increase in public opposition to the ERA in the unratified states" between 1976–77 and 1980–81. Bolce and his colleagues (1986) attribute this shift to the rise of the New Right in general, as manifested in increasing Southern congressional opposition to the ERA and the conservative reaction to the 1977 International Women's Year Conference in Houston in particular. Gray and Conover (1983) also point to the rise of the New Right as pivotal, crediting traditionalist conservatives for expanding the ERA's substantive meaning in ways that created and intensified opposition to the amendment. This analysis is consistent with Mansbridge's hypothesis that the New Right successfully linked the ERA to expansive interpretations of existing constitutional provisions in controversial areas such as busing, criminal defendants' rights, and abortion, contributing to fears that the ERA would open a Pandora's box of radical and undesirable changes. She also notes that attitudes toward the ERA became increasingly polarized along partisan lines in the late 1970s, especially among legislators and activists.

Even before 1977, there was some disagreement among the amendment's supporters over its likely effects on law and society. As the Supreme Court interpreted the Fourteenth Amendment to invalidate many sex-based legal classifications, supporters as well as opponents increasingly began to expand their accounts of the amendment's likely impact, forecasting effects on highly controversial areas like abortion and the military draft (Mansbridge 1986). Further, as Deborah Rhode observed, "it is by no means clear that those responding" to questions about the ERA "had a clear appreciation of the content or plausible consequences of the amendment" (Rhode 1983, 2, n. 3).

Thus, the structure of public opinion on the ERA mirrored many of the new political alignments of the period. As Mansbridge (1986, 15–16) observes, "Support for the ERA...split along lines that would become familiar in the new politics of the 1980s: religious fundamentalists and heavy churchgoers against agnostics and Jews, people with many children against those with none, old people against young, country against city dwellers," and Southerners versus non-Southerners. Similarly, Bolce and colleagues (1986) showed that correlates of opposition to the ERA included conservative political ideology, frequent church attendance, opposition to equal roles for women, negative feelings toward the women's liberation movement, preference for individual training over collective action to overcome discrimination, the belief that civil rights had been pushed too fast, and opposition to abortion. The strength of each of these correlations, the authors found, increased between 1976 and 1980. Bolce and his colleagues also studied the relationship between views on abortion and support for the ERA from 1976 to 1982, comparing four groups of respondents: those who favored abortion rights and the ERA ("feminists"), those who opposed unrestricted abortion and opposed the ERA ("tradition-alists"), those who supported abortion rights but opposed the ERA ("secular conservatives"), and those who opposed unrestricted abortion but supported the ERA ("dissonants"). Their findings confirmed the initial hypothesis that, at least among whites, the greatest attitude change toward the ERA in non-ratifying states occurred among "dissonants," who brought their views on the ERA into line with their opposition to abortion.

Although women in both ratifying and nonratifying states were initially less supportive of the ERA than men, Bolce and colleagues (1987) found that this gap had closed by 1980. African Americans in both ratifying and nonratifying states were significantly more likely to favor the ERA than were whites and were both more enthusiastic and less volatile in their support. Crucially, as Bolce and his colleagues found, ERA opponents were both more aware of and more interested in the issue than were ERA proponents. For instance, in nonratifying states, opponents were almost twice as likely as proponents to correctly describe the amendment's status in their state's legislature (Bolce et al. 1987).

Women and Military Service

Although the ERA's demise cannot be attributed to any one factor, Mansbridge (1984) hypothesized that the projected impact of the amendment on women's role in the military played a significant part in the ratification failure. Between 1972 and 1982, she observed, less than a quarter of Americans believed that women should be sent into combat on an equal basis with men. Indeed, when the Supreme Court issued its opinion in *Rostker v. Goldberg* (1981) upholding draft registration limited to men, the majority opinion specifically cited public opposition to women serving in combat as one reason that Congress chose to exempt women. The opinion quoted a Senate report to the effect that "[t]he principle that women should not intentionally and routinely engage in combat is fundamental, and enjoys wide support among our people."

At least three factors complicate analysis of public opinion and the drafting of women. The first is the lack of surveys with consistent question wording over time. As Stiehm (1984) observed, the difficulties in comparing pre- and post-1970 survey items regarding women and military service are considerable: questions asked before 1970 assume a limited military role for women, whereas after 1970 more expansive duties, including combat, are contemplated. Moreover, it is impossible to know respondents' background assumptions about the military roles women would perform, if drafted. Whether respondents assume that women may fill traditional positions as nurses and clerks or instead anticipate female draftees serving alongside men in combat is likely to have a profound effect on their answers to questions about a draft. It is difficult to determine how question-wording effects and current political context might affect these background assumptions. Finally, questions that attempt to measure opinion on women and the draft often trigger respondents' attitudes toward war (both in the abstract and with respect to a particular conflict). Respondents may be against drafting women either because they are against the draft or because they think drafting only men is discriminatory.

Torres-Reyna and Shapiro (2002) provide an overview of polls on attitudes toward women and military service that include questions about the draft. They found that egalitarian responses to the question "If a draft were to become necessary, should young women be required to participate as well as young men, or not?" rose between 1979 (when 43% said "yes") and 1991 (50%) and again through 1998 (54%). A poll taken in December 2001, after the attacks of September 11, reported 46% yes and 50% no. The small overall variation of attitudes toward drafting women contrasts starkly with the long-term change in abstract gender role attitudes discussed previously.[7]

Though there are few studies of long-term trends in attitudes toward women in the military, we do have occasional snapshots of public opinion on these issues. For instance, several authors have analyzed the 1982 survey by the National Opinion Research Center (NORC), which provided an unusually extensive exploration of the topic. The survey found that 42% of the population favored a return to the draft "at this time," with 47% supporting a draft "if there were a national emergency." Of those who favored a draft in case of emergency, 54% would have conscripted women as well as men. The poll also canvassed public views on particular military assignments for women and found that 62% of Americans supported women serving as fighter pilots, 59% endorsed women missile gunners, and 57% favored allowing women to serve on fighting ships (Wilcox 1992). Fifty-eight percent supported women serving as base commanders, and the presence of women in nontraditional, noncombat roles like air transport and mechanic positions received 73% and 83% support, respectively (Wilcox 1992). Further, 35% of respondents to the NORC poll endorsed the assignment of qualified women to ground combat—a result that Stiehm (1984) called "astounding."

The next high-profile assessment of public opinion about women in military service came a decade later, when the Presidential Commission on the Assignment of Women in the Armed Forces (PCAWAF) commissioned the Roper organization to measure attitudes among both civilians and military personnel. This 1992 poll found that 52% of the public supported drafting women in the event of national emergency or threat of war and 39% opposed including women in military conscription (PCAWAF 1992, D-1). In general, to the extent that the public approved of women's combat service, they preferred that it be voluntary rather than mandatory (PCAWAF 1992, D-2).

The survey also revealed significant differences of opinion between civilians and military personnel and between various branches of the armed services.[8] Civilians were more supportive of women serving in combat than were military personnel, though those in the military were less likely to support exempting women from combat because of family circumstances (Sadler 1993). The Navy was the most supportive of equal roles for women in the military, followed by the Air Force and the Army; the Marines were in a distant last place (Sadler 1993).

Our findings suggest that over the last twenty years, the structure of opinion on women and the draft appears to have remained largely unchanged. Table 6.2 arrays three surveys, conducted between 1982 and 2003, that asked

Table 6.2
Support for Inclusion of Women in a Military Draft, 1982, 1991 and 2003

		1982	1991	2003
All respondents		50.7%	51.5%	48.6%
Sex	Males	57.2%	55.4%	51.2%
	Females	45.7%	47.5%	46.0%
Race	Blacks	39.2%	45.7%	40.8%
	Whites	54.5%	52.0%	49.0%
Age	18 to 29	51.7%	51.9%	39.6%
	30 to 49	55.4%	53.2%	48.1%
	50 to 64	49.2%	51.7%	54.5%
	65 and over	43.5%	46.5%	49.2%
Education	< High school	42.8%	47.1%	35.6%
	HS grad	48.6%	53.0%	44.3%
	Some college	60.0%	47.6%	49.5%
	College grad	59.7%	55.2%	52.9%

Question wording and sources for data:
1982: Combination of "If we should return to a draft in a national emergency" and "If we should return to a military draft at this time" (GSS).
1991: "If a military draft were to become necessary" (Gallup/Newsweek).
2003: "If a military draft is reinstated" (Newsweek).

Sources: GSS, Gallup, Newsweek.

whether women should be drafted. Despite differences in question wording (see note to Table 6.2), the cross-tabulations (and multivariate analysis not presented here) suggest some consistent differences in opinion that correlate with gender, race, education, and age.

The gender divide on the question of drafting women is currently roughly 5 percentage points, with men more supportive of the idea. These data extend Stiehm's (1984) findings that women were more likely to support the draft between 1940 and 1969 but that in the 1970s men became more likely to support drafting women. Stiehm offered three nonexclusive possible explanations for the gender gap in the 1980s: that the ERA debate precipitated a view among men that women should assume equal responsibilities in exchange for equal rights, that women are more opposed to military service—particularly compulsory military service—for both men and women, and that women would prefer to avoid the obligations of equal citizenship. Stiehm found evidence pointing toward the first two explanations, but given that women are as opposed to conscription for men as for women, she concluded that the third explanation is probably baseless. Notably, Wilcox (1992) found considerable heterogeneity between and among men and women in the 1982 survey data. Although generally liberal attitudes on women's equality (e.g., support for the ERA or egalitarian responses to the GSS items on gender) were generally significant predictors of egalitarian attitudes on women and the military, black women who displayed feminist attitudes were more opposed to drafting women than those who held more traditional views about gender roles. Wilcox also found age to be a significant predictor of women's attitudes but not men's.

Blacks and whites differ consistently in their support for inclusion of women in the draft. The difference is about 8 percentage points, with nearly half of whites, compared with 41% of blacks, supporting women's inclusion in the draft. This difference holds even when controlling for other demographic variables, such as age and education.

Although age is often inversely related to support for egalitarian policies toward women, both the oldest (over 65) and the youngest (age 18 to 29) respondents are generally less supportive of drafting women than respondents aged thirty to sixty-four. The very youngest respondents might be guided by self-interest, given that they would be most directly affected by a draft. For the oldest respondents, the cohort effects regarding gender roles, discussed earlier, might explain their traditionalist views on conscripting women.

Finally, education is a strong predictor of egalitarian attitudes on drafting women. Support among college graduates is 17 percentage points higher than among those who did not finish high school, and at each additional level of education, support increases for including women in the draft. Education also remains a significant predictor of opinion even when all other demographic factors are controlled for.

Conclusions

The last four decades have seen significant changes in women's economic and political participation and in the degree to which gender definitively restricts women's opportunities in the workplace and in public life. The public opinion data discussed here reflect, to some degree, those profound shifts. Though egalitarian attitudes are not shared by all demographic groups, most Americans are now unwilling to endorse abstractly worded traditional positions on the proper roles of men and women. However, these opinion shifts did not translate into the ratification of an Equal Rights Amendment to the federal Constitution, nor did they portend increasingly egalitarian attitudes on the concrete issue of whether women should be drafted into the military on the same basis as men. The story of incremental change in gender role attitudes provides an example of how constitutionally relevant beliefs might evolve over time, without any dramatic short-term effects in opinion produced by court decisions or other discrete events. The story of attitudes toward the ERA reveals how important the underlying structure of public opinion can be to the success or failure of an attempt to amend the Constitution. The case of public opinion about women and the military draft suggests that focusing exclusively on abstract measures of gender-related attitudes may obscure greater continuity in the acceptance of certain concrete manifestations of legal inequality.

APPENDIX A
Disagreement with Traditional Gender Roles, 2004

All Respondents		63.4%
Sex	Males	62.4%
	Females	64.2%
Race	Blacks	64.7%
	Whites	62.6%
Age	18 to 29	72.2%
	30 to 49	66.3%
	50 and Over	55.8%
Region at age 16	South	55.8%
	Non-South	66.9%
Had a Working Mother	Yes	67.8%
	No	55.0%
Mother's Education	Mother Has at Least a Bachelor's Degree	76.0%
	Mother Has Less than a Bachelor's Degree	61.9%
Marital Status	Married	59.4%
	Never Married	74.1%

Appendix A Table
(continued)

All Respondents		63.4%
	Widowed	49.1%
	Separated/Divorced	67.1%
Number of children	Do Not Have Children	77.2%
	One or Two Children	62.9%
	More than Two Children	51.5%
Education	At Least a Bachelor's Degree	75.0%
	Less than a Bachelor's Degree	59.4%
Attendance of Religious Services	At Least Once a Week	47.3%
	Less than Once a Week but at Least Once a Month	64.7%
	Less than Once a Month	71.8%
Ideology	Liberal	79.6%
	Moderate	61.4%
	Conservative	55.0%
Party Identification	Democrat	67.6%
	Republican	59.1%

Source for data: General Social Survey. Question Wording: See Table 6.1.

Notes

1. Significant Title VII sex discrimination cases that reached the Supreme Court during the 1970s and 1980s include, among others, *Phillips v. Martin-Marietta* (1971), *Gilbert v. General Electric* (1976), *Meritor Savings Bank v. Vinson* (1986), *Johnson v. Transportation Agency of Santa Clara* (1987), *Price-Waterhouse v. Hopkins* (1989), and *Automobile Workers v. Johnson Controls* (1991). In 2003, the Supreme Court upheld the Family and Medical Leave Act as a valid exercise of congressional power under section 5 of the Fourteenth Amendment in *Nevada Department of Human Resources v. Hibbs*.

2. There are exceptions: for example, pollsters have canvassed public opinion on issues like Title IX, which prohibits discrimination based on sex in publicly funded education, including athletic programs, but they have not done so consistently over time.

3. We note here that the Gallup data reported for the 1930s and 1940s are biased toward the opinions of whites, men, and other groups more likely to vote, as these polls were conducted with the goal of representing the views of the electorate, not the U.S. population as a whole (Berinsky 2006).

4. This question was not asked in the years between 1945 and 1969.

5. In addition to the generic "women's role" questions, the question most consistently asked by pollsters that taps attitudes about gender equality concerns whether the respondent would be willing to vote for a woman for president. When Gallup first asked the question in 1937, only 33% of the respondents said they would vote for an otherwise qualified woman. Today the figure is closer to 88%. Interestingly, this is somewhat lower than the share of the public willing to vote for a Catholic, Jewish, or black candidate.

6. Analysis of GSS data over the past thirty years (not presented here) yields broadly similar findings as described in this section, leading us to agree with Bolzendahl and Myers's (2004) conclusion that "for the most part, the determinants of feminist opinion have been stable over time."

7. Although not all the questions have consistent wording, they are all relatively similar. The main variation in the question is the setup, with the three most common questions starting with: "If a military draft were to become necessary," "If the military draft were reinstated," and "If we should return to a military draft in a national emergency"; each ends with essentially the same question: whether young women should be included, as well as young men.

8. The poll also canvassed views on women's service in particular military occupations, including crew member of aircraft carrier, submarine, or destroyer (public support: 69%; military support: 66%); pilot/crew member of bomber or fighter aircraft (public: 69%; military 62%); member of Special Forces operating behind enemy lines (public: 59%; military: 34%); tank crew member (public: 59%; military: 40%); artillery gunner (public: 58%; military: 46%); Marine landing on shore to attack the enemy (public: 42%; military: 27%); and infantry soldier fighting the enemy in close ground combat (public: 38%; military 25%) (Sadler 1993, 53).

As this book went to press, Gallup released the results from its September 2007 poll, which included a question about women in the military. The poll found that 74% of Americans agreed that women should be allowed to hold combat jobs in the armed forces.

References

Bennett, Stephen Earl, and Linda L. M. Bennett. 1992. "From Traditional to Modern Conceptions of Gender Equality in Politics: Gradual Change and Lingering Doubts." *Western Political Quarterly* 45: 93–111.

Berinsky, Adam J. 2006. "American Public Opinion in the 1930s and 1940s: The Analysis of Quota-Controlled Sample Survey Data." *Public Opinion Quarterly* 70: 499–529.

Bolce, Louis, et al. 1987. "The Equal Rights Amendment, Public Opinion, and American Constitutionalism." *Polity* 19: 551–69.

Bolce, Louis, et al. 1986. "ERA and the Abortion Controversy: A Case of Dissonance Reduction." *Social Science Quarterly* 67: 299–314.

Bolzendahl, Catherine I., and Daniel J. Myers. 2004. "Feminist Attitudes and Support for Gender Equality: Opinion Change in Women and Men, 1972–1998." *Social Forces* 83: 759–90.

Brewster, Karin L., and Irene Padavic. 2000. "Change in Gender-Ideology, 1977–1996: The Contributions of Intra-Cohort Change and Population Turnover." *Journal of Marriage and the Family* 61: 477–87.

Ciabattari, Teresa. 2001. "Changes in Men's Conservative Gender Ideologies: Cohort and Period Influences." *Gender & Society* 15: 574–91.

Daniels, Mark, et al. 1982. "The ERA Won. At Least in the Opinion Polls." *PS* 15: 578–84.

Erskine, Hazel. 1971. "The Polls: Women's Role." *Public Opinion Quarterly* 35: 275–90.

General Social Surveys, 1972—2004, General Social Surveys (release 2, January 2006). [computer file.] National Opinion Research Center [producer]. Storrs, CT: Roper Center for Public Opinion Research, University of Connecticut [distributor].

Gray, Virginia, and Pamela Johnston Conover. 1983. *Feminism and the New Right.* New York: Praeger.

Greeley, Andrew M. 1989. Religious Change in America. Cambridge: Harvard University Press.

Hoffmann, John P., and Alan S. Miller. 1997. "Social and Political Attitudes among Religious Groups: Convergence and Divergence Over Time." Journal for the Scientific Study of Religion 36: 52–70.

Hoffmann, John P., and Alan S. Miller. 1998. "Denominational Influences on Socially Divisive Issues: Polarization or Continuity?" *Journal for the Scientific Study of Religion* 37: 528–46.

Kane, Emily W. 2000. "Racial and Ethnic Variations in Gender-Related Attitudes." *Annual Review of Sociology* 26: 419–39.

Kane, Emily W. 1992. "Race, Gender, and Attitudes Toward Gender Stratification." *Social Psychology Quarterly* 55: 311–20.

Mansbridge, Jane. 1986. *Why We Lost the ERA*. Chicago: University of Chicago Press.

Mansbridge, Jane. 1984. "Who's in Charge Here? Decision by Accretion and Gatekeeping in the Struggle for the ERA." *Politics & Society* 13: 343–82.

Mason, Karen Oppenheim, and Yu-Hsia Lu. 1988. "Attitudes toward Women's Familial Roles: Changes in the United States, 1977–1985." *Gender & Society*. 2: 39–57.

Mason, Karen Oppenheim, John L. Czajka, and Sara Arber. "1976. Changes in U.S. Women's Sex-Role Attitudes, 1964–1974." *American Sociological Review* 41: 573–96.

Mayeri, Serena. 2004. "Constitutional Choices: Legal Feminism and the Historical Dynamics of Change." *California Law Review* 92: 755–839.

Newsweek Magazine. July 25–26, 1991. Gallup/Newsweek Poll # 1991–205012: Women in Combat. [computer file.] Gallup Organization [producer]. Storrs, CT: Roper Center for Public Opinion Research, University of Connecticut [distributor].

Newsweek Magazine. January 23–24, 2003. PSRA/Newsweek Poll # 2003-NW02: Iraq and George W. Bush. [computer file.] Princeton Survey Research Associates [producer]. Storrs, CT: Roper Center for Public Opinion Research, University of Connecticut [distributor].

Presidential Commission on the Assignment of Women in the Armed Forces. 1992. Report to the President.

Rhode, Deborah. 1983. "Equal Rights in Retrospect." *Law & Inequality* 1: 1–72.

Sadler, Georgia C. 1993. "The Polling Data." *Proceedings of the United States Naval Institute* 119: 51–54.

Sapiro, Virginia, and Pamela Johnston Conover. 2001. "Gender Equality in the Public Mind." *Women and Politics* 22: 1–36.

Stiehm, Judith Hicks. 1984. "Public Opinion about Women and the Military." *Minerva* 2(1): 139.

Torres-Reyna, Oscar, and Robert Y. Shapiro. 2002. "The Polls—Trends: Women and Sexual Orientation in the Military." *Public Opinion Quarterly* 66: 618–32.

USA Today. December 2001. Gallup/CNN/USA Today Poll # 46: Admirable Leaders/Economy/Terrorism/Religion. [computer file.] Gallup Organization [producer]. Storrs, CT: Roper Center for Public Opinion Research, University of Connecticut [distributor].

Wilcox, Clyde. 1992. "Race, Gender, and Support for Women in the Military." *Social Science Quarterly* 73: 310–23.

Wilkie, Jane Riblett. 1993. "Changes in U.S. Men's Attitudes toward the Family Provider Role, 1972–1989." *Gender & Society* 7: 261–79.

7

Affirmative Action

Loan Le and Jack Citrin

From *University of California Regents v. Bakke* in 1978 to *Grutter v. Bollinger* twenty-five years later, the Supreme Court's decisions on affirmative action have wrestled with one overriding question: under what conditions are race-conscious employment or admission policies consistent with the constitutional guarantee of equal protection of the law? The justices' positions varied from Brennan and Marshall's relaxed "almost always" answer to Scalia and Thomas's "almost never" rejoinder, with first Powell and then O'Connor casting the ambiguous though decisive "sometimes" vote. The subject of this chapter is the relationship between the preferences of the Supreme Court and the court of public opinion. Did the Supreme Court lead or follow vox populi in the matter of affirmative action? Specifically, did the public consider affirmative action to be more or less legitimate in the aftermath of Court decisions, or did public opinion remain unchanged? And if aggregate opinion was largely unmoved by the Court's balancing act, is there evidence of structural change in the form of increased partisan or racial polarization? Given that the Supreme Court generally has enjoyed greater public confidence than the other branches of government (Hibbing & Theiss-Morse 1995), one hypothesis is that the public might follow its lead on affirmative action. Yet given that the messages sent from the deeply divided Court have been so unclear, what signal was the public to follow?

One difficulty in assessing public attitudes toward affirmative action is the ambiguity of the term. Is affirmative action intended to foster equality of opportunity or equality of results? Does it refer to policies that prescribe specific quotas for minorities in jobs or college admissions or refer merely to increased efforts in recruiting and training minority applicants? At the same time that Supreme Court justices adjudicate these nuanced arguments about the constitutionality of diverse legislative and administrative mandates of affirmative action, many polling organizations ask respondents simply whether they favor or oppose "affirmative action," leaving the respondents to supply their own definitions. Illustrating the ambiguity of the term, a Newsweek poll conducted in January 2003 found that 38% of the sample said they thought of affirmative action as setting quotas for minorities, whereas 44% said they perceived it as increasing outreach efforts to find qualified minorities. Thus survey questions that merely ask about affirmative action in the abstract are of little value to predicting the public's views of specific policies or its agreement with particular Supreme Court decisions. Sound methodology proscribes asking questions with vague "objects" (Schuman & Presser 1996), so this chapter concentrates on survey items that name specific race-conscious actions and justifications for them, although we recognize that these questions may not perfectly mimic the types of policies that the Court has adjudicated.

One important distinction is between "hard" affirmative action that explicitly provides for ethnic or gender preferences and "soft" affirmative action that allows for measures that help minorities and women compete for scarce positions or government contracts without guaranteeing a protected category a designated share of such benefits. One way of capturing the difference can be seen in Justice O'Connor's contrasting votes in *Gratz v. Bollinger* and *Grutter v. Bollinger*, both of which dealt with admission to the University of Michigan. O'Connor viewed the "hard" affirmative action undergraduate admissions procedures attacked by *Gratz* as giving an applicant's race too heavy and precise a weight, whereas the law school's "soft" affirmative action policy addressed in *Grutter* could be accommodated by Powell's opinion in *University of California Regents v. Bakke* that the "proper" use of race as "just one" factor in the admissions decision was constitutional.

In agreement with Justice O'Connor, public opinion is substantially more hostile to the "harder" forms of affirmative action. The authors of California's Proposition 209 recognized this when they named their proposal the "California Civil Rights Initiative" and wrote an opening sentence that prohibited state and local government agencies from discriminating *for* as well as *against* an individual or group on the grounds of race, ethnicity, or gender. Years of polling show that how questions about affirmative action are framed powerfully affects the distribution of responses. Because the policy involves the collision of two widely held values—the principle of judging people as individuals and the desire for social equality—question wording strongly influences how survey respondents make the trade-off.

Gamson and Modigliani (1987) have tracked the efforts of the antagonists in the battle over public opinion to frame the affirmative action issue to political advantage. A "frame" is a package of symbols and arguments that interpret the meaning of policies and events. In a sense, framing an issue means classifying it or telling people how to categorize it. In the present instance, framing affirmative action refers to how its purposes and consequences are highlighted. Examining the content of television broadcasts, official statements, newsmagazine articles, editorial cartoons, and opinion columns, Gamson and Modigliani identify the main alternative frames for affirmative action as 1) remedial action to compensate for institutional racism or 2) opposition to preferential treatment. The "remedial action" frame stresses the role of prior discrimination in disadvantaging blacks, other ethnic minorities, and women. Because of past inequities, there is a need to make a special effort to recruit and train minority applicants for jobs and for higher education. The "no preferential treatment" frame variously highlights reverse discrimination against whites and the stigmatization of blacks and other minorities as the negative consequences of affirmative action. Gamson and Modigliani document the growing dominance of the reverse discrimination theme in the early 1980s, when the Reagan administration tried to roll back affirmative action programs.

The survey evidence is clear that there is virtually no support in the United States today for legal discrimination on the basis of race or gender, a huge shift in outlook in the fifty years since *Brown v. Board of Education* (see chapter 1). Support for formal discrimination against blacks had collapsed by the end of the 1960s, with the percentage of whites who believed that they themselves should have the "first chance" at jobs falling from 55% in 1942 to 3% in 1972 (Sears et al. 2000, 10). Although respondents thirty years ago began showing almost uniform opposition to formal discrimination, that impulse has not translated into majority support for affirmative action or racial preferences.

In 2003, when *Grutter* was decided, a June Gallup Poll found that 60% of respondents in a national sample agreed that applicants should be admitted to college solely on the basis of merit. Only 35% felt that an applicant's racial and ethnic background should be considered to help promote diversity on college campuses, the position accepted by the five to four majority in *Grutter*. An even more one-sided division of opinion emerged in a poll conducted in a joint effort by the *Washington Post*, Kaiser, and Harvard in 2001: 92% of respondents agreed that hiring, promotion, and college admissions should be based on merit and other qualifications besides race or ethnicity. Of course, the meaning of "merit" itself is debated, as is the validity of the dichotomy between merit and racial preference. Nevertheless, this 2001 result, which confirms those of earlier polls, demonstrates widespread rejection of overt ethnic and racial preferences. Compensating for present or past discrimination is a more acceptable justification for affirmative action, but even so, another poll by the *Washington Post*, Kaiser, and Harvard in 1995 found that more than 60% of white respondents denied that racism was a "big problem today" or that whites had an obligation to make up for past discrimination (Fiorina et al. 2006, 117). And large majorities of those rejecting the standard justifications for affirmative action said they wanted Congress to act to limit these programs. Summarizing the results of National Election Studies between 1986 and 1992, the General Social Surveys between 1972 and

1996, and their own Race and Politics National Survey conducted in 1991 by the Survey Research Center at the University of California, Berkeley, Sniderman and Carmines (1997) conclude that a majority of the public endorsed affirmative action when limited to encouragement, such as making a special effort to recruit minority applicants, while at the same time strongly opposing "preferences" or "quotas."

Affirmative action policy developed with key decisions often made out of public view in administrative agencies or courts rather than through legislation (Skrentny 2004). The Supreme Court's position on affirmative action has oscillated on a wide range of controversies, including minority set-asides,[1] employment preferences,[2] and (as mentioned earlier) university admissions. Because the Court has not broadcast a consistent position on affirmative action—and because affirmative action has deeply divided the Court's justices—the conditions for the Court to dramatically influence public opinion seem absent. Without a clear sign that everyone on the Court agreed "that's the way it is," the public understandably might be confused or react in ideological terms.

The low salience of many important decisions also constrains the Court's potential influence. In tracking the interplay of the Court's behavior and public attitudes, therefore, one factor to take into account is the degree to which particular cases were publicized and visibly politicized. The *Gratz* and *Grutter* cases on university admissions were argued and decided in an atmosphere resembling an election campaign, with both sides mobilizing supporters to file amicus briefs; write letters, editorials, and op-ed pieces; obtain endorsements from politicians and business leaders; and organize public rallies and protests. Ironically, at the end of the day, the two decisions tugged in different directions, and the cloudiness emanating from *Bakke* remained.

The chapter begins with a description of public opinion leading up to the first major Court decision on affirmative action, the *Bakke* case in 1978, and then tracks trends in public opinion over the next quarter century. We concentrate on assessing the extent to which public opinion moved after major cases were decided in 1978, 1995, and 2003. The main empirical questions are whether the Supreme Court's decisions boosted public support for its positions, how reactions of significant demographic and political groups varied, if at all, and whether shifts in opinion about affirmative action reflected how policies were framed by proponents, critics, and the media. A discussion of the trends in public opinion is followed by a multivariate analysis of the underlying structure of public attitudes.

The analysis of opinion trends relies mainly on the questions included in the biennial American National Election Studies (ANES) and the General Social Survey (GSS). Both studies have asked the same questions on affirmative action over a series of years and rely on national samples. The evidence from these surveys is supplemented with data from other national polls that have probed the affirmative action issue. A full-text search of *Newsweek* and the *New York Times* in the Lexis-Nexis and ProQuest databases is used to track media coverage of affirmative action.

Our review of polls over time finds little change in public opinion toward affirmative action. In 2006, as in 1978, most Americans favor equal rights and equal opportunity, but they oppose the use of preferential treatment for particular groups to achieve those ideals. If anything, there has been a slight overall decline in support for "racial preferences," particularly—and perhaps remarkably—among blacks. By and large, majority opposition to "preferences" and "quotas" has remained steady in the face of Supreme Court rulings on a range of affirmative action programs in government, business, and education over the last three decades. Despite the Court striking down or upholding a variety of such programs and often applying different constitutional rules, public opinion on affirmative action has remained largely unchanged.

Public Opinion at the Birth of Affirmative Action

Seymour Martin Lipset and William Schneider (1978) reviewed the results of public opinion polls about affirmative action conducted before the Supreme Court decided *Bakke* in 1978, providing us with a snapshot of Americans' attitudes before the Court's intervention on this issue. Their results and data from later surveys consistently indicate a combination of widespread support for the principle of racial equality and opposition to compensation through "preferential treatment." A 1977 National Opinion Research Center nationwide poll found that 85% of Americans agreed that "Negroes have a right to live wherever they can afford to" and that "white and Negro students should go to the same schools" (Lipset & Schneider 1978, 39). But only 13% favored efforts by local government to help blacks buy homes in the suburbs.

An October 1977 Gallup Poll asked this question about affirmative action: "Some people say that to make up for past discrimination, women and members of minority groups should be given preferential treatment in getting jobs and places in college. Others say that ability, as determined by test scores, should be the main consideration. Which point of view comes closest to how you feel about this matter?" Fully 84% of whites favored selection on ability, compared with 55% of blacks. A question asked by Cambridge Survey Research in 1976 framed the issue without such a stark contrast between preferences and ability: "Some large corporations are required to practice what is called affirmative action. This sometimes requires employers to give special preference to minorities or women when hiring. Do you approve or disapprove of affirmative action?" By 51% to 35%, the sample disapproved (Lipset & Schneider 1978, 40).

A July 1977 Roper poll of 2,000 Americans asked respondents whether they agreed that "quota programs are necessary to increase the numbers of minorities in colleges and graduate programs and make up for past discrimination" or whether they believed that "this practice discriminates against whites who cannot be considered for the places in the quota." The results showed 25% in support of quotas, 54% opposed, and 15% who volunteered that they had "mixed feelings." There was a wide gap between the views of whites and blacks.

On the other hand, Lipset and Schneider found that Americans were more favorable to compensation for past deprivations in the form of special training and recruitment programs. For example, 63% of whites and 88% of blacks in a New York Times/CBS News survey carried out in October 1977 approved of requiring large companies to set up special training programs for members of minority groups, and similar percentages approved of colleges giving special consideration to the "best" minority applicants to help their admission. More generally, the closer a program comes to granting official preferences or special advantages for blacks, the more public opposition increases: "a majority of whites approve of programs that channel resources to specific racial minorities, but draw the line at absolute preference" (Lipset & Schneider 1978, 43). Below, we show that the pattern of public opinion evident before the Supreme Court's first major ruling on affirmative action persists today.

Media Coverage of Supreme Court Decisions

Members of the public depend on the media to inform them about Supreme Court decisions (Franklin & Kosaki 1995; Caldeira 1986). How the media frame an issue taken up by the Court and the reactions of the contending parties should affect the public's response to these decisions. Sometimes coverage emphasizes just a single theme; on other occasions, coverage draws upon and displays competing frameworks for thinking about an issue.

In an analysis of the coverage of affirmative action by the *New York Times* and *Newsweek*, we find that Supreme Court cases have often driven the intensity of media coverage for the issue. Figure 7.1 plots the number of stories per thousand mentioning the term "affirmative action" in both publications from 1976 through 2006. As shown in the graph, the intensity of media interest in affirmative action cases was high in the late 1970s, receded in the decade after *Bakke*, and grew again in the mid-1990s (when, in addition to ruling in *Adarand Constructors v Pena*, the Supreme Court refused to review the highly publicized *Hopwood v. State of Texas* case; and California voters banned the use of affirmative action by their state and local governments with Proposition 209). In 2003, media attention again spiked with the *Grutter* and *Gratz* cases. The cases that have drawn the most coverage by the two media outlets are *Bakke*, *Adarand*, and *Grutter* and *Gratz*.

Although measuring the frequency of references to affirmative action is straightforward, assessing how the media have framed the policy is more complex. The methodology we employed was a keyword search that counted the proportion of affirmative action stories that also included one of five framing terms: "past discrimination," "diversity," "merit," "quota," or "reverse discrimination."[3] These terms, we argue, are indicators of the type of frame

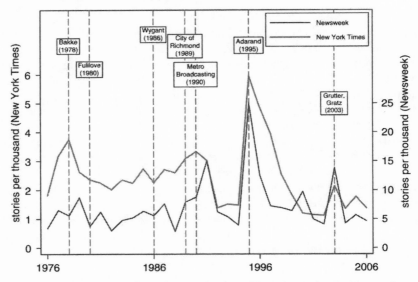

Figure 7.1. Proportion of Articles Mentioning Affirmative Action in *Newsweek* and the *New York Times*, 1976–2006. Sources: Lexis-Nexis, ProQuest.

used by the *Times* to cover the affirmative action controversy. "Past discrimination" and "diversity" are terms that both provide justification for affirmative action, whereas the terms "merit," "quota," and "reverse discrimination" are used in arguments against affirmative action. The relative frequency of usage, therefore, is a crude indicator of whether coverage emphasized the positive or negative aspects of affirmative action.[4]

Figure 7.2 breaks out the positive and negative frames to show the relative incidence over time for each of the main categories. As shown in Figure 7.2, the dominant interpretation of affirmative action in media coverage by the *Times* varied throughout this period. Until the mid-1990s, when *Adarand* was decided, negative frames were noticeably more common. From 1996 on, media coverage was about equally balanced as stories with positive frames proportionately increased, primarily because the diversity theme gradually became the most prominent of all frames. As for the frequency of references to particular frames, to some extent this depended on the nature of the cases decided by the Court. The increasing focus on "diversity" in stories about affirmative action clearly is associated with the nature of legal debates over college admissions policy.

Bakke

Affirmative action was a contentious issue before *Bakke*. The media reported on the opinions of prominent individuals and groups at the forefront of the debate, including Milton Friedman, George Will, and the NAACP. One *Newsweek* article

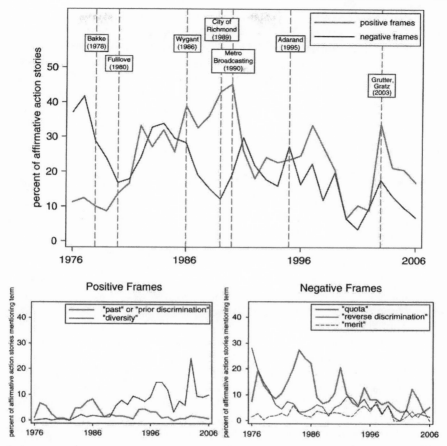

Figure 7.2. Positive and Negative Frames in *New York Times* Coverage of Affirmative Action, 1976–2006. Sources: Lexis-Nexis, ProQuest Direct.

went so far as to suggest that opposition to affirmative action was a reason for the renewed strength of the Ku Klux Klan (Williams, Clift, & Schmidt 1976).

Before *Bakke*, a *Newsweek* article remarked on the media's intense focus on an emotion-charged case from California that took on "a symbolic significance" (Footlick, Camper, & Howard 1978, 19). Despite the obvious interest in the *Bakke* case, the Court's ruling, a five-to-four decision with multiple partial concurrences and dissents, failed to provide a clear signal about the constitutionality of affirmative action. The Court majority declared that strict quotas for minority applicants in college admissions were unconstitutional. Justice Powell provided the decisive fifth vote for this portion of the opinion, but he also wrote that the "proper" use of race as one, but not the sole, factor in the selection process in order to enhance the diversity of the student body was legitimate. On the one hand, journalists portrayed the Court as having sent out "confusing signals" (Footlick, Camper, & Howard 1978, 19), making it unlikely that there would be a sharp shift in public opinion one way or the other. On the other hand, *Bakke* was accompanied by negative coverage in the *Times*. As shown in Figure 7.2, the newspaper's coverage of *Bakke* was dominated by references to "reverse discrimination" and "quotas." Stories that framed affirmative action as a quota system made up approximately 40% of affirmative action frames between 1977 and 1979, and this remained strong through much of the 1980s. Mentions of "reverse discrimination" in the *Times* declined quite sharply after the late 1970s.

Adarand

In the *Richmond v. Croson* case decided in 1989, Justice O'Connor's majority opinion about the constitutionality of set-asides in public contracting established a difficult standard for affirmative action programs. The rights guaranteed by the Fourteenth Amendment, she wrote, were individual rights that applied equally to members of all racial groups. Minority set-aside programs had to be "narrowly tailored" to compensate for egregious discrimination committed by the state actor now seeking to rectify past injustices. In cases prior to *Adarand Constructors v. Pena* (1995), the Supreme Court had suggested that affirmative action programs at the federal level might be given more leeway than those at the state and local level. In *Adarand*, however, the Court applied to federal government set-asides the same strict rules set forth in *Richmond v. Croson*.

The five-to-four *Adarand* decision was complex, but it did represent another step toward limiting federal affirmative action programs, which were "already being slowly dismantled by regulatory fiat, court order and political action" (Samuelson 1995, 51). The Court itself "did seem to insist…that the public dialogue take account of the heightened suspicion of these programs" (Klein 1995, 23).

Adarand shifted the media's focus on the interpretation of affirmative action as a system of preference. In a separate analysis (not shown on our graphs) of the incidence of the word "preference" in the *Times* coverage of affirmative action, we found a large increase in mentions of the term in the wake of *Adarand*. In part, this term is used simply as a description of an affirmative action program, particularly with regard to set-asides, but it also is the case that the detractors of affirmative action often deride the practice as "preferential treatment." In some contexts, "preference" clearly is a negative term, albeit less explicitly so than "quota" or "reverse discrimination."

Grutter and Gratz

In the high-profile cases of *Grutter* and *Gratz* decided in 2003, the Court reaffirmed the diversity rationale elaborated by Justice Powell in *Bakke*. The majority opinion in *Grutter* concluded that the educational benefits of "diversity" constituted a compelling interest, justifying some race-conscious procedures. That is, the University of Michigan's law school could use race as a factor in admitting students because "attaining a diverse student body is at the heart of the law school's proper institutional mission." In *Gratz*, however, the Court ruled against the university's undergraduate admissions policy because it was not sufficiently narrowly tailored.

The Court admitted that some of its signaling in these two cases might confuse observers in light of past decisions, but it underscored the importance of diversity in its consideration of case merits. In the *Grutter* case, O'Connor wrote that "we have never held that the only governmental use of race that can survive strict scrutiny is remedying past discrimination." The majority opinion in *Grutter* emphasized instead that universities inhabit a special niche that justifies affirmative action for a time to achieve diversity in their student bodies. Even though the combination of rulings in *Grutter* and *Gratz* may have been confusing, an emphasis on diversity became the dominant frame in media coverage of affirmative action at this time (see Figure 7.2). Richardson and Lancendorfer (2004) conclude that "remedial action" and "no preferential treatment," two frames that guided affirmative action discussions in news media through the mid-1990s, "were overshadowed in 2003 newspaper editorials by *diversity*" (p. 74). This growing tendency to frame affirmative action as contributing to diversity prevailed in a separate examination we conducted of *USA Today* and *Newsweek* between 2001 and 2006 (not shown here). Given that the diversity rationale had been for the most part applied to the education context, it is unsurprising that the University of Michigan cases led to a reframing of affirmative action along these lines.

Trends in Public Opinion

Earlier we argued that the way survey questions are worded engage particular meanings of affirmative action. How questions are framed is crucial because while some frames engage widely held cultural values, others are more contentious, and in these circumstances there generally is variation across individuals and groups in how persuasive a particular frame is. "Some [people] will find the particular metaphors and moral appeals invoked more compelling, others less, depending on their point of view. A person who attaches a higher priority to equality than to individual achievement will find the framing of affirmative action as 'leveling the playing field' more compelling than one who has the reverse set of priorities" (Sniderman & Theriault 2004, 141). Here we review public opinion on three broad affirmative action themes and note important changes over time.

Affirmative Action as "Special Efforts" for Minorities

As noted earlier, "softer" varieties of affirmative action that refer to expanding the pools of applicants and helping in the training of disadvantaged

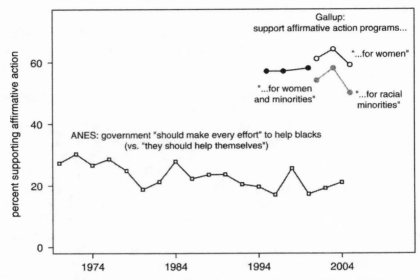

Figure 7.3. Support for Affirmative Action and Government Efforts to Help Blacks, 1970–2005. Question wording: see text. Sources: American National Election Studies; Gallup.

minorities tend to receive greater support from the American public than do "harder" versions that mention "quotas" or "preferences." In addition, the highly general term "affirmative action," when undefined, has symbolic appeal. In 2005, 59% of respondents told the CBS/New York Times poll that they favored the general proposition that "in order to make up for past discrimination, [there should be] special efforts to help minorities get ahead." Similarly, a Gallup question asking, "Do you generally favor or oppose affirmative action programs for racial minorities?" elicited a favorable response from 50% of survey participants in 2005, while an identical Gallup question regarding affirmative action programs for women found 59% in favor. As shown in Figure 7.3, opinion on these topics has remained relatively stable over the past ten years.

But such majority support for the general idea of assisting minorities does not appear when survey questions pose a choice between competing fundamental values. Consider for example an ANES question asking whether the government "should make every possible effort to improve the social and economic position of blacks" or whether no "special effort to help blacks" is necessary because "they should help themselves." With the value of individual responsibility invoked, support for such "efforts" is quite low (21% in 2004) and appears to have declined slightly over the past thirty years. Thus, support founders for even soft forms of affirmative action when a fundamental competing value is presented in the same question.

Affirmative Action as Quotas

Analyses of public opinion about affirmative action following Lipset and Schneider's original summary in 1978 create a sense of déjà vu. Steeh and Krysan, writing in 1996, confirmed that quotas remained overwhelmingly opposed by the American public. In 1986 and in 1992, the ANES surveys showed that when respondents were asked their opinion after being told that "Some people say that because of past discrimination, it is sometimes necessary for colleges and universities to reserve openings for Black students [whereas] others oppose such quotas because they say quotas give Blacks advantages they haven't earned," only 30% approved of the affirmative action position. Roper polls in 1977 and in 1985 asking about approval for quotas for minority students in college and graduate school programs in light of concerns about reverse discrimination against whites also found less than 30% support for setting aside places for minorities.

When affirmative action is explicitly distinguished from absolute preference, public acceptance can be high—69% in a 1982 Harris Poll asking about approval for "federal laws requiring affirmative action for women and minorities in employment provided there are no rigid quotas." Approval rose to 76% for affirmative action programs in higher education without rigid quotas for blacks. By contrast, in a CBS/New York Times poll in 1997 that asked about programs that did "impose quotas for racial minorities" in order to make up for past discrimination, only 19% approved.

Mass opinion in the United States is invariably opposed to overt preferential treatment for deprived groups, including blacks whose current disadvantages because of historical oppression are acknowledged and deplored. One reason for this is the political culture's emphasis on individual achievement. Americans favor meritocracy and individual competition over group-oriented solutions. For this reason, when a Gallup Poll in 2001 asked about support for "setting quotas for the number of racial minorities hired or accepted, but requiring them to meet the same standards as others," an overwhelming 70% of respondents approved, compared with only 26% support for quotas in a context where lower standards for racial minorities were permitted.

Affirmative Action as Preferences

The American public exhibits a similar resistance to "preferences" as it does for "quotas," even when these are portrayed as a remedy for past discrimination. Between 1985 and 1997, approval of "preference in hiring and promotion" for blacks "where there has been job discrimination in the past" dropped from 34% to 24% according to our analysis of CBS News/New York Times polls (see Figure 7.4). A similar decline appears to have occurred regarding preferences for women in employment, but Americans are more supportive of these initiatives for women than they are for racial minorities. The gap in popularity between affirmative action programs for these two groups results in a strong

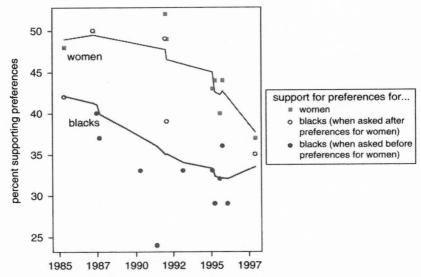

Figure 7.4. Support for Preferences in Hiring and Promotion for Women and Blacks Where There Has Been Job Discrimination in the Past, 1985–1997. Question wording: see text. Source: CBS News/New York Times Poll.

question-order effect in the CBS News/New York Times polls. In some administrations of the survey, respondents were asked about preferences for women before being asked about preferences for minorities (these polls are plotted with white points in Figure 7.4). In other surveys, the question about preferences for minorities came first (plotted with black points in Figure 7.4). Our analysis estimates that the effect of asking about women first boosts support for preferences for racial minorities by more than 9 percentage points. Ironically, although affirmative action developed as a corrective for racial inequity, programs designed exclusively to assist racial minorities are less popular than those with a broader set of beneficiaries.

Similarly, six times between 1977 and 1991, the Gallup Organization asked whether to make up for past discrimination, "minorities and women should be given preferences in getting jobs and places in college" or whether "ability as determined by test scores should be given the main consideration." In each survey, only 10% or 11% said that there should be preferential treatment for minorities, and there were no differences in the views of men and women (Lipset 1997, 125). Furthermore, by a majority of 70% to 19%, a national sample in a January 2003 Newsweek poll believed that as a result of affirmative action, less qualified candidates are admitted to colleges. Opposition to affirmative action increases when programs are perceived as sacrificing merit.

Whatever the nuances of the Supreme Court's affirmative action decisions, the pattern of public opinion remained substantially intact. A striking example of this continuity is the fact that in both 1994 and 2004, a mere 16% of a national sample opted for the affirmative action position when asked: "[Some say that] because of past discrimination, blacks should be given preference in hiring and promotion. Others say that such preference in hiring and promotion of blacks is wrong because it discriminates against others. What about your opinion?" (General Social Survey polls). It is possible to portray the overall record of the Court on affirmative action as roughly corresponding to the dominant pattern of public opinion: opposition to the harder forms of preferential treatment, such as quotas, combined with acceptance of more informal procedures to compensate for the disadvantages experienced by minorities (Stoker 1998). The public has not been moved from its predominant commitment to the values of individual responsibility and achievement, even if these fail to produce more equality of results.

With respect to *Grutter* itself, the available survey data suggest considerable public opposition, even when the questions concerning the affirmative action programs at issue use the diversity frame. A question in an NBC News/Wall Street Journal poll in January 2003 posed the trade-off confronted by the justices in the University of Michigan cases: "As you may know, the US Supreme Court will be deciding whether public universities can use race as one of the factors in admissions to increase diversity in the student body. Do you favor or oppose this practice?" Most respondents (65%) opposed the use of race as a factor in admissions decisions, with just 26% in favor. A 2003 Gallup Poll came to similar conclusions when it asked whether "applicants [to a college or university] should be admitted solely on the basis of merit, even if that results in few minority students being admitted" or whether "an applicant's racial and ethnic background should be considered to help promote diversity on college campuses, even if that means admitting some minority students who otherwise would not be admitted." This question produced a majority of 61% to 35% against the use of affirmative action in such circumstances. A month after the *Grutter* decision, opinion had shifted slightly against affirmative action, with 69% favoring admissions based on academic records alone and just 27% supporting the use of race as a factor to achieve more diversity. Other polls confirm that the public disagrees with the Court's conclusion as to the uniquely compelling nature of diversity in some educational settings. A 2003 national survey conducted by the Los Angeles Times found that 57% of the public favored admitting students into college solely on the basis of their academic record, with just 33% agreeing that "some students should be admitted in [an] attempt to balance the student body by looking at geographic location, ethnicity or gender [as well]."

Given these results, it is not surprising that despite the opposition of the state's political, business, and academic establishments, Michigan voters responded to *Grutter* by passing an anti–affirmative action initiative modeled after California's Proposition 209 by a vote of 58% to 42%. Access for minorities and diversity in the workplace are positive symbols; quotas and the erosion of merit are negative symbols. But when Americans are forced to choose between these values, they consistently eschew affirmative action by roughly a two-to-one margin.

Group Differences in Opinion

A large and heated scholarly literature has examined the opinions different groups hold regarding affirmative action (Sears, Sidanius, & Bobo 2000; Sniderman & Carmines 1997; Kinder & Sanders 1996). The scholarly argument about how to interpret differences in outlook centers on the influences of self-interest, political ideology, and racial prejudice. Specifically, researchers have sought to determine the reasons whites were more opposed to affirmative action than blacks: was it because whites were the targets and not the beneficiaries of such programs, because of their political values, or because of their prejudice against blacks?

Before briefly commenting on these complex questions, we track group differences in support for affirmative action, focusing on the size of these differences and whether they have widened or narrowed over time. Of particular interest are changes in the racial gap and in ideological polarization. Affirmative action programs provide benefits for designated groups, and so it seems plausible that there are racial and gender differences in reactions to Supreme Court decisions. In addition, at the elite level, liberals and conservatives have taken different stances on affirmative action, so it is important to determine whether this divergence of opinion is replicated among ordinary citizens. Given the deep divisions within the Court, one possibility to explore is that liberals and conservatives move in opposite directions after an important case is decided.

Figures 7.5, 7.6, and 7.7 track public approval of affirmative action, measured as the proportion of respondents in the ANES from 1986 to 2004 who say they approve of racial preferences in hiring and promotion. By comparing responses to the identical questions over time, the ANES surveys delineate the fluctuations in opinion in the aftermath of specific Court decisions, as well as confirm that there was little overall change over the eighteen-year period. In 1986, only 22% of the national sample supported racial preferences in hiring; support dipped to 14% in 1994, the year of a Republican electoral victory, before rising to 18% in 2004. The racial gap in opinion was substantial throughout the period, as shown in Figure 7.5. In 1986, the margin was 49 percentage points, and in 2004 blacks were still more likely to favor racial preferences in hiring by 36 percentage points. The narrowing of the racial gap, then, was mainly due to a 16% decline in support for affirmative action in hiring among blacks. Data from the General Social Survey (which has asked a virtually identical question since 1994) confirm these results. Black support for preferences in hiring and promotion declined from 51% to 42% between 1994 and 2004. Similarly, the National Black Election Studies conducted in 1984 and 1996, with much larger

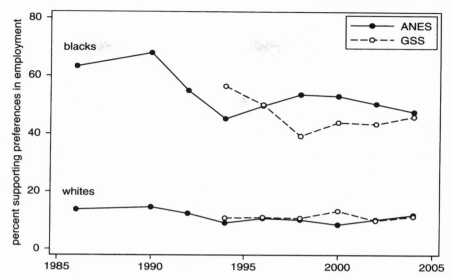

Figure 7.5. Black Support for Affirmative Action Declines, 1986–2004. Question wording: (source: American National Election Studies) Some people say that because of past discrimination blacks should be given preference in hiring and promotion. Others say that such preference in hiring and promotion of blacks is wrong because it gives blacks advantages they haven't earned. What about your opinion—are you for or against preferential hiring and promotion of blacks? (source: General Social Survey) Some people say that because of past discrimination, blacks should be given preference in hiring and promotion. Others say that such preference in hiring and promotion of blacks is wrong because it discriminates against whites. What about your opinion—are you for or against preferential hiring and promotion of blacks?

samples of black respondents, show a 5% drop in support for "special consideration" in hiring for jobs "because of past discrimination."

With regard to age, sex, and region, little change has taken place in aggregate public opinion on affirmative action over the past eighteen years. Small differences in opinion exist across age cohorts. Younger respondents were slightly more supportive of affirmative action throughout most of the period between 1986 and 2004. In 1986, women were more likely than men to support affirmative action for racial minorities, by 25% to 18%; in 2004, the two groups had virtually identical outlooks (19% and 17% support). Southerners were more likely to favor affirmative action than non-Southerners, by 4 percentage points in 1986 and by 8 percentage points in 2004, but these differences reflect regional contrasts in the proportion of black respondents.

As shown in Figure 7.6, preferences in employment consistently earn greater support among less educated respondents than among those who attended or graduated from college, partly because of the correlation between race and educational attainment. This gap reached its maximum in 1998, although the gap

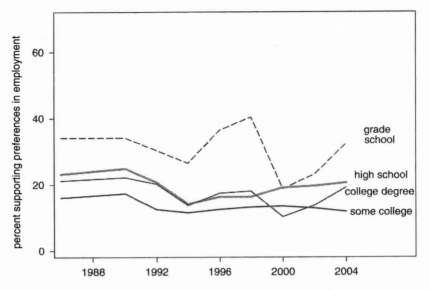

Figure 7.6. Support for Affirmative Action by Education Level, 1986–2004. Question wording: see ANES item in Figure 7.5. Source: American National Election Studies.

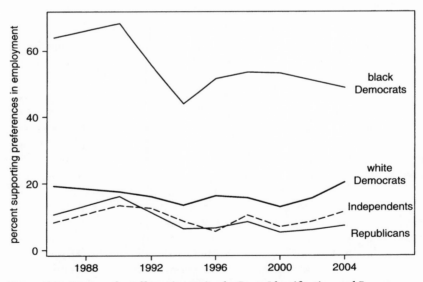

Figure 7.7. Support for Affirmative Action by Party Identification and Race, 1986–2004. Question wording: see ANES item in Figure 7.5. Source: American National Election Studies.

between those with college degrees and those with just a grade school level of education (eighth grade or less) was 13 percentage points in both 1986 and 2004.

Data on the association between affirmative action opinions and party affiliation indicate a consistent gap of roughly 15 to 20 percentage points between Democrats (strong, weak, and independents who lean toward the party) and Republicans. This partisan gap, however, is due substantially, though not entirely, to the fact that almost all blacks identify themselves as Democrats. Sixty-four percent of self-identifying black Democrats supported preferences in jobs and hiring in 1986, but this number had dropped to 47% in 2004; in contrast, a much lower but steady proportion of white Democrats expressed support for preferences (19% in 1986 and 20% in 2004; see Figure 7.7). The differences between white Democrats and white Republicans are much smaller—10 percentage points in 1986 and 15 percentage points in 2004 (not shown in figure). The so-called "pure" independents who say they lean toward neither party have opinions almost identical to those of Republicans. With respect to ideology, a large, consistent gap of more than 20 percentage points between self-identified conservatives and liberals persisted throughout the period, with self-styled moderates closer to conservatives on this issue than to liberals. The Supreme Court's affirmative action decisions were not polarizing; rather, they seemed to have very little impact on underlying public opinion, which shifted just a little between 1986 and 2004, with concurrent fluctuations in all social and political groups.

Predicting Support for Affirmative Action

To determine the degree of stability in the underpinnings of support for affirmative action, we conducted a multivariate analysis of responses to the questions about preferences in hiring (Table 7.1) and college admissions (Table 7.2) in the ANES surveys between 1986 and 2004. For the "hiring and promotion" question, the 1986, 1992, and 2004 samples were analyzed; for the "college admissions" question, only the 1986 and 1992 studies were considered because ANES dropped this item after 1992. The estimation procedure was a probit regression and proceeded in two phases. The first equation included demographic variables (race, Hispanic ethnicity, gender, age, income, trade union membership, region of residence, education, and level of political information) as predictors. A second equation added party identification, self-reported political ideology, and an indicator of positive affect for blacks measured by a "feeling thermometer" that records the respondent's warmth toward a specific social group. All variables were recoded to be scored from 0 to 1.

There is great consistency in the predictors of preferences for affirmative action over time and across the two issues (see Table 7.1). Race is always a powerful predictor, with blacks more favorable toward affirmative action, even after controls for the other demographic and attitudinal predictors are included in the equation. Hispanic ethnicity had statistically significant

Table 7.1

Predicting Support for Affirmative Action in Hiring and Promotion, 1986–2004

Variable	1986		1992		2004	
	I	II	I	II	I	II
Age	−.005	.012	−.043	−.009	.008	.023
Black	.546***	.466***	.421***	.296***	.389***	.268***
Hispanic	.245**	.164*	.223***	.217***	.042	.003
Female	.068*	.061*	−.040	−.048	.011	.008
South	−.047	−.034	−.037	−.029	.019	.024
Education level	−.043	−.064	.050	.045	.076	.012
Level of information	.096	.095	.035	.006	−.074	−.055
Family income	−.061	−.021	−.062	−.032	−.063	−.011
Union	−.029	−.024	−.047	−.053	.054	.030
Democrat to Republican		−.093**		−.082*		−.124***
Liberal to conservative		−.093*		−.068*		−.095**
Black thermometer		.231**		.230**		.176*
N	925	820	861	799	877	815
Pseudo R^2	.17	.21	.11	.14	.11	.18
Log likelihood	−413.77	−338.05	−390.05	−346.24	−378.14	−320.61

Question wording: See ANES question in figure 7.5
Cells contain probit coefficients. All variables are coded from 0 to 1. Black, Hispanic, female, South, and union are dummy variables (1 = present, 0 = absent). Cases with missing data are excluded. $*p < .05$, $**p < .01$, $***p < .001$

Source: American National Election Studies.

effects on support for affirmative action in 1986 and in 1992 but not in 2004. With few exceptions, gender and region did not have a significant association with beliefs about affirmative action. Finally, party identification, political ideology, and group affect always have statistically significant effects, with Republicans, conservatives, and people with relatively cool feelings toward blacks as a group (an indicator of racial prejudice and/or resentment) less likely to favor affirmative action. These data conform to the results of prior research on diverse samples (Sears, Sidanius, & Bobo 2000). Public opinion about affirmative action is embedded in a combination of ethnic group interests, political values, and entrenched hostility toward blacks. Fluctuations in the position of the Supreme Court have done nothing to weaken these roots of public opinion.

Conclusion

A precise definition of affirmative action would confine the term to policies that formally recognize the use of race, ethnicity, or gender in the selection process

Table 7.2
Predicting Support for College and University Quotas, 1986 and 1992

Variable	1986		1992	
	I	II	I	II
Age	−.113	−.079	−.047	−.015
Black	.518***	.498***	.493***	.349***
Hispanic	.155	.129	.257***	.263***
Female	.040	.006	.082*	.060
South	−.091*	−.096*	−.033	−.026
Education level	.038	.008	.080	.033
Level of information	−.068	−.051	.038	.024
Family income	−.069	−.048	−.173**	−.142*
Union	−.025	−.038	.007	−.012
Democrat to Republican		−.055		−.100*
Liberal to conservative		−.147**		−.112**
Black thermometer		.293**		.486***
N	920	820	845	787
Pseudo R²	0.12	0.15	0.12	0.16
Log likelihood	−536.35	−454.23	−476.99	−421.23

Question wording: "Some people say that because of past discrimination, it is sometimes necessary for colleges and universities to reserve openings for Black students. Others oppose such quotas because they say quotas give Blacks advantages they haven't earned. What about your opinion—are you for or against quotas to admit Black students? "
Cells contain probit coefficients. All variables are coded from 0 to 1. Black, Hispanic, female, South, and union are dummy variables (1 = present, 0 = absent). Cases with missing data are excluded. $*p < .05$, $**p < .01$, $***p < .001$.
Source: American National Election Studies.

for recruitment, admissions, employment, or promotion. Thirty years of survey evidence tells the same story: despite their embrace of the principle of racial equality, a large majority of Americans oppose the use of racial preferences or quotas. Softer forms of affirmative action that do not trigger the visceral reaction against preferences or quotas receive much higher levels of support.

Supreme Court decisions generally have hewed to this line, but regardless of how the Supreme Court has tried to straddle the issue, public opinion has remained unmoved. Affirmative action policy is a case in which the Supreme Court's conflicting and subtle decisions, even when countermajoritarian, produced neither a strong backlash nor increased polarization in public opinion. This is in many ways surprising, given the gap between elite and mass opinion and the fact that over time media coverage of the issue seemingly changed to frame affirmative action in a more favorable way by linking the policy to the benefits of diversity. One possible reason for the stability of public opinion is that affirmative action is not a highly salient issue for the general public. The Civil Rights and Race Relations Survey conducted by the Gallup Organization in November 2003 posed to a national sample of respondents: "Please tell me if you believe that any of the following things have ever happened to you as a result of affirmative action programs which favor minorities." Among white respondents, low proportions expressed that they had not been offered a job (14%), were passed over for a promotion (11%), or were not admitted to a school (2%). Another possible explanation is that notwithstanding media coverage of major decisions, only a small segment of the public was attentive to or received pertinent information. The Supreme Court's nuanced decisions on affirmative action appear to have had a limited impact on the lives of most Americans and have thus failed to engender changes in opinions that are rooted in group identification and fundamental values. Finally, to the extent that opinions about affirmative action are embedded in fundamental values and group identifications, policy preferences are unlikely to change in response to divided Supreme Court decisions in which each side can find arguments sustaining their prior point of view.

Notes

1. See *Fullilove v. Klutznick* (1980), *Richmond v. Croson* (1989), and *Adarand v. Pena* (1995).

2. *United Steelworkers of America v. Weber* (1979), *Wygant v. Jackson School Board of Education* (1986).

3. Stories that included more than one of the terms were counted multiple times. Our counts of the mentions of "past discrimination" incorporate mentions of "prior discrimination" but do not include those of "reverse discrimination." Because doing so returns a more accurate count of applicable articles, we employed a simple search for "reverse discrimination" mentions, as opposed to a joint search for "reverse discrimination" and "affirmative action."

4. We also searched for stories that included references to both affirmative action and the general term "discrimination." There were a substantial number of such stories, but in sampling their content, we found that the term was used variously in neutral, positive, and negative senses. For this reason, we do not include those stories in the count, so the figure underreports the total number of stories and confines itself to those that can be more readily categorized as either favorable or unfavorable to affirmative action.

References

Caldeira, G. A. 1986. "Neither the Purse nor the Sword: Dynamics of Public Confidence in the Supreme Court." *American Political Science Review* 80:1209–1226.

Fiorina, M. P., P. E. Peterson, D. S. Voss, and B. Johnson. 2006. *America's New Democracy*, 3rd ed. New York: Longman/Penguin Academics.

Footlick, J. K., D. Camper, and L. Howard. 1978. "The Landmark Bakke Ruling." *Newsweek*, July 10, 19.

Franklin, C. H., and L. C. Kosaki. 1995 "Media, Knowledge, and Public Evaluations of the Supreme Court." In *Contemplating Courts*, edited by L. Epstein. Washington, D.C.: Congressional Quarterly Books.

Gamson, W.A. and A. Modigliani, 1987. "The Changing Culture of Affirmative Action." *Research in Political Sociology* 3:137–177.

Hibbing, J. R., and E. Theiss-Morse. 1995. *Congress as Public Enemy: Public Attitudes toward American Political Institutions*. Cambridge: Cambridge University Press.

Kinder, D. R., and L. M. Sanders. 1996. *Divided by Color: Racial Politics and Democratic Ideals*. Chicago: University of Chicago Press.

Klein, J. 1995. "Affirmative Inaction?" *Newsweek*, June 26, 23.

Lipset, S. M. 1997. American Exceptionalism: A Double-Edged Sword. New York: W. W. Norton.

Lipset, S. M., and W. Schneider. 1978. "The Bakke Case." *Public Opinion* 1:38–44.

Richardson, J. D., and K. M. Lancendorfer. 2004. "Framing Affirmative Action: The Influence of Race on Newspaper Editorial Responses to the University." *Harvard International Journal of Press/Politics* 9:74–94.

Samuelson, R. 1995. "Affirmative Action as Theater." *Newsweek*, August 14, 51.

Schuman, H., and S. Presser. 1996. *Questions & Answers in Attitude Surveys: Experiments on Question Form, Wording, and Context*, reprinted. Thousand Oaks, Calif.: Sage.

Sears, D. O., J. Hetts, J. Sidanius, and L. Bobo. 2000. "Race in American Politics: Framing the Debates." In *Racialized Politics: The Debate about Racism in America*, edited by D. O. Sears, J. Sidanius, and L. Bobo. Chicago: University of Chicago Press.

Skrentny, J. D. 2004. *The Minority Rights Revolution*. Cambridge: Harvard University Press.

Sniderman, P. M., and E. G. Carmines. 1997. *Reaching beyond Race*. Cambridge: Harvard University Press.

Sniderman, P. M., and S. M. Theriault. 2004. "The Structure of Political Argument and the Logic of Issue Framing." In *Studies in Public Opinion: Attitudes, Nonattitudes, Measurement Error, and Change*, edited by W. E. Saris and P. M. Sniderman. Princeton, N.J.: Princeton University Press.

Steeh, C., and M. Krysan. 1996. "Trends: Affirmative Action and the Public, 1970–1995." *Public Opinion Quarterly*. 60:128–158.

Stoker, L. 1998. "Understanding Whites' Resistance to Affirmative Action: The Role of Principled Commitments." In *Perception and Prejudice: Race and Politics in the United States*, edited by J. Hurwitz and M. Peffley. New Haven: Yale University Press.

Williams, D. A., E. Clift, and W. Schmidt. 1976. "The South: The Klan Also Rises." *Newsweek*, January 12, 33.

8

Flag Burning

Peter Hanson

With its 1989 decision in *Texas v. Johnson* holding that burning the American flag is a form of speech protected by the First Amendment, the Supreme Court took a stand at odds with a great majority of the American public. The ruling catalyzed a highly salient debate in Congress over the adoption of a constitutional amendment to prohibit flag burning. But repeated attempts to approve such an amendment have failed in Congress—albeit by slim margins—and the public's support for the measure has declined steadily.

Opinion on the amendment is structured by a set of key variables: education, party identification, political ideology, belief in limited government, moral traditionalism, and, as one might expect, patriotism. It is noteworthy that although the Supreme Court and most scholars think of flag burning as political speech, the public does not frame the issue that way. Rather, most ordinary Americans think of flag burning in moral terms, the same way they think of pornography. Over time, the salience of the flag burning controversy has declined, even as Congress has taken up the proposed amendment year after year. *Texas v. Johnson* thus serves as an important instance of the power of the Supreme Court to make unpopular policy that endures in the face of a hostile public.

History of the Flag-Burning Controversy

Protecting the American flag from desecration has a long history of support in the United States, and numerous state and federal laws prohibited flag burning (Goldstein 1995). Defendants challenged the Texas law after the arrest of Gregory Johnson in 1984 for burning an American flag in protest of Reagan administration policies. After his conviction under the Texas statute, Johnson's appeal was heard by the U.S. Supreme Court, and on June 21, 1989, the court ruled in a five-to-four decision that flag burning was a form of speech protected by the First Amendment to the Constitution (*Texas v. Johnson* 1989).

No polls were taken on flag burning prior to the Court's action, but polls taken immediately after the decision show high levels of awareness of the case and overwhelming public opposition to the Court's decision. According to the Pew Research Center for the People and the Press, news of the Court's decision was followed "very closely" by 51% of the public—more than any other Court decision in the ten-year period under study (Pew 1997). Moreover, the public was deeply unhappy with the Court's action. Only 28% of the public agreed with the Court that flag burning was unconstitutional, and 71% said they favored a constitutional amendment to prohibit flag burning. Reaction among political elites was similarly intense and one-sided.

The day after the Court's ruling, Congress passed resolutions condemning the decision in virtually unanimous votes, and a bipartisan debate ensued over the proper way to overturn the decision. Two strategies emerged. The first approach, favored by congressional Republicans and President George H. W. Bush, was to override the Court by passing a constitutional amendment. For their part, Democrats proposed a new federal statute to prohibit flag burning that would pass constitutional muster. The debate over these alternative approaches came to a head in October 1989, when the Democratic-controlled House and Senate endorsed the statutory approach by passing the Flag Protection Act and rejecting Republican-sponsored constitutional amendments.

The new law was immediately challenged. On June 11, 1990, the Supreme Court overturned the Flag Protection Act in *U.S. v. Eichman* and again held that the Constitution protected flag burning. Once again, polls showed overwhelming public disapproval for the decision, and the president and members of Congress condemned the Court's action. With the statutory approach discredited, attention in Congress turned to a constitutional amendment to prohibit flag burning. In much closer votes in June 1990, majorities in the Democratic-controlled House and Senate voted in favor of the amendment, but fell short of the two-thirds vote required for passage. These votes ended the debate until Republicans took control of Congress in 1994. Over the next twelve years, the amendment passed the House six times and fell to defeat in the Senate three times, most recently by just one vote in June 2006.

Previous studies of public opinion suggest that public affection and respect for the flag can have political ramifications. Although flag burning did not receive substantial public attention or media attention prior to *Texas v. Johnson*, the Court's ruling sparked intense media interest, a public outcry, and congressional action (Flemming, Bohte, & Wood 1997). Sullivan, Fried, and Dietz (1992) argue that respect for the American flag is a politically potent weapon in political campaigns. In the 1988 presidential campaign, Vice President George Bush's attacks on Governor Michael Dukakis for vetoing a law requiring schoolchildren to recite the Pledge of Allegiance appear to have been effective, winning Bush additional votes from those for whom patriotism was important.

Grosskopf and Mondak (1998) analyzed three Harris polls to determine whether the Court's decisions in *Texas v. Johnson* and *U.S. v. Eichman* led to a long-term decline in confidence in the Court. They conclude that people who disagreed with the Court's rulings expressed lower confidence in the Court and that these feelings did not decay in the six weeks between the two polls taken soon after the decision.

General Trends in Public Opinion

The best time-series data on flag burning, spanning 1989 to 2006, comes from six data sets available from Gallup, three from Harris Associates, and eight from a media institute known as the Freedom Forum.[1] Data sets including questions on flag burning are also available for surveys conducted by the American National Election Studies (ANES), CBS/New York Times, and NBC/Wall Street Journal in 1990 and by ABC/Washington Post in 1989 and 1995. Also, marginal results are available for polls taken in June 2006 by Gallup/USA Today, CNN, the Pew Research Center, and Fox News.

Most of the polls measure support for a constitutional amendment to prohibit flag burning. Five polls ask about agreement with the Supreme Court's decisions. Several also measure whether a politician's position on flag burning would influence the way a respondent votes. These surveys are useful for establishing broad trends in opinion, although, regrettably, most of them lack the standard set of demographic variables and repeated questions over time necessary for more in-depth statistical analysis. Fortunately, a rich set of variables is available in the 1990 ANES, and a standard set of demographic variables and consistent question wording over time is available in the series of Freedom Forum surveys.

The Supreme Court's decisions protecting flag burning were rejected by the vast majority of the American people. A Gallup survey immediately after *Texas v. Johnson* found that 65% of respondents disagreed with the court, and subsequent surveys by Harris Associates and ABC/Washington Post found disagreement with the court at even higher levels: 77%, 75%, and 79%, respectively (see Table 8.1). One year later, in the wake of the Court's second decision in *U.S. v. Eichman*, Gallup again found substantial disagreement (58%) with the Court.

These findings leave no doubt that a majority of the American people disagreed with both decisions. But what accounts for the substantial gap between the findings of Gallup and the other polling organizations, particularly between the polls from the summer of 1989? It appears that differences in question wording are the likely reason for the variation in the findings.

Table 8.1

Opinion on the Supreme Court's Flag Burning Rulings, 1989 and 1990

Poll	Date	% Disagreeing with Ruling
Texas v. Johnson		
Gallup/Newsweek	June 23, 1989	65.3
Business Week/Harris	July 7, 1989	77.1
Harris	August 18, 1989	74.6
ABC-Washington Post	August 17–21, 1989	78.5
U.S. v. Eichman		
Gallup/Newsweek	June 13–14, 1990	58.0

Question wording: see Appendix A.

The Gallup wording uses relatively less provocative language about flag burning and clear language about the Constitution (see Appendix A) and appears to raise more uncertainty in the minds of respondents, as evidenced by the poll's higher "don't know" rates. Alternatively, lower "don't know" rates in later polls may be because respondents had more time to learn about the decision and form an opinion on it.

Turning to opinion about a constitutional amendment to reverse *Texas v. Johnson*, the two best sources of data on opinion are the Gallup Poll and the Freedom Forum, both of which have polled on flag burning for many years. These polls indicate a steady downward trend in support for the amendment from 1989 to the present (see Figure 8.1). More significantly, these surveys illustrate the dramatic difference in results that stems from different ways of asking respondents whether they support an amendment. As shown in Figure 8.1, the two survey houses have used three different versions of a question regarding an amendment. The simplest question wording (version 1) was used by Gallup immediately after *Texas v. Johnson* in June 1989 and immediately after *U.S. v. Eichman* in June 1990. These polls show the highest levels of support recorded by Gallup for the amendment, at 71% and 69%. Later, Gallup adopted a more nuanced question wording (version 2), which it posed in five surveys between 1989 and 2006. The trend of responses to this version shows a slight but steady decline in support for the amendment, falling from 65% in October 1989 to 56% in June 2006.

The Freedom Forum measures public support for a constitutional amendment in its annual "State of the First Amendment" surveys. This survey (which includes a series of questions on the right to freedom of speech) uses a third question version that presents brief statements supporting and opposing an amendment before asking respondents for their opinions. As shown in Figure 8.1, the free speech context of the Freedom Forum survey and the argument version 3 presents in support of flag burning as political expression appear to reduce support for the amendment by more than 10 percentage points compared with the other question versions. Further confirmation of the significance of question wording comes from the unique split-sample survey Gallup conducted in June 2006, in which half

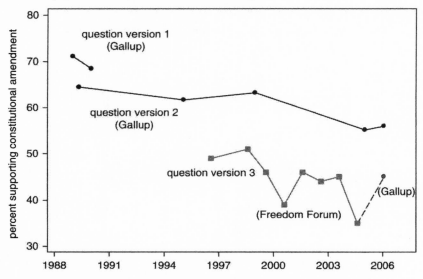

Figure 8.1. Support for a Constitutional Amendment to Prohibit Flag Burning, 1989–2006. Question version 1. Do you think we should pass a constitutional amendment to make flag burning illegal, or not? (source: Gallup 1989, 1990). Question version 2. Do you favor or oppose a constitutional amendment that would allow Congress and state governments to make it illegal to burn the American flag? (source: Gallup 1989–2005). Question version 3. Some people feel that the U.S. Constitution should be amended to make it illegal to burn or desecrate the American flag as a form of political dissent. Others say that the U.S. Constitution should not be amended to specifically prohibit flag burning or desecration. Do you think the U.S. Constitution should or should not be amended to prohibit burning or desecrating the American flag? (Sources: Freedom Forum 1996–2005, Gallup 2006).

of respondents were asked question version 2 and half were asked version 3. Those asked version 2 supported the amendment at a level of 56%, compared with 45% of those who were asked version 3.

Seven other polls—most, unfortunately, employing a unique question wording—measured support for a flag-burning amendment between 1990 and 2006. Support for an amendment in these polls ranged between 51 and 70%, with the lowest level of support measured by two ABC/Washington Post polls in 1995 and 1998. Unlike any of the other polls, these surveys asked respondents to choose between whether the country "should amend the Constitution" or "leave the Constitution alone"—a choice set that undoubtedly tempered some respondents' enthusiasm for change. Complete results for all polls are reproduced in Appendix B.

This evidence suggests that support for a flag-burning amendment has been falling since 1989 and that Americans are torn between their desire to protect the flag and their reluctance to tinker with the Constitution. Despite its reputation as a hot-button issue, support for the flag amendment depends in a significant way on how the topic is presented. Constitutional reform is a process that people endorse only reluctantly. As we will see, only those with a particularly intense love of the flag overcome this more general respect for preserving the Constitution.

The Structure of Opinion on Amending the Constitution

Table 8.2 displays attitudes regarding the adoption of an amendment to the Constitution among various demographic groups. Not surprisingly, support for a flag-protection amendment is consistently higher among Republicans

Table 8.2
Support for Flag Burning Amendment Among Demographic Groups, 1989–2005

Survey House	Percent in Support of Amendment
Freedom Forum (1997–2005 average)	
Party identification	
Republicans	
w/ H.S. diploma	54
w/ College degree	49
Democrats	
w/ H.S. diploma	48
w/ College degree	32
Religiosity	
Identify with a religion	53
Do not identify with a religion	40
American National Election Studies (1990–1992)	
Moral traditionalism	
High	85
Low	59
Ideology	
Conservative	84
Moderate	77
Liberal	66
Love of country	
Extremely strong	77
Not very strong	31

Question wording: Freedom Forum: see Figure 8.1. ANES: Would you favor or oppose a Constitutional amendment making it illegal to destroy the flag for political reasons?

than among Democrats. But more notably, education is associated with higher levels of opposition to the amendment among Democrats but not among Republicans. Although support for the amendment among Democrats with only a high school education averaged 16 percentage points higher than among college-educated Democrats in the Freedom Forum polls conducted between 1997 and 2005, there was very little difference between Republicans based on their level of education. In fact, the typical views of non-college-educated Democrats resemble those of Republicans.

Support for the amendment also is associated with a cluster of social and political attitudes, such as social conservatism and patriotism. Most polls do not measure these variables directly, but multivariate analysis (not shown here) indicates that one commonly measured variable, religiosity, acts as a proxy for these beliefs because it encapsulates many attitudes that predict support for the amendment. Between 1997 and 2005, respondents who identified with a religion were far more likely to support the amendment (at an average level of 53%) than respondents who did not identify with a religion (40%).

Our analysis of ANES data collected in 1990 and 1992 found that opposition to the amendment is concentrated among those who are politically liberal and more tolerant of people whose moral standards differ from their own. Patriotism is one of the strongest predictors of support for a constitutional amendment: 77% of those who told the ANES that their love for the United States is "extremely strong" support the proposal for an amendment banning flag burning.

Using the block recursive approach described in Appendix C, we derived the models shown in Table 8.3. It illustrates the impact of different variables using first differences, or the difference in the probability of supporting the amendment when moving from the minimum to the maximum value of the variable. The most striking finding is the importance of education in explaining opinion toward a Constitutional amendment prohibiting flag burning. The more highly educated a person is, the less likely he or she is to support an amendment. As estimated in Model II, holders of an advanced degree are fully 51 percentage points less likely to support an amendment than people who have not completed high school (holding other variables constant at their means), and this effect diminishes only modestly when additional variables are added.

Social values and political beliefs also structure opinion on the amendment. In limited versions of the model, beliefs linked with support for the amendment are encapsulated by attendance at religious services. Controlling for other variables, those who attend religious services are 10 percentage points less likely to support the amendment than those who do not (model II). However, this effect disappears in models III and IV, which include attitudes such as moral traditionalism, conservative political ideology, and patriotism, suggesting that religiosity acts as a proxy for these variables. In these models, moral traditionalists and conservatives are significantly more likely to support an amendment, holding other variables constant. Notably, belief in

Table 8.3

Predicting Support for a Constitutional Amendment to Prohibit Flag Burning
ANES 1990–1992 Panel Study

Variables	I	II	III	IV
Immutable demographic characteristics				
Age	**.22****	.11	.12	.06
Black	**−.13***	−.16*	−.15*	−.09
Male	**−.04**	−.02	−.03	−.03
Long-term social characteristics				
South		**−.03**	−.05	−.06
West		**.01**	−.02	−.03
North central		**−.01**	−.03	−.03
Urbanicity		**−.11**	−.10	−.08
Married/widowed		**.07**	.04	.05
Divorced/separated		**.04**	.03	.02
Children in household		**−.12**	−.15*	−.15*
Education		**−.51****	−.48***	−.48***
Income		**.05**	.06	.06
Union household		**.02**	.02	.02
Attendance at religious services		**.10****	.06	.06
Values and political orientation				
Egalitarianism (1992)			**−.04**	−.02
Moral traditionalism (1992)			**.17****	.15**
Belief in limited government			**−.22****	−.20**
Political ideology			**.23****	.20*
Party identification			**−.08**	−.08
Feelings toward U.S.				
Patriotism (1992)				**.33****
Log likelihood	−528.02	−481.50	−463.23	−454.14
Pseudo-R^2	.02	.11	.14	.16
N	878	878	878	878

Cell entries are first differences derived from logit analysis. They are estimates of the change in probability of supporting a constitutional amendment to prohibit flag burning, given a shift from the minimum to the maximum value of each independent variable, holding all other variables constant at their means. Cell entries in bold are a variable's total effect—that is, the effect of a variable on support for an amendment before the consideration of mediating effects of any intervening variables.

Effects are significantly different from zero at *p<.05, **p<.01, ***p<.001.

Source: American National Election Studies Panel Study, 1990–1992.

Question wording: see wording for ANES item in Table 8.2.

limited government is associated with a steep (22-point) reduction in support for the amendment, holding other variables constant (Model IV). This may help explain why several U.S. senators who are otherwise considered quite conservative have consistently cast votes against the amendment.

The model also illustrates the role played by patriotism in the flag debate. Model IV shows that Americans who report having an "extremely strong" love for their country are 33% more likely to support the amendment than those who say their love for their country is "not very strong." The effect of adding patriotism to the model is noteworthy. Comparing Model III with Model IV, there is only a slight decline in the effect of variables measuring values and political orientation. These findings suggest that these values have a strong effect independent of patriotism on support for the amendment, indicating that for many Americans, being patriotic and supporting an amendment to prohibit flag burning are not the same thing.

Unlike our analyses of other polls, here we find no statistically significant effect of party identification on opinions toward flag burning once we control for respondents' other political and ideological attributes. One explanation is that the apparent effect of party is explained by the other attitudinal variables included in the model. Another possibility is that respondents were reacting to the anti–flag-burning rhetoric of congressional Democrats when the survey was conducted in the early 1990s. Even those Democratic legislators who ultimately voted against the flag amendment typically qualified their vote with a strong condemnation of the Court's ruling, and it is likely that Democratic adherents did not absorb the nuance of the party's anti-amendment message.

As noted before, we also found no effect of age on attitudes toward the amendment in models II, III, and IV. It is reasonable to suppose that older Americans might be more likely to be offended by flag burning and that the young might be more tolerant, but there is no evidence that simply getting older has any influence on opinion.[2] Although age is significant in model I, the effect disappears once factors associated with age—such as increased levels of education and attendance at religious services—are taken into account.

Finally, race is a significant factor in limited versions of the model. In model II, blacks are 16 percentage points more likely than whites to oppose the amendment. The fact that this effect dissipates in model IV suggests that the relatively lesser degree of emotional attachment measured among blacks in other studies explains this change (Citrin, Sears, Muste & Wong 2001).

The Contours of Support for a Constitutional Amendment

The Freedom Forum survey offers the single best source of data over time on attitudes toward a constitutional amendment to prohibit flag burning.[3] The survey poses a two-part question on a constitutional amendment to prohibit flag burning. It challenges respondents who indicate their support for

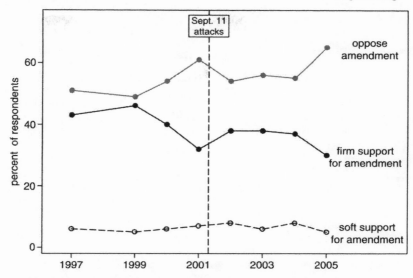

Figure 8.2. American Opinion on a Constitutional Amendment to Prohibit Flag Burning, 1997–2005. Question wording: Figure 8.1. Source: Freedom Forum. Questions asked as part of extensive survey about the First Amendment.

an amendment (in question version 3 in Figure 8.1) with the following additional information:

> FOLLOW UP QUESTION: If an amendment prohibiting burning or desecrating the flag were approved, it would be the first time any of the freedoms in the First Amendment have been amended in over 200 years. Knowing this, would you still support an amendment to prohibit burning or desecrating the flag? (Freedom Forum)

We considered yes answers to both questions as constituting "firm" support for an amendment; a yes to the first question followed by a no to the follow-up question constituted "soft" support. The data from the Freedom Forum show an overall decline in firm support for a constitutional amendment to prohibit flag burning between 1997 and 2005, although a significant spike in support occurred after the attacks of September 11, 2001 (see Figure 8.2). Soft support for an amendment remains steady during the period, indicating that the effect of challenging respondents with the follow-up question was constant over the time period, lowering support for the amendment by 6 percentage points on average. The level of opposition to an amendment (65% in the Freedom Forum's most recent poll in 2005) is consistently higher than that found by other survey houses, indicating that the Freedom Forum's battery of questions about the First Amendment is cuing respondents as expected.

Table 8.4

Support for Constitutional Amendment to Prohibit Flag Burning, 1997–2005

	Level of Education				
	Below High School	High School	Some College	College Grad	Graduate Degree
% supporting amendment	50.2	48.0	46.0	37.3	24.9
% supporting amendment after hearing argument against it	42.2	40.9	40.5	34.5	23.0
Difference	8.0	7.2	5.4	2.9	1.9

Source: Freedom Forum.

Question wording: see Appendix B.

What distinguishes firm from soft supporters of the constitutional amendment? Education. As shown in Table 8.4, those with less education are more likely to change their minds about the amendment after being informed that such a measure would be the first time the First Amendment has been altered in the Constitution's entire history. This finding is probably due to the fact that awareness of the First Amendment and its connection to flag burning are more widespread among the highly educated to begin with and that therefore the follow-up question does not convey any new information to these respondents. It also comports with other research indicating that people with less education are less likely to hold steady opinions on public affairs. This finding holds up in multivariate analysis (not shown here) that controls for party identification and typical demographic variables.

We conducted another set of multivariate analyses that uncovered interesting differences in the determinants of disagreement with the Court's flag-burning rulings, on the one hand, and support for a constitutional amendment on the other. The Gallup Poll conducted in June 1990 first asked respondents their opinion on the Supreme Court's ruling in *U.S v. Eichman* (as shown in Table 8.1, 58% disagreed). It then asked respondents if a constitutional amendment should be passed to make flag burning illegal (as shown in Figure 8.1, 69% supported an amendment).

Table 8.5 shows the results of logit analyses in which disagreement with the Court's ruling and support for the amendment are predicted with political and demographic variables. Estimates are presented as first differences as described previously and in Appendix C. Notably, older Americans were 15 percentage points *more* likely to disagree with *U.S. v. Eichman* than younger Americans, but they were *less* likely than the young to support the amendment—although the results for support of the amendment do not reach standard levels of significance. All other things being equal, education and partisanship had no statistically significant role in explaining variation in agreement with the decision

Table 8.5

Predicting Disagreement with *U.S. v. Eichman* and Support for a Constitutional Amendment, June 1990

Variable	Disagree with Decision	Support Amendment
Age	.15*	−.10
Black	−.38***	−.22*
Male	−.01	−.04
Education	−.04	−.23**
Democrat	−.05	−.16*
Independent	−.04	−.12*
South	.04	.02
Religion	.09	.07
Log Likelihood	−354.38	−313.39
Pseudo R²	.06	.05

Cell entries are first differences derived from logit analysis.
Effects are significantly different from zero at *$p<.05$, **$p<.01$, ***$p<.001$. $N = 577$.

Source: The Gallup Poll.

Question wording: see Appendix B.

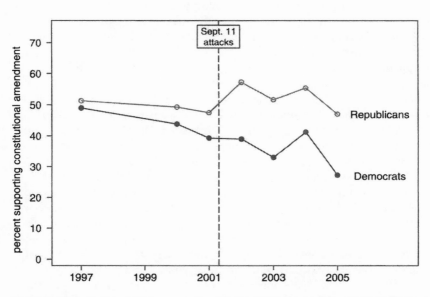

Figure 8.3. American Opinion on a Constitutional Amendment to Prohibit Flag Burning, 1997–2005. Question wording: see Figure 8.1. Source: Freedom Forum. Question asked as part of extensive survey about the First Amendment.

but were significant in explaining support for an amendment. Better-educated Americans, as well as Democrats and Independents, may not have liked the Court's decision, but they were substantially less willing than others to overturn it by amending the Constitution. Blacks were far less likely than others to disagree with the decision and were also less likely to support the amendment.

Much as political polarization has increased generally in recent years, the relationship between party identification and the public's attitudes regarding a constitutional amendment has grown stronger over time. As shown in Figure 8.3, there was little difference between Democrats and Republicans over amending the constitution in the mid-1990s.[4] But a partisan gap in opinion has grown steadily since then. Most notably, Republicans responded to the September 11 attacks by literally "rallying around the flag": their support for an amendment grew by 9 percentage points. Democrats' support remained flat and continued to fall precipitously in the years that followed. A 20-point gap now exists between Republicans and Democrats on amending the constitution. We confirmed this growing partisan divide with year-by-year multivariate analyses (not shown here) in which we controlled for typical demographic variables.

What Kind of "Free Speech" Is Flag Burning?

The Supreme Court has ruled that flag burning is protected by the First Amendment because it qualifies as political speech. Do Americans see it this way? The Freedom Forum surveys also allow us to investigate how the public views flag burning in comparison with other free speech issues. In 1997, the survey asked respondents whether ten different forms of controversial speech should be permitted (see Figure 8.4; specific question wording may be found in Appendix D). Support for controversial speech varies widely by category, but overall there is a generally low level of support for offensive speech. As shown in Figure 8.4, more than 90% of Americans claim to support the right of people to express "unpopular opinions" in the abstract, but support drops drastically once concrete examples are introduced. Of the ten items, Americans are least likely to view flag burning as permissible: only 21% of respondents believe it should be allowed as a form of political protest.

Further investigation revealed that it is unlikely that Americans view these forms of speech through the same lens. Through factor analysis, we assessed the extent to which these responses are generated by different sets of underlying, unobserved "factors," which we claim are distinct values that Americans hold regarding offensive speech. Table 8.6 displays the "loadings" associated with responses on the ten forms of speech, which are estimates of how strongly these responses are associated with the underlying factors.[5]

Three issues load highly onto the first factor: broadcasting nudity on television, Internet pornography, and burning the flag. Although the first two of these issues involve what Chief Justice Warren Burger once called "prurient interest"—that is, sexual content—flag burning does not. By contrast, flag

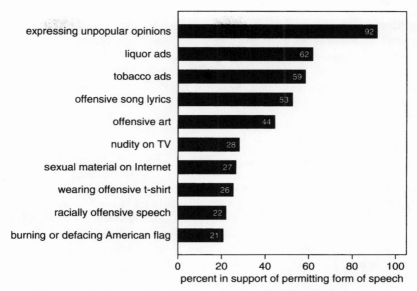

Figure 8.4. Support for Permitting Controversial Speech, 1997. Question wording: see Appendix D. Source: Freedom Forum. Questions asked as part of extensive survey about the First Amendment.

Table 8.6
Controversial Speech Factor Loadings (rotated), 1997

Type of Speech	Loadings on:			Uniqueness
	Factor 1	Factor 2	Factor 3	
Sexual material on Internet	**.76**	−.03	.01	.45
Nudity on TV	**.71**	.02	.03	.47
Burning or defacing American flag	**.59**	−.02	−.06	.59
Offensive song lyrics	.50	**.31**	.04	.42
Wearing offensive T-shirt	.27	**.40**	−.05	.68
Offensive art	.39	**.39**	.01	.47
Expressing unpopular opinions	.22	.22	.08	.81
Racially offensive speech	.39	.17	.06	.58
Tobacco ads	.01	−.05	**.88**	.26
Liquor ads	.02	.03	**.85**	.24

Source: Freedom Forum.

Question wording: see Appendix D.

burning and pornography do not load at all onto factor 2, the factor that appears to describe the expression of unpopular ideas, including offensive song lyrics, offensive T-shirts, and offensive art. Instead of being viewed as an unpopular idea, flag burning—like pornography—is seen as a threat to the moral order. It is not surprising, then, that the public needs to be prodded to see flag burning as a free-speech issue.

Salience of a Flag Amendment

Since *Texas v. Johnson*, support for an amendment to prohibit flag burning has attracted the public's strong support. Yet the adoption of such an amendment does not rank high on the public's list of priorities. After an initial burst of enthusiasm in 1989 and 1990, the public attention given to a constitutional amendment almost disappeared. Immediately after *Texas v. Johnson*, flag burning was thought to be the most important of four major policy issues in a Gallup survey. But a year later, even in the immediate wake of *U.S. v. Eichman*, the percentage of Americans who said that flag burning was "one of the most important issues" or a "very important" issue in deciding how to vote dropped by more than 10 percentage points. The salience of this issue continued to drop over the next two decades. As Congress once again debated the flag amendment in 2006, the public ranked it last in importance of five issues surveyed by Fox News, last

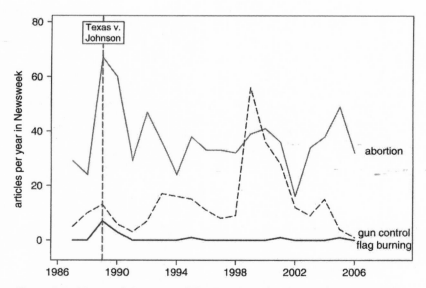

Figure 8.5. *Newsweek* Coverage of Flag Burning, Abortion, and Gun Control, 1987–2006. Source: Lexis-Nexis.

of seven in a poll by NBC News and the Wall Street Journal, and fourteenth among the nineteen issues surveyed by the Pew Research Center (Taylor 2006). Media attention to the issue has also plummeted since 1989, when, according to the Pew Center for People and the Press (1997), flag burning was one of the most followed stories. For a rough measure of media interest, we counted the number of stories in *Newsweek* from 1987 to 2006 that discussed "flag burning" and compared it to the counts for two other controversial constitutional issues, "abortion" and "gun control" (see Figure 8.5). After a burst of attention to the decisions in 1989 and 1990, flag burning received minimal coverage in *Newsweek* compared to abortion and gun control. Similar trends pertain for other national print media, such as *USA Today* and the *New York Times*.

Despite the public's low level of interest, flag burning amendments continue to be introduced in Congress. The sponsors' goal, it would seem, is not to win mass support for the amendment but to force opponents of the amendment to go on the record and take an unpopular stand—which makes for a sharp "attack ad" during the next election cycle. That the amendment failed by only one vote in June 2006 suggests that even if flag burning is not at the top of the public agenda, politicians still view the measure as a potent weapon.

Conclusion

In the nearly two decades since *Texas v. Johnson*, public opposition to flag burning has not changed. But support for an amendment to overturn the decision has waned, and the public no longer views flag burning as a high-priority issue. The public has not been persuaded by the Supreme Court's arguments that flag burning is a legitimate form of political speech, but many people are loath to tinker with the Constitution—even to prevent something they despise. Absent public support, the Senate has not been able to muster the two-thirds vote required for a constitutional amendment.

Predictably, supporters of the amendment are more likely to be Republican, moral traditionalists, people who are highly patriotic, and those with less education. Opponents of the amendment are more likely to be Democratic and people with high levels of education. But the partisan split emerged only in 2000 and 2001, in the wake of the contested presidential election and September 11. There are divisions within the parties as well. Among Democrats, those with only a high school education are much more likely to support the amendment than those with a college education. Among Republicans, social conservatives are likely to support the amendment, and libertarians who believe in limited government are likely to oppose it. This cleavage is reflected in the Senate votes on the amendment, in which an unlikely coalition of liberal and conservative Republicans joined with most Democrats to defeat the amendment.

Finally, although the courts and scholars view flag burning as political speech, Americans do not. Our evidence indicates that Americans think of flag burning in moral terms, the same way they think of pornography.

This finding also helps to explain why the amendment garnered sixty-six votes in the Senate in 2006, even as public support fell to the lowest point on record. As long as permitting flag burning is viewed through the same lens as allowing sexually explicit content on the nation's airwaves and the Internet, few politicians will see any advantage in protecting a form of speech that deeply offends so many Americans.

Appendix A. Disagreement with Decision Question Wording

Gallup June 1989 and June 1990. "The Supreme Court ruled this week that burning the American flag, though highly offensive, is protected under the free speech guarantee of the First Amendment to the Constitution. Do you agree or disagree?"

Harris July and August 1989. "Do you agree or disagree with a recent Supreme Court decision that said while the flag was a symbol of patriotism, one of the freedoms an individual has is the right to desecrate and even burn the flag, as part of the First Amendment guaranteeing freedom of expression."[6]

Washington Post August 1989. "As you may know, the U.S. Supreme Court has ruled that citizens have the constitutional right to destroy or burn the American flag as a form of political protest if they so choose. Do you favor or oppose the Court's decision? Do you favor/oppose it strongly or only somewhat?"

Appendix B.   Poll-by-Poll Results for Support for Amendment

1. Gallup Polls

Table A1.
Gallup Polls, 1989–2006

Poll	Date	Support for Amendment	N	Question Wording
Gallup/Newsweek	June 23, 1989	71	500	1
Gallup	October 5—8, 1989	64	1,234	2
Gallup/Newsweek	June 13—14, 1990	69	604	1

Table A1.
(continued)

Poll	Date	Support for Amendment	N	Question Wording
Gallup/CNN/USA Today	July 7–9, 1995	60	1,127	2
Gallup/CNN/USA Today	June 25–27, 1999	63	1,016	2
Gallup/CNN/USA Today	June 24–26, 2005	55	1,009	2
Gallup/USA Today	June 23–25, 2006	56/45	484/516	2/3

Question 1. Do you think we should pass a constitutional amendment to make flag burning illegal, or not?

Question 2. Do you favor or oppose a constitutional amendment that would allow Congress and state governments to make it illegal to burn the American flag?

Question 3. Some people feel that the U.S. Constitution should be amended to make it illegal to burn or desecrate the American flag as a form of political dissent. Others say that the U.S. Constitution should not be amended to specifically prohibit flag burning or desecration. Do you think the U.S. Constitution should or should not be amended to prohibit burning or desecrating the American flag?

Note: In the June 23–25, 2006 poll, two separate questions on the flag amendment were asked to two subsamples of respondents.

2. State of the First Amendment Polls

Table A2.
State of the First Amendment Polls, 1997–2005

Poll	Date	Question 1 Support Amendment	Question 2 Support Amendment	N
SOFA 1997	July 17—August 1, 1997	49	43	1,026
SOFA 1999	February 26—March 24, 1999	51	46	1,001
SOFA 2000	April 13—20, 2000	46	40	1,015
SOFA 2001	May 16—June 6, 2001	39	32	1,012
SOFA 2002	June 12—July 5, 2002	46	38	1,000
SOFA 2003	June 3—June 15, 2003	44	38	1,000
SOFA 2004	May 6—June 6, 2004	45	37	1,000
SOFA 2005	May 13—May 23, 2005	35	30	1,003

Question 1. Some people feel that the U.S. Constitution should be amended to make it illegal to burn or desecrate the American flag as a form of political dissent. Others say that the U.S. Constitution should not be amended

to specifically prohibit flag burning or desecration. Do you think the U.S. Constitution should or should not be amended to prohibit burning or desecrating the flag?

Question 2. If an amendment prohibiting burning or desecrating the flag were approved, it would be the first time any of the freedoms in the First Amendment have been amended in over 200 years. Knowing this, would you still support an amendment to prohibit burning or desecrating the flag? [Asked only of those who respond "yes" to Question 1.]

Note: The results for Question 2 are the percentage of the <u>total</u> sample supporting the amendment. Since several of the datasets lack a variable for weighting, the findings in the table are based on the Freedom Forum's reported marginal results, which are weighted.

3. Other Organizations

Table A3.
Individual Polls from Other Organizations, 1990–2006

Poll	Date	Support for Amendment	N
CBS/New York Times	May 22–24, 1990	59	1,140
Business Week/Harris	June 21, 1990	57	1,255
NBC News/Wall Street Journal	July 6–10, 1990	57	1,555
ANES	November 1990	70	878
ABC/Washington Post	July 14–17, 1995	51	1,548
ABC/Washington Post	July 9–12, 1998	51	1,511
CNN	June 8–11, 2006	56	1,031

CBS/New York Times

Question 1. Should flag burning or destroying the American flag as a form of political protest be legal, or should it be against the law?

Question 2. If the only way to make flag destruction illegal was to change the Constitution, would you favor or oppose a Constitutional amendment making it illegal to destroy the flag for political reasons? (Asked only of respondents who respond with "against the law" to the previous question.)

Note: Responses for these two questions were combined to determine the percentage of the full sample that supported the amendment.

Business Week/Harris

Do you favor or oppose passing a constitutional amendment to prohibit the burning of the American flag?

NBC News/Wall Street Journal

Do you favor or oppose a constitutional amendment to make it illegal or burn or deface the flag?

Note: Registered voters only. All other polls are national adult sample.

ANES

Question 1. Should burning or destroying the American flag as a form of political protest be legal, or should it be against the law?

Question 2. Would you favor or oppose a Constitutional amendment making it illegal to destroy the flag for political reasons? (asked only of people who respond with "against the law" to the previous question.)

Note: Responses for these two questions were combined to determine the overall percentage of the 878 respondents used for the bloc recursive analysis in this chapter that supported the amendment.

ABC/Washington Post

As you may know, the Supreme Court has ruled that burning the American flag is a form of free speech that's protected by the U.S. Constitution. Do you think the country should amend the Constitution to make flag-burning illegal, or do you think it should leave the Constitution alone, even if that means flag-burning stays legal?

CNN

Do you favor or oppose passing a constitutional amendment which would make it illegal to burn the American flag?

Appendix C.   Methodology of Block Recursive Model

In the block recursive model of support for a constitutional amendment, we conduct a series of four logit estimates on four blocks of variables using support for a constitutional amendment to prohibit flag burning coded 0 or 1 as the dependent variable. The first model includes immutable demographic characteristics such as age, race and sex. Model II includes all variables from Model I and adds long-term social characteristics including place of residence, education, marital status, income, attendance of religious services, living in a union household and having children in the house. Model III includes all variables from Model I and II, and adds variables for values and political orientation such as egalitarianism, moral traditionalism, belief in limited government, political ideology and party identification. Finally, Model IV includes all previous blocks and adds a variable for patriotism. Because these models build upon each other, the virtue of this approach is that it builds a model of public opinion of increasing complexity that illustrates both the total effect of long-term characteristics like age and the direct effect of intervening variables such as education or place of residence.[7]

Data for this model come from the 1990–1992 American National Elections Study. In this panel study, researchers questioned a group of respondents in 1990 and again in 1991 and 1992. The survey only asked questions about flag burning in 1990, so we drew all data for the model from the initial 1990 survey with the exception of questions on patriotism and political values. Complete data for these questions were only available in the 1992 survey.

The 1990 NES asks two questions in regard to flag burning, reproduced above, that we use to construct a dependent variable for this analysis: v900471 and v900472. The model also includes variables for "Values and Political Orientation" including measures of egalitarianism, moral traditionalism and patriotism. The full question wording for each variable is reproduced in Appendix D. The NES asked appropriate questions to measure egalitarianism (v900426) and moral traditionalism (v900503) only to a subset of respondents in the 1990 survey, and asked questions measuring patriotism (v926131) only in 1991 and 1992. As a result, using only 1990 responses for our analysis reduced the sample size substantially. To secure a higher sample size, we used observations for egalitarianism and moral traditionalism from the 1992 survey (V926116 and V926024) in place of the 1990 equivalent variables in the model.[8]

While the approach of substituting variables from the 1992 round of the study is not ideal, we adopted this approach because it allowed the use of a larger sample size. In addition, we compared regression coefficients using both approaches and found there was not a substantial amount of difference between the two models when only 1990 variables were used as compared to a mix of 1990 and 1992 variables. Given that fact, we chose the larger number of observations for use in this analysis.

Question Wording for ANES Variables

Moral Traditionalism. 926116. "We should be more tolerant of people who choose to live according to their own moral standards even if they are very different from our own." (5 point scale, agree/disagree)

Egalitarianism. 926024. "Our society should do whatever is necessary to make sure that everyone has an equal opportunity to succeed." (5 point scale, agree/disagree)

Patriotism. 926131. "How strong is your love for your country...extremely strong, very strong, somewhat strong, or not very strong?"

Belief in Limited Government. 900452. "Some people think the government should provide fewer services, even in areas such as health and education in order to reduce spending. Other people feel it is important for the government to provide many more services even if it means an increase in spending. Where would you place yourself on this scale, or haven't you thought much about this?" (7 point scale, more/fewer services)

Appendix D. Question Wording for Controversial Forms of Speech

(1) people should be allowed to express unpopular opinions; (2) companies should be allowed to advertise tobacco; (3) companies should be allowed to advertise liquor and alcohol products; (4) the media should be allowed to broadcast pictures of nude or partially clothed persons; (5) musicians should be allowed to sing songs with words that others might find offensive: (6) people should be allowed to place sexually explicit material on the Internet; (7) people should be allowed to burn or deface the American flag as a political statement; (8) school students should be allowed to wear a t-shirt with a message or picture that others may find offensive; (9) people should be allowed to use words in public that might be offensive to racial groups; and (10) people should be allowed to display in a public place art that might be offensive to others.

Notes

1. The Freedom Forum was established by Allen Neuharth, the founder of the newspaper *USA Today*, to promote First Amendment rights. It operates the Newseum in Arlington, Virginia, and the First Amendment Center at Vanderbilt University.

2. Some evidence does suggest a curvilinear relationship between age and support for the amendment, as other chapters in this book find.

3. A disadvantage of the survey is that it is focused on First Amendment issues and thus it cues respondents to oppose the amendment by placing the controversy in a free speech context.

4. This is a finding consistent with our analysis of the 1990 ANES data (not shown), which found no partisan differences on amending the Constitution at that time.

5. Space considerations make it impossible to present a complete description of factor analysis here. See Kim and Mueller (1978a, 1978b) for an accessible discussion of the technique.

6. In July 1989, the flag amendment question was in a list of decisions about which respondents were asked. In August 1989, the flag amendment was asked about as a stand-alone question.

7. The author wishes to thank Pat Egan for his assistance in the preparation of this section of the paper.

8. Although these responses came from the same individuals, the fact that the observations were made at a different point in time than the initial response on flag burning raised concerns about the stability of opinions. Major intervening events such as the Gulf War and the 1992 presidential campaign could have changed the minds of some of those responding to the survey. A comparison of available 1990 responses and the resurvey of those individuals in 1992 using a Pearson's correlation in which a $1/-1$ equals a perfect correlation and a 0 indicates no correlation shows moderate levels of stability. The 1990 response for moral traditionalism was correlated with the 1992 response at a level of .43. The 1990 response for egalitarianism was correlated with the 1992 response at a level of .32. Patriotism was measured in 1991 and 1992, and was correlated at .53.

References

ABC News/Washington Post. ABC NEWS/WASHINGTON POST POLL, AUGUST 1989. [computer file.] Radnor, Pa.: Chilton Research Services [producer], 1989. Ann Arbor, Mich.: Inter-University Consortium for Political and Social Research [distributor], 1991.

——. July 14–17, 1995. ABC NEWS/THE WASHINGTON POST POLL. 1996 ELECTION. [computer file]. Radnor, Pa.: Chilton Research Services [producer]. Storrs: Roper Center for Public Opinion Research, University of Connecticut [distributor].

——. July 9–12, 1998. ABC NEWS/THE WASHINGTON POST POLL. [computer file.] Radnor, Pa.: Chilton Research Services [producer]. Storrs: Roper Center for Public Opinion Research, University of Connecticut [distributor].

Battle, Michelle. 1989. "Poll: 69% want flag protected." *USA Today*, June 23, 1A.

Business Week Magazine. July 1989. HARRIS 1989 (JULY) BUSINESS-WEEK SURVEY, STUDY NUMBER 891203 [computer file]. Louis Harris and Associates [producer]. Chapel Hill, N.C.: The Howard W. Odum Institute for Research in Social Science [distributor].

——. June 21–26, 1990. HARRIS 1990 (JUNE) BUSINESS WEEK SURVEY, STUDY NUMBER 901206 [computer file.] Louis Harris and Associates [producer]. Chapel Hill, N.C.: The Howard W. Odum Institute for Research in Social Science [distributor].

Cable News Network and USA Today. July 7–9, 1995. GALLUP/CNN/USA TODAY POLL. 1996 ELECTION/FEDERAL DEFICIT. [computer file.] Gallup Organization [producer]. Storrs: Roper Center for Public Opinion Research, University of Connecticut [distributor].

——. June 25–27, 1999. GALLUP/CNN/USA TODAY POLL #9906032. 2000 ELECTION/CONFIDENCE IN INSTITUTIONS. [computer file.] Gallup Organization [producer]. Storrs: Roper Center for Public Opinion Research, University of Connecticut [distributor].

——. June 24–26, 2005. GALLUP/CNN/USA TODAY POLL #2005–29. NASA/IRAQ/ UPCOMING TRIAL OF SADDAM HUSSEIN/SUPREME COURT. [computer file.] Gallup Organization [producer]. Storrs: Roper Center for Public Opinion Research, University of Connecticut [distributor].

CBS News/The New York Times. CBS NEWS/NEW YORK TIMES MONTHLY POLL, MAY 1990 [Computer file]. New York, NY: CBS News [producer], 1990. Ann Arbor, Mich.: Inter-university Consortium for Political and Social Research [distributor], 1991.

Citrin, Jack and David Sears, Christopher Muste and Cara Wong. 2001. "Multiculturalism in American Public Opinion." *British Journal of Political Science*. 31, (2). 247–275.

The First Amendment Center. 1997. STATE OF THE FIRST AMENDMENT 1997 [computer file]. Storrs: Center for Survey Research and Analysis, University of Connecticut [producer and distributor].

——1999. STATE OF THE FIRST AMENDMENT 1999 [computer file]. Storrs: Center for Survey Research and Analysis, University of Connecticut [producer and distributor].

——. 2000. STATE OF THE FIRST AMENDMENT 2000 [computer file]. Storrs: Center for Survey Research and Analysis, University of Connecticut [producer and distributor].

——. 2001. STATE OF THE FIRST AMENDMENT 2001 [computer file]. Storrs: Center for Survey Research and Analysis, University of Connecticut [producer and distributor].

——. 2002. STATE OF THE FIRST AMENDMENT 2002 [computer file]. Storrs: Center for Survey Research and Analysis, University of Connecticut [producer and distributor].

——. 2003. STATE OF THE FIRST AMENDMENT 2003 [computer file]. Storrs: Center for Survey Research and Analysis, University of Connecticut [producer and distributor].

——. 2004. STATE OF THE FIRST AMENDMENT 2004 [computer file]. Storrs: Center for Survey Research and Analysis, University of Connecticut [producer and distributor].

——. 2005. STATE OF THE FIRST AMENDMENT 2005 [computer file]. Nashville, Tenn.: First Amendment Center [producer and distributor].

Flemming, Roy, John Bohte, and B. Dan Wood. 1997. "One Voice among Many: The Supreme Court's Influence on Attentiveness to Issues in the United States, 1947–92." *American Journal of Political Science* 41(4), 1224–1250.

Gallup Organization. October 5–8, 1989. GALLUP NEWS SERVICE SURVEY #1989–89139-W1. ABORTION/GUN LAWS. [computer file.] Gallup Organization [producer]. Storrs: Roper Center for Public Opinion Research, University of Connecticut [distributor].

Goldstein, Robert Justin. *Saving "Old Glory": The History of the American Flag Desecration Controversy*. Boulder, Colo.: Westview, 1995.

Grosskopf, Anke, and Jeffrey Mondak. 1998. "Do Attitudes toward Specific Supreme Court Decisions Matter? The Impact of *Webster* and *Texas v. Johnson* on Public Confidence in the Supreme Court." *Political Research Quarterly* 51(3), 633–654.

Kim, Jae-On, and Charles W. Mueller. 1978a. *Factor Analysis: What It Is and How to Do It*. Thousand Oaks, Calif.: Sage.

——. 1978b. *Factor Analysis: Statistical Methods and Practical Issues*. Thousand Oaks, Calif.: Sage.

Louis Harris and Associates. 1989. HARRIS 1989 (AUGUST) PUBLIC OPINION SURVEY, STUDY NUMBER 891105 [computer file]. Chapel Hill, N.C.: The Howard W. Odum Institute for Research in Social Science [distributor].

NBC News and the Wall Street Journal. July 6–10, 1990. NBC NEWS/WALL STREET JOURNAL POLL. [computer file.] Hart-Teeter Research Companies [producer]. Storrs: Roper Center for Public Opinion Research, University of Connecticut [distributor].

Newsweek Magazine. June 23, 1989. GALLUP/NEWSWEEK POLL #1989–89193. FLAG BURNING. [computer file.] Gallup Organization [producer]. Storrs: Roper Center for Public Opinion Research, University of Connecticut [distributor].

———. June 13–14, 1990. GALLUP/NEWSWEEK POLL #1990–125006. FLAG BURNING/OBSCENITY. [computer file.] Gallup Organization [producer]. Storrs: Roper Center for Public Opinion Research, University of Connecticut [distributor].

Pew Research Center for the People and the Press. May 17, 1997. "Ten Years of the Pew News Interest Index." Available at http://people-press.org/reports/print. php3?ReportID=107. Accessed August 7, 2007.

Sullivan, John, Amy Fried, and Mary Dietz. 1992. "Patriotism, Politics and the Presidential Election of 1988." *American Journal of Political Science* 35(1), 200–234.

Taylor, Paul. 2006. "No Clamor for Amendment from Flag-Waving Public." Pew Research Center, June 28. Available at http://pewresearch.org/obdeck/?ObDeckID=32. Accessed August 7, 2007.

Texas v. Johnson, 491 U.S. 397 (1989). No 88–155.

9

Federalism

Megan Mullin

Federalism has occupied a large portion of the Supreme Court's caseload in recent years, but unlike other issues addressed in this book, it has remained off the public agenda. The Court's federalism decisions lack three elements that would prompt a public opinion response: high levels of salience, strong reaction from elites, and an impact that is discernible from other political activities with respect to federalism. Federalism is about the process of governance more than the substance of policy, and questions about the reach of federal power and the appropriate allocation of responsibilities among levels of government have little salience for most of the public. As Samuel Beer has observed, federalism "is an instrumental, not a consummatory value."[1] Court decisions addressing questions about the bounds of federal authority typically provoke little reaction from political elites, and the Court is just one of multiple venues in which these boundaries are subject to ongoing negotiation and readjustment. Political efforts to devolve responsibility to the states, such as those under Presidents Reagan and Nixon, are likely to be more visible and more comprehensible than Court rulings defining interstate commerce or preemption.

An additional reason for the public's inattention to federalism jurisprudence is the abundance and complexity of the decisions themselves. The case history for federalism does not consist of a few discrete, visible decisions. Instead, the Court has acted incrementally through frequent rulings on a broad set of constitutional questions. Many of the Court's decisions address issues related to the reach of federal power, even as they involve other legal questions as well. Melnick (2003) estimates that half to two thirds of the full opinions issued by the Court each term involve federalism issues. The decisions that are most significant for federalism jurisprudence often receive little public attention because of the substance of the policy question; for example, some of the most important recent decisions relate to state employment practices, a policy area that is unlikely to capture public attention. At the same time, Americans may not perceive high-profile cases about the regulation of abortion, medical marijuana, and assisted suicide as questions of federalism. Moreover, the constitutional questions underlying federalism jurisprudence are multifaceted and complex. The Court has used a wide range of constitutional grounds to interpret the scope of congressional power and define the rights of states, resulting in a highly technical set of opinions that is the subject of ongoing scholarly debate.

Thus for reasons related to both the nature of public opinion about federalism and the content of decisions themselves, Court activity on federalism attracts little public attention. If the Court is not shaping public opinion on this issue, then what is? Does coherent public opinion about the division of governmental responsibilities even exist? This chapter examines public attitudes about the allocation of powers within the American federalist system. Previous research has shown that public perceptions of the responsibilities and performance of specific levels of government are weakly held and often inconsistent. To the extent that people have an opinion about federalism, the literature suggests that it is influenced by persistent attitudes about race and political trust. This analysis focuses on beliefs about the strength of the federal government in order to disentangle the influence of these long-term, generalized attitudes from more immediate responses to political institutions. On the whole, I find that Americans' perceptions of federal power are largely determined by their orientation toward government itself. Short-term assessments of political leaders also help to shape opinion about the scope of federal authority, and assessments of the Supreme Court have as much influence as opinion about the president and Congress. People are less critical of federal power when they have a positive affect toward current political leaders.

Federalism in Politics and the Courts

The idea underlying federalism as a system of governance is the division of political authority between a central government and constituent units; disputes over federalism involve how that power should be divided. Federalism is promoted as a means for advancing any number of values—individual liberty, economic efficiency, policy innovation, and governmental responsiveness, among others—and upholding federalism is widely perceived as protecting states' rights against the nationalistic tendencies of the federal government.

Both the courts and the political branches have acted to limit the reach of federal authority and to protect state autonomy. Neither set of institutions offered much resistance to the federal government's rapid expansion beginning in the 1930s. In a series of decisions during the early stages of the New Deal, the Court attempted to rein in federal power to address the economic and social consequences of the Great Depression. After Franklin Roosevelt famously threatened to "pack the Court" with new members to guarantee himself a nationalist majority, the Court began to issue opinions allowing expansion of federal power to regulate the economy. That trend culminated in the 1942 decision of *Wickard v. Filburn*, which interpreted Congress's power to regulate interstate commerce as including even the amount of wheat a farmer grew for his own consumption. Over subsequent decades, the Court's liberal view of federal government authority grew to include a broader set of doctrinal elements, and its willingness to defer to congressional interpretation of Congress's own enumerated powers facilitated the growth of federal activity in areas such as civil rights protection, welfare state expansion, and regulatory policy through the 1970s.

Political institutions acted earlier than the Court in attempting to rein in this expansion of federal authority and shift some power back to the states. As part of his New Federalism initiative, President Nixon instituted revenue-sharing programs intended to give state and local governments more autonomy in decisions about spending federal dollars. Nixon convinced Congress to pass the State and Local Assistance Act, which delivered billions in undedicated funds to state and local governments, and he consolidated dozens of categorical grant programs into block grants to encourage states and municipalities to design their own programs. A decade later, President Reagan promoted further devolution of grant-making authority to the states and called for dramatic reductions in federal regulatory activity and social spending. The Nixon and Reagan initiatives differed in their policy goals, but both administrations explicitly framed their efforts in terms of federalism. Nixon believed that states and localities would be more efficient and responsive to local preferences if given authority over spending decisions, and the Reagan administration argued more generally for a reduction in the scope of federal power. Attention to federalism came principally from political venues through the 1970s and 1980s, as the Burger Court largely continued its predecessors' tolerance for expansion of national government powers. The most notable exception to this nationalist approach came in the Court's 1976 decision in *National League of Cities v. Usery*, holding that Congress lacks the authority to regulate states in areas of traditional state government functions. The Court reversed itself less than a decade later, though, in *Garcia v. San Antonio Metropolitan Transit Authority* (1985).

Justice William Rehnquist, who wrote the majority opinion in *National League of Cities*, had long had an interest in protecting states' rights. With the appointment of Clarence Thomas in 1991, Rehnquist—then Chief Justice—obtained a five-vote majority that would support him at least to some degree in scaling back the power of the national government. Over the next fourteen years, the Rehnquist Court conducted what many have called a "federalism revolution," reasserting a strong role for the judiciary in carving out areas of state sovereignty and placing limits on congressional authority. This revolution occurred across a range of constitutional domains, including a revival of Tenth Amendment protections of state sovereignty, restrictions on federal court jurisdiction under the Eleventh Amendment, and narrowing constructions of congressional authority under the commerce clause and Section Five of the Fourteenth Amendment.

The federalism revolution is likely to be remembered as the core legacy of the Rehnquist Court. But despite its significance for legal doctrine, its impact on the public's view of states' rights and the power of the federal government is unclear. One reason is the low salience of the policy questions addressed in most of the cases in the Rehnquist Court's federalism jurisprudence. The structural relationship among levels of government does not capture public attention on its own, and many of the cases the Court used to redefine the scope of national authority involved complex policy issues such as state employment practices,[2] intellectual property,[3] and the management of low-level radioactive waste.[4] The exception is a set of cases that struck down some highly visible laws related to crime policy—the Gun Free School Zones Act (*United States v. Lopez* (1995)), the Violence against Women Act (*United States v. Morrison* (2000)), and the Brady Handgun Violence Prevention Act (*Printz v. United States* (1997))—but the Court's rulings in these cases had only marginal substantive impact. Moreover, as Whittington (2001) points out, the public tends to attribute responsibility for fighting crime to local and state governments and is unlikely to punish the Court for impeding federal efforts on this issue. In general, the Rehnquist Court's federalism decisions did not take on fundamental issues about the relationship between the national government and private citizens. Melnick (2003) describes: "The bottom line is that the Court has placed very few constitutional restrictions on Congress's power to regulate private conduct, to tax private citizens, and to spend for the 'public welfare.' The New Deal and most of the Great Society are perfectly safe" (113–14).

The Rehnquist Court's federalism jurisprudence not only addressed relatively obscure policy questions; the doctrinal foundation of the opinions themselves was complex and difficult to decipher. The overall trend was to limit the authority of the federal government, but the Court did not rule consistently in favor of the states, as members of the five-vote majority would peel off based on the merits of a particular case. Taken as a whole, the Court's record on federalism is mixed. Although careful Court-watchers would agree that the Rehnquist Court made important steps in limiting congressional authority, that larger trend may not have been evident to the mass public.

Another reason that the public might not have paid attention to the Court's federalism decisions is the lack of response from policy elites. The Court's leadership did not spark a broad public debate over the proper allocation of powers among levels of government.[5] Indeed, the topic of federalism received little attention outside scholarly communities while the Rehnquist revolution was taking place. When the Court started overturning congressional

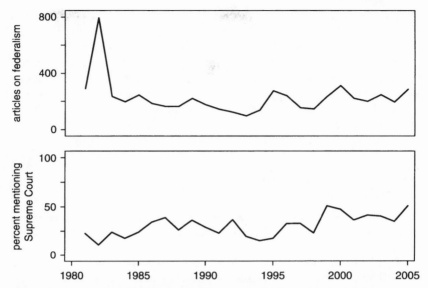

Figure 9.1. Coverage of Federalism in the *New York Times* and the *Washington Post*, 1981–2005. Source: Lexis-Nexis.

statutes on federalism grounds after sixty years of deference, policy makers largely looked the other way. With the exception of *Lopez*, Congress did not recraft legislation to achieve the original policy goals within constitutional constraints set by the Court, even though in many cases it would have been feasible to do so (Dinan 2002).

Media coverage also did not signal to the public that an important change was taking place in the balance of governmental authority. Figure 9.1 shows coverage of federalism issues in the *New York Times* and the *Washington Post* from 1981 through 2005. The top line shows the total number of articles in both newspapers mentioning "federalism" or "states' rights," culled to include only articles about the United States. The lower line shows the percentage of those articles that mention "Supreme Court." The graph illustrates that during this period, and especially after 1995, courts increasingly became the focus for activity related to federalism. In the early 1980s, just one in every five articles about federalism mentioned the Court, rising to more than half the articles in 2005. But while the Court's efforts to set constraints on national power have received greater attention in hindsight than did the Reagan administration's devolution policies, the public received less information about the Court's activities. Overall media attention to federalism reached its peak in 1982, when President Reagan proposed in his State of the Union speech to turn over more than forty federal programs to state and local governments. The *Times* and the *Post* featured nearly four times as many articles about federalism that year than their average through the rest of the period. The level of coverage after

1982 remained fairly constant, with annual fluctuations. Indeed, the papers wrote less about federalism during the early 1990s, as the Court began its federalism charge, than during the years immediately prior. Coverage picked up somewhat beginning in 2000 but remained far less extensive than during President Reagan's devolution efforts. With the media dedicating little attention to the Court's efforts to protect and expand state sovereignty, Americans had few clear signals upon which to form opinions about the allocation of power under federalism.

Consistency and Contradiction in Public Opinion about Federalism

Given the low level of attention that Americans dedicate to politics, we would not expect to see evidence of strongly held attitudes about the distribution of responsibilities and authority among levels of government. Indeed, one reasonably might ask whether the public makes distinctions at all among federal, state, and local jurisdictions in assessing governmental performance.

Results from previous research are mixed. It does appear that people make distinctions in their affect toward different levels of government. Although trust in the federal government has declined since the 1960s, attitudes toward subnational governments have held steady or even improved (Cole & Kincaid 2006; Conlan 1988; Hetherington & Nugent 2001; Reeves & Glendening 1976; Roeder 1994). State and local governments historically inspired little public confidence, but surveys conducted in recent decades reveal rising public support relative to feelings toward Washington. Given a choice among levels of government, survey respondents are increasingly likely to express faith and confidence in states and localities (Hetherington & Nugent 2001) and to perceive them as being closer to the people (Conlan 1988) and giving more for the public's money (Cole & Kincaid 2006).

A few studies have attempted to explain support for states. Using data from a 1995 survey on trust in government conducted by the *Washington Post*, the Kaiser Family Foundation, and Harvard University, Uslaner (2001) shows that trust in government is highly correlated across institutions; respondents are consistent in expressing trust or lack of trust in both state and federal governments. In a forced choice, white, conservative, and more highly educated respondents were more likely to prefer states over the federal government. Hetherington and Nugent (2001) examine whether support for states can be explained by attitudes toward the federal government. In a multivariate analysis using the 1996 ANES survey, they find that low levels of trust in Washington make it more likely that a respondent will express more faith and confidence in state and local governments, rather than the federal government, in a forced choice. Republican partisanship and conservative ideology also predict support for subnational governments in their analysis, but measures of actual state capacity and effectiveness do not. Historically, race has played an important role in public opinion about federalism because of the framing of slavery and segregationist policies as issues of states' rights (Jennings & Zeigler 1970; Riker 1964), but analyses of more recent surveys have revealed no evidence of greater support for the federal government among African Americans (Hetherington & Nugent 2001; Schneider & Jacoby 2003).

Generalized support for subnational governments does not necessarily translate into calls for devolution of policy responsibility, however. Public attitudes about the proper allocation of governmental authority are weakly held and inconsistent. As Cantril and Cantril (1999) describe, "Clear and abiding preferences are hard to find in public opinion regarding which level of government should take the lead in dealing with different issues. Questions along these lines have been included in polls for years and frequently have produced widely varying results" (37). In their own 1997 national survey, respondents expressed a preference for reduced federal activity in broad terms but supported a larger federal role when asked about specific government functions. A survey of Michigan residents produced the same result: respondents supported devolution in the abstract but endorsed federal involvement in nearly all the specific functions the survey named (Thompson & Elling 1999). Although Schneider and Jacoby (2003) find a latent attitude dimension that predisposes individuals to support or oppose national over state policy leadership, the relationship between people's general beliefs and their specific attitudes about federal power and responsibilities is weak.

Some of the inconsistency evident in attitudes about policy responsibility may arise from question wording, which often asks about broad policy domains that are in fact shared responsibilities among multiple levels of government. These questions suggest a dual federalism model in which federal and state powers are clearly specified and well defined. The public may prefer a marble cake federalism model that rests more on intergovernmental cooperation rather than divided powers (Grodzins 1966; Thompson & Elling 1999). It is difficult to discern whether inconsistency in responses is evidence of nonopinion or an indication that the question wording in surveys is not capturing the public's true preference for shared policy responsibility among governments (Reeves 1987).

Perceptions of government performance also may contribute to attitudes about the allocation of authority. Using data from national surveys conducted between 1987 and 1989, Roeder (1994) finds a relationship between people's assessments of the levels of government and their preference about who should have responsibility for specific policies. Arceneaux (2005) shows that individuals make determinations about the level of government that has the greatest policy responsibility, and if they are satisfied with that government's performance, then they favor giving it more responsibility. Opinions about who should have power are based in large part on perceptions of who does have power, whether or not those perceptions are correct. Thus it is possible that how people perceive the existing distribution of government power explains some of the inconsistency in opinion about policy responsibility.

In short, much remains unknown regarding public opinion about federalism. The states do not appear to have experienced the sharp decline in public confidence that the federal government has suffered in recent decades, but the improved stature of subnational governments may be attributable in part to survey question wording that often requires respondents to make a choice among levels of government. Increased pessimism about politics in Washington may produce higher estimations of state and local governments by default. The public seems to form opinions about the allocation of power and responsibility based on perceptions of governmental performance, but the resulting opinions are weakly held and may be contradictory. We know little about public assessments of the power of the federal government.

The analysis that follows makes several contributions to the state of knowledge on public opinion about federalism. First, it assembles data from dozens of surveys in order to track public opinion over time and detect trends that correspond with political and legal efforts to change the balance of power between national and state governments. It compares trends across poll questions to evaluate the relationship between trust in different levels of government and assessments of their performance. The analysis then directs attention to perceptions of federal government power, an important element of public opinion about federalism and one that has received little previous attention in the literature. Finally, I examine the role of race in contemporary political attitudes about federalism and show that race is no longer decisive in determining support for states' rights.

Public Attitudes about Trust and Government Performance

Measurement issues are critical in analyzing public opinion about federalism. The public's affection for an institution is not necessarily consistent with its assessment of that institution's performance, and it is not clear what relationship either of those opinions has with attitudes about the abstract principle related to the division of power.

In general, Americans' support for state government has grown over time. Figure 9.2 shows the change in attitudes over sixty years about where power should be located in the American system. In a 1995 survey conducted by the Council for Excellence in Government (CEG), 64% of respondents reported favoring a theory of government that concentrates power in state government rather than in the federal government.[6] Preference for state over federal power had risen from a 56% majority responding to the same question in a 1981 Gallup poll. When Gallup asked the question during the New Deal, respondents expressed greater support for a division of power that favored Washington. As shown in the figure, in 1937 a plurality (46%) preferred federal to state authority. Support for concentrating power in the states has thus grown by a remarkable 30 percentage points since the New Deal.[7]

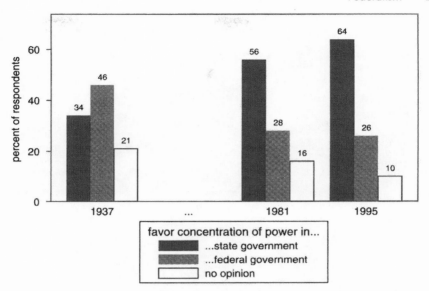

Figure 9.2. Americans' Favored Theory of Government, 1937, 1981, and 1995. Question wording: Which theory of government do you favor—concentration of power in the federal government or concentration of power in state government? Sources: Gallup (1937, 1981); Council for Excellence in Government (1995).

Consistent with the more widely shared preference for state power in the abstract, the public expects that shifting policy responsibility to the states will lead to better performance. In 1995, 50% of CEG respondents thought that shifting responsibility for some domestic programs from federal to state government would improve the quality of those programs. Only 9% predicted that quality would decline, and 34% anticipated no change.[8] This poll was conducted in the midst of the debate over welfare reform, a period when the media regularly featured stories about successful state welfare programs. Nine years earlier, Cambridge Reports/Research International asked a similar question but included the possibility of shifting programs to state and local governments. Respondents to that survey were less optimistic about the capacity of subnational governments: a plurality of 34% expected program quality to decline, and just 27% anticipated an improvement.

This is a surprisingly low level of support for devolution during Reagan's second term, so the result may reveal more about Americans' confidence in local governments than their attitudes toward federalism. But a question-wording effect also would be surprising, because the public typically gives high scores on the performance of local governments. When respondents have to make a forced choice about the level of government that does the best job in dealing with the problems it faces, they are most likely to name local governments.[9] States also perform well, but over the course of three surveys

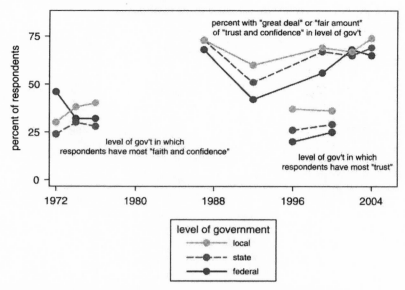

Figure 9.3. Trust in Local, State, and Federal Governments, 1972–2005.
Question wording: see text. Sources: ACIR, ANES, Democratic Leadership
Council, NBC News/Wall Street Journal poll, and Cole, Kincaid et al., 2002, 2004.

conducted between 1981 and 1997, a plurality always gave the highest performance assessment to local governments. The gap between subnational and
national governments expanded during that period, and by 1997 just 14% of
respondents thought the federal government did the best job among the three
levels of government.

Previous studies have focused on trust in state governments as a measure of public support for federalism (Hetherington & Nugent 2001; Uslaner
2001). States have not suffered the sharp declines in public trust that affected
attitudes toward the federal government in recent decades. The topmost three
lines in Figure 9.3 show the percentage of respondents in a series of polls conducted between 1987 and 2004 who reported having "a great deal" or "a fair
amount" of trust and confidence in each level of government to carry out
its responsibilities.[10] The general trend is the same for all levels of government: a decline in trust in the early 1990s, rebounding later that decade with
a continued rise through 2004. The dip in support is much larger for the federal government, however, and smallest for local governments. Confidence in
states fell between federal and local governments in 1992, but by 1999 states
ranked nearly as high as local governments. The one departure from the trend
is the sharp increase in trust in the federal government reported in 2002, likely
stemming from a rally effect following the September 11 attacks. By 2004,
the federal government again ranked lowest among levels of government but
enjoyed higher levels of trust than during the 1990s.

The other sets of lines in Figure 9.3 depict trust data during two shorter time periods, in this case as responses to a forced-choice question asking survey respondents which level of government inspires the most faith and trust. The lines on the left display data from three ANES surveys conducted in the 1970s, and those on the right illustrate responses from two more recent surveys conducted in 1996 and 2000.[11] As the Watergate scandal was just beginning to unfold in 1972, nearly half of all ANES respondents expressed the most faith and confidence in the federal government. Two years later, faith in the federal government had dropped off sharply, mostly to the benefit of local government, and it changed little by 1976. Trust in Washington suffered another decline over the next twenty years, however, and opinion expressed in the two more recent surveys has a pattern similar to the longer series on political trust. The federal government ranked well below states and localities in the public's esteem, but its scores showed some improvement between 1996 and 2000.

On the whole, it appears that public attitudes toward states and localities respond to some of the same forces that affect opinion about the federal government but that the federal government is more susceptible to strong opinion shifts.[12] The most dramatic shifts that occurred in recent decades are attributable at least in part to Watergate and the September 11 attacks, highly salient political events. But those events cannot explain the steady decline in public support for the federal government through the 1980s and early 1990s. State governments suffered some loss of public trust during this period, but to a much lesser extent. And if we focus on government performance, assessments of the federal government showed no signs of rebounding as of the late 1990s, while opinion about the states was rising.

How do these attitudes toward individual levels of government affect public opinion about federalism? Does distrust in the federal government make it more likely that people will view the federal government as too strong? And do perceptions of federal power respond to political and judicial efforts to change the scope of that power? Whittington (2001) argues that increased confidence in states during a period of declining trust in the federal government helped create a favorable environment for the Rehnquist Court's federalism revolution. It is not clear that the causal relationship operates in reverse: trust in states and the federal government have moved in parallel since the late 1970s, and it is difficult to say whether the Court's protection of state sovereignty contributed to the continued decline in perceptions of federal government performance in the 1990s. To assess the influence of politics, trust, and the Court on public opinion about federalism, it is necessary to focus on a survey question that directly measures attitudes about federal power.

Public Opinion about Federal Power

The small body of literature on public opinion about federalism has focused on measures of affect toward different levels of government and judgments about the allocation of specific policy responsibilities. These attitudes have only a loose connection to political and judicial efforts to scale back the scope of national authority. Survey respondents might express low confidence in the federal government but still prefer centralization of power to the variable policy outcomes that would arise under state sovereignty. They might support state funding and administration of education or welfare policy but still see an important role for the federal government in protecting individual liberties and civil rights in all policy areas. Questions that specifically address the scope of federal authority should reveal more about public response to changes in the balance of power under federalism.

Citizens seem to have taken note of the expansion of federal power over the latter half of the twentieth century. In a 1964 survey sponsored by the Institute for International Social Research, the 40% of respondents who said the federal government was interfering too much with state and local matters were outnumbered by the 48% who disagreed.[13] A 1997 Pew Research Center survey showed a 53% majority agreeing that interference was excessive. The majority opinion was weakly held, however, with just 12% of respondents reporting that they "completely agree" instead of "mostly agree."[14]

The overall rise in perceptions of national supremacy that is evident in these questions about federal interference conceals important fluctuations in opinion during this period. Figure 9.4 shows the percentage of respondents agreeing that the federal government is too powerful in polls conducted by seven different survey houses between 1970 and 2005, accompanied by a smoothed trend line.[15] The survey houses employed different versions of the question, but the trend in responses is consistent. Just after Watergate in the early 1970s, the percentage of Americans saying that the federal government was too strong sharply increased, reaching nearly half the respondents in the 1980 ANES survey. Concern about federal government power dropped off during the Reagan administration and then rose again through the 1990s to reach its peak during President Clinton's second term. It had already begun to recede prior to the September 11 attacks that galvanized support for strong national action, support that seemed to be in decline by the mid-2000s.

The trend in perceptions of federal government power during this period suggests that the public may be more attentive to political efforts regarding federalism than to judicial efforts. Concern about federal power reached a low during the 1980s, when President Reagan cut federal domestic spending and devolved grant-making authority to the states. Intense media coverage raised public awareness about these activities. In contrast, perceptions of excessive federal power were widespread during the period when the Rehnquist Court focused its attention on federalism. These perceptions eased in the early 2000s following a set of important Court rulings, but the rulings probably had less influence than a new presidential administration and heightened public concern about national security.

Few survey questions tap attitudes about the role of different institutions in safeguarding federalism. Polls conducted in 1982 showed strong support—topping 60% for most question wordings—for the Reagan administration's

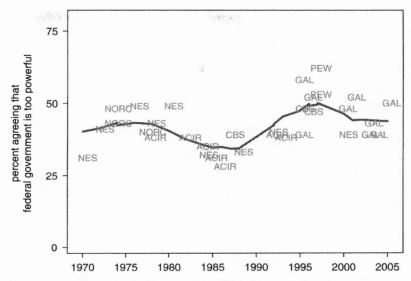

Figure 9.4.   Belief That Federal Government Is Too Powerful, 1970–2005.
Question wording and sources: see text.

ambitious devolution proposals. But the public also seems to support a role for the Supreme Court in guarding the interests of states. Anticipating retirements from the Rehnquist Court, in 2003 ABC News asked whether the next nominee should favor giving state governments more authority than the federal government or the reverse. Fifty-seven percent of respondents hoped for a nominee who would endorse the authority of states.[16]

The public seems to accept a role for both political and judicial institutions in negotiating the boundaries of federal government power. It is possible that people's attitudes about federal power derive from their assessments of current political and judicial leaders. Another factor may be an individual's generalized feelings of trust toward the political system as a whole. Trust and affect toward political institutions are probably correlated with one another, however, and other factors such as partisanship and political ideology are also likely to have an influence on opinion about the power of the federal government. The following section introduces multivariate analysis in order to disentangle these relationships and measure the impact of both long-term, generalized attitudes and contemporary political assessments on perceptions of federal power.

The Structure of Public Opinion about Federal Power

The models employ data from ANES surveys conducted around the 1980, 1988, and 2000 elections to examine the structure of public opinion regarding federal power. This set of surveys allows comparison of opinion at three points in time: the beginning and end of the Reagan administration and the conclusion of Clinton's presidency. Intervening and later years are not included because relevant questions did not appear on ANES surveys in those years. The dependent variable is a dichotomous measure indicating agreement with the proposition that the government in Washington is getting too powerful for the good of the country and the individual person. The analysis includes only respondents who indicated in a filtering question that they have an opinion on this issue; excluding nonresponses removes between a third and half of the ANES sample in each of the three years. Across the three surveys, 69% of those responding consider federal power to be excessive.

The probit models regress perception of federal power on three sets of independent variables. The first set includes demographic characteristics of individuals, including race, residence in the South, gender, income, education, and age. The model also interacts race with residence in the South to fully assess the role of race and region in contemporary attitudes about states' rights. The second set of variables contains political and social attitudes. Party identification is a 7-point scale with strong Republicans scored at the highest value. Political ideology is measured using a liberal-conservative index constructed from group feeling thermometer scores that survey respondents assign to liberals and conservatives. It ranges from 0 for the most liberal respondents to 97 for the strongest conservatives.[17] Racial affect is an indicator of negative attitudes toward African Americans, again to evaluate the legacy of federal civil rights legislation in influencing attitudes about federalism. It is measured as the difference in the group feeling thermometer scores assigned to whites and blacks.[18] Also included among political and social attitudes is an index constructed from four questions measuring trust in government.[19] The trust index is scored from 0 (least trusting) to 100 (most trusting). The final set of variables measures affect toward political institutions, as measured with feeling thermometer questions that ask respondents to rate the president, Congress, and the Supreme Court on a scale of 0 (cold) to 97 (warm).

Table 9.1 presents the structure of public opinion about federal power for each survey year, as well as estimates from an analysis using pooled data across all three survey years. Results are shown as first differences, or differences in the predicted probability of agreeing that the government in Washington is too powerful associated with a shift from the minimum to the maximum value of each independent variable, holding all other variables at their mean values.[20]

Holding constant political and social attitudes and affect toward national institutions, the demographic characteristics of individual survey respondents exercise very little direct effect on perceptions of federal power. Only two of the variables have coefficients that are statistically significant in any of the models. Gender is the most important of the demographic variables, with an effect that is significant at the 95% confidence level in 1988 and in the pooled model. Across all survey years, women are 4 percentage points less likely than men

Table 9.1
Determinants of Public Opinion about Federal Power, 1980–2000

Variables	1980	1988	2000	Pooled
Demographic Characteristics				
Black (among Southerners)	−.04	−.12	−.02	−.09
Black (among non-Southerners)	−.19	−.12	.06	−.11
South (among blacks)	.14	.05	−.13	.04
South (among nonblacks)	−.01	.05	−.04	.02
Female	−.03	−.07*	−.03	−.05*
Income	−.07	−.12	−.01	−.06
Education	.11	.11	−.25***	−.01
Age	.12	−.10	−.01	−.00
Political and Social Attitudes				
Party identification	.18**	−.10	.02	.07*
Political ideology	.52***	.43***	.74***	.59***
Racial affect	−.18	−.18	−.20	−.15
Trust index	−.33***	−.55***	−.54***	−.50***
Affect toward Political Institutions				
President	−.01	.07	−.35***	−.18***
Congress	−.22*	−.11	−.26*	−.14*
Supreme Court	−.14	−.28**	.01	−.18***
N	660	773	668	2,101
Log likelihood	−299.15	−459.11	−326.56	−1124.17
Pseudo R^2	.15	.09	.24	.14

Cell entries show the difference in predicted probability of agreeing that the government in Washington is too powerful associated with a shift from the minimum to the maximum value of each independent variable, holding all other variables at their mean values. Probabilities are based on estimates from probit models. Estimates are significant at *p <.05, **p <.01, ***p <.001.

Question wording: Some people are afraid the government in Washington is getting too powerful for the good of the country and the individual person. Others feel that the government in Washington is not getting too strong. Do you have an opinion on this, or not?

Source: American National Election Studies.

to perceive the federal government as too powerful, controlling for political attitudes. Education has a powerful effect in 2000 only, when college graduates were 25 percentage points less likely to express concern about national power than people who had completed grade school or less. That effect is not evident in other survey years or in the pooled model. Confirming the results of other recent studies, the effect of race on attitudes about federal power is not significant in any of these models, nor is region, age, or income. These variables may indirectly affect opinion about federal power through their influence on political orientation and assessments of political leaders, however, a possibility that will be explored in more detail later.

Political and social attitudes are more powerful in explaining opinion about federalism. The most important political predispositions are ideology and trust, which have large and highly significant effects in all years. In the pooled model, the most conservative respondents are 58 percentage points more likely than those furthest on the left to perceive the government in Washington as too strong, even with partisan orientation and other political attitudes held constant. The influence of ideology varies over time, and its importance reaches a peak at the close of the Clinton administration in 2000. Party identification is less important; its influence is restricted to 1980, when strong Republicans were 18 points more likely to express concern about government power than strong Democrats. In 1988 and 2000, partisanship does not exercise an independent effect on opinion about federalism. Generalized trust toward government makes it less likely that an individual will perceive the federal government as too strong. This relationship holds across all survey years but is least powerful in 1980, when perceptions of excess federal power were widely held. Consistent with the results on race, racial affect demonstrates no direct effect in any model, and moreover the direction of the relationship between racial affect and attitudes about federal power are counter to expectation.

Finally, the models estimate the relationship between Americans' feelings toward national political institutions and their attitudes about national power. These contemporary assessments have less influence than long-held political beliefs, but opinion about the leadership in Washington helps to shape perceptions of the power of the federal government. In the pooled model, "warm" feelings toward each branch of federal government directly reduce the likelihood of perceiving federal power as excessive. A shift from 0 to 97 on the feeling thermometer score for the president or Congress is associated with a decline of approximately 16 percentage points in the likelihood of saying that the government in Washington is too strong. Affect toward the Supreme Court is somewhat more influential, with respondents who are most supportive of the Court being 20 points less likely to express concern about federal power.

These results offer evidence that public perceptions of federal power reflect both long-term, generalized attitudes toward the political system and more immediate assessments of national institutions. However, to the extent that Americans consider the performance of current political leaders when evaluating the state of federalism, they do not appear to respond directly to the efforts of those leaders to alter the balance of power between the national government and the states. If those efforts directly influenced attitudes about federalism, we should see stronger relationships between affect toward an institution and perception of national power subsequent to action by the institution. For example, if the Rehnquist Court's federalism revolution changed public perceptions of federal power, then people who view the Court in a positive light would be most likely to respond. We should see a relationship between esteem for the Court and concern about the strength of the national government—either a positive relationship if the Court's actions heightened concern about federal power or a negative relationship if the public felt that the Court's actions had solved the problem. In fact, affect toward the Supreme Court has its strongest relationship with perception of federal power prior to the Rehnquist Court's initial decisions broadening state sovereignty. More-over, warm feelings toward the president have no relationship with opinion about federal strength at the start and close of the Reagan administration, before and after a period of executive activity to address the size and scope of the federal government, but they do in 2000. Assessments of political leaders help shape opinion about the scope of federal authority, but not in response to the efforts of those leaders to change federal authority.

In sum, these results suggest that perceptions of the scope of national power have little connection to specific government activities—Court deci-sions or policy changes—that actually alter the reach of federal authority. Instead, these perceptions are a product of relatively stable political and social beliefs. Holding other factors constant, the relationship between trust in gov-ernment and satisfaction with federal power is strong. More variable opinions about specific institutions also play a role in explaining perceptions of fed-eral authority, but not in a pattern that would indicate responsiveness to the actions of those institutions on issues related to federalism. Without panel data measuring individuals' perceptions of federal power over time, it is impossible to unravel the causal direction in many of these relationships. Moreover, with the exception of the model analyzing data from 2000, the overall fit of these models is fairly weak, with the pseudo-R^2 for each model falling between .09 and .25. However, the models do shed light on the role of political attitudes and affect toward political institutions in explaining public opinion regarding the scope of national power.

The Role of Race in Contemporary Public Opinion about Federalism

Given the importance of civil rights policy in structuring discussions about federalism over much of the twentieth century, it is worthwhile to consider more carefully the role of race in explaining contemporary attitudes about federal power. While the federal government and the Supreme Court were leading the way in protecting the rights of African Americans in the South during the 1950s and 1960s, advocating for the rights of states was viewed as a statement of racial intolerance. Indeed, Riker (1964) viewed racial con-siderations as so essential to the operation of federalism in the United States that it prompted him to question whether the costs of state autonomy might outweigh its many benefits. As he famously concluded his study of federalism, "[I]f in the United States one approves of Southern white racists, one should approve of American federalism.... [I]f in the United States one disapproves of racism, one should disapprove of federalism" (155).

The analysis presented in the previous section suggests that the impor-tance of race in shaping opinion about federalism has diminished with time. Opposition to a strong national government no longer seems to be equiva-lent to endorsement of Jim Crow laws or other discriminatory public policies.

African American respondents in the samples analyzed here were no less likely than respondents of other races to agree that the federal government is too powerful, regardless of whether they lived in the South or elsewhere. Respondents expressing more favorable opinion toward whites than blacks were no more likely to demonstrate concern about federal encroachment.

Is race no longer relevant in conversations about federalism? A few recent studies have indicated that race does not have a direct effect on differences in trust across levels of government (Hetherington & Nugent 2001) or opinion about the division of responsibilities between governments (Schneider & Jacoby 2003).[21] But important differences might still exist between members of different racial groups or people with varying levels of racial prejudice because of the influence of racial considerations on intervening variables such as ideology or opinion about national leaders. These recent studies and the models presented earlier both estimate only the direct effects of race, holding constant political attitudes that develop after the determination of an individual's race. To fully understand how race structures contemporary public opinion about federalism, we must consider the indirect effects of race as it operates through intervening variables, as well as its direct effect on attitudes about federal power.

To measure the total effect of race on opinion about federal power, the following analysis employs a block recursive approach that estimates the effects of each set of variables described earlier in causal order.[22] The data set for this analysis is the pooled ANES data from the 1980, 1988, and 2000 elections. The first regression in this model includes only a respondent's demographic characteristics, including race, residence in the South, and an interaction between them. This equation estimates the total effect of each characteristic on perceptions of federal power. The second equation adds in long-term political and social attitudes, and the third equation introduces affect toward national institutions. The complete equation including all three sets of variables measures the direct effect of each variable, and it produces the pooled sample results that appeared in Table 9.1.

Table 9.2 presents first differences in the predicted probability of agreeing that the government in Washington is too strong as each independent variable changes from its lowest to highest value, holding values of the other variables in the equation constant at their mean. The total effect of each variable appears in bold. Subtracting the direct effect that appears in the final column from the variable's total effect produces an estimate of the indirect effect of that variable as it operates through intervening attitudes and/or assessments of political institutions.

The model indicates that race continues to play a role in opinion formation about federalism but racial prejudice does not. African Americans are 18 percentage points less likely to perceive the federal government as too strong, 20 points if they live in the South. The effect of race is mediated through intervening variables, however, primarily political ideology. Blacks tend to be more liberal and therefore more likely to support a strong and active national

Table 9.2
A Multi-stage Model of Opinion about Federal Power, 1980–2000

Variables			
Demographic Characteristics			
Black (among Southerners)	−.20***	−.12	−.09
Black (among non-Southerners)	−.18***	−.13*	−.11
South (among blacks)	.02	.02	.04
South (among nonblacks)	.04	.01	.02
Female	−.04	−.05**	−.05*
Income	−.02	−.06	−.06
Education	−.07	.01	−.01
Age	−.03	−.04	−.00
Political and Social Attitudes			
Party identification		.09*	.07*
Political ideology		.58***	.59***
Racial affect		−.17	−.15
Trust index		−.61***	−.50***
Affect toward Political Institutions			
President			−.18***
Congress			−.14
Supreme Court			−.18***
N	2,101	2,101	2,101
Log likelihood	−1294.41	−1152.09	−1124.17
Pseudo R²	.01	.12	.14

Cell entries show the difference in predicted probability of agreeing that the government in Washington is too powerful associated with a shift from the minimum to the maximum value of each independent variable, holding all other variables at their mean values. Probabilities are based on estimates from probit models using pooled data from the 1980, 1988, and 2000 ANES surveys. Estimates are significant at *p <.05, **p <.01, ***p <.001.

Question wording: see Table 9.1.

government. Controlling for ideology and other political and social orientations, the effect of race declines for all respondents and loses significance among Southerners. African Americans in the rest of the country remain less critical of the strength of the federal government, even holding ideology constant, but the effect of race loses significance after introducing controls for attitudes about political institutions. The positive feelings that African Americans have for Congress and the Court mediate the effect of race on perceptions of federal power.

Thus although race does not appear to have a direct influence on opinion about federalism, it is an important factor in the development of political attitudes that help explain opinion about the strength of Washington. The same does not hold true for racial prejudice. Riker's (1964) assessment of the importance of racism in shaping opinion about federalism no longer seems to hold true: using a simple measure of racial prejudice, the total effect of viewing whites more favorably than blacks is insignificant.[23]

Conclusion

As the size and scope of the federal government expanded over the latter half of the twentieth century, more Americans began to perceive federal power as excessive and to support a concept of federalism that favors concentrating power with the states. Within this long-term trend, opinion about federal power fluctuated periodically. The sharpest changes in opinion occurred after Watergate and after the September 11 attacks, but polling data provide some evidence to suggest that public opinion responded to real shifts in the balance of power between federal and state governments when those shifts received public attention. Americans reacted favorably to President Reagan's initial proposals for devolving federal power to the states, and over the course of the Reagan administration, perceptions that the federal government was too powerful declined markedly. A similar trend is not evident in response to the Rehnquist Court's federalism decisions, which received far less attention from Congress and the media.

Much remains unexplained by an account that focuses only on national political events, however. In this chapter, I have considered individual-level factors that contribute to the structure of public opinion on issues of federalism. In particular, I have compared the relative influence of long-held political attitudes and short-term assessments of national institutions. People's stable orientations toward government matter the most in explaining their assessment of federal government power; liberal ideology and high levels of political trust contribute to lower levels of concern about the strength of the government in Washington. Affect toward political institutions matters as well. Although the relationships between opinion about federal power and perceptions of each branch of government vary over time, overall the president, Congress, and the Court have nearly equal importance in helping to shape attitudes about federal power.

Thus the performance of the Supreme Court does have an influence on how Americans perceive issues of federalism, even if the public does not respond specifically to the Court's federalism decisions. And while public opinion about federalism is often inconsistent and weakly held, the Court appears to be in step with the general mood of Americans regarding the scope of federal power. When the public expressed little concern about the strength of the national government, the Court largely deferred to Congress's efforts to expand its own authority. The Court then allowed the executive branch to take the lead in scaling back federal activity and devolving more policy responsibility to the states. Watergate interfered with President Nixon's efforts in this area, but the public responded favorably to the Reagan administration's devolution agenda, at least as originally conceived. The Court did not take its own action to rein in federal authority until the 1990s, when public concern about the power of the national government began to rise once more. It is unlikely that the Court took signals from public opinion as it reached into this complex area of constitutional law, but the Court nonetheless acted in a manner that was consistent with the latent views of the mass public.

At the time of this writing, it is unclear whether the Roberts Court will continue to use its power to protect the states from federal intrusions, return to the nationalist approach of Rehnquist's predecessors, or simply turn its attention to other constitutional matters. If it attempts to continue the legacy of the federalism revolution, its actions would probably receive the quiet consent of a public that supports the states.

Notes

I am grateful to Bill Draper for tracking down polling data on federalism and to Yphtach Lelkes for valuable research assistance. This chapter benefited from helpful comments by the editors.

1. Samuel H. Beer, "Introduction," in Conlan (1988), p. xii.

2. *Gregory v. Ashcroft* (1991), *Alden v. Maine* (1999), *Kimel v. Florida Board of Regents* (2000), *Board of Trustees of the University of Alabama v. Garrett* (2001).

3. *College Savings Bank v. Florida Prepaid Postsecondary Education Expense Board* (1999).

4. *New York v. United States* (1992).

5. It is notable that in a political landscape littered with charges of judicial activism, the Court's leadership on federalism also did not prompt questions about whether the Court should be determining the allocation of powers between national and state governments. The Court itself questioned that role in *Garcia*. The majority endorsed the political safeguards approach to federalism (Kramer 2000; Wechsler 1954) in arguing that the limitation on federal authority is the participation of states in the political process: "State sovereign interests...are more properly protected by procedural safeguards inherent in the structure of the federal system than by judicially created limitations on federal power" (*Garcia v. SAMTA*). The pro-federalism majority on the Rehnquist Court clearly rejected that view.

6. Question wording: "Which theory of government do you favor—concentration of power in the federal government or concentration of power in state government?"

7. Not shown in the figure are results from a 1936 Gallup poll that posed the same question but apparently did not offer respondents a "no opinion" option. In that poll, Americans favored federal authority to state authority by 56% to 44%.

8. Question wording in 1995: "If responsibility for some domestic programs were shifted from the federal to state government, do you think the quality of the programs shifted to the state would get better, get worse, or stay about the same?" In 1986: "As some services and programs are shifted from the federal government to state and local governments, do you think the quality of those services and programs will get better, get worse, or will the quality of those services and programs stay about the same?"

9. Question wording from CBS News/New York Times polls conducted in 1981, 1986, and 1997: "Which level of government—federal, state, or local—does the best job of dealing with the problems it faces?"

10. Data from 1987 and 1992 were collected by the U.S. Advisory Commission on Intergovernmental Relations (ACIR), which ceased operations in 1996. Later surveys were conducted by Cole, Kincaid, and their colleagues (Cole & Kincaid 2000; Cole, Kincaid, & Parkin 2002; Cole, Kincaid, & Rodriguez 2004; Kincaid & Cole 2005) using the ACIR instrument. The question asked, "Overall, how much trust and confidence do you have in the federal government, your state government, and your local government [respectively] to do a good job in carrying out its responsibilities?"

11. Data from 1972, 1974, and 1976 are from an American National Election Studies (ANES) question asking, "We find that people differ in how much faith and confidence they have in various levels of government in this country. In your case, do you have more faith and confidence in the national government, the government of this state, or in the local government around here?" Data sources and question wording for the remaining years:

- 1996, Democratic Leadership Council: "Thinking generally, which level of government do you trust more—the federal government, your state government, or your local government?"
- 2000, NBC News/Wall Street Journal: "Which level of government do you currently have the most trust in—the federal government, your state government, or your local government?"

12. Two methodological factors might contribute volatility to public opinion about the federal government. First, most of the questions that survey organizations have repeated over time require respondents to choose which level of government they trust the most or which does the best job. If these questions in fact measure approval of the federal government rather than independent assessments of each level of government, then states and local governments both become default categories. As support for the federal government declines, the esteem expressed for both states and localities rises, but the change for each is smaller as they share the respondents who do not favor Washington. Alternatively, if responses do reflect separate assessments of each government level, scores for the federal government should be most volatile because the object of assessment is constant across respondents. Opinion about the fifty states and thousands of localities should average out, based on the varied performance of those governments. A good year in Sacramento might produce high trust scores for state government from California respondents, while stalemate in Richmond prompts Virginians to lose confidence in their state leadership. In the national samples for the surveys discussed here, there is good reason to expect sharper opinion changes for the federal government as the public responds to national political debate and real conditions of national security and economic prosperity.

13. Question wording: "Here are several statements that people critical of the government sometimes make. Just tell me whether, in general, you agree or disagree. The federal government is interfering too much in state and local matters. Do you agree or disagree?"

14. Question wording: "I'm going to read you a few statements some people have made about government. The federal government is interfering too much in state and local matters. Do you completely agree, mostly agree, mostly disagree, or completely disagree?"

15. Question wording:

- ACIR (Advisory Commission on Intergovernmental Relations): "Which of these statements comes closest to your view about government power today—the federal government has too much power, the federal government is using about the right amount of power meeting today's needs, or the federal government should use its power more vigorously to promote the well being of all segments of the people?"

- CBS (CBS News/New York Times): "Think about the relationship between the states and the federal government. Does the federal government have too much power, do the states have too much power, or is the balance about right?"
- GAL (Gallup), 1995, 1996, 2000, 2001, 2003: "Do you think the federal government has become so large and powerful that it poses an immediate threat to the rights and freedoms of ordinary citizens, or not?"
- GAL (Gallup), 1995, 2002, 2003, 2005: "Do you think the federal government today has too much power, has about the right amount of power, or has too little power?"
- ANES (American National Election Studies): "Some people are afraid the government in Washington is getting too powerful for the good of the country and the individual person. Others feel that the government in Washington is not getting too strong. Do you have an opinion on this or not?...What is your feeling, do you think the government is getting too powerful or do you think the government is not getting too strong?"
- NORC (National Opinion Research Center), 1974: "Some people are afraid the government in Washington is getting too powerful for the good of the country and the individual person. Others feel that the government in Washington is not getting too strong for the good of the country. Have you been interested in this enough to favor one side over the other?...What is your feeling, do you think the government is getting too powerful or do you think the government is not getting too strong?"
- NORC (National Opinion Research Center), 1974, 1978: "Some people are afraid the government in Washington is getting too powerful for the good of the country and the individual person. They would be at point 1. Others feel that the government in Washington is not getting too strong for the good of the country. They would be at point 7. Where would you place yourself?" (1–3 coded as agreement).
- PEW (Pew Research Center): "The federal government is too powerful. Do you completely agree, mostly agree, mostly disagree, or completely disagree?"

16. Question wording: "Do you think the next person nominated to join the U.S. Supreme Court should be someone who favors giving state governments more authority than the federal government, or someone who favors giving the federal government more authority than the state government?...Do you feel that way strongly, or somewhat?"

17. I rely on the liberal-conservative thermometer index rather than self-reported ideology because there is less missing data for the index variable. This is especially true for 2000, when the NES administered its traditional 7-point scale question on ideology to only half its respondents; the other half of the sample received a branching series of questions to measure ideology. The main results reported here are consistent using either the index or the 7-point scale.

18. The racial affect measure is a simple indicator of racial prejudice (Sears et al. 1997), but unlike some alternative measures, it avoids confounding the analysis by introducing preferences about whether the government should act to ameliorate the effects of racial discrimination.

19. Four items comprise the trust index: (1) "How much of the time do you think you can trust the government in Washington to do what is right—just about always, most of the time or only some of the time?"; (2) "Would you say the government is pretty much run by a few big interests looking out for themselves or that it is run for the benefit of all the people?"; (3) "Do you think that people in the government waste a lot of money we pay in taxes, waste some of it, or don't waste very much of it?"; and (4) "Do you think that quite a few of the people running the government are crooked, not very many are, or do you think hardly any of them are crooked?" Scale reliability (Cronbach's α) for the index is .66.

20. Predicted probabilities are based on a probit model estimated using the CLARIFY routine in STATA (King, Tomz, & Wittenberg 2000; Tomz, Wittenberg, & King 2001).

21. In fact, Schneider and Jacoby (2003) produce the unexpected result that blacks in South Carolina are more likely to prefer state government leadership in a variety of policy areas.

22. For more detail on this approach, see chapter 10.

23. This result remains after introducing a fourth stage to the analysis and treating racial affect as causally prior to party identification, political ideology, and trust. Racial affect continues to have no effect.

References

Arceneaux, Kevin. 2005. "Does Federalism Weaken Democratic Representation?" *Publius: The Journal of Federalism* 35: 297–312.

Cantril, Albert H., and Susan Davis Cantril. 1999. *Reading Mixed Signals: Ambivalence in American Public Opinion about Government.* Washington, D.C.: Woodrow Wilson Center Press.

Cole, Richard L., and John Kincaid. 2000. "Public Opinion and American Federalism: Perspectives on Taxes, Spending, and Trust—An ACIR Update." *Publius: The Journal of Federalism* 30: 189–201.

Cole, Richard L., and John Kincaid. 2006. "Public Opinion on U.S. Federal and Intergovernmental Issues in 2006: Continuity and Change." *Publius: The Journal of Federalism* 36: 443–59.

Cole, Richard L., John Kincaid, and Andrew Parkin. 2002. "Public Opinion on Federalism in the United States and Canada in 2002: The Aftermath of Terrorism." *Publius: The Journal of Federalism* 32: 123–48.

Cole, Richard L., John Kincaid, and Alejandro Rodriguez. 2004. "Public Opinion on Federalism and Federal Political Culture in Canada, Mexico, and the United States, 2004." *Publius: The Journal of Federalism* 34: 201–21.

Conlan, Timothy. 1988. *New Federalism: Intergovernmental Reform from Nixon to Reagan.* Washington, D.C.: Brookings Institution.

Dinan, John. 2002. "Congressional Responses to the Rehnquist Court's Federalism Decisions." *Publius: The Journal of Federalism* 32: 1–24.

Grodzins, Morton. 1966. "Centralization and Decentralization in the American Federal System." In *The American System: A New View of Government in the United States,* edited by Daniel J. Elazar. Chicago: Rand McNally.

Hetherington, Marc J., and John D. Nugent. 2001. "Explaining Public Support for Devolution: The Role of Political Trust." In *What Is It about Government That Americans Dislike?* edited by John R. Hibbing and Elizabeth Theiss-Morse. New York: Cambridge University Press.

Jennings, M. Kent, and Harmon Zeigler. 1970. "The Salience of American State Politics." *American Political Science Review* 64: 523–35.

Kincaid, John, and Richard L. Cole. 2005. "Public Opinion on Issues of U.S. Federalism in 2005: End of the Post-2001 Pro-Federal Surge?" *Publius: The Journal of Federalism* 35: 169–85.

King, Gary, Michael Tomz, and Jason Wittenberg. 2000. "Making the Most of Statistical Analyses: Improving Interpretation and Presentation." *American Journal of Political Science* 44: 347–61.

Kramer, Larry D. 2000. "Putting the Politics Back into the Political Safeguards of Federalism." *Columbia Law Review* 100: 215–93.

Melnick, Shep. 2003. "Deregulating the States: Federalism in the Rehnquist Court." In *Evolving Federalisms: The Intergovernmental Balance of Power in America and Europe.* Syracuse, N.Y.: Campbell Public Affairs Institute, Maxwell School of Citizenship and Public Affairs, Syracuse University.

Reeves, Mavis Mann. 1987. "Public Opinion and Federalism, 1986." *Publius: The Journal of Federalism* 17: 55–65.

Reeves, Mavis Mann, and Parris N. Glendening. 1976. "Areal Federalism and Public Opinion." *Publius: The Journal of Federalism* 6: 135–67.

Riker, William H. 1964. *Federalism: Origins, Operation, Significance.* Boston: Little, Brown.

Roeder, Phillip W. 1994. *Public Opinion and Policy Leadership in the American States.* Tuscaloosa: University of Alabama Press.

Schneider, Saundra K., and William G. Jacoby. 2003. "Public Attitudes toward the Policy Responsibilities of the National and State Governments: Evidence from South Carolina." *State Politics and Policy Quarterly* 3: 246–69.

Sears, David O., Colette Van Laar, Mary Carrillo, and Rick Kosterman. 1997. "Is It Really Racism? The Origins of White Americans' Opposition to Race-Targeted Policies." *Public Opinion Quarterly* 61: 16–53.

Thompson, Lyke, and Richard Elling. 1999. "Let Them Eat Marblecake: The Preferences of Michigan Citizens for Devolution and Intergovernmental Service-Provision." *Publius: The Journal of Federalism* 29: 139–53.

Tomz, Michael, Jason Wittenberg, and Gary King. 2001. CLARIFY: Software for Interpreting and Presenting Statistical Results. Version 2.0. Cambridge, MA: Harvard University, June 1. Available at http://gking.harvard.edu. Accessed August 10, 2007.

Uslaner, Eric M. 2001. "Is Washington Really the Problem?" In *What Is It about Government That Americans Dislike?* edited by John R. Hibbing and Elizabeth Theiss-Morse. New York: Cambridge University Press.

Weschler, Herbert. 1954. "The Political Safeguards of Federalism: The Role of the States in the Composition and Selection of the National Government." *Columbia Law Review* 54: 543–60.

Whittington, Keith. 2001. "Taking What They Give Us: Explaining the Court's Federalism Offensive." *Duke Law Journal* 51: 477–521.

10

Gay Rights

Patrick J. Egan, Nathaniel Persily, and Kevin Wallsten

The controversy surrounding gay rights represents the most recent chapter in the long story of often unpopular attempts by courts to protect minorities from discrimination and to broaden the constitutional guarantees concerning freedom of intimate associations. While debating whether these cases represent examples of unwarranted judicial activism or classic attempts to protect equal rights, supporters and opponents alike compare the recent gay rights cases to historical precedents dealing with desegregation, gender equality, and abortion. As with those contexts, the questions arise: did the courts go too far, and will a public backlash overwhelm the civil rights gains?

In this chapter, we trace the remarkable rise in attitudes favorable toward gay people and gay rights over the past thirty years. We then explore the relationship between court decisions on gay rights and public opinion, with a close examination of the trajectory of opinion before and after two critical Supreme Court decisions regarding gay sex: *Bowers v. Hardwick* (1986) and *Lawrence v. Texas* (2003). In particular, we focus on how *Lawrence*—although nominally about sodomy laws—instead catalyzed a highly salient debate over gay marriage, a debate that intensified after the Massachusetts Supreme Judicial Court issued a landmark decision granting gays and lesbians marriage rights in that state (*Goodridge v. Department of Health*). Same-sex marriage continued to dominate the headlines throughout the 2004 campaign season, which ended with voters in thirteen states passing bans on gay marriage. We close by noting the ambivalence with which analysts and advocates alike view the effects of these consequential court decisions on the long-term prospects for gay rights in the United States.

Public Opinion on Gay Rights

Lawrence and *Goodridge* were handed down in 2003 in the wake of a remarkable, decades-long shift in American attitudes regarding gays and lesbians. Over the past thirty years, American public opinion regarding gay people, gay rights, and gay sex has moved unambiguously toward acceptance and tolerance (Brewer & Wilcox 2005; Egan & Sherrill 2005; Brewer 2003; Wilcox & Wolpert 2000; Yang 1997). However, Americans remain deeply more uncomfortable with gays than with other demographic groups, and their support for gay rights does not extend as strongly to the domains of sexuality and relationships.

Any discussion of public opinion regarding gays and lesbians must begin with the fact that Americans view homosexual behavior through a strong moral lens: in 2004, according to the General Social Survey, 57% of the public believed that same-sex relations are "always wrong." However, this disapproval has declined in a relatively steady fashion since the late 1980s, when it peaked at 78%. Notably, the decline in morally traditionalistic views regarding homosexuality has not been accompanied by increasing permissiveness on other matters of private behavior related to sexuality. Opinion regarding discretionary abortion, premarital sex, and pornography has remained relatively steady over the past thirty years—and Americans' condemnation of adultery has risen during this time period (see Figure 10.1). Instead, the

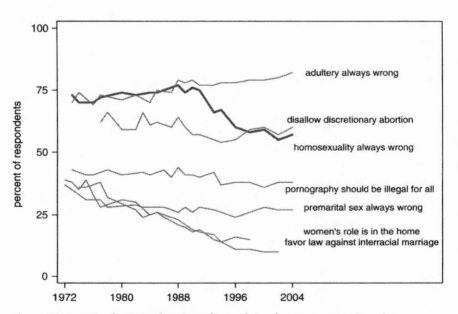

Figure 10.1. Attitudes Regarding Sexuality and Gender, 1972–2004. Question wording: see Appendix C. Source: General Social Survey.

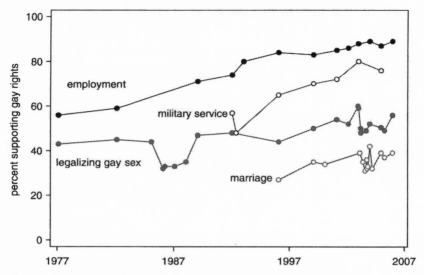

Figure 10.2. Support for Gay Rights, 1977–2006. Question wording: see Appendix C. Source: Gallup.

trend line of Americans' views on homosexuality roughly parallels (though lags behind) their opinions on issues like interracial marriage and the proper role for women in society—issues that are generally framed in terms of equal treatment as opposed to individual rights.

Over the same time period, more Americans have come to believe that homosexuality is an aspect of identity rather than a lifestyle choice. In 1983, 16% of the public told the Los Angeles Times poll that homosexuality is "something that people are born with;" that figure rose to 32% in 2004. The proportion who said homosexuality is "just the way some people prefer to live" was relatively unchanged: 37% in 1983 and 35% in 2004. Overwhelming majorities of Americans have also come to believe that gay people deserve equal employment rights, including employment in the military, medicine, and politics and (to a lesser extent) as teachers or clergy. Yet on aspects of gay rights that have to do with gay relationships and sexuality, Americans are less supportive, and their opinions have changed more slowly. For example, a solid majority of Americans have supported equal opportunities for gays in employment and military service since the late 1980s, but support for legalizing homosexual sex and same-sex marriage has risen less dramatically (see Figure 10.2). (Later in this chapter, we show how the variation in responses to the legalization question during the late 1980s and early 1990s is due to question-ordering effects rather than actual opinion change.)

The rise in Americans' tolerance of homosexuality and their embrace of some aspects of the gay rights agenda has been accompanied by and perhaps derives from a growing familiarity and comfort with gay and lesbian people. In 1985, 54% of Los Angeles Times poll respondents said they knew of no friends, family members, or coworkers who were gay. By 2004, this figure dropped to 27%. As more Americans have come to realize that they do know gay people, they have also become more comfortable with them. The proportion of Times poll respondents reporting that they were "sometimes" or "always" uncomfortable around gay people fell from 38% in 1983 to 20% in 2004 (Los Angeles Times Poll 2004).

By a widely used measure of sentiment toward demographic groups—the so-called feeling thermometer—Americans have grown decidedly warmer toward gays and lesbians over the past twenty years. Surveys with feeling thermometers ask participants to rate groups on a scale of 0 (cold) to 100 (warm), with a score of 50 considered neutral. The average thermometer score assigned to gays and lesbians by participants in the American National Election Studies (ANES) has increased sharply, from 30 "degrees" in 1984 to 49 in 2004 (see Figure 10.3). However, ANES respondents have consistently ranked gays and lesbians either last or next to last among all demographic groups in every administration of the survey since gays were first included in its battery of feeling thermometer questions in 1984. In 2004, for example, Americans rated groups such as "rich people," "feminists," "fundamentalists," "people on welfare," and "Muslims" more warmly than gays and lesbians (Egan & Sherrill, 2005).

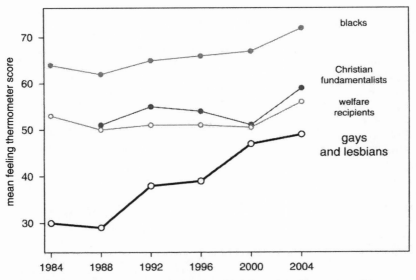

Figure 10.3. Feeling Thermometer Ratings for Selected Groups, 1984–2004. Source: American National Election Studies.

Four demographic variables have been shown to be consistent, strong predictors of individuals' attitudes toward gays and lesbians: education, religiosity, political ideology, and year of birth (cohort).[1] All things being equal, religiosity and conservative ideology are associated with cooler feelings toward gay people and with opposition to gay rights, whereas later birth and higher educational attainment are associated with warmer feelings and support (see Table 10.1). Overall, there is far more public support for equal rights in employment, including military service, than for gay marriage or the rights of gay couples to adopt children.

Table 10.1
Attitudes on Gay Rights by Education, Birth Cohort, Ideology and Religiosity, 2004

Categories	Mean feeling thermometer score assigned to gays and lesbians	% agreeing same-sex couples should be allowed to marry	% agreeing that gay couples should be legally allowed to adopt children	% favoring law to protect gays from job discrimination	% agreeing gays should serve in armed forces
Education					
Less than HS diploma	36	27	28	68	75
HS diploma	47	30	46	74	79
College degree	55	45	59	75	86
Postgraduate study	56	53	68	84	92
Birth cohort (year born)					
Before 1927	32	8	14	55	69
Between 1927 and 1942	42	21	37	72	75
Between 1943 and 1958	49	31	47	72	83
Between 1959 and 1974	48	37	52	76	81
After 1974	53	50	60	82	85
Ideology					
Conservative	43	20	35	68	77
Moderate	47	35	48	73	77
Liberal	56	57	69	85	88

Table 10.1
(continued)

Categories	Mean feeling thermometer score assigned to gays and lesbians	% agreeing same-sex couples should be allowed to marry	% agreeing that gay couples should be legally allowed to adopt children	% favoring law to protect gays from job discrimination	% agreeing gays should serve in armed forces
Religiosity (attendance at religious services)					
Every week	39	14	25	61	69
Almost every week	46	15	39	70	78
Once/twice per month	48	30	44	75	81
Few times per year	54	45	66	83	93
Never	51	51	62	81	85
All respondents	47	34	48	75	81

Source for data: American National Election Studies.
Question wording: see Appendix C.

Gay Rights, the Courts, and Public Opinion

Although majorities of Americans have supported equal rights for gays and lesbians in employment and military service for several decades, these views have not been reflected in policy making at the national level. Successive attempts to adopt a federal law banning employment discrimination have failed in Congress for more than twenty years. Furthermore, the military's "don't ask, don't tell" policy forbids lesbian and gay military personnel from being open about their sexual orientation. According to a 2005 report by the Government Accountability Office, nearly a thousand gay service members are dismissed by the military annually under the policy (United States Government Accountability Office 2005). State and local governments have been more receptive to gay rights: through 2007, nineteen states and hundreds of cities and counties had prohibited discrimination on the basis of sexual orientation in employment (National Gay and Lesbian Task Force 2007; also see Wald, Button, & Rienzo 1996). In addition, by the time *Lawrence v. Texas* struck down state laws banning gay sex in 2003, all but a handful of states had already rescinded such laws (as noted by Justice Antonin Scalia in his *Lawrence* dissent).

Gay rights advocates have recently won a series of highly publicized cases in the courts. When Colorado voters approved a constitutional amendment in 1992 to prevent gays from achieving certain civil rights protections, the Supreme Court threw out the amendment (*Romer v. Evans*, 1996). Rulings by state high courts requiring the legal recognition of same-sex couples were delivered in Hawaii (1993), Vermont (1999), Massachusetts (2003), and New Jersey (2006). The Massachusetts decision led to that state's historic granting of marriage licenses to same-sex couples beginning in 2004, and the Vermont and New Jersey cases resulted in those states creating "civil unions," which extend to gay couples the same rights accorded to heterosexuals in civil marriages. (The Hawaii ruling was rendered void by a state constitutional amendment adopted by voters in 1998.) California (2003), Maine (2004), Connecticut (2005), and New Hampshire (2007) have established legal statuses for same-sex couples without the imperative of a court order.

Conservatives have criticized the courts for making policy and for devising policies at odds with the public will, and gay rights supporters are concerned that the rulings have led to a backlash against their movement. Both sides point to voters' eager adoption of state statutes and constitutional amendments banning same-sex marriage (and in many cases, any legal recognition of same-sex couples) as evidence that the American public rejected and resented the landmark court decisions. By 2007, forty-three states had enacted these bans—a development that raises a significant obstacle to future efforts to expand legal recognition.

Here we focus on whether public opinion was affected by two U.S. Supreme Court cases that adjudicated the constitutionality of state bans on sodomy. The earlier case, *Bowers v. Hardwick* (1986), found no constitutional problem with the arrest of a Georgia man pursuant to that state's ban on sodomy. But in *Lawrence v. Texas* (2003), the Court reached the opposite result and struck down a Texas ban on sex between same-sex couples with an opinion that explicitly repudiated *Bowers*.

In Gallup polls conducted immediately after *Bowers* and *Lawrence*, public support for decriminalizing consensual gay sex declined (see Figure 10.4). Some researchers have argued that these shifts are evidence of the Supreme Court's ability to affect aggregate levels of public opinion and to polarize it along ideological, religious, and other demographic lines (Stoutenborough, Haider-Markel, & Allen 2006). But our analysis uncovered a confounding condition: Gallup changed the order in which it asked questions about gay rights in the surveys it conducted immediately after *Bowers*. Specifically, Gallup began asking its question on legalizing gay sex first, before any other gay rights questions. Before *Bowers*, the legalization question had been preceded by other questions about gay rights. As shown in Figure 10.4, respondents are more likely to agree that gay sex should be decriminalized if they are first asked a question about employment rights or other gay rights issues: in polls administered between 1977 and 1993, the size of this question-order effect was about 12 percentage points.

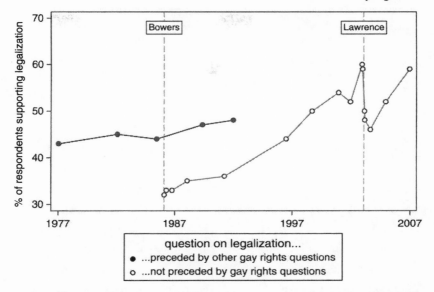

Figure 10.4. Opinion on Legalizing Gay Sex, 1977–2006. Question wording: Do you think homosexual relations between consenting adults should or should not be legal? Source: Gallup.

The change in question order makes it difficult to assess whether attitudes about legalization actually shifted after *Bowers*.[2] However, it is clear from the data that *Lawrence* significantly disrupted the upward trend in public opinion regarding decriminalization. Although the Court considered very similar constitutional issues in *Bowers* and *Lawrence*, the prominence, context, and effect of the decisions were quite different in ways that would lead us to expect the two rulings to have dissimilar impacts on public opinion. *Bowers*, which reinforced the constitutional status quo, was (as we will show) a low-salience news event that was quickly forgotten by the media and the public. By contrast, *Lawrence*, which created a new constraint on state laws regulating sex, catalyzed a highly salient national debate—a debate not about decriminalizing gay sex but about legalizing same-sex marriage. Research on the content of the media's coverage of *Lawrence* has found that it was very negative toward the notion of gay marriage (Haider-Markel 2004). During this debate, attitudes regarding gays became polarized, and aggregate support for gay rights dropped.

We begin by noting that *Bowers* was not a highly salient news event. Media coverage mentioning "sodomy" (a term likely to correlate with newspaper stories describing the Court's ruling) declined to pre-*Bowers* levels within three weeks after the announcement of the Court's decision on June 30, 1986 (see Figure 10.5).

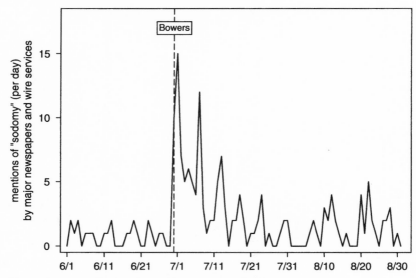

Figure 10.5. Media Coverage of *Bowers v. Hardwick*, Summer 1986.
Source: Lexis-Nexis.

Media coverage of the *Lawrence* decision followed a similar trajectory: a short burst of coverage during the week of the decision and then a tapering off to predecision levels soon after (see Figure 10.6). But the *Lawrence* decision quickly became enmeshed in the media coverage of gay marriage: nearly fifty stories concerning gay marriage ran in major U.S. newspapers on the day after *Lawrence*.[3] *Lawrence* became, in effect, the first event in a series that generated extensive coverage of the gay marriage issue (see Figure 10.7). During the two years following *Lawrence*, coverage of gay marriage spiked after the Vatican's condemnation of gay marriage in August 2003; the first *Goodridge* opinion in November 2003; the second *Goodridge* opinion on February 4, 2004; the decision by San Francisco Mayor Gavin Newsom to issue marriage licenses (February 12); President Bush's announcement of support for a constitutional amendment banning same-sex marriage (February 23); the granting of marriage licenses to gays in Massachusetts on May 17; the defeat in the U.S. Senate of a proposed constitutional amendment banning gay marriage (July 14); and the November 2004 elections. Notably, all of these events generated *more* coverage regarding same-sex marriage than the *Lawrence* decision.

Throughout this period of intense media scrutiny, the public soured noticeably on the notion of gay marriage. Public support for same-sex marriage fell in the months following the *Lawrence* decision, continued to fall in the aftermath of *Goodridge* and through the 2004 election, and began to approach pre-*Lawrence* levels only in the summer of 2005 (see Figure 10.8).

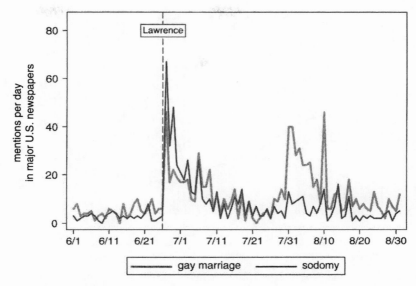

Figure 10.6. Media Coverage of *Lawrence v. Texas*, Summer 2003. Source: Lexis-Nexis.

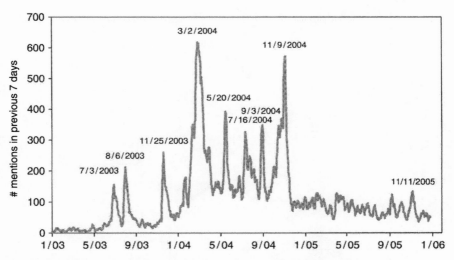

Figure 10.7. Coverage of Gay Marriage in Major U.S. Newspapers, 2003–2005. Source: Lexis-Nexis.

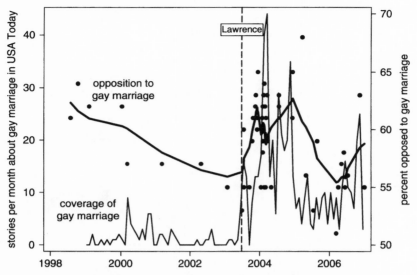

Figure 10.8. Media Coverage and Opposition to Gay Marriage, 1998–2006. Question wording varies. Sources: Lexis-Nexis, Bowman (2006), PollingReport.com.

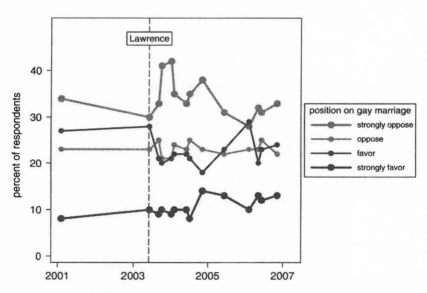

Figure 10.9. Polarization of Attitudes on Gay Marriage, 2001–2006. Question wording: Do you strongly favor, favor, oppose, or strongly oppose allowing gays and lesbians to marry legally? Source: Pew Research Center.

Between 2004 and 2006, public opposition to gay marriage rose and fell with the level of media coverage.

The period immediately following the *Lawrence* decision was notable not only for the aggregate change in public opinion but also for the polarization of opinion: in particular, the proportion of the population that "strongly opposed" gay marriage increased, with the levels of intensity receding to pre-*Lawrence* levels two years later (see Figure 10.9). Throughout, strong opponents outnumbered strong supporters: between 30% and 40% of Americans say they strongly oppose legalization of gay marriage, and only 8% to 14% consider themselves strong supporters of gay marriage. Moreover, opponents of gay marriage are more likely to say that they would be unwilling to vote for a candidate who disagreed with them on the issue (Pew Research Center 2004).

The Structure of Opinion on Gay Marriage

To study the structure of opinion on gay marriage, we reviewed the survey data collected by the Pew Center, which repeatedly asked its respondents questions about same-sex marriage in surveys conducted between 2001 and 2006. We also reviewed the 2004 American National Election Study (ANES) survey, which was conducted during the 2004 presidential election season.[4] Because the issue of gay marriage figured so prominently during this campaign, the ANES data are probably unrepresentative of American opinion at times when the issue is less salient.[5] But the ANES has several items unavailable in the Pew surveys, including those designed to capture three core political values—egalitarianism, moral traditionalism, and belief in limited government—as well as the aforementioned "feeling thermometer" rating for gays and lesbians. In this section, we use the ANES to estimate a causal model of attitude formation, as shown in Table 10.2.

The four blocks of variables in Table 10.2 are listed in causal order: immutable demographic characteristics (block I), long-term social characteristics (II), values and political orientation (III), and feelings toward gays and lesbians (IV). By organizing the analysis in this way, we can assess the direct effects of each block on attitudes on same-sex marriage, as well as the indirect effects of blocks earlier in the chain of causality, as mediated through the variables in the intervening groups.[6] For example, higher levels of educational attainment are associated with higher levels of support for gay marriage. However, education probably has both a direct effect on attitudes toward gay marriage and an indirect effect through the intervening variable of egalitarianism, which is correlated with both education and support for gay marriage.

The estimates in Table 10.2 are derived from probit analyses in which the dependent variable is scored 1 for support of gay marriage and 0 for opposition. The table presents "first differences," which are calculated from the probit estimates and are the estimated change in probability of supporting gay marriage, given a shift from the minimum to the maximum value of each independent variable, holding all other variables in the model constant

Table 10.2
The structure of support for same-sex marriage, 2004

Variables	I	II	III	IV (direct effects)
Immutable demographic characteristics				
Age	−.44***	−.30**	−.24*	−.20
Black	−.15**	−.07	−.16**	−.16**
Hispanic	−.05	−.01	−.09	−.11
Female	.04	.08*	.09*	.03
Long-term social characteristics				
South		−.10	−.06	−.02
West		−.03	−.03	−.04
Midwest		−.13*	−.11	−.08
Urbanicity		.07	−.01	.02
Married/widowed		−.05	−.02	−.04
Divorced/separated		−.01	−.03	−.04
Children in household		−.07	−.05	−.02
Education		.41***	.35***	.27**
Income		−.06	−.02	−.07
Union household		.01	.01	.01
Attendance of religious services		−.38***	−.21***	−.20***
Values and political orientation				
Egalitarianism			.12	.08
Moral traditionalism			−.85***	−.80***
Belief in limited government			.10	.13*
Political ideology			.15**	.14**
Party identification			.13**	.12*
Feelings toward gays				
Gay/lesbian feeling thermometer score				.63***
Log likelihood	−501.20	−438.21	−338.65	−306.88
Pseudo-R²	.05	.17	.36	.42
N	805	805	805	805

Cell entries are first differences derived from probit analyses. They are estimates of the change in probability of supporting gay marriage, given a shift from the minimum to the maximum value of each independent variable, holding all other variables constant at their means. Cell entries in bold are a variable's total effect—that is, the effect of a variable on support for gay marriage before the consideration of the mediating effects of any intervening variables. Probit coefficients are significantly different from zero at *p< .05, **p<.01, ***p<.001.

Source: American National Election Studies.

Question wording: see Appendix C.

at their mean value.[7] For example, in model IV we see that the direct effect of a shift in education from its minimum value (eighth grade or less) to its maximum value (postgraduate study) is a 27 percentage point increase in the probability of supporting gay marriage, holding all other variables constant at their means. We can compare this direct effect with the total effect of education (estimated in model II at 41 percentage points) and thus calculate the indirect effect of education through the intervening variables in blocks III and IV as 41–27 ≈ 14 percentage points.

Demographic Characteristics

We consider first the effects of three immutable demographic characteristics: sex, race, and age. With respect to sex, we confirm what others have found: women tend to be more supportive of gay rights than men (Haider-Markel & Joslyn 2005). The total effect of sex is small, but among those with similar long-term social characteristics and political values, women are significantly more likely to support same-sex marriage than men, as shown in model III. Once we control for warmth toward gays and lesbians, women and men are statistically indistinct (model IV).

With respect to race, differences in opinion on same-sex marriage are more pronounced (see Figure 10.10). Hispanics are typically more supportive of gay marriage than whites or African Americans. However, Hispanics' high level of support appears to reflect the fact that they tend to be younger than other racial and ethnic groups. As shown in Table 10.2, model I, Hispanics are actually less supportive of same-sex marriage than whites once we control for age and sex, and they remain so after controlling for intervening factors (model IV). African Americans are distinctly opposed to same-sex marriage, even after controlling for intervening variables such as attendance at religious services, moral traditionalism, and living in the South (model III). As shown in Figure 10.10, support for gay marriage among African Americans dropped substantially in the period following *Lawrence*: in August 2004, only 19% of blacks told Pew that gay marriage should be legal. Recently African American support for same-sex marriage has risen to pre-*Lawrence* levels.

As discussed earlier, birth cohort (which is equivalent to age in a cross-sectional survey such as the 2004 ANES) is one of the strongest predictors of attitudes on same-sex marriage. Holding sex and race constant, there is a 44-point gap in support for gay marriage between the oldest and youngest survey respondents (model I). This effect diminishes once controls are added for intervening variables—in particular, education, because later generations are currently better educated than earlier generations.

Long-Term Social Characteristics

Of several long-term social characteristics that are often linked to attitudes on gay rights, only two of those shown in Table 10.2—education and religiosity

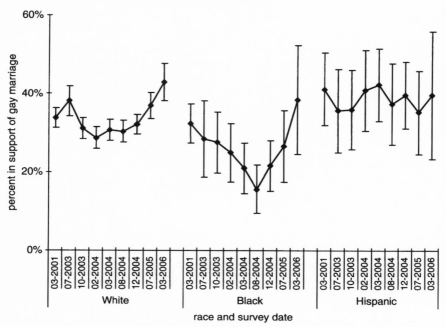

Figure 10.10. Support for Gay Marriage by Race, 2001–2006. Bars represent 95% confidence intervals. Note: For space considerations, time periods of unequal length appear equal in this figure. Question wording: See Figure 10.9.
Source: Pew Research Center.

(measured by attendance at religious services)—have significant, substantial total effects on individuals' opinions on same-sex marriage. A shift from the minimum to maximum value of education has the total effect of raising the probability of supporting same-sex marriage by 41 percentage points (model II). A similar shift in religiosity lowers support for gay marriage by 38 points. As shown in Table 10.3 (which combines responses to all waves of the Pew Center surveys), the relationship between attendance of services and opposition to same-sex marriage holds across the nation's major religious denominations—among which there is substantial variation in opinion. Jews are by far the most supportive of gay marriage, followed by those who have no religious preference. At the other end of the spectrum, evangelical Protestants and black Protestants express the least support.

Religiosity has also affected the dynamics of opinion change during the post-*Lawrence* period. Although support for gay marriage fell sharply after *Lawrence*, support among the less religious—those attending services less than once per month on average—rebounded in 2005. Moreover, by 2006, their support rose to a level 10 percentage points higher than before *Lawrence* (see Figure 10.11). By contrast, support among the more religious has remained low even as the issue has faded in the national debate.

Table 10.3
Support for Same-Sex Marriage by Religious Preference and Attendance
of Services, 2001–2006

Religious preference		Attendance of religious services		
		At least once per month	Less than once per month	Totals
Evangelical Protestant* (24% of respondents)		10%	24%	12%
Mainline Protestant*	(21%)	35%	44%	40%
Black Protestant	(8%)	21%	38%	25%
Roman Catholic	(24%)	35%	54%	42%
Jewish	(2%)	67%	84%	79%
Other religion	(10%)	25%	60%	39%
No religion/agnostic/atheist	(11%)	43%	71%	69%
Totals		24%	52%	36%

*These categories do not include Black Protestants.
$N = 15,014$. Data are weighted.

Source: Pew Research Center.

Question wording: see Figure 10.9.

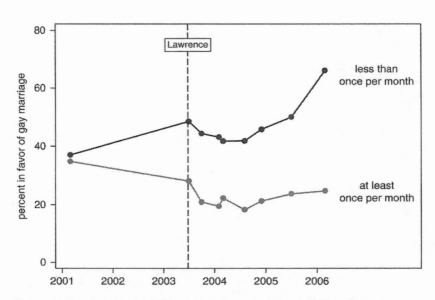

Figure 10.11. Attitudes on Gay Marriage by Attendance at Religious Services,
2001–2006. Question wording: See Figure 10.9.
Source: Pew Research Center.

Frequency of church attendance, of course, is only one way to measure religiosity. One could also look at the difference between those who call themselves born again or evangelical (only 17% supported same-sex marriage over the 2001–2006 period in the Pew Center surveys) and those who do not (43%). Attitudes toward the authority of the Bible show the religious differences most starkly. Of those who say the "Bible is the actual word of God and is to be taken literally," 14% supported legalization of same-sex marriage in the July 2005 Pew Center survey, whereas 77% of those who said the "Bible was written by men" supported same-sex marriage.

Values and Political Orientation

Political ideology is an important predictor of opinion on same-sex marriage, and its effect rose over the period of controversy precipitated by *Lawrence*. Averaged over the 2001–2006 period, 67% of those who described themselves as "liberal" or "very liberal" were in favor of same-sex marriage, and 83% of those calling themselves "conservative" or "very conservative" opposed it. To illustrate the effect of ideology, Figure 10.12 shows ideological trends among whites—the racial group for whom ideology has the strongest association with attitudes on gay marriage; as a reference, we include the trend for blacks. Among whites, support for same-sex marriage declined in all ideological groupings in the immediate post-*Lawrence* period (between the July 2003 and October 2003 Pew polls). By 2006, white conservatives and moderates had just barely recovered to their

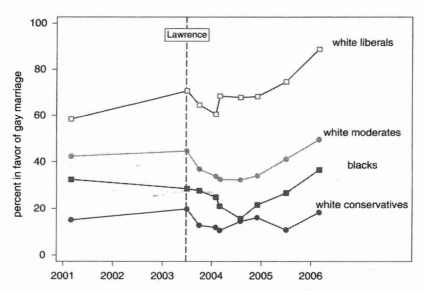

Figure 10.12. Attitudes on Gay Marriage by Ideology and Race, 2001–2006.
Question wording: See Figure 10.9.
Source: Pew Research Center.

pre-*Lawrence* levels, and white liberals had emerged from the nationwide debate as much more supportive of same-sex marriage—an increase in support of 25 percentage points since 2001. These trends lend themselves to two interpretations that lead to substantially different conclusions. On one hand, the controversy may have catalyzed support among liberals. But on the other, it may have interrupted a steady rise in support for same-sex marriage among all ideological groups—an interruption from which only liberal opinion has recovered.

The multivariate analyses in Table 10.2 allow a more nuanced understanding of how values influence attitudes on same-sex marriage. In model III, we find that the ANES "moral traditionalism" index (a battery of questions presented in Appendix B, which assess respondents' views on changing social mores and tolerance of other moral views) is a very strong predictor of attitudes: a shift from the least traditional to most traditional moral views raises opposition to same-sex marriage by 85 percentage points. (Brewer (2003) finds the moral traditionalism index to be a strong predictor of a range of attitudes regarding gay rights that do not include marriage.) This effect is more than five times the size of a similar shift on the ideological spectrum from liberal to conservative, which raises opposition by 15 points. As model IV also shows, those who believe in limited government are more likely to support same-sex marriage, holding all other variables constant at their means—a result that is notable given that legalized same-sex marriage would extend government regulation of private relationships. As we would expect, given the partisan rancor over the issue of gay rights, party identification also distinguishes same-sex marriage opponents from supporters (models III and IV), even when controlling for values and ideology. Surprisingly, no direct, statistically significant relationship exists between egalitarian beliefs (as measured by another ANES index) and attitudes concerning same-sex marriage, which suggests that most of the power of egalitarianism as an explanatory variable may be subsumed by ideology, party identification, and moral traditionalism.[8]

Warmth toward Gays and Lesbians and Attitudes about Homosexuality

Of course, those who express "warm" feelings toward gays are much more likely to be in favor of same-sex marriage than those who express "cool" feelings. Of ANES respondents who gave gays a rating between 0 and 45 on the feeling thermometer, 88% were opposed to same-sex marriage in 2004. Only 31% of those who assigned ratings between 61 and 100 opposed same-sex marriage. A move from the lowest to the highest feeling thermometer score increases the probability of being in favor of same-sex marriage by 63 percentage points, holding other variables at their means.

The warmth one feels toward gays and lesbians is clearly itself the effect of other variables earlier in the causal chain. It is notable, then, that the inclusion of respondents' feelings toward gays (in Table 10.2, model IV) does not undermine the direct effect that most of the values and political orientation variables have on attitudes toward same-sex marriage. In contrast, age and gender (but not race) decline to statistical insignificance once we include feelings toward gays in the model, indicating that age and gender have an effect on respondents' attitudes toward gays but not an independent and direct effect on their attitudes toward same-sex marriage.

Several researchers have recognized a relationship between individuals' beliefs as to the origins of homosexuality and their support for same-sex marriage (Tygart 2000; Haider-Markel & Joslyn 2005; Bergeron 2005). Those studies find, for example, that respondents who see homosexuality as the result of genetic or biological factors, rather than as the result of situational factors and personal choices, were more likely to support same-sex marriage and domestic partnership laws. Indeed, Haider-Markel and Joslyn (2005) find that support for same-sex marriage has gone up almost in parallel with rates of response attributing homosexuality to genetics instead of upbringing.

Our analysis of the October 2003 Pew Center survey confirms these findings. That survey asked, "In your opinion, when a person is homosexual is it something they are born with, something that develops because of the way people are brought up or just the way that some people prefer to live?" Respondents were also asked, "Is homosexuality something that can be changed?" Answers to both these questions are highly correlated with attitudes on gay rights: those who consider homosexuality a fixed identity rather than a changeable preference are more likely to support same-sex marriage (see Table 10.4). Of course,

Table 10.4
Explanations of Homosexuality and Same-Sex Marriage Attitudes, 2003

	Opinion on Same-Sex Marriage			
	Strongly Oppose	Oppose	Support	Strongly Support
Beliefs about causes of homosexuality				
Fixed at birth (30% of respondents)	18.2	22.4	38.1	21.2
Due to upbringing (15%)	51.5	25.0	18.2	5.2
The way some people prefer to live (43%)	47.8	28.9	19.4	3.8
Don't know (12%)	43.1	29.3	21.3	6.3
Beliefs about whether homosexuality can be changed				
Can be changed (42% of respondents)	53.3	27.0	16.4	3.3
Cannot be changed (43%)	23.0	23.1	36.6	17.4
Don't know (16%)	42.6	35.1	17.3	5.1

$N = 1,390$. Data are weighted.

Source: Pew Research Center.

Question wording: *Marriage:* See Figure 10.9. *Causes:* In your opinion, when a person is homosexual is it something that people are born with, or is it something that develops because of the way people are brought up, or is it just the way that some people prefer to live? *Changed:* Do you think a gay or lesbian person's sexual orientation can be changed or cannot be changed?

Table 10.5
Contact with Gays and Attitudes toward Same-Sex Marriage, 2003

Do you have a friend, colleague or family member who is gay?	Opinion on Same-Sex Marriage			
	Strongly Oppose	Oppose	Support	Strongly Support
Yes (54.2% of respondents)	30.3	21.0	33.1	15.6
No (43.8%)	42.3	32.4	20.8	4.4
Not Sure/Refused (2.0%)	32.5	53.2	14.4	0.0

$N = 2,073$. Data are weighted.
Source: Pew Research Center.
Question wording: see Figure 10.9.

answers to these two questions are also correlated with the demographic and political variables that predict attitudes about same-sex marriage. But in multivariate analysis (not shown here), we find that beliefs about nature, nurture, and preference remain significantly associated with opinion on gay marriage even after controlling for ideology, education, and other characteristics.

The July and October 2003 Pew surveys also asked, "Do you have a friend, colleague or family member who is gay?" Respondents who answered yes were about twice as likely to support same-sex marriage as those who said they did not know someone who was gay (49% versus 25%)—but a full 51% of respondents who have gay friends, colleagues, or family members were opposed to extending marriage to gay couples (see Table 10.5). Although "yes" responses are highly correlated with liberalism, education, region, and other factors, we find that the variable is still a statistically significant predictor of attitudes toward gay marriage ($p<.001$) when included in a multivariate analysis with these other variables.

Opinion on Civil Unions and Amending the Constitution

The heated debate surrounding same-sex marriage produced an important outcome favorable to gay rights activists: an unmistakable rise in the public's support for some legal recognition of same-sex couples (see Figure 10.13). Support for civil unions—which provide a legal status that falls short of marriage—grew between mid-2003 and mid-2005 (see Cimino & Segura 2005). During this same period, political elites across the ideological spectrum expressed support for civil unions. For example, in the 2004 presidential campaign, both major candidates stated their support for civil unions (Bumiller 2004). Also during this period, a growing number of Americans began to see eventual legal recognition of same-sex marriage as possible, if not probable: in March 2004, 59% of Americans told the Los Angeles Times poll that legal recognition of same-sex marriage was "inevitable."

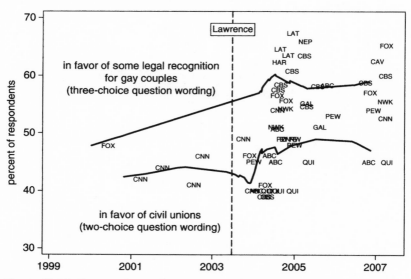

Figure 10.13. Support for Legal Recognition of Gay Couples, 2000–2007. Question wording varies. Sources: Bowman (2006), PollingReport.com.

Surveys that offer an up-or-down choice on civil unions tend to find less support for some kind of legal recognition of gay couples than do surveys that offer three options (marriage, civil unions, or no legal recognition); see Figure 10.13.When the question is asked in the three-option format, a majority supports some form of legal recognition: in surveys conducted in 2006, about 20% to 28% say they favor marriage, 24% to 35% are in favor of civil unions, and 35% to 45% believe gay couples should have no legal recognition. In other words, offering three options draws people away from the extremes, a phenomenon familiar to survey researchers (Kalton, Roberts, & Holt 1980, Presser & Schuman 1980). In a related vein, respondents are more likely to support same-sex marriage if they are asked a question on this topic before being asked a question on civil unions. When respondents are asked a question about civil unions first, their support for marriage declines in subsequent questions (Rutgers-Eagleton Poll 2006).

A second important effect of question wording is that survey participants are more supportive of granting gay couples specific marriage-like rights than they are of allowing either same-sex marriage or creating civil unions. Steady majorities of Americans favor inheritance rights, social security survivor benefits, hospital visitation, and other specific rights for gay couples (see Bowman 2006).

Regardless of how the question was asked in opinion surveys, civil unions became markedly more popular in the year when same-sex marriage received great attention in the courts and in the media. In a multivariate analysis conducted with data from four Pew surveys,[9] we found that the structure of support for civil unions is very similar to that for same-sex marriage: education, liberal ideology, and Democratic party identification are significantly associated with support for civil unions, holding other variables constant. Those most opposed to civil unions included the more religious, lower income earners, and males. Among the determinants of attitudes regarding gay marriage, only the variable of age did not emerge as a significant predictor of support of civil unions.

Among issues related to gay marriage, question wording has the largest effect on survey responses regarding a constitutional amendment to ban gay marriage. Support for a constitutional amendment banning same-sex marriage has varied between 40% and 60%. Questions that stress either the dramatic nature of a constitutional amendment or the effect on state autonomy elicit a much lower level of support than less detailed questions that emphasize the proposed amendment's definition of marriage.

Questions that describe the proposed amendment as "defining marriage as between a man and a woman" usually elicit majority support for the amendment. For example, the share of the population giving a favorable response to the question posed by the Gallup Poll—"Would you favor or oppose a constitutional amendment that would define marriage as being between a man and a woman, thus barring marriages between gay or lesbian couples?"—has hovered between 48% and 57%. By contrast, questions that encourage respondents to think about federalism or the exceptional nature of a constitutional amendment attract less support. The Annenberg National Election Study released data three times in 2004 on responses to the following question: "Would you favor or oppose an amendment to the U.S. Constitution saying that no state can allow two men to marry each other or two women to marry each other?" Only 40% to 42% of the population said they favored such an amendment.[10] For the most part, when controlling for question-wording effects, support for a constitutional amendment is consistently lower than opposition to legalization of same-sex marriage but follows the same pattern: a rise post-*Lawrence* and through to the 2004 election and then a decline by the summer of 2005.

In sum, a core 35% to 40% of Americans would favor almost any measure to prevent the legal recognition of same-sex relationships, even a constitutional amendment to prevent states from recognizing gay marriages. In the middle are the 25% to 30% of the population who oppose attaching the word "marriage" to gay and lesbian relationships but who would not support a constitutional amendment and who are open to the concept of civil unions. About 25% to 30% of Americans support gay marriage and civil unions and oppose constitutional amendments to ban them. About 5% to 10% of Americans do not have an opinion on any of these issues.

Conclusions

The changes in public opinion following *Lawrence* and *Goodridge* appear to constitute instances of short-term backlash to judicial decisions. Unlike *Bowers*, which did not alter the tide of opinion, *Lawrence* temporarily reversed a trend in favor of decriminalizing gay sex and legalizing same-sex marriage. Given the extensive media coverage of same-sex marriage following *Lawrence*, we argue (but cannot prove) that the framing of gay rights issues in terms of marriage led to this temporary backlash. Levels of public disapproval of same-sex marriage continued to increase in response to the Vatican's pronouncement, the two *Goodridge* decisions, the same-sex marriage ceremonies in San Francisco, and President Bush's call for a constitutional amendment restricting marriage to heterosexual couples. Our analysis suggests that the rise in the salience and coverage of same-sex marriage temporarily moved public opinion in a direction against gay marriage and gay rights.

The sharp backlash appears to have been short-lived, but aggregate opinion remains highly sensitive to the prominence of same-sex marriage as a topic of national debate. When the salience of the issue is low, the long-term trend of slow, steady growth in support for gay rights resumes. But when courts, political elites, or other actors put the issue back into the national spotlight, support for gay rights declines. Despite these ups and downs, support for gay marriage is now quite strong among the less religious as well as liberals, and majority support has materialized for some legal recognition of same-sex relationships.

We have been careful here not to overemphasize the independent effect of the *Lawrence* decision on the backlash we observe. Although Justice Scalia's dissent tied the majority's opinion to the marriage issue, the case after all was not about marriage. The decision became about marriage because the media and political elites began to talk about same-sex marriage in its aftermath. A similar discussion might have been provoked by other relevant events over the subsequent year. Absent the *Lawrence* decision, moreover, the backlash probably would have materialized somewhat later in 2003 following *Goodridge*, and absent *Goodridge*, the backlash that began after *Lawrence* might have subsided earlier than it eventually did.

We also do not answer the question whether the short-term backlash following these decisions somehow made the constitutional litigation for protections for gays' rights to have sex or to get married counterproductive. We cannot answer that question because there is no objective way to measure the benefits of these decisions against the costs of the temporary backlash. These legal fights produced tangible benefits for the plaintiffs involved and for those who otherwise might be subject to a subordinate legal status. Moreover, they led to a favorable change in public opinion on civil unions, appear to have only temporarily interrupted a long-term liberalizing trend in opinion on gay rights (including marriage), and perhaps accelerated legal change in some states in a direction amenable to some legal recognition of gay relationships. At the same time, the period of short-term backlash was characterized by intense activism by gay marriage opponents who achieved their goal of codification of gay marriage bans in most states and the creation of gay marriage as an issue for candidate campaigns. We cannot say whether the court decisions discussed here will ultimately be considered to have furthered the cause of gay rights—or if they will someday be seen by advocates and scholars alike as having led to a setback for the gay rights movement.

Appendix A

Support for legalization of gay marriage, July 2005

	Strongly Favor	Favor	Oppose	Strongly Oppose	DK/ Refused
TOTAL	11.8	22.3	23.5	30.5	11.9
GENDER					
Male	10.8	21.3	24.9	32.8	10.1
Female	12.7	23.2	22.2	28.3	13.6
RACE					
White	12.1	22.1	23.8	30.7	11.4
Black	6.9	18.5	24.6	36.2	13.8
Hispanic	14.7	22.1	24.2	28.4	10.5
Other	12.4	26.8	17.5	26.8	15.5
AGE					
18–29	21.3	25.0	17.6	31.4	4.8
30–40	17.2	24.8	20.0	28.0	10.0
40–50	10.3	23.8	23.2	30.8	11.9
51–62	11.8	26.0	22.3	26.6	13.3
63+	5.5	14.0	29.3	35.9	15.3
EDUCATION					
Less than High School	10.0	11.1	26.7	41.1	11.1
High School	8.8	18.1	27.4	34.7	11.0
Some College	8.8	22.2	22.7	32.2	14.1
College+	17.0	27.3	20.4	24.5	10.8
INCOME					
~ $30,000	10.4	20.4	25.3	30.0	13.9
$30,000–50,000	13.2	20.6	26.5	31.2	8.5
$50,000–100,000	11.9	23.5	20.9	33.5	10.3
$100,000+	19.8	29.3	21.6	21.6	7.8
HAVING CHILDREN					
No Child	11.6	22.7	23.4	29.9	12.4
Have children	12.8	21.4	22.8	32.3	12.4
REGION					
Northeast	12.2	29.9	22.6	21.2	14.2
Midwest	10.1	21.7	24.6	31.3	12.2
South	8.9	16.4	23.8	38.6	12.4
West	18.0	26.0	22.6	24.5	8.9
RELIGION					
Protestant	6.7	16.9	27.2	38.3	10.9
Catholic	10.6	26.5	22.3	27.4	13.2
Other	5.5	16.4	34.2	39.7	4.1
EVANGELICAL					
Yes	4.9	10.0	24.9	52.0	8.3
No	11.4	27.8	27.2	20.5	13.1

(*continued*)

	Strongly Favor	Favor	Oppose	Strongly Oppose	DK/ Refused
ATTENDANCE OF RELIGIOUS SERVICES					
More than once a week	4.6	6.7	21.4	60.9	6.3
Once a week	6.2	16.4	26.2	40.8	10.5
Once or twice a month	13.0	22.6	26.0	22.6	15.9
A few times a year	12.0	29.7	26.3	20.5	11.6
Seldom/Never	20.7	33.1	19.4	13.4	13.4
IDEOLOGY					
Very Liberal	46.2	33.8	1.5	12.3	6.2
Liberal	33.2	34.0	10.5	9.3	13.0
Moderate	8.3	28.8	26.8	22.1	14.0
Conservative	2.7	10.8	31.4	47.2	7.9
Very Conservative	2.9	2.9	16.5	74.8	2.9
PARTY IDENTIFICATION					
Republican	3.2	11.8	31.1	45.8	8.2
Independent	14.8	26.8	19.1	26.2	13.1
Democrat	17.7	27.7	20.1	21.1	13.5
NEWS ATTENTION (Scale)					
Low	13.0	22.7	19.5	32.5	12.2
Medium	10.6	24.9	27.8	25.3	11.4
High	12.8	19.3	23.7	33.3	10.9

Source: Pew Research Center. Question wording: see Figure 10.9.

News Attention Scale (derived from 5 items);

News about the current situation in Iraq
The retirement of Supreme Court Justice Sandra Day O'Connor
The move by a Chinese firm to buy the American oil company Unocal
Recent hurricanes that have affected the Gulf Coast of the United States
The terrorist bombings in London, England

Appendix B
Demographic Breakdown of Support for Gay Marriage, Fall 2004

	Support
TOTAL	34.1
GENDER	
Male	32.8
Female	35.5

	Support
RACE	
White	35.0
Black	29.5
Hispanic	39.2
Asian	46.4
AGE	
18–29	50.2
30–39	41.2
40–49	30.4
50–64	30.8
65+	15.1
EDUCATION	
Less than High School	26.6
High School Diploma	30.0
College Degree	44.6
Postgraduate study	53.4
HOUSEHOLD INCOME	
< $25,000	32.9
$25,000–$49,999	33.1
$50,000–104,999	34.8
$105,000+	38.0
MARITAL STATUS	
Married	28.7
Widowed	19.6
Divorced	35.8
Separated	25.0
Never Married	51.4
NUMBER OF CHILDREN	
No Children	34.6
1 Child	27.1
2+Children	36.7
REGION	
Northeast	42.8
North Central	26.4
South	27.8
West	46.3
URBANICITY	
Rural	25.1
Small Town	33.6
Suburb	34.7
Large City	43.4
Inner City	36.2

(*continued*)

	Support
RELIGION	
Protestant	22.8
Catholic	38.2
Jewish	72.5
Other	55.0
None	57.7
ATTENDANCE OF RELIGIOUS SERVICES	
Every Week	14.3
Almost Every Week	15.3
Once or Twice per Month	30.0
A Few Times per Year	44.6
Never	51.4
BIBLE	
Bible is actual word of God and is to be taken literally	11.6
Bible is the word of God but should not be taken literally	38.9
Bible is written by men	72.4
IDEOLOGY	
Liberal	56.9
Moderate	34.7
Conservative	19.7
PARTY IDENTIFICATION	
Republican	19.1
Independent	38.5
Democrat	45.8
EGALITARIANISM (Scale)	
Low	24.1
Medium	28.9
High	50.4
MORAL TRADITIONALISM (Scale)	
Low	63.4
Medium	30.9
High	10.7
BELIEF IN LIMITED GOVERNMENT (Scale)	
Low	40.9
Medium	30.1
High	29.5
FEELING THEROMOMETER ON GAYS AND LESBIANS	
0–49	6.9
50	33.8
51–100	63.0

Source: American National Election Studies. Question Wording: See "same-sex marriage" in notes to Table 10.1 in Appendix C.

Wording of questions for egalitarianism, moral traditionalism, and limited government scales:

Egalitarianism (six agree/disagree items):
- Our society should do whatever is necessary to make sure that everyone has an equal opportunity to succeed.
- We have gone too far in pushing equal rights in this country.
- One of the big problems in this country is that we don't give everyone an equal chance.
- This country would be better off if we worried less about how equal people are.
- It is not really that big a problem if some people have more of a chance in life than others.
- If people were treated more equally in this country we would have many fewer problems.

Moral traditionalism (four agree/disagree items):
- The world is always changing and we should adjust our view of moral behavior to those changes.
- The newer lifestyles are contributing to the breakdown of our society.
- We should be more tolerant of people who choose to live according to their own moral standards, even if they are very different from our own.
- This country would have many fewer problems if there were more emphasis on traditional family ties.

Belief in limited government (three forced choice items):
- Agree more with: ONE, the main reason government has become bigger over the years is because it has gotten involved in things that people should do for themselves; OR TWO, government has become bigger because the problems we face have become bigger.
- Agree more with: ONE, we need a strong government to handle today's complex economic problems; OR TWO, the free market can handle these problems without government being involved.
- Agree more with: ONE, the less government, the better; OR TWO, there are more things that government should be doing?

APPENDIX C. Wording of Questions in Figures and Tables

Figure 10.1

homosexuality: What about sexual relations between two adults of the same sex—do you think it is always wrong, almost always wrong, wrong only sometimes, or not wrong at all?

pornography: Which of these statements comes closest to your feelings about pornography laws? Illegal for all, illegal for those under 18, or legal for all?

interracial marriage: Do you think there should be laws against marriages between (Negroes/Blacks/African-Americans) and whites?

discretionary abortion: Please tell me whether or not you think it should be possible for a pregnant woman to obtain a legal abortion if...the woman wants it for any reason?

premarital sex: There's been a lot of discussion about the way morals and attitudes about sex are changing in this country. If a man and woman have sexual relations before marriage, do you think it is always wrong, almost always wrong, wrong only sometimes, or not wrong at all?

adultery: What is your opinion about a married person having sexual relations with someone other than the marriage partner—is it always wrong, almost always wrong, wrong only sometimes, or not wrong at all?

women's role: Do you agree or disagree with this statement? Women should take care of running their homes and leave running the country up to men.

Figure 10.2

employment. As you may know, there has been considerable discussion in the news regarding the rights of homosexual men and women. In general, do you think homosexuals should or should not have equal rights in terms of job opportunities?

military service. Do you think homosexuals should or should not be hired for each of the following occupations...the armed forces?

gay sex. Do you think homosexual relations between consenting adults should or should not be legal?

marriage. Do you think marriages between same-sex couples should or should not be recognized by the law as valid, with the same rights as traditional marriages?

Table 10.1

feeling thermometer. I'd like to get your feelings toward some of our political leaders and other people who are in the news these days. I'll read the name of a person and I'd like you to rate that person using something we call the feeling thermometer. Ratings between 50 degrees and 100 degrees mean that you feel favorable and warm toward the person. Ratings between 0 degrees and 50 degrees mean that you don't feel favorable toward the person and that you don't care too much for that person. You would rate the person at the 50 degree mark if you don't feel particularly warm or cold toward the person....How would you rate...GAY MEN AND LESBIANS, that is, homosexuals?

same-sex marriage. Should same-sex couples be ALLOWED to marry, or do you think they should NOT BE ALLOWED to marry?

adoption. Do you think gay or lesbian couples, in other words, homosexual couples, should be legally permitted to adopt children?

job discrimination. Do you FAVOR or OPPOSE laws to protect homosexuals against job discrimination?

serve in armed forces. Do you think homosexuals should be allowed to serve in the United States Armed Forces or don't you think so?

Notes

1. Egan and Sherrill (2005) present evidence that the gay-supportive attitudes of younger survey respondents are due to cohort effects (that is, membership in a given historical generation), not life cycle effects (that is, age at the time of the survey).

2. Specifically, any assessment of whether opinion shifted after *Bowers* requires assumptions about how attitudes were trending over time. In multivariate analysis not shown here, we found that estimates of the size of a *Bowers* effect were highly sensitive to these assumptions. Some of these analyses indicated that opinion did not change in any statistically significant way after *Bowers*.

3. The Lexis-Nexis "Major Papers" archive has limited coverage of U.S. newspapers from 1986. To augment this data, we added stories from the "News Wires" archive in constructing Figure 10.5. Because we did not face the problem of limited coverage for 2003, Figure 10.6 includes only stories in the "Major Papers" archive.

4. The ANES question on gay marriage is the following: "Should same-sex couples be ALLOWED to marry, or do you think they should NOT BE ALLOWED to marry?"

1. Should be allowed
2. Should not be allowed
3. Should not be allowed to marry but should be allowed to legally form a civil union [VOLUNTEERED]
4. Other [VOLUNTEERED] (SPECIFY)
5. Don't know
6. Refused

The analysis in Table 10.2 includes only those who chose responses 1 or 2.

5. One might also suppose that the existence and eventual success of anti-same-sex marriage referendums in thirteen states would also make the preelection period exceptional in several respects. However, our analysis of the ANES data in the thirteen referendum states (available on request) indicates that trends in opinion on gay marriage were not affected in any detectable way by the referendum campaigns in these states.

6. This analysis, conducted in what is known as a "block recursive" approach, is performed with a series of four probit estimations that have the binary choice of support for gay marriage (with value 1) or opposition (with value 0) as the dependent variable. For a description of this technique, see Davis (1985) and Miller and Shanks (1996). The first estimation (model I) includes only the variables from block I. Each subsequent analysis adds an additional block in the causal chain, until the final model (IV) includes all independent variables of interest. The *total effect* of any variable is estimated via the model that controls for all variables causally prior to it but that does not control for any intervening variables. These effects are presented in boldface type in Table 10.2. Model IV, which controls for the effects of all the variables, provides estimates of the *direct effects* of all variables. The *indirect effect* of a variable through intervening factors is calculated by subtracting the variable's direct effect from its total effect.

7. For more on this approach to presentation, see King, Tomz, and Wittenberg (2000) and Long (1997).

8. Wording of questions for egalitarianism, moral traditionalism, and limited government scales is provided in Appendix B.

9. The Pew survey question on civil unions is: "Do you strongly favor, favor, oppose, or strongly oppose allowing gay and lesbian couples to enter into legal agreements with each other that would give them many of the same rights as married couples?" The surveys were administered in October 2003, March 2004, August 2004, and July 2005.

10. A similar result comes from the ABC/Washington Post poll, which asked: "Would you support amending the U.S. Constitution to make it illegal for homosexual couples to get married anywhere in the U.S., or should each state make its own laws on homosexual marriage?" Only 38% supported such an amendment in January of 2004, and 46% supported it a month later.

References

Bergeron, Joe. 2005. "Examining Determinants of American Support for Same-Sex Marriage." Paper presented at the annual meeting of the American Political Science Association, Washington, D.C.

Bowman, Karlyn. 2006. "Attitudes about Homosexuality and Gay Marriage." AEI Studies in Public Opinion. Washington, D.C.

Brewer, Paul R. 2003. "The Shifting Foundations of Public Opinion about Gay Rights." *Journal of Politics* 65: 1208–20.

Brewer, Paul R., and Clyde Wilcox. 2005. "The Polls-Trends: Same-Sex Marriage and Civil Unions." *Public Opinion Quarterly* 69: 599–616.

Bumiller, Elisabeth. 2004. "The 2004 Campaign: Same-Sex Marriage; Bush Says His Party Is Wrong to Oppose Gay Civil Unions." *New York Times*, Oct. 26, A21.

Cimino, Ken, and Gary M. Segura. 2005. "From Radical to Conservative: Civil Unions, Same-Sex Marriage, and the Structure of Public Attitudes." Paper presented at annual meeting of the American Political Science Association, Washington, D.C.

Davis, James A. 1985. *The Logic of Causal Order.* Thousand Oaks, Calif.: Sage.

Egan, Patrick J., and Kenneth Sherrill. 2005. "Neither an In-Law Nor Outlaw Be: Trends in Americans' Attitudes toward Gay People." *Public Opinion Pros* (February). Available online at http://www.publicopinionpros.com. Accessed August 15, 2007.

Haider-Markel, Donald P. 2004. *Media Coverage of Lawrence v. Texas: An Analysis of Content, Tone, and Frames in National and Local News Reporting.* New York: GLAAD Center for the Study of Media and Society.

Haider-Markel, Donald P., and Mark Joslyn. 2005. "Attributions and the Regulation of Marriage: Considering the Parallels between Race and Homosexuality." *PS: Political Science and Politics* 38: 233–40.

Kalton, G., Julie Roberts, and D. Holt. 1980. "The Effects of Offering a Middle Response Option with Opinion Questions." *Statistician* 29: 65–78.

King, Gary, Michael Tomz, and Jason Wittenberg. 2000. "Making the Most of Statistical Analyses: Improving Interpretation and Presentation." *American Journal of Political Science* 44: 341–55.

Long, J. Scott. 1997. *Regression Models for Categorical and Limited Dependent Variables.* Thousand Oaks, Calif.: Sage.

Los Angeles Times Poll. 2004. "National Presidential Politics/Gay Issues/Corporate Scandals." Poll 501. March 27–30. available online at http://www.latimesinteractive.com/pdfarchive/nationworld/la-poll041104-pdf.pdf. Accessed September 23, 2007.

Miller, Warren E., and J. Merrill Shanks. 1996. *The New American Voter.* Cambridge: Harvard University Press.

National Gay and Lesbian Task Force. 2007. "State Nondiscrimination Laws in the U.S." Available online at http://www.thetaskforce.org/reports_and_research/nondiscrimination_laws.Accessed August 15, 2007.

Pew Research Center for the People and the Press. 2004. "Constitutional Amendment Rates as Low Priority: Gay Marriage a Voting Issue, but Mostly for Opponents." February 27. Available online at http://www.people-press.org/reports/pdf/204.pdf. Accessed August 15, 2007.

Presser, G. Stanley Presser, and Howard Schuman. 1980. "The Measurement of the Middle Position in Attitude Surveys." *Public Opinion Quarterly* 44: 70–85.

Rutgers-Eagleton Poll. 2006. "New Jerseyans Now Support Civil Unions by 2–1." Press release. June 23. Available online at http://eagletonpoll.rutgers.edu/polls/release_06–23–06.pdf. Accessed August 15, 2007.

Stoutenborough, James W., Donald P. Haider-Markel, and Mahalley D. Allen. 2006. "Reassessing the Impact of Supreme Court Decisions on Public Opinion: Gay Civil Rights Cases." *Political Research Quarterly* 59: 419–33.

Tygart, C. E. 2000. "Genetic Causation Attribution and Public Support of Gay Rights." *International Journal of Public Opinion Research* 12: 259–75.

United States Government Accountability Office. 2005. "Military Personnel: Financial Costs and Loss of Critical Skills Due to DOD's Homosexual Conduct Policy Cannot Be Completely Estimated." Washington, D.C. Available online at http://www.gao.gov/new.items/d05299.pdf. Accessed September 23, 2007.

Wald, Kenneth D., James W. Button, and Barbara A. Rienzo. 1996. "The Politics of Gay Rights in American Communities: Explaining Antidiscrimination Ordinances and Policies." *American Journal of Political Science* 40: 1152–78.

Wilcox, Clyde, and Robin Wolpert. 2000. "Gay Rights in the Public Sphere: Public Opinion on Gay and Lesbian Equality." In *The Politics of Gay Rights*, edited by Craig A. Rimmerman, Kenneth D. Wald, and Clyde Wilcox. Chicago: University of Chicago Press.

Yang, Alan S. 1997. "Trends—Attitudes toward Homosexuality." *Public Opinion Quarterly* 61: 477–507.

11

The Right to Die

Joshua A. Green and Matthew G. Jarvis

The "right to die" has been part of our national lexicon for only three decades, but in that time we have seen a dramatic shift of public opinion toward high, stable supermajority support—often across partisan and ideological lines—for some individual right to determine the timing and manner of one's death. For the most part, the Supreme Court has left questions about physician-assisted suicide and the right to die to the states. In doing so, the Court has left to the political process the protection of a right that an increasing share of the American public has begun to deem fundamental.

Court cases regarding the right to die have catalyzed intense media coverage that has played a crucial role in crafting a shifting set of frames that define what the "right to die" means. These cases often bring attention to compelling stories about terminally ill or vegetative patients and their desire—or their families' desire—to remove life support, to refuse medical treatment, or to enlist a physician's help in ending a patient's life. Their sympathetic subjects—including Karen Ann Quinlan, Nancy Cruzan, and Terri Schiavo—have challenged the public continually to reevaluate their own beliefs about the relationship between the state and the individual concerning the apportionment of authority to make heartrending end-of-life determinations.

However, there is little evidence that these cases and the media coverage have accelerated or dampened the steady increase in the public's support for the right to die. Only one major news story appears to have noticeably affected public opinion: the widely publicized controversy over Dr. Jack Kevorkian's nine-year campaign to assist (by his claim) more than 100 of his terminally ill patients in committing suicide. The media's coverage of his efforts reframed the issue from the "right to die" to the less palatable "assisted suicide," and during this period support for the right to die fell slightly. There is some evidence that the controversy about removing Terri Schiavo's feeding tube led to a resurgence in support for the right to die, but the polling data are relatively sparse.

In this chapter, we examine both the structure of public opinion on the right to die and how different framings of the issue affect that structure. In general, respondents are much more likely to support the right to die or assisted suicide when asked about a hypothetical case that involves a terminal illness or extreme pain, a painless method of "exit," and consultation with family. Support for the right to die is considerably weaker among opponents of abortion, opponents of the death penalty, blacks, women, Republicans, and people scoring high on measures of religiosity. Rulings by the Supreme Court do not seem to have had any effect on Americans' attitudes toward end-of-life issues.

Trends in Aggregate Opinion

Polling data on the right to die are scarce before the mid-1970s. A scattering of surveys from the New Deal era indicate that nearly half of Americans believed that assisted suicide was morally wrong. In 1936, when Gallup asked Americans whether they favored "mercy deaths under government supervision for hopeless invalids," 45% said they did not, and 38% said they did. In a similar poll Gallup conducted in 1939, 45% favored such "mercy deaths," but we can find no substantive explanation for this change, and it may represent a sampling error. In addition, two Gallup polls in the 1940s found only a minority of Americans willing to allow a doctor to end the life of a patient with an "incurable disease" at the patient's request.

Responses to the three survey questions that have been asked consistently over the longest period demonstrate that support for the right to die—with or without the assistance of a doctor—has risen dramatically since pollsters began fielding questions on the issue. Those three questions, the responses from which form Figure 11.1, are:

- General Social Survey (GSS): "Do you think a person has the right to end his or her own life if this person: Has an incurable disease?"
- Gallup: "When a person has a disease that cannot be cured, do you think doctors should be allowed by law to end the patient's life by some painless means if the patient and his family request it?"
- GSS: When a person has a disease that cannot be cured, do you think doctors should be allowed by law to end the patient's life by some painless means if the patient and his family request it?[1]

As documented by Benson (1999) and Duncan and Parmelee (2006), support for assisted suicide grew most sharply in the early 1980s and has remained

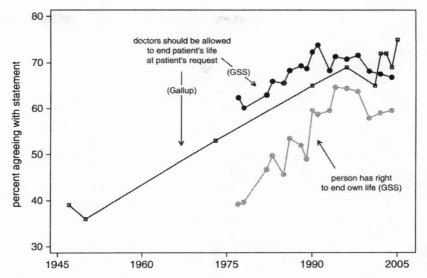

Figure 11.1. Support for the Right to Die for a Person with an Incurable Disease, 1947–2005. Question wording: see Appendix. Sources: Gallup, General Social Survey.

stable since, with the exception of a slight dip in public support during the Kevorkian controversy in the late 1990s. Americans have been consistently more supportive of the right to die with the assistance of a doctor than without such assistance.

Major Court Cases

The courts first became involved in the consideration of end-of-life issues in the 1970s, when life-support technology made it possible to extend, sometimes for many years, the life of a person who was in a persistent vegetative state. The courts were called on to adjudicate various conflicts between the rights of patients, the rights of a patient's family, the ethics of medical practitioners, the policies and practices of hospitals, and the state's interest in protecting life.

The starting point for the modern right-to-die debate is the 1976 New Jersey Supreme Court decision on the fate of Karen Ann Quinlan, a twenty-two-year-old woman who had lapsed into a persistent vegetative state, induced, it seems, by a combination of alcohol and drugs. Her parents asked her doctors to remove her from a respirator, but the doctors refused, on the grounds that she was not "brain dead." After being denied legal guardianship of their daughter, the Quinlans argued in court that their daughter had a constitutionally protected right to die. The New Jersey Supreme Court agreed, in a decision that established that New Jersey families could act on behalf of an incapacitated patient. Karen Ann Quinlan was subsequently removed from the respirator, and she survived, comatose but breathing on her own, for eight years.

Similar litigation in other states extended the legal principle that family members had the right to act as proxies for an incapacitated patient (Glick 1992). Thus began a slow expansion of the courts' influence on how state laws apply to patients, especially those unable to voice their own preferences. Policy makers hoped to reduce conflict over end-of-life care with the introduction of advance directives ("living wills"), in which individuals describe the conditions under which they wish to forgo life-sustaining treatment, should they be unable to participate in medical decisions.[2]

During the 1980s, no right-to-die cases gained national attention, but there was a steady flow of such cases in the state appellate courts. Using an empirical analysis of court decision citations for right-to-die cases, Glick (1992) claims that the Quinlan case stimulated a period of judicial policy making in the 1980s in twelve to fifteen "early adopter" states. Media attention and salience then motivated other states to consider end-of-life issues.

The Supreme Court made its first definitive statement on the right to die in 1990 in the case of Nancy Beth Cruzan (*Cruzan v. Missouri Department of Health*), in a ruling that permitted states to require clear and convincing evidence of a patient's intent before allowing removal of life support. Like Quinlan, Cruzan was a young woman who, after an accident (in this instance, a car crash), was in a persistent vegetative state. Cruzan's parents asked that her feeding tube be removed, and the case turned on the question of what type of evidence family members should be required to present to prove that an incompetent patient would want to end his or her life. The Missouri Supreme Court found "inherently unreliable" the Cruzans' evidence that their daughter would not wish to live in a vegetative state, and the Court concluded that "Missouri's interest in preserving life outweighed Cruzan's liberty interest. A diminished quality of life does not support a decision to cause death." Although hinting at an individual's right to refuse medical treatment, the U.S. Supreme Court nevertheless upheld Missouri's statutory requirement that "clear and convincing evidence" of an incompetent person's intent be demonstrated before life support could be terminated. In the four years following *Cruzan*, advocates placed initiatives to allow physician-assisted suicide on the ballots in three states on the West Coast. Those in Washington (1991) and California (1992) failed, but Oregon's Death with Dignity Act prevailed at the polls in 1994.[3]

In subsequent rulings on the right to die, the Supreme Court continued to defer to the states. In a pair of cases decided in 1997 (*Vacco v. Quill* and *Washington v. Glucksberg*), the Court denied doctors' attempts to overturn state bans on physician-assisted suicide. In these cases, the Court found no constitutional "right to die," separating the circumstances of withdrawal of medical treatment (e.g., *Quinlan* and *Cruzan*) from voluntary euthanasia. The Court rejected the physicians' arguments that such a right could be drawn from Fourteenth Amendment protections of due process and equal protection.

These cases illustrate several aspects of the relationship between court rulings and public opinion. In its initial ruling in *Washington v. Glucksberg*, the Ninth Circuit Court of Appeals supported the physicians' argument for a constitutional right to assisted suicide. The appeals court decision includes a section labeled "Current Societal Attitudes" that cites "increasingly widespread support for allowing the terminally ill to hasten their deaths and avoid painful, undignified and inhumane endings to their lives" (*Compassion in Dying v. Washington*, 1996). In noting the "growing movement to restore humanity and dignity to the process by which Americans die," the Ninth Circuit indicated its sense that jurisprudence must adjust its perspective to changing mores.

In *Washington v. Glucksberg*, the Ninth Circuit held that the state of Washington's ban on assisted suicide was unconstitutional because it denied a liberty interest—"the right to choose a humane, dignified death"—that was protected by the Fourteenth Amendment. But the Supreme Court, in a unanimous decision, reversed the Ninth Circuit and held that Washington's assisted-suicide ban did not violate the due process or equal protection clauses. With the goals of protecting "vulnerable groups" and averting an increase in euthanasia, the Court accepted the state restrictions. Although a majority of Americans may have supported some right to die at the time, the Court considered this issue one best left to the states and the political process. As Chief Justice Rehnquist wrote for the Court in *Glucksberg*, "throughout the Nation, Americans are engaged in an earnest and profound debate about the morality, legality, and practicality of physician-assisted suicide. Our holding permits this debate to continue, as it should in a democratic society." (The Court's rulings were unpopular at their time and remain so today: Harris polls taken over the past ten years have found support for the decision to range between 32% and 35%.)

As was true with *Quinlan* and the cases concerning Jack Kevorkian discussed later, the case of Theresa Marie Schiavo demonstrates that lower level court decisions on this issue can often exceed Supreme Court decisions in their salience and notoriety. Schiavo had suffered heart failure and subsequent brain damage in 1990. She lost consciousness and left no advance directive. Fifteen years later, she remained alive in a hospice in Florida, while her husband and legal guardian, Michael Schiavo, fought with her parents in state courts to have her feeding tube removed. In three separate instances, Schiavo's parents petitioned the Supreme Court to intervene, but the Court refused to hear the case. The Court's final refusal to review came in the wake of an extraordinary intervention by Congress and President George W. Bush, who signed legislation giving federal courts jurisdiction in the Schiavo case in March 2005. Schiavo died on March 31, 2005, nearly two weeks after her feeding tube was removed for the final time (University of Miami Ethics Programs 2007).

In 2006, the Supreme Court again deferred to state law when it ruled in favor of the state of Oregon and against the U.S. Department of Justice in *Gonzales v. Oregon*. Voters in Oregon had approved physician-assisted suicide in 1994 and reapproved it in 1997. But in 2001, U.S. Attorney General John

Ashcroft asserted that physicians who prescribed medications to assist the suicide of terminally ill patients were in violation of the federal Controlled Substances Act because such prescriptions did not have a "legitimate medical purpose." The Court, in a six-to-three decision, held that the statute did not authorize the attorney general to prosecute doctors who were otherwise behaving legally under Oregon law by assisting patients who wanted to end their lives. Although not foreclosing the possibility that a federal law could constitutionally regulate the practice of assisted suicide, the Court did not find the Controlled Substances Act did so, and therefore states were free to experiment with regulatory regimes akin to Oregon's.

With the few notable exceptions mentioned here, the Supreme Court has been a minor player in the national debate over the right to die. The Court has left to the state courts and legislatures the task of resolving most of the major controversies concerning when persons can terminate their own lives or the evidence necessary for one to act on behalf of an incompetent patient. Over this period of general acquiescence by the Court, however, public opinion on the issue has changed considerably, often in tandem with media coverage of efforts and cases at the local level.

Media Coverage and Public Opinion

Starting in the 1990s, several court decisions in right-to-die and assisted-suicide cases attracted intense media coverage. Figure 11.2 depicts the number of stories appearing on these issues in the *New York Times* and *Washington Post* since 1970, although the pattern is similar if most major newspapers are included. For the most part, media coverage spikes with highly salient court cases or controversies such as those spurred on by Jack Kevorkian, and it increases somewhat above average during ballot measure campaigns, such as those in Washington, California, and Oregon.

In the early 1990s, the media's predominant frame for the issue switched from "right to die" to "assisted suicide." Both terms, of course, refer to actions taken to end a terminal patient's life. But "right to die" evokes a patient's request for the withdrawal of life-support equipment, and "assisted suicide" connotes patient-doctor decision making in the prescription and consumption of a lethal dose of drugs. The latter involves an active choice to end one's life; the former implies that the person would probably die naturally. Survey data indicate that the American public is much more uncomfortable with active, compared with passive, means to end life. The change in frame, we note, was accompanied by dips in support for the right to die by the end of the 1990s (see Figure 11.1).

Kevorkian's many arrests and trials over a nine-year period sustained media interest in the right to die. A Gallup poll taken in 1993, at the height of media coverage of his activities, showed that 43% of Americans supported Kevorkian's "actions."[4] The public's attitude toward Kevorkian did not soften,

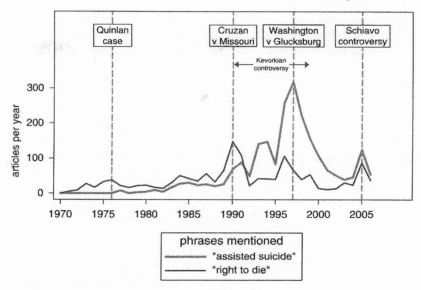

Figure 11.2. Coverage of Right to Die and Assisted Suicide in the *New York Times* and *Washington Post*, 1970–2006. Source: Lexis-Nexis, ProQuest Direct.

even though general support for the rights of terminal patients remained high. In the GSS conducted in 1993, for example, 68% of respondents supported the principle that doctors should be allowed to assist patients with incurable diseases to end their lives, and 59% said that such patients should be allowed to end their lives themselves. In effect, the public supported the message but not the messenger. In 1998, a CBS/New York Times poll showed that the public still disapproved of Kevorkian, with only 43% supporting his actions. Media coverage of the right to die and assisted suicide declined after Kevorkian was sent to prison in 1999. Coverage of right-to-die issues gripped readers when a specific person was involved, either a dying patient or a crusading doctor (cast as a villain or a hero). But after Kevorkian's trial, no new story lines emerged until the final stages of the dispute over Terri Schiavo in 2005.

The Schiavo case, which monopolized the headlines for several months in 2005, put the right to die back on the national agenda. The controversy also seems to have strengthened the public's resolve to keep government out of what most considered a family decision. The Pew Research Center asked 1,500 adults in July and November 2005 whether Congress "did the right thing" in getting involved in the Schiavo case. Large majorities—74% in July and 72% in November—said that Congress "should have stayed out" of it, with only 17% of the November respondents saying Congress "did the right thing." In a Harris poll in April 2005, the public also expressed disapproval of government interference: 33% approved of the actions of the Florida legislature, 35%

approved of the conduct of the U.S. Congress, and 49% approved of the behavior of the U.S. Supreme Court. In a Time Magazine poll days after Schiavo's death, 54% of respondents said they were "less likely" to vote for their congressional representative if he or she had voted to move the Schiavo case to the federal courts, 21% said they were more likely to vote for such a representative, and 18% said that their representative's vote on this issue "doesn't matter."

In several polls, the majority of respondents shied away from extreme positions, which suggests that a mainstream effect has settled on the side of favoring the right to die. For example, in a Fox News poll after Schiavo's death, 20% of respondents were unsure whether they agreed or disagreed with the decision to remove her feeding tube, but when given a choice of whether to characterize the outcome as an act of "murder" or "mercy," only 29% of all respondents called it murder.

When news stories receive the widespread media coverage that the Schiavo case did, salience sharply spikes for short periods of time. In the March 2005 Time Magazine poll, 76% said they had followed the Terri Schiavo case "very closely" or "somewhat closely." Survey data suggest that this intense media attention may have been accompanied by a rise in the public's support for the right to die. As shown in Figure 11.1, support for assisted suicide as measured by the Gallup poll rose to a historic high of 75% in a survey administered in May 2005. GSS data for 2006 show support for the right to die when requested by a patient at 68%, while 61% believed that a patient has a right to end his or her own life. CBS/New York Times polls taken between 2003 and 2006 also demonstrate that media attention can shift public opinion significantly. In all iterations of the survey, respondents were asked: "If a person has a disease that will ultimately destroy their mind or body and they want to take their own life, should a doctor be allowed to assist the person in taking their own life, or not?" In November 2004, before the media attention to Terri Schiavo, 46% of respondents said that assisted suicide should be allowed. By July 2005, three months after Schiavo's death, 54% said that assisted suicide should be allowed. And in January 2006—in a survey conducted three days after the Court announced its opinion in *Gonzales v. Oregon*—support for assisted suicide reached 56%.

Evidence from other polls also suggests that support for the right to die increases with increased attention and public debate. The Pew Research Center (2006) reports that more people were talking about "end of life" issues in 2005 than had done so fifteen years earlier. More important, those who said that they talked about these issues "a great deal" were much more likely to support the right to die. In both 1990 and 2005, overall support for right-to-die laws was high (79% in 1990; 84% in 2005), but those who thought about end-of-life issues "a great deal" were even more supportive of the right to die (87% in 2005). This group also showed the greatest increase in support (8 percentage points) between 1990 and 2005; among those who thought about end-of-life issues "not much or not at all," support for the right to die rose by 4 percentage points. On the more controversial issue of physician-assisted suicide, the gap between those paying high attention to the issue and those paying low attention was even wider. In the 2005 survey, 57% of those who had thought about end-of-life issues "a great deal" approved of physician-assisted suicide, compared with 45% of those who paid "some" attention and 35% of those who had thought about the issue "not much or not at all."[5]

Framing and Question Wording Effects

The "right to die" refers to a constellation of issues that concern the laws governing how individuals may determine the timing and manner of their deaths.[6] Public opinion surveys tend to focus on two types of situations: (1) the withdrawal of life support when an unconscious patient is in a "persistent vegetative state" and (2) the ending of a terminally ill patient's life with the conscious agreement of the patient. In general, the public is much more comfortable with allowing a patient, or a patient's family, to request the withdrawal of life support than with allowing a patient to arrange for physician-assisted suicide. Although most of the high-profile court cases discussed in this chapter involve the first situation, most of the opinion polls address the second situation.

Research on the decisions of mentally competent patients to end their lives (e.g., MacDonald 1998) notes an important but subtle difference in public opinion on voluntary active euthanasia (in which a patient asks a doctor to administer fatal drugs) and assisted suicide (in which the doctor writes a prescription but the patient administers the drugs). According to Benson (1999), support for voluntary euthanasia reaches 60% or higher, and support for assisted suicide is between 45% and 59%, depending on the poll. Though one might expect more support for the practice that allows patients more control over the process, Benson argues that people's instinctive and religious-based aversion to suicide may depress support for the practice. It may also be that the presence of the word "doctor" provokes a more positive response. Despite high levels of support for assisted suicide, only 32% of respondents said that they would consider assisted suicide if they had a terminal disease, and only 14% said that they would help a friend end his or her life in the same circumstances (Benson 1999).

Polling questions that ask about physician-assisted suicide without adding qualifying circumstances (e.g., incurable disease) garner much lower support—between 5 and 10 percentage points—than questions that include such circumstances. These circumstances—which may be as simple as an extra word or description in a particular question—seem to soften respondents' aversion to suicide. For example, one GSS question asks: "When a person has a disease that cannot be cured, do you think doctors should be allowed by law to end the patient's life by some painless means if the patient and his family request it?" This question elicits strong support, but when the question is asked without the "softening" circumstances—"Do you think a person has the right to end his or her own life if this person has an incurable disease?"—approval fell by nearly 10 percentage points in recent surveys. Thus, there is a clear distinction between "soft" questions, which give the respondent the ability to empathize with the subject of the question or validate only the specific situation in the question, and "hard" questions, which force subjects to either state an absolute or confront the term "suicide." (See Appendix for more examples of "hard" and "soft" questions.)

Question-wording effects also arise when we compare responses to questions that reference the right to die as a refusal of medical treatment and those that reference physician-assisted suicide. In a survey conducted in 2005, the Pew Research Center (2006) found that 84% of respondents approved of right-to-die laws that allow patients to decide to end their lives by refusing medical treatment. Support fell to 60% when respondents were asked whether patients have the "moral right" to end their lives if they "suffer great pain with no hope of improvement," and support fell again, to 53%, when respondents were asked about a patient who "has an incurable disease" without any mention of great pain. Other circumstances greatly suppress support for a patient's decision. When asked about patients who "are ready to die because living is a burden" and patients who "are an extremely heavy burden on family," only 33% and 29%, respectively, agreed that such patients had a moral right to end their lives. Regardless of question wording, support increased at least 4 percentage points (with the exception of the "heavy burden on family" question) from a similar Pew poll taken in 1990.

Over the past thirty years, high-profile cases and intense media attention have led more families to talk about end-of-life issues, including life-support technology and living wills. Even since 1990, there has been a marked increase in respondents who have talked with family members about their wishes for end-of-life treatment. In 1990, only half of Pew Center respondents reported discussing the issue with a spouse. By 2005, more than two thirds (69%) had done so.

The distinctions among responses to different types of questions regarding end-of-life issues are substantial. But what is remarkable is that regardless of how it is assessed, the over-time trend in public opinion on these issues has been to give terminally ill patients and their families more control over how and when they end their lives.

Structure of Right-to-Die Opinion

Support has been rising for the right to die, but this support is not uniform across all demographic and ideological groups. Singh (1979) first documented that blacks are much less likely to approve of assisted suicide than whites, and research by Ostheimer (1980) and Blendon, Szalay, and Knox (1992) replicated this finding. Blendon and colleagues found that blacks were less likely than whites to support voluntary euthanasia by an average margin of 20 percentage points. Before MacDonald (1998), most researchers assumed that this gap was due to cultural and religious differences, including a fear of giving others power to end one's life. MacDonald finds that measures of "biblical ethicalism" (a measure of how important the Bible is in making life decisions) and political conservatism also explain blacks' lack of support for assisted suicide. He notes that because blacks have historically voted Democratic in the twentieth century and hold more liberal views on most social issues (with the exception of attitudes toward homosexuality), the size of the gap between blacks and whites on the right to die might be larger after controlling for views on other social and economic issues.

Our findings are consistent with other research on the structure of right-to-die opinion, although we introduce a new approach that helps to illuminate *why* opinion is structured the way it is. Support for a right to die is noticeably lower among the more religious (as measured by church attendance, as well as by responses to questions of fundamentalism or biblical literalism), conservatives, older people, women, the less educated, Republicans, and particularly African Americans (mostly because of higher levels of biblical ethicalism and belief that "life belongs to God"). Our findings here are quite consistent with those of all of these previous researchers, to the extent our data allow testing of their findings. However, we also introduce a new approach to the question that shows the similarity in opinion on the question of a right to die and opinion on two other life-and-death questions: abortion and the death penalty.

Among respondents to the GSS since 2000, a majority of almost all major demographic and opinion groups support physician-assisted suicide, including those groups that we might expect to oppose this practice: fundamentalists (54% support), blacks (50%), and those who attend religious services every week (52%). (See Table 11.1.) All of these groups, however, reject the premise that a person has the right to end his or her life, and that opinion also predominates among people who take a pro-life position on abortion, those over age 65, and those with less than a high school diploma.

On the issue of physician-assisted suicide, support is 8 percentage points higher among men than among women and 13 percentage points higher among the youngest group than among the oldest group. Conservatives' support for assisted suicide is 23 percentage points lower than liberals' support. Support among those who attend church weekly is 30 percentage points lower than those who never attend. Also notable is the 30-percentage-point difference between pro-life and pro-choice respondents. Overall, though, support for assisted suicide has increased nearly uniformly across the board since the late 1970s, with the exception of a trend indicating an increased ideological polarization on the issue. As shown in the last few rows of Table 11.1, the gap between liberals' and conservatives' attitudes on assisted suicide is now much larger than it was three decades ago.

The next step in analyzing these differences is to sort out the independent contribution of each variable by using block-recursive logit equations. Table 11.2 displays "first differences"—the effect associated with a shift from the minimum to the maximum value of each independent variable, holding all others at their 2004 means. In these models, we follow the approach suggested by Campbell, Converse, Miller, and Stokes (1960) and model various

Table 11.1
Support for Right to Die for a Person with an Incurable Disease, 1977–2004

	Doctors should be allowed to end patient's life at patient's request ("soft" support for right to die)				Person has right to end own life ("hard" support for right to die)			
	Before 1990	1990–1999	2000– present	Change	Before 1990	1990–1999	present	2000– Change
All respondents	65	71	68	3	46	63	59	12
Sex								
Male	69	75	72	3	52	68	64	12
Female	61	68	64	3	42	59	54	12
Race								
White	67	74	71	4	48	66	63	14
Black	45	52	50	5	30	45	37	7
Attendance of religious services								
Never	78	86	82	5	65	81	74	9
Monthly	71	77	68	–3	51	67	59	8
Weekly	52	56	52	0	29	44	40	10
Religious fundamentalist	53%	58	54	1	33	48	42	9
Abortion opinion*								
Pro-choice	81	87	86	4	68	82	80	11
Pro-life	54	57	56	3	31	44	45	14

Death penalty opinion

Favor	69	76	74	4	50	67	64	14
Oppose	52	58	57	5	38	52	51	13
Age								
18–29	74	77	72	−2	57	68	63	6
30–44	68	74	70	2	54	67	61	7
45–64	58	70	67	9	38	61	61	23
65 plus	55	61	59	4	31	48	43	12
Party identification								
Democrat	62	70	68	6	42	61	57	15
Independent	68	75	72	3	53	66	63	10
Republican	64	69	61	−3	45	59	54	9
Education								
<HS	56	62	60	4	33	49	44	11
HS diploma	68	73	68	0	49	63	58	9
BA	70	74	72	3	62	71	69	7
Political views								
Liberal	69	80	79	10	54	74	72	18
Moderate	67	74	71	3	45	63	59	14
Conservative	61	64	56	−4	42	55	50	8

*Categorized by response to the statement: It should be possible for a pregnant woman to obtain a legal abortion if the woman wants it for any reason. Those responding yes are categorized as "pro-choice"; those responding no are categorized as "pro-life."

Source: General Social Survey. Question wording: see text.

Table 11.2
Predicting "Soft" Support for the Right to Die

	I	II	III
Immutable characteristics			
Female	**−.07*****	**−.04****	−.04***
Age	**−.26*****	**−.17*****	−.19***
Black[+]	**−.24*****	**−.17*****	−.20***
Other race[+]	**−.05****	−.03	−.03
Long-term social characteristics			
Married		**−.01**	.01
Parent		**.06****	.05**
Number of children		**−.16*****	−.12**
Education		**.07*****	.03*
Catholic[++]		**−.03****	−.03*
Jewish[++]		**.07**	−.02
Religious fundamentalist		**−.09*****	−.08***
Attendance at religious services		**−.38*****	−.33***
Political attitudes and views			
Ideology			**−.08*****
Party identification			**−.04****
Opposition to legal abortion			**−.26*****
Opposition to death penalty			**−.18*****
N	11,822	11,822	11,822
Pseudo R^2	.04	.11	.15
Pseudo log likelihood	−7129.74	−6584.78	−6196.79

[+] Base category: white; [++] base category: Protestant/other.
Cell entries are first differences derived from logit analyses. They are estimates of the change in probability of supporting the right to die, given a shift from the minimum to the maximum value of each independent variable, holding all other variables constant at their 2004 means. The analyses also include variables for a linear and a quadratic time trend (not shown). Cell entries in bold are a variable's total effect—that is, the effect of a variable on support for the right to die before the consideration of the mediating effects of any intervening variables. Logit coefficients are significantly different from zero at *p< .05, **p<.01, and ***p<.001. Analyses incorporate weights supplied by GSS.
Source: General Social Survey. Question wording: see text.

contributing factors to a person's opinion on the right to die in stages based on where the variable would fall in the "funnel of causality." Thus, we model race, age, and sex (physical characteristics) in the first stage; include demographics such as education, religion, and family in the second stage; and study political attitudes and views on particular issues (in this case, abortion and the death penalty) in the final stage. In all stages of the analysis, we also control for the effects of time (not shown in the table).

Most of the findings here are consistent with those of earlier researchers. Holding other immutable characteristics constant, women, older respondents, and blacks are less supportive of assisted suicide (Model I in Table 11.2). These associations remain significant even as other variables are added to the analysis (in Models II and III): for example, blacks are 20 percentage points less likely to support the right to die than are similarly situated whites. In model II, variables associated with moral traditionalism—including being a parent, having more children, Catholicism, religious fundamentalism, and attendance at religious services—all predict less support for assisted suicide. With the exception of parenthood, the effects of all these variables remain significant when we control for political attitudes and views (in Model III). Not surprisingly, conservatives, Republicans, and those holding pro-life views on abortion are less supportive of the right to die. But opposition to the death penalty (usually a liberal stance) is associated with opposition to the right to die. Of all of these effects, those associated with age,[7] African American identity, religiosity, and attitudes on abortion and the death penalty are the largest by the first differences measure.[8] But many of the differences in Table 11.2 are relatively modest. Men are only 5 percentage points more likely to support assisted suicide than women, a finding consistent with those of Sawyer and Sobal (1987), Finlay (1995), and MacDonald (1998).[9]

On other points, our analysis differs from that of other scholars. Some have claimed (Sawyer & Sobal 1987; Ostheimer 1980; MacDonald 1998), for example, that college graduates are more likely to support assisted suicide than high school graduates. The results for Model II seem to concur, but once opinions on abortion and the death penalty are introduced, the effect of educational attainment becomes much smaller. This suggests that perhaps education changes people's views of life and death issues in general.

The very large effects associated with people's opinions on abortion and the death penalty and their support for the right to die illustrate the ramifications of beliefs about the sanctity of life. The 30-point difference in support for physician-assisted suicide among abortion rights supporters and abortion rights opponents is not substantially due to demographic correlates of abortion opinion; when physical characteristics, demographics, and political frameworks are controlled for, these two groups are predicted to differ in their level of support by 26 percentage points. The size of the effect associated with opposition to the death penalty is also large: 18 percentage points. Introduction of the abortion and death penalty variables into the model cuts the effect of the religious variables (denomination, religious fundamentalism, and attendance at services). In other words, much of the effect of religion is channeled through opinion on abortion and the death penalty.[10] This suggests that people's responses to all three issues reflect some belief about the "sanctity of life" or some other aspect of religious belief that the surveys have not captured—such as MacDonald's (1998) finding that a component of disapproval of a right to die is a belief that "life belongs to God."

Conclusion

Public opinion data from the last three decades show a consistent rise in the support for the right to die, although the levels of support depend on how the question is posed. There is also a strong correlation between opposition to abortion, opposition to the death penalty, and opposition to the right to die, suggesting that there is a "sanctity of life" thread that may somewhat temper conventional ideological distinctions.

Court cases at both the state and federal levels regarding right-to-die issues have contributed to impressive spikes in media attention that bring the controversy to the forefront of national debate. With the possible exception of the small effects observed during the Kevorkian and Terri Schiavo controversies, court cases have done little to interrupt or accelerate the strong upward trend in support for the right to die over the past thirty years.

The profound national debate over the right to die that the Supreme Court acknowledged in *Glucksberg* has continued in the ten years since that decision. It has continued in the courts with cases such as Terri Schiavo's, as well as outside the courts with ballot campaigns or proposed bills to enact rights into law that courts have not recognized in the state or federal constitution. Court cases, in this realm as in others, place a human face on an otherwise quite abstract philosophical and legal controversy. In doing so, they have spurred media coverage, elite action, and a national discussion that has expressed itself in rising support for an individual's right to determine the timing and manner of one's death.

Appendix: Categorization of "Hard" and "Soft" Questions

The diversity of question wording has prompted us to categorize individual questions as either being "hard" or "soft" in order to draw some substantive conclusions. We have included for interested readers an explanation of how this sorting occurred.

Hard questions are those that seek to measure a respondent's opinions on an absolute right to die, stripped of any frames or words that may allow the respondent to respond "yes, but only under certain circumstances specified." In some cases, those questions that choose to use words with negative associations (most notably, "suicide" or "doctor-assisted suicide") are considered "hard." Example of hard questions, with key language in italics:

> General Social Survey: "Do you think a person has the right to *end his or her own life* if this person: Has an incurable disease?"
>
> Fox: "Do you favor or oppose legalizing physician-assisted *suicide* for terminally ill patients?"

Harris Question on *Glucksberg* and *Vacco:* "In 1997, the U.S. (United States) Supreme Court ruled that individuals do not have a constitutional right to *doctor-assisted suicide*. Do you agree or disagree with this decision?"

Pew Research Center for the People & the Press, Right to Die II Survey: "In some states, it's legal for doctors to prescribe lethal doses of drugs that a terminally ill patient could use themselves to *commit suicide*. Do you approve or disapprove of laws that let doctors assist patients who want to end their lives this way?"

Soft questions are those that include language that allow a respondent to respond "yes, but only under the terms specified in the question." No soft questions include the word "suicide," and all refer to qualifying circumstances that may lead someone who is undecided or against the right to die to lean toward support. Examples of qualifying soft questions, with key language in italics:

Gallup: "When a person has a disease *that cannot be cured*, do you think doctors should be allowed by law to end the patient's life *by some painless means* if the patient *and his family* request it?"

CBS/New York Times: "If a person has a disease *that will ultimately destroy their mind or body* and they want to take their own life, should a doctor be allowed to *assist the person in taking their own life*, or not?"

Harris: "Do you think that the law should allow doctors *to comply with the wishes of a dying patient in severe distress* who asks to have his or her life ended, or not?"

General Social Survey: When a person has a *disease that cannot be cured*, do you think doctors should be allowed by law to end the patient's life *by some painless means if the patient and his family request it?*

CBS News/New York Times Poll: "If a person has a disease that will ultimately destroy their mind or body and they want to take their own life, should a doctor be allowed to assist the person in taking their own life, or not?"

Pew Research Center for the People & the Press, Right to Die II Survey: "In some states, it's legal to stop medical treatment that is keeping a *terminally ill patient* alive, or never start the treatment in the first place, if that's what the patient wants. Do you approve or disapprove of laws that let PATIENTS decide about being kept alive through medical treatment?"

"Do you think a person has a moral right to end his or her own life under any of the following circumstances?

a. when this person has a disease that is incurable?
b. when this person is suffering great pain and has no hope of improvement?
c. when this person is an extremely heavy burden on his or her family?
d. when this person is ready to die because living has become a burden?

Notes

1. The different questions from the General Social Survey (GSS) introduce a distinction between what we term "hard" versus "soft" support for the right to die. We explore this distinction later in this chapter.

2. The term "advance directive" had been introduced in 1969 in a law journal article by Louis Kutner, an American lawyer active in the Euthanasia Education Fund. The use of advance directives was furthered by the Patient Self-Determination Act of 1991, by which Congress required many hospitals and nursing homes to advise incoming patients of their rights to advance directives under state law.

3. Voters in Michigan (in 1998) and Maine (2000) defeated assisted suicide laws, and efforts to pass bills legalizing assisted suicide failed in the state legislatures of Hawaii, Vermont, and Wisconsin. For a time line of events, including legislative efforts to legalize assisted suicide, see http://www.deathwithdignity.org/historyfacts/chronology.asp.

4. The question asked: "Do you approve or disapprove of the actions taken by Doctor Kevorkian (who assists terminally ill people commit suicide)?" The poll was taken December 4–6, 1993. Question accessed through Lexis-Nexis; question ID USGALLUP.422024, Q 38.

5. See Appendix for poll question wording in the Pew survey.

6. For a particularly lucid discussion of the medical profession's positions on the various practices discussed here, see Benson 1999.

7. It is likely that the effects associated with age are "cohort" rather than "life cycle" effects. In their analysis of GSS data, Duncan and Parmelee (2006) find that members of all birth cohorts increased their support for the right to die between 1977 and 2004—a finding inconsistent with the hypothesis that people become less supportive of assisted suicide as they grow older.

8. Although the first difference associated with the "number of children" variable is large, very few families actually have the maximum number of children of respondents to the GSS (eight children). Thus the first difference associated with this variable is an artificially high measure of its effect on the typical GSS respondent. For example, calculations (not shown) derived from Model III estimate that each additional child is associated with a decline in the probability of support for assisted suicide of approximately 1.4 percentage points.

9. Ostheimer (1980) contends that the data show no differences between men and women, but his analysis is confined to marginals and does not control for other factors.

10. Although opinions on the death penalty and abortion are strongly associated with opinion on the right to die, and although the Roman Catholic Church takes strong stances on abortion, the death penalty, and end-of-life issues, identification as a Roman Catholic has only a small effect on attitudes regarding the right to die.

References

Benson, John M. 1999. "Trends: End-of-Life Issues." *Public Opinion Quarterly* 63(2): 263–77.

Blendon, Robert J., Ulrike S. Szalay & Richard A. Knox. 1992. "Should Physicians Aid Their Patients in Dying? The Public Perspective." *JAMA: Journal of the American Medical Association* 267: 2658–2662.

Campbell, Angus, Philip E. Converse, Warren E. Miller, and Donald E. Stokes. 1960. *The American Voter.* New York: Wiley.

Duncan, O. D., and L. F. Parmelee. 2006. "Trends in Public Approval of Euthanasia and Suicide in the U.S., 1947–2003." *Journal of Medical Ethics* 32: 266–72.

Finlay, Barbara. 1985. "Right to Life vs. the Right to Die: Some Correlates of Euthanasia Attitudes." *Sociology and Social Research* 69: 548–60.

Glick, Henry R. 1992. "Judicial Innovation and Policy Re-Invention: State Supreme Courts and the Right to Die." *Western Political Quarterly* 45(1): 71–92.

Kutner, Louis. 1969. "Due Process of Euthanasia: The Living Will, a Proposal." *Indiana Law Journal* 44: 539.

MacDonald, William L. 1998. "The Difference between Blacks' and Whites' Attitudes toward Voluntary Euthanasia." *Journal for the Scientific Study of Religion* 37(3): 411–26.

Ostheimer, John M. 1980. "The Polls: Changing Attitudes toward Euthanasia." *Public Opinion Quarterly* 44(1): 123–28.

Pew Research Center for the People and the Press. 2006. "Strong Public Support for Right to Die." News Release. Available online at http://people-press.org/reports/pdf/266.pdf. Accessed April 16, 2007.

Sawyer, Darwin & Jeffery Sobal. 1987. "Public Attitudes Toward Suicide Demographic and Ideological Correlates" *The Public Opinion Quarterly* 51: 92–101.

Singh, K. 1979. "Correlates of Attitudes toward Euthanasia." *Social Biology* 26: 247–54.

University of Miami Ethics Programs. 2007. "Key Events in the Case of Theresa Marie Schiavo." Available online at http://www6.miami.edu/ethics/schiavo/timeline.htm. Accessed March 20, 2007.

12

Government Takings of Private Property

Janice Nadler, Shari Seidman Diamond,
and Matthew M. Patton

In June 2005, the U.S. Supreme Court decided *Kelo v. City of New London*, which held that the government can force the sale of private property for the purpose of economic development. Although the ruling was largely in line with established legal precedent regarding "takings"—the extent to which the government can take private property or otherwise regulate its use for a public purpose—news of the *Kelo* decision was highly salient, and the public's reaction was uniformly negative. *Kelo* thus stands as a rare instance in which a Supreme Court ruling that reaffirmed the status quo nevertheless raised the awareness and ire of a previously inattentive public.

At issue in the case was a plan by the City of New London, Connecticut, to redevelop the waterfront neighborhood of Fort Trumbull. But some homeowners in the area refused to sell. The City of New London sought to use its power of eminent domain to condemn the properties. The homeowners objected on the grounds that taking their property would violate their rights under the Fifth Amendment of the U.S. Constitution, which states: "nor shall private property be taken for public use without just compensation." The Supreme Court has interpreted the Fifth Amendment to mean that the government can take private property only for a public use and only if it pays the owner just compensation. The City of New London claimed that it was justified in taking the homeowners' property because the proposed development promised to bring jobs and tax revenue to the city. The homeowners argued that this justification did not constitute a "public use" within the meaning of the Fifth Amendment.

In a five-to-four decision, the Supreme Court decided the case in favor of the City of New London and held that the proposed development constituted a public use. Public reaction to the case was surprisingly strong and uniform across the political spectrum. An overwhelming majority of citizens were astonished and dismayed by the decision. At the same time, most legal scholars and practitioners viewed the decision as a logical product of established precedent in the Supreme Court's earlier takings jurisprudence, in which the "public use" requirement was already very relaxed.

Rarely has a single U.S. Supreme Court decision triggered such a wave of popular outrage and immediate legislative response. In testimony before Congress, property scholar Thomas Merrill commented that *Kelo* "is unique in modern annals of law in terms of the negative response it has evoked" (U.S. Senate 2005). What explains the extreme public reaction to the *Kelo* case, given that the outcome matched what most legal experts expected? One possibility is that prior Supreme Court eminent domain cases did not receive much attention, leaving the public generally unaware of the long history of Court decisions approving government takings for a variety of purposes. For example, in 1954 in *Berman v. Parker*, the Court permitted the taking of two non-blighted stores in Washington, D.C., on the grounds that the neighborhood in which the stores were located was blighted and that the redevelopment of the neighborhood was necessary. The Court issued a sweeping ruling, holding that Congress was not required to "take a piecemeal approach" but rather had broad authority to condemn the entire area. As a result, thousands of poor black residents were pushed out of their homes (Kanner 2006; Pritchett 2003). Remarkably, the decision received little notice in the press.

Little is known about public impressions of takings prior to *Kelo*, largely because takings occur on the local level, affecting local communities. A local government taking might provoke sharp controversy, but the controversy would be reported mostly in the local press. Before *Kelo*, there was almost no polling on eminent domain or on takings.

This chapter discusses the conflict between the public's expectations about the circumstances under which government should be permitted to exercise its power of eminent domain to effect an outright taking of private property, on the one hand, and the U.S. Supreme Court's Fifth Amendment "public use" jurisprudence, on the other. We focus largely on outright takings in which the government forces the sale of private property—a situation that usually arises when the government feels it necessary to assemble parcels that have a particular configuration (Dana & Merrill 2002; Fischel 2004). To prevent private property owners from refusing to sell or from holding out for an unreasonably high price, the government can exercise its power of eminent domain to force the sale of the land and go forward with the project. The Fifth Amendment to the U.S. Constitution limits the power of eminent domain to situations in which the government takes land for "public use," a requirement that the Supreme Court has long interpreted quite loosely. The toothlessness of the public use requirement went mostly unnoticed by the general public until the Supreme Court declared in *Kelo* that taking homes for the purpose of economic development satisfies the public use requirement. The *Kelo* decision seemed to trigger a sudden collective recognition of the Court's public use doctrine, and in this chapter we explore the possible reasons for this change.

We note, however, that forced sale of private property by the government is not the only instantiation of the government's power to control private property. Local land-use regulations restrict the use of private property, and sometimes those restrictions are so burdensome that courts have declared them to constitute "takings" under the Fifth Amendment, which requires the government to pay just compensation. These regulatory takings cases provide an important comparison with forced-sale takings cases, in part because the former are often perceived to stem from local government decisions that are responsive to the majority of voters, rather than the product of special interests such as developers (Fischel 2004). In recent years, the Supreme Court has decided many more regulatory takings cases than forced-sale takings cases. Public opinion data on land-use regulation therefore offer useful insights into attitudes toward private property and the government's right to control it, and as we will see, those attitudes pose a counterpoint to the strong public reaction to *Kelo*.

We begin by discussing the data available about public opinion in reaction to eminent domain prior to *Kelo*, and we then turn to the backlash that followed the decision. We show that the backlash was remarkably uniform across virtually all dimensions of identification, including political party, race, income, and education. We note the ongoing efforts—through legislation and voter initiative campaigns—to curb government eminent domain powers. Interestingly, many of these efforts go well beyond the issue of the circumstances under which property can be condemned, attempting more broadly to curb land-use regulation, including environmental regulation and zoning restrictions. We argue that the nearly uniform popular denunciation of *Kelo* suggests that the decision was perceived to violate fundamental cultural values, which we attempt to identify. We conclude by speculating why the Court ended up with a position so out of step with the opinions of the American public.

Public Opinion about Takings Prior to *Kelo*

Before *Kelo*, pollsters and academic researchers who study public opinion did not focus on public reaction to the use of the power of eminent domain to take property. Some scholars did, however, study and address public reaction to urban renewal programs—"slum clearance"—that promised to create healthier, more modern, and more beautiful urban communities. During this period, the power of eminent domain was a key tool in the effort to reinvigorate areas deemed blighted. Critiques of urban renewal did not generally take issue with the use of eminent domain per se, but rather with the focus of redevelopment officials on clearance of minority communities and the creation of new, racially segregated neighborhoods (Pritchett 2003).

Examples include the construction of the interstate highway network beginning in the late 1950s. In urban areas, there was a concerted effort to reduce blight by routing the interstate highway through poor neighborhoods (Mohl 1993). Until the rise of the neighborhood preservation movements of the late 1960s, the plans to raze minority communities met little resistance, and that resistance was mostly futile. Opponents' objections were not so much to the use of eminent domain, but rather to the policies that were perceived to work to the detriment of poor or otherwise powerless communities.

To our knowledge, only two public opinion polls asked about eminent domain prior to *Kelo*. One was a poll in Montana that addressed a local issue with a unique history. In the western United States, state and local governments sometimes delegated their power of eminent domain to private developers of mines and electric power lines (Fischel 2004). A summary, but not the language, of a 1975 poll of Montanans is reported by Calvert (1979). Respondents were asked if they favored or opposed a law that would take from private corporations their right to exercise the power of eminent domain, primarily for mining and power line construction. Eighty percent of respondents favored this law, and this percentage did not vary substantially across political party identification. More recently, in 1997, a national poll asked whether the government adequately compensates owners when property is taken for public use (as is required by the Fifth Amendment to the U.S. Constitution). Thirty-five percent of respondents thought that the government does not adequately compensate in these situations (Wisconsin Public Television/Princeton Survey Research 1997).[1]

In contrast, information on public opinion about government regulation of private property is more readily available. In an early national survey (Gallup poll, 1964), 40% of respondents agreed with the statement "The government is interfering too much with property rights."[2] Like questions in many of the early polls and some of the post-*Kelo* polls, this question was highly abstract.

Focusing more specifically on regulation, 59% of respondents in a 1995 national Harris poll said that the government should not have the right to regulate private property.[3] It is not clear, however, what meaning respondents attached to this question because when the next question asked whether the government should have the right to prevent owners of private land from developing the land if it would harm the environment, 79% of respondents agreed. As a general matter, in the pre-*Kelo* era, a substantial minority of Americans expressed some concern that governmental action poses a threat to private property.

The sanctity of private property to Americans is well documented. For example, in 1974 a Time/Yankelovich national poll gave respondents a series of "statements which represent some traditional American values," and 70% said they strongly believed in the statement "The right to private property is sacred." (By comparison, 62% said they strongly believed that "The American way of life is superior to that of any other country," and

57% said they strongly believed that "Belonging to some organized religion is important in a person's life.") Similarly, in a 1973 Harris Survey, 88% of respondents rated "allowing people to own private property" as a major contributor to making America great. Other qualities also rated high were "rich natural resources" (88%), "hard-working people" (90%), and "industrial know-how and scientific progress" (90%), but the ability to own private property rated higher than "free education for all qualified" (74%), "high quality products and services" (69%), and "outstanding political leaders" (63%).

Some polls focused on specific regulatory concerns. For example, in a 1977 Cambridge Reports poll, respondents were asked whether they favored or opposed various "measures for dealing with growth and population problems." Sixty-one percent of respondents said they opposed the government "restricting the ways people can use their land or property."[4] Yet this general reaction is misleading; public opinion depends on the type of restriction. In response to a question in a 1973 Harris poll concerning "restrictions on the size of house lots and houses to prevent overcrowding," only 37% of respondents said they opposed such a restriction.

Conflicts between environmental concerns and private property rights attracted the most frequent polling in the pre-*Kelo* era. National polls conducted in 1995 (Gallup/CNN/USA Today), 1999 (Gallup/U.S. News and World Report/CNN), and 2001 (Los Angeles Times) asked the same question: "Which is more important—protecting endangered species from extinction or protecting the ability of property owners to do what they want with their land?" The percentage of respondents who selected protecting property owners as more important ranged from 33% to 41%. Thus, a substantial minority of the respondents saw the rights of property owners as sufficient to overcome at least some competing environmental values.

Another national poll (Times Mirror/Roper, 1992) examined the influence of context on people's choices. The survey described five situations pitting specific environmental interests against specific property owner desires and asked respondents: "Which is more important—protecting the environment or the owner's rights?" (see Table 12.1). Respondents consistently rated the owner's rights as less important than environmental protection, but the percentage favoring the owner varied substantially, with far greater support for an owner who was an individual rather than a developer or a logging company. It appeared to make little difference what use the owner had in mind (a golf course or a barn) or the environmental interest that was threatened (an endangered species or a wetland).

The Fifth Amendment to the U.S. Constitution requires that property owners receive just compensation for any government taking of property, and some public opinion polls explored perceptions of the adequacy and propriety of the compensation offered. In 1997, a national poll (conducted by Wisconsin Public Television/Princeton Survey Research) asked whether the government adequately compensates owners when the property is taken for

Table 12.1
Opinion on Hypothetical Conflicts Pitting Property Rights Against
Environmental Concerns, 1992

Property owner	Owner's desired use	Threatened Environmental Interest	More important to protect...		
			The environment	The owner's rights	Don't know
Developer	Build 50 homes for middle-class families	Land designated as an official wetland area	71%	20%	9%
Logging company	Harvest timbers in forest it own	Harm endangered bird species	68%	23%	9%
Private individual	Build golf course	Harm endangered butterfly species	53%	37%	10%
Homeowner	Build barn behind house	Damage wetland area	52%	39%	9%
Homeowner in financial trouble	Develop 1 acre to raise money	Damage wetland area	48%	40%	12%

Source: Times Mirror/Roper poll, 1992.
Question wording: see text.

public use. Thirty-five percent of respondents thought that the government does not adequately compensate in these situations.

Responses to the question of whether compensation should be required at all for a regulatory taking varied considerably, depending on what information was made salient in the framing of the question. For example, an Electorate Survey in 1994 (conducted by League of Conservation Voters/Mellman, Lazarus & Lake) asked about compensation for regulation (as opposed to actual forced sale). This poll framed the issue as a contrast between whether private landowners have the right to do what they want with their land, so that restrictions must be compensated, versus whether restrictions without payment (such as prohibiting the building of a toxic dump) are justified to keep neighborhoods healthy and safe and to protect endangered habitats. On this question, a majority (55%) responded that payment was not justified, and only 28% responded that property owners have the right to do what they wish with their land.

Salient Takings Cases Prior to *Kelo*

In the past several decades, the Supreme Court has addressed the use of eminent domain to accomplish outright condemnation of property only a few times. Instead, the Court has more often turned its attention to the question of when government regulation of property becomes a "taking" for purposes of the Fifth Amendment, requiring payment of compensation to the owner. Cases involving regulatory restrictions on property use provoked little public attention, despite the fact that the Supreme Court has decided several such cases in the past twenty years (see Table 12.2). The most notable feature of these regulatory takings cases is that the media attention they received did not even approach the media attention generated by *Kelo*. Prior to *Kelo*, the public's concern with government encroachment on property rights was largely unaffected by questions of entitlement to compensation for land-use regulations. That lack of concern has changed markedly in the western United States since the introduction of a variety of post-*Kelo* voter initiatives that would require compensation for a much larger set of regulations—an issue we return to later.

Prior to *Kelo*, the U.S. Supreme Court had decided very few cases in recent decades involving the use of eminent domain to force the sale of property. During the early twentieth century, large American cities used eminent domain to revitalize areas that were considered slums. Controversy over housing and highway projects seemed to focus more on debates about location, rather than questioning the more basic premise that the government is entitled to use the power of eminent domain for large, ambitious projects such as these. This premise, however, was explicitly questioned in connection with an enormous urban renewal project in the nation's capital that led to the U.S. Supreme Court's 1954 decision in *Berman v. Parker*. The Supreme Court permitted the project to go forward, even though it meant that nonblighted stores would be condemned, thousands of predominantly African American residents would be displaced, and the land would be turned over to a private developer. No public opinion polls assessed the reaction to the decision or the plan itself. Press coverage of the decision appears to consist of two short articles in the *Washington Post* and one in the *Chicago Tribune*, none of which were critical of the case or the plan.

The other main legal pillar on which the *Kelo* decision rests is *Hawaii Housing Authority v. Midkiff* (1984), in which the Supreme Court issued a unanimous decision holding that a property redistribution plan in Hawaii was constitutional under the public use clause. We are aware of no public opinion polls following *Midkiff*, but the public reaction largely seemed to favor the land redistribution plan.

A final case, *Poletown Neighborhood Council v. City of Detroit* (1981), is important because it involved the forced sale (not just restricted use) of residential property by relatively powerless homeowners—and it, like *Kelo*, sparked public opposition. In *Poletown*, the Michigan Supreme Court ruled in favor of

Table 12.2
News Coverage of Prominent U.S. Supreme Court Takings Decisions, 1981–2005

U.S. Supreme Court Case (Year)	Holding	Perceived "Victim" of Regulation	Decision in favor of property owner or government	News stories (1 month) / (6 months)*	
Keystone Bituminous Coal (1987)	Restriction on coal removal is not a taking (must leave 50% of coal for structural safety)	Coal company	Government	3	7
First English (1987)	Government must pay retroactive compensation after removing restriction on flood area without compensation	Church	Property owner	16	20
Nollan (1987)	Conditions on building permits must be related to proposed construction (cannot require easement for beach access as a condition for lifting building height restriction)	Beachfront landowners	Property owner	14	23
Lucas (1992)	Regulation that denies all economically productive use of land is a taking (involving prohibition on beachfront construction without compensation)	Beachfront landowner	Property owner	15	23
Dolan (1994)	Conditions on building permits must be related to impact of proposed development (cannot require bike path as condition of parking lot permit)	Small business owner	Property owner	23	32
Palazzolo (2001)	Landowner can challenge regulations even if regulations predated purchase	Beachfront landowner	Property owner	8	8
Tahoe-Sierra (2002)	Moratorium on construction is not a per se taking	Developers	Government	12	15

(*continued*)

Table 12.2
(*continued*)

U.S. Supreme Court Case (Year)	Holding	Perceived "Victim" of Regulation	Decision in favor of property owner or government	News stories (1 month) / (6 months)*	
Lingle v. Chevron (2005)	A regulation need not "substantially advance" government interests (rent control on gas stations is not a taking even though it might not substantially advance governmental interest)	Chevron Corporation	Government	4	8
Kelo (2005)[†]	Forced sale of private property to promote economic development is permissible	Middle-class homeowners	Government	64	107

* Number of stories appearing within one month and six months after the decision in five major newspapers—*New York Times, Washington Post, Los Angeles Times, Chicago Tribune,* and *Wall Street Journal*—identified by using the following search terms: ([name in case] & property & "supreme court").

† We include the *Kelo* case for comparison purposes, although it is not a regulatory takings case.

a city redevelopment plan involving the forced sale of homes in Detroit's working-class Poletown neighborhood. Eminent domain was invoked to require the removal of more than 4,000 residents and the condemnation of more than 1,000 homes and businesses, as well as several churches, to make room for a new General Motors assembly plant. Public reaction to the *Poletown* decision was strongly negative. By comparison, *Kelo* arguably was a less egregious case: many fewer people, homes, and businesses were displaced, the neighborhood was less tight-knit, and the influence of large corporate interests was less explicit. Nonetheless, public disapproval of *Poletown* in Michigan foreshadowed the national backlash that ensued when the U.S. Supreme Court decided *Kelo*.

Media Coverage of *Kelo*

One dimension of the public outrage in response to the *Kelo* decision was the high level of public awareness of the case, an awareness that reflects the

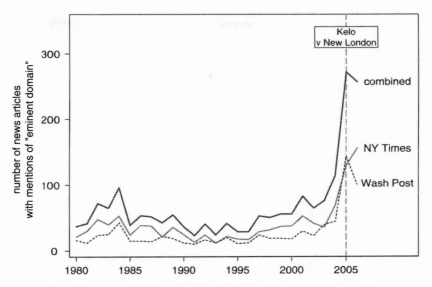

Figure 12.1. Coverage of Eminent Domain by the *New York Times* and *Washington Post*, 1980–2006. Source: Lexis-Nexis.

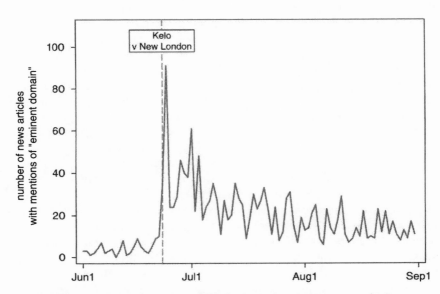

Figure 12.2. Coverage of *Kelo v. New London* by Major Newspapers and Wire Services, Summer 2005. Source: Lexis-Nexis.

intensity of media coverage. More newspapers editorialized about *Kelo* than any other takings case. The *Economist* reported that *Kelo* "has set off a fierce backlash that may yet be as potent as the anti-abortion movement" ("Hands off Our Homes" 2005).

After the Court announced its opinion, there was a sudden burst of national coverage of eminent domain controversies (see Figure 12.1) and extensive coverage of the *Kelo* case, coverage that persisted throughout the summer (see Figure 12.2). By the end of August, coverage had dropped off, but it still remained substantially higher than before the decision was announced. Part of the reason for the continued media focus on eminent domain was the introduction of various federal and state legislative proposals in response to *Kelo*.

Public Opinion on *Kelo*

The intense media coverage given to the *Kelo* decision in the summer of 2005 was accompanied both by a rise in the public's interest in the case and by opposition to the ruling that crossed ideological, partisan, and demographic lines. In a July 2005 poll conducted by NBC News and the *Wall Street Journal*, 42% of respondents listed "private property rights" as one of the one or two issues before the Court in which they were most interested at the time—a proportion much greater than other contenders, including cases involving parental notification for abortions by minors (34%), display of the Ten Commandments on public property (32%), and right-to-die laws (24%).

Of the controversial cases decided by the U.S. Supreme Court in the 2004–2005 term, *Kelo* was identified in this poll as the most controversial. At the same time, it is worth noting that, except for a brief period during the New Deal, the Supreme Court's agenda has scarcely overlapped the public's agenda (Schauer 2006). According to a Gallup poll in July 2005, the "most important problem[s]" facing the country at that time, as perceived by ordinary Americans, were the economy and unemployment, the war with Iraq, terrorism, and fear of war. The issues decided by the Supreme Court are generally not the same policy issues that are of primary concern to the public, and features of Supreme Court cases that are of public concern do not necessarily correspond to the legal aspects of the case considered by the judiciary.

Nonetheless, the decision in *Kelo* touched a nerve. Indeed, *Kelo* has proven to be one of the most unpopular decisions of the Rehnquist court. Table 12.3 displays the results of polling data regarding *Kelo*. As shown in the table, disapproval of *Kelo* averaged well above 80%, higher than the disapproval rating for such controversial cases as *Brown v. Board of Education*, the school prayer cases, *Webster* (1989, affirming abortion rights), and *Texas v. Johnson* (1989, protecting flag burning).[5] Furthermore, a large majority in one national and two local polls—ranging from 69% to 89%—favored legislation restricting the

Table 12.3

Opposition to *Kelo* and Support for Legislative Reform, Summer and Fall 2005

Poll Name	Sample	% Disagreeing with *Kelo*	% Favoring Legislation Restricting Eminent Domain
Saint Index	National	81%	N/A
American Survey	National	N/A	69%
NH Granite State	NH	92%	N/A
Quinnipiac	CT	88%	89%
Mason-Dixon	FL	88%	89%

Question wording:

Saint Index: The U.S. Supreme Court recently ruled that local governments can take homes, business and private property to make way for private economic development if officials believe it would benefit the public. How do you feel about this ruling? [Strongly Support, Somewhat Support, Somewhat Oppose, Strongly Oppose, Don't Know]

American Survey: As you may have heard, the Supreme Court recently announced a decision saying federal, state, and local governments may take away private property and give it to developers for commercial development even if the homeowners object, so long as the homeowners receive compensation for their homes. Congress is considering legislation that would say the federal government cannot take private property for private commercial development if homeowners object. It also would say state and local governments cannot take private property for private commercial development against homeowners' wishes if any federal funds are being used in the project. What about you, would you favor or oppose Congress placing these limits on the ability of government to take private property away from owners?

New Hampshire Granite State: Recently, the Supreme Court ruled that towns and cities may take private land from people and make it available to businesses to develop under the principle of eminent domain. Some people favor this use of eminent domain because it allows for increased tax revenues from the new businesses and are an important part of economic redevelopment. Other people oppose this use of eminent domain because it reduces the value of private property and makes it easier for big businesses to take land. What about you? Do you think that towns and cities should be allowed to take private land from the owners and make it available to developers to develop or do you oppose this use of eminent domain?

Quinnipiac: As you may know, the Court ruled that government can use eminent domain to buy a person's property and transfer it to private developers whose commercial projects could benefit the local economy. Do you agree or disagree with this ruling?

Mason Dixon: In that Connecticut case, the U.S. Supreme Court ruled government can use the power of eminent domain to acquire a person's property and transfer it to private developers whose commercial projects could benefit the local economy. Do you agree or disagree with this ruling?

power of eminent domain. A majority of New Jersey residents (66%) stated support for a temporary moratorium on eminent domain until further study (Monmouth University/Gannet, 2005).

Other questions during this time period reflect specific anxieties that the *Kelo* decision seemed to trigger. For example, New Jersey residents were overwhelmingly opposed to the prospect of government takings of low-value homes to build a shopping center (90%) or to build high-value homes (86%) (Monmouth University/Gannet, 2005). Responses to other questions reflect dissatisfaction with current local eminent domain practices. For example, 65% of New Jersey residents thought that property owners were not given fair market value when their property was taken (Monmouth University/Gannet, 2005).

The *Kelo* decision seems to have provoked concern that the Court had endorsed a kind of "reverse Robin Hoodery," whereby, in Justice O'Connor's words, "the government now has license to transfer property from those with fewer resources to those with more" (Kanner 2006, 358). Consistent with this concern, 76% of New Jersey residents endorsed the statement that "eminent domain in my area has benefited private developers more than local communities." Aside from the perception that *Kelo* would encourage exploiting those who are particularly vulnerable, the polls convey a general sense of skepticism about, if not outright opposition to, the power of eminent domain in any form whatsoever. Thus, 61% of Connecticut residents and 53% of Florida residents reported that they were opposed to "the longstanding practice" of eminent domain in which the government takes private property "for important public projects" and pays just compensation. A smaller but still substantial number (39%) of New Jersey residents reported that it was never acceptable for the government to exercise its eminent domain power.

Public disapproval of *Kelo* is notable in its uniformity across traditional political cleavages. The percentage of Democrats, Republicans, and Independents who oppose the *Kelo* decision was nearly equal in national and state polls conducted in 2005, hovering between 80 and 85%.[6] We further confirmed the uniformity of opposition in a multivariate regression analysis (not shown here) performed with data from a national poll conducted by the Saint Consulting Group in 2005. The question was: "The US Supreme Court recently ruled that local governments can take homes, business and private property to make way for private economic development if officials believe it would benefit the public. How do you feel about this ruling?" Responses were measured on a 4-point scale (1 = strongly support; 4 = strongly oppose). This analysis found that variables which typically predict attitudes on public affairs—such as political affiliation, age, sex, education, income, and home ownership—collectively explained less than 5% of the variation in opinion regarding *Kelo*. The subgroup least opposed to the decision was respondents with incomes of $150,000 and over, and yet even these respondents opposed the decision on average (mean = 3.12). The subgroup that expressed the greatest disapproval (mean = 3.64) was the Native American respondents (N = 28), which is consistent with previous examples of Native American resistance to government efforts to place a dollar value on forced relocation.[7] On the other hand, the small absolute difference between these two extremes illustrates what the regression analysis confirms: that group membership is not a strong predictor of opposition to *Kelo*.

The Complexity of the *Kelo* Decision and the Nuances of Attitudes Regarding Eminent Domain

Because the *Kelo* decision endorsed either explicitly or implicitly a complex set of propositions (including the purposes for which property can be acquired by eminent domain, the characteristics of properties that can be acquired, the processes that comport with the requirements of due process, and the determinations of just compensation), writing a single polling question that fairly characterizes the decision is perhaps impossible. But many of the polls either intentionally or unintentionally slanted the presentation of *Kelo* by using inflammatory language to frame the question or by omitting important elements that might affect responses. For example, in a survey conducted in Minnesota by Decision Resources Ltd. of Minneapolis, respondents who indicated they were not aware of the recent Supreme Court decision on eminent domain (31% of the sample) received the following explanation before being asked their opinion:

> The U.S. Supreme Court recently ruled that local governments have the right to take land from private owners for not only public purposes, but also to support private development. For example, under this decision a city could condemn an existing business property or residential neighborhood in order to create a new privately-owned shopping center. Supporters of this decision say that city council members should have the authority to make decisions about the best kinds of development for their community. Opponents say that governments should only be allowed to take land away from private owners for truly public purposes, such as a new highway or a government building.

All respondents were then asked whether they supported "allowing local governments to use eminent domain to take private property for another private development project." This explanation of *Kelo* was misleading. Contrary to the first sentence in this description, *Kelo* requires a public purpose, and the issues addressed in *Kelo* were whether economic development could constitute a sufficient public purpose and whether a public purpose was sufficient to meet the constitutionally required standard of public use. Moreover, the description used in the survey suggests that any transfer of property to a private business would be permissible; by contrast, *Kelo* requires an asserted public benefit. Finally, the description does not mention that if the government exercises its power of eminent domain, it must fairly compensate the owner of the property. Not surprisingly, 91% of respondents said they would not support the use of eminent domain.

Some of the polls further misled respondents by describing eminent domain takings as "seizures." In a follow-up question on the Minnesota survey, respondents were asked whether they were likely to support a candidate who "voted to restrict the power of local governments to use eminent domain to seize private property." Although the exercise of the power of eminent domain constitutes a taking, rather than a voluntary sale, certain procedures must be followed before the property can be taken. The use of the word "seize" arguably implies the absence of process or compensation. Eighty-three percent of the Minnesota respondents said they would be more likely to support a candidate who would vote to restrict the power to seize private property. We note that although the misleading wording of questions regarding eminent domain undoubtedly affected survey responses, the broad opposition to the *Kelo* decision found in the polls shown in Table 12.3 was nevertheless consistent across a wide range of question wordings regarding the ruling (see appendix).

Some polls sought to assess opposition to *any* form of eminent domain for *any* purpose. In a poll conducted by the Monmouth University Polling Institute, the interviewer explained, "Eminent domain is the process by which towns take control of property after paying compensation in order to use the land for other purposes to benefit the public good." Although one might quarrel with the assumption that such takings actually benefit the public good or whether government personnel are always properly motivated, the characterization includes neutral language describing the taking and acknowledges that the property owner is compensated for the loss. After hearing this description, respondents were asked, "In general, do you agree or disagree that there are times when it is O.K. to use eminent domain to rebuild an area?" and 39% disagreed. The Florida survey by Mason-Dixon obtained a similar level of rejection for any form of eminent domain (43%). The level of rejection was even higher (61%) in the Quinnipiac survey conducted in Connecticut, the state where *Kelo* originated.

The rejection rate of any form of eminent domain by two out of five respondents is misleading, however. The Monmouth poll also asked each respondent about four of eight hypothetical situations that combine different types of property and possible uses (see Table 12.4). Approval or disapproval of these takings begins to reveal the contours of the opposition to *Kelo*. Reaction depends on what is taken (whether land or a business or a home) and how it will be used. For example, the use of eminent domain to take vacant land and run-down buildings for a school garnered almost uniform support (88%) and minimal outright rejection (7%). Part of this strong support might be explained by the minimal harm to the owner because of the nature of the property taken—vacant land. When low-value homes rather than vacant land would be taken to build a school, support dropped from 88% to 33%. Thus, a large proportion of respondents reject the idea of taking homes, even for an important use. The proposed use of the land did affect reaction to takings, however. Although using eminent domain to take low-value homes to build a school garnered the support of 33% of respondents, support dropped to 7% when low-value homes were to be taken to build high-value homes, and to 4% when low-value homes were to be taken to build a shopping center. The proposed shopping center garnered far more support (55%) when the property taken would be vacant land and run-down buildings.

Table 12.4
Attitudes regarding eminent domain in hypothetical situations (New Jersey residents)

Use eminent domain to take	In order to	O.K.	Not O.K.	Depends/ Don't Know
Vacant and run-down buildings	Build a school	88%	7%	4%
Land from a developer	Preserve open space	65%	28%	8%
Land from a business to keep it from expanding	Prevent noise and traffic	43%	48%	8%
Low-value homes from people	Build a school	33%	55%	11%
Low-value homes from people	Build higher value homes	7%	86%	8%
Low-value homes from people	Build a shopping center	4%	90%	7%

The order of the items was rotated. N = 800 New Jersey adults.

Source: Monmouth University/Gannett New Jersey Poll, Fall 2005.

Question wording: I'm going to read you some situations where eminent domain might be used. Please tell me whether you think using eminent domain is O.K. in each case. Is it O.K. or not O.K. to use eminent domain to [READ ITEM]?

These results suggest that beneath the vigorous public opposition to *Kelo* lay a more nuanced evaluation of government takings—a complex structure of public attitudes not easily gauged at an abstract level by simply measuring attitudes toward eminent domain in general. In particular, the level of support for use of eminent domain appears to depend on, among other things, the nature of the property (homes, vacant land, etc.) and the proposed use for the property (a school, a shopping center, etc.). The complete rejection of eminent domain by 40% to 60% of respondents answering a general question probably reflects the salience of the *Kelo* facts and the outrage in response to its perceived unfairness rather than a wholesale rejection of the legitimacy of eminent domain.

Elite Opinion and Spillover into Regulatory Takings Initiatives in the Western United States

The legal academy recognized that the *Kelo* decision took the public by surprise, and scholars sought to assure the public that the decision changed nothing.[8] After all, most legal academic commentators understood that the Supreme Court's interpretation of the phrase "public use" in the takings clause did not meaningfully restrict the exercise of the eminent domain power (Mahoney, 2005),[9] and the Court's prior "public use" cases contained language that seemed to rule out a decision for the property owners in *Kelo*. For example, in 1984, the Court proclaimed, "[W]here the exercise of eminent domain power is rationally related to a conceivable public purpose, the Court has never held a compensated taking to be proscribed by the Public Use Clause" (*Midkiff*, 241). Because of this sweeping language, many observers in the legal academy correctly predicted that the Court would rule against the property owners in *Kelo*. A notable feature of the reaction to *Kelo*, then, is the large disparity between elite opinion and popular opinion.

Two prominent newspapers echoed legal commentators and editorialized in favor of the *Kelo* decision. The *Washington Post* acknowledged that the result for the property owners in the case was "quite unjust" but "the court's decision was correct" ("Eminent Latitude" 2005). The *New York Times* ("The Limits of Property Rights" 2005) also called the result in *Kelo* correct; however, as others have noted, the *Times* recently had been the beneficiary of New York City's exercise of eminent domain, which enabled construction of a new, subsidized *Times* headquarters in midtown Manhattan (Kanner 2006). In conceding that the outcome for the plaintiffs was harsh, even those who supported the decision in *Kelo* seem to acknowledge, either implicitly or explicitly, that the case posed a challenge to important cultural values, such as the sanctity of the home. The Court's majority opinion, authored by Justice Stevens, insisted that "we do not minimize the hardship that condemnations may entail."

The public backlash quickly generated a multitude of legislative proposals to limit the exercise of eminent domain for the purpose of economic development, in state legislatures as well as the U.S. Congress.[10] Losing *Kelo* energized opponents of takings. Less than a week after the decision, the Institute for Justice, a libertarian public interest law firm that represented Susette Kelo before the U.S. Supreme Court, announced that it would spend $3 million, about half of its annual budget, to "combat eminent domain at the state and local level" (Institute for Justice 2005). Americans for Limited Government, another libertarian group, also saw an opportunity to gain support for opposition to regulatory takings and has funded state groups in Arizona, California, Idaho, Michigan, Montana, Nevada, North Dakota, and Washington "to protect property rights" in the wake of *Kelo* (Americans for Limited Government 2005). Within a few months after *Kelo*, some states had passed broad prohibitions on the use of the eminent domain power to transfer property to private parties,[11] and others made procedural changes.[12] The trend gathered steam in November 2006, when residents of twelve states were asked to vote on proposals for constitutional amendments,[13] changes in statutory language,[14] and other measures that would limit the ability of governments to exercise the power of eminent domain.

Ten of the twelve propositions passed (all except California and Idaho). Many of these referendums were stimulated by political interest groups, particularly libertarian and small-government organizations, which used the concerns generated by *Kelo* as an opportunity to press for legal limits on government that exceeded the concerns raised by *Kelo* (Brady 2006). For example, the referendums in Arizona, California, and Idaho included a regulatory takings component that would have required governments to compensate owners not only when their property was taken outright under eminent domain but also when their property values were reduced by land-use regulations. Other referendums inserted additional protections for property owners who might be subject to a legitimate governmental taking under *Kelo*. For example, the Michigan referendum on a state constitutional amendment provided that if a government takes an individual's principal residence for public use, the individual must be paid at least 125% of the property's fair market value.

Voters' reaction to these referendums provides an indication of public opinion on *Kelo*-related matters—but this indication is imperfect, as Arizona Proposition 207 demonstrates. The proposition, which passed with 65.2% of the vote, appeared on the ballot under the title of an initiative "relating to eminent domain." Voters had the following choice:

> A "yes" vote shall have the effect of [1] establishing additional rights for individuals whose property is taken by the government for public use (eminent domain), [2] defining "public use," [3] prohibiting the taking of property for economic development, [4] requiring primary residences taken by eminent domain be replaced by a comparable dwelling, [5] requiring compensation for property values reduced by land use laws, [6] requiring attorneys' fees in eminent domain lawsuits, and [7] allowing attorneys' fees in property value reduction lawsuits. A "no" vote shall have the effect of retaining the current eminent domain law.

Thus, the "yes" vote choice began with a general description of the initiative as providing rights for individuals. A "yes" vote supported prohibiting takings for economic development, yet also endorsed a requirement of compensation for reductions in property values brought about by regulation (fifth element). Voters' response to this initiative offers little insight into how they might evaluate each of the seven elements covered by the statutory amendment. The elements themselves are shorthand descriptions, and even if each were offered separately, it would have been difficult for voters to have evaluated each element beforehand. In preparation, some voters might have braved the Arizona Secretary of State's detailed description of each proposed measure, in this case nineteen pages including the proposed amendment itself (four pages), an analysis by legislative counsel, a fiscal impact statement, and fourteen pages of arguments submitted by identified private individuals, officials, and organizations favoring (fifteen) and opposing (twenty-one) the measure.

It would be surprising, however, if many voters performed a thorough examination of this information (Magleby 1995). More likely, the broad news coverage of *Kelo* made it easy to characterize a proposal limiting eminent domain and protecting property rights as worthy of support. The upshot is that the proposal obtained support from two thirds of the voters for limits on condemnation and also endorsed costs to be imposed on governments exercising their regulatory powers.

The difficulty of educating the electorate on a complex referendum has received substantial scholarly attention (e.g., Cronin 1989; Magleby 1984, 1995), and it may explain the last-minute shifts in public opinion in California on a similar referendum. In November 2006, California voters defeated the proposed referendum by a narrow margin (47.5% to 52.5%), and polls taken among likely voters in July and October showed a substantial shift from 46% in favor in July to 35% in favor in October (23% undecided at each point).

Conclusion

The real story in the *Kelo* backlash is the remarkable consistency of opinion across political and demographic subgroups. Something about *Kelo* spoke to core values shared by Americans of various racial, ethnic, religious, and ideological groups.

The first value threatened by *Kelo* is the sacredness of the home. Although most of the public knew little about the nuances of the *Kelo* decision, they seemed to have implicitly understood that the Supreme Court's eminent domain jurisprudence afforded no special protection for ordinary homeowners, and some might have felt disappointed that the Supreme Court declined to act to protect their rights against what they perceived to be local government encroachment. This is borne out by the strong opposition to hypothetical takings of homes, as compared with other types of property, illustrated in Table 12.4 and discussed earlier. The cultural importance of homeownership also helps to explain the high public disapproval rating for the *Kelo* decision, because there was little in the media reports about the decision that suggested any natural limit on whose home could be targeted in the future for government condemnation. Alarming headlines such as "Your Home Could Be Up for Grabs" made many ordinary citizens feel vulnerable. The fact that the plaintiffs in *Kelo* were white middle-class residents whose homes were well maintained probably exacerbated the public's feelings of vulnerability (Pritchett 2006).

A second value concerns the expectation that the Supreme Court will protect ordinary citizens from overreaching governmental power. The public's sense of equity is challenged by takings whose purpose diverges from public use archetypes like schools and post offices. The more the proposed use for the targeted property appears speculative, vague, or for the benefit of private parties, the more unfair the taking will be perceived.

A most unusual feature of the public backlash following *Kelo* is that it signified overwhelming opposition to a ruling that respected local control, a decision in which the Court declined to interfere with the act of a local government and let stand a permissive policy of a state. The structure of the majority's decision is consistent with principles of federalism, in which the federal government defers to the states to develop and experiment with their own policies. The popular backlash, by contrast, seemed to object to this hands-off approach and instead called for the Court to step in and impose limits on eminent domain powers, which have historically been seen as properly residing in state and local governments. Unlike other controversial court decisions involving abortion, gay marriage, and school integration, where courts have overturned legislative action, in *Kelo* the Court endorsed local and state control, and it was the Court's *failure* to intervene that has upset the public.

Judge Richard Posner has called the public indignation engendered by the *Kelo* decision "surprising because it is a restrained decision that leaves the states free to curtail their eminent domain powers" (Posner 2006). In a comment in a law review, Justice John Paul Stevens, the author of the majority *Kelo* opinion, said, "Though much criticized, the *Kelo* opinion was surely not an example of 'judicial activism' because it rejected arguments that federal judges should review the feasibility of redevelopment plans, that they should evaluate the justification for the taking of each individual parcel rather than the entire plan, and that they should craft a constitutional distinction between blighted areas and depressed areas targeted for redevelopment" (Stevens 2006).

A difficult aspect of drawing general lessons from an examination of the popular reaction to *Kelo* is that, in some sense, the backlash seems to have come out of nowhere. Unlike prominent debates implicating cultural values like the role of race and religion in the social order (implicating desegregation, affirmative action, and school prayer), the meaning of family and marriage (implicating gay rights and gender equality), and the sanctity of human life (implicating the death penalty, the right to die, and abortion), debates about the sanctity of property were not featured prominently in public discourse prior to *Kelo*.

But the *Kelo* decision seems to have tapped into existing concerns about the sanctity of the home, government overreaching, and tensions between protecting public goods (like the environment) and protecting private rights. In some sense, *Kelo* was a "perfect storm" because all of these issues were directly implicated in the decision, a circumstance highlighted by Justice O'Connor's dissent, in which she warned, "Nothing is to prevent the State from replacing any Motel 6 with a Ritz-Carlton, any home with a shopping mall, or any farm with a factory." These images were invoked in hundreds of news stories on the decision and the flurry of legislative proposals that followed.

Everyone could find something to hate about the *Kelo* decision. Middle-class homeowners identified with the middle-class homeowners who were the plaintiffs in *Kelo*. For urban residents and members of communities that had been displaced by urban renewal programs, the decision renewed fears that a new era of displacement was afoot. In his dissent, Justice Thomas noted that the racially discriminatory nature of urban renewal had caused many to refer to these programs as "Negro removal," and he predicted that the *Kelo* decision would exacerbate these effects. The decision also troubled residents of the western states who were already concerned about excessive government regulation of private property, and the numerous post-*Kelo* voter initiatives that would restrain regulatory power reflect this concern. As a result, *Kelo* generated the perfect storm that, for different reasons and toward different ends, brought liberals, conservatives, and libertarians to seek shelter under the same umbrella.

Acknowledgment

We thank David Dana, Stewart Diamond, Tom Marshall, Nate Persily, and Len Rubinowitz for useful comments. We thank Natasha Murashev for excellent research assistance, and the American Bar Foundation for financial assistance.

APPENDIX

University of New Hampshire Granite State Poll, July 2005. "Recently, the Supreme Court ruled that towns and cities may take private land from people and make it available to businesses to develop under the principle of eminent domain. Some people favor this use of eminent domain because it allows for increased tax revenues from the new businesses and are an important part of economic redevelopment. Other people oppose this use of eminent domain because it reduces the value of private property and makes it easier for big businesses to take land. What about you? Do you think that towns and cities should be allowed to take private land from the owners and make it available to developers to develop or do you oppose this use of eminent domain?"

Quinnipiac University Poll, July 2005. (A preliminary question asked whether the respondent was familiar with the *Kelo* case.) "As you may know, the Court ruled that government can use eminent domain to buy a person's property and transfer it to private developers whose commercial projects could benefit the local economy. Do you agree or disagree with this ruling? Do you agree/disagree strongly or somewhat?"

Mason-Dixon Polling & Research, October 2005. (A preliminary question on familiarity asked: "A recent U.S. Supreme Court decision involving a Connecticut case held that local government could also use its eminent domain power to acquire homes and businesses for redevelopment projects which could benefit the local economy. Do recall hearing of this decision in the news?") "In that Connecticut case, the U.S. Supreme Court ruled government can use the power of eminent domain to acquire a person's property and transfer it to private developers whose commercial projects could benefit the local economy. Do you agree or disagree with this ruling?"

Saint Consulting Group, October 2005. "The US Supreme Court recently ruled that local governments can take homes, business and private property to make way for private economic development if officials believe it would benefit the public. How do you feel about this ruling?"

Notes

1. Nineteen percent thought people were overcompensated, 38% thought compensation was about right, and 8% did not know.

2. Thirty-eight percent disagreed, and 23% did not know.

3. Thirty-eight percent said the government should have the right, and 3% were not sure.

4. Thirty percent were in favor, and 10% did not know.

5. For example, opposition to *Brown v. Board of Education* was about 40%–45% (see chapter 1, this volume), disapproval of the school prayer decisions ranged from 52% to 67% (see chapter 3, this volume), disapproval for *Webster* ranged from 35% to 46% (see chapter 4, this volume), and disapproval for *Texas v. Johnson*) ranged from 65% to 79% (see chapter 8, this volume).

6. These include polls conducted by the Saint Consulting Group (national sample), Quinnipiac (Connecticut residents), Mason-Dixon (Florida), and the University of New Hampshire (New Hampshire).

7. See, for example, Espeland (1998).

8. Harvard Law School professor David Barron wrote that despite the un-American-sounding headlines reporting the case, such as "Court Authorizes Seizure of Homes," the *Kelo* decision "affirmed principles as old as the Constitution" (Barron 2005). Professor Eugene Volokh at UCLA Law school said *Kelo* did not represent much of a change in law (Canellos 2005). University of Connecticut law professor Jeremy Paul said, "I think the worries for individual homeowners are exaggerated" (Tuohy 2005).

9. Mahoney cites Ackerman (1977) ("any state purpose otherwise constitutional should qualify as sufficiently 'public' to justify a taking"), Tribe (2000) (noting that the Court in modern times "refuses to give 'teeth' to the public use requirement"), and Merrill (1986) ("most observers today think the public use requirement is a dead letter"). For a dissenting view, see Epstein (1985).

10. As of early 2007, the Private Property Rights Protection Act (PRPA) has been passed by the House but not by the Senate. Under the act, state and local governments that use eminent domain for economic development would lose federal economic development funds for two years. Even if PRPA is enacted, its effects may be small because of the small amounts of federal funds that offending state and local governments stand to lose. By one estimate, PRPA applies only to about 1.8% of all federal grants to states and localities (Somin 2007).

11. For example, South Dakota.

12. For example, Georgia and Utah moved decisions on takings from appointed boards to elected officials. As of early 2007, twenty-seven state legislatures have enacted post-*Kelo* reforms. However, many of these reforms are purely symbolic, because they

only nominally forbid "economic development" condemnations but permit them to continue under another name (e.g., "blight reduction") (Somin 2007).

13. California, Florida, Georgia, Louisiana, Michigan, New Hampshire, and South Carolina.

14. Arizona, Idaho, Nevada, Oregon, and Washington.

References

Ackerman, B. 1977. *Private Property and the Constitution*. New Haven: Yale University Press.

Americans for Limited Government. 2005. "Protecting Property Rights across the Country." Available online at http://www.getliberty.org/campaigns/propertyrights/index.php. Accessed August 17, 2007.

Barron, D. 2005. "High Court's Ruling Has Ample Precedent." *Orlando Sentinel*, July 8, A23.

Brady, J. 2006. "Western Voters Consider Property Rights Changes." National Public Radio. Available at online http://www.npr.org/templates/story/story.php?storyID=6102255. Accessed August 17, 2007.

Calvert, J. W. 1979. "The Social and Ideological Bases of Support for Environmental Legislation: An Examination of Public Attitudes and Legislative Action." *Western Political Quarterly* 32: 327–37.

Canellos, P. 2005. "High Court Backs Seizure of Land for Development." *Boston Globe*, June 24, A1.

Cronin, T. E. 1989. *Direct Democracy: The Politics of Initiative, Referendum, and Recall*. Cambridge: Harvard University Press.

Dana, D. A., and T. W. Merrill. 2002. *Property: Takings*. New York: Foundation Press.

"Eminent Latitude." 2005, *Washington Post*, June 24, A30.

Epstein, R. A. 1985. *Takings: Private Property and the Power of Eminent Domain*. Cambridge: Harvard University Press.

Espeland, W. 1998. "Commensuration as a Social Process." *Annual Review of Sociology* 24: 313–43.

Fischel, W. A. 2004. "The Political Economy of Public Use in *Poletown*: How Federal Grants Encourage Excessive Use of Eminent Domain." *Michigan State Law Review* 2004: 929.

"Hands off Our Homes: Property Rights and Eminent Domain." 2005. *Economist*, August 20.

Institute for Justice. 2005. "IJ's $3 Million National Campaign Tells Lawmakers: "Hands off My Home." Available at http:ij.org/private_property/castle/6_29_05pr.html. Accessed August 17, 2007.

"The Limits of Property Rights." 2005. *New York Times*, June 24, A22.

Kanner, G. 2006. "The Public Use Clause: Constitutional Mandate or "Hortatory Fluff"?" *Pepperdine Law Review* 33: 335–384.

Magleby, D. B. 1984. *Direct Legislation: Voting on Ballot Propositions in the United States*. Baltimore: Johns Hopkins University Press.

———. 1995. "Governing by Initiative: Let the Voters Decide? An Assessment of the Initiative and Referendum Process." *University of Colorado Law Review* 66: 13.

Mahoney, J. D. 2005. "*Kelo's* Legacy: Eminent Domain and the Future of Property Rights." *Supreme Court Review* 103–33.

Merrill, T. W. 1986. "The Economics of Public Use." *Cornell Law Review* 72: 61.

Mohl, R. A. 1993. "Race and Space in the Modern City." In *Urban Policy in Twentieth Century America,*" edited by Arnold R. Hirsch and Raymond A. Mohl. New Brunswick, N.J.: Rutgers University Press.

Posner, R. A. 2006. "Judicial Autonomy in a Political Environment." *Arizona State Law Journal* 38: 1.

Pritchett, W. E. 2003. "The 'Public Menace' of Blight: Urban Renewal and the Private Uses of Eminent Domain." *Yale Law & Policy Review* 21: 1.

——. 2006. "Beyond *Kelo*: Thinking about Urban Development in the 21st Century." *Georgia State Law Review* 22: 895.

Schauer, F. 2006. "The Court's Agenda—And the Nation's." *Harvard Law Review* 120: 4–64.

Somin, I. 2007. "The Limits of Backlash: Assessing the Political Response to *Kelo.*" Working paper, on file with authors.

Stevens, J. P. 2006. "Learning on the Job." *Fordham Law Review* 74: 1561.

Tuohy, L. 2005. "5–4, For the Takings; High Court: City Can Seize Homes to Boost Economy." *Hartford Courant,* June 24, A1.

Tribe, L. H. 2000. *American Constitutional Law,* 3rd ed.^

U.S. Senate. 2005. "The *Kelo* Decision: Investigating Takings of Homes and Other Private Property." Hearing before the United States Senate Committee on the Judiciary, September 20. Testimony of Thomas Merrill, Columbia Law School.

13

The War on Terror and Civil Liberties

Darshan Goux, Patrick J. Egan, and Jack Citrin

As Hamilton noted in *Federalist* No. 8, when a nation's security is at stake, even those nations with the most devout attachment to civil liberties find that "to be more safe, they at length become willing to run the risk of being less free." After the terrorist attacks of September 11, 2001, Americans again considered how far to limit the civil liberties of groups or individuals deemed to pose a threat to public safety or national security. The issue is not new; indeed, the Supreme Court has considered civil liberties cases arising out of every major war the country has fought from the Civil War to the present. Whether it was assessing the scope of President Lincoln's authority to suspend the writ of habeas corpus (Ex Parte *Milligan* (1866)), the constitutionality of the speech restrictions of the Espionage and Sedition Acts in World War I (*Schenk v. United States* (1918)), the due process rights of both citizens and noncitizens during World War II (Ex Parte *Quirin* (1942); *Korematsu v. United States* (1944)), the power of the president to seize the steel mills during the Korean War (*Youngstown Sheet and Tube v. Sawyer* (1952)), or the rights of journalists during the Vietnam War (*New York Times v. United States* (1971)), the Supreme Court has played a critical role in defining constitutional guarantees in the context of threats to national security.

The "War on Terrorism" is no different in that regard. Since September 2001, America's political institutions have grappled with the boundaries of executive power to combat the threat of terrorism through wiretapping, limiting the rights of imprisoned suspects, and obtaining information about financial transactions and diverse political activities. Both legislative and executive actions have been challenged in the courts, and the Supreme Court has issued opinions in several notable cases involving the rights of those held on suspicion of involvement in terrorist activities: *Hamdan v. Rumsfeld* (2006), *Hamdi v. Rumsfeld* (2004), *Rasul v. Bush* (2004), and *Rumsfeld v. Padilla* (2004). Each of these cases required the Court to consider the degree to which the civil liberties guarantees of the Constitution place constraints on the government's ability to hold or to prosecute those it suspects pose a threat to national security.

Hamdan v. Rumsfeld and *Rasul v. Bush* each concerned the rights of non-citizens who were being held by the United States as enemy combatants. In *Hamdan*, the Court invalidated the military commissions established by the government to try enemy combatants. In *Rasul*, the Court found that U.S. courts have authority to rule in cases filed on behalf of foreign citizens held at Guantánamo Bay, Cuba, because the United States has complete authority over the military base. *Hamdi v. Rumsfeld* and *Rumsfeld v. Padilla* involved the rights of U.S. citizens. In *Hamdi*, the Court ruled that under the Fifth Amendment, U.S. citizens who were apprehended on a foreign battlefield and detained as enemy combatants have the right to contest their detention before a neutral decision maker. On procedural grounds, the Court rejected the appeal in *Rumsfeld v. Padilla*, a case that involved the apprehension and detention inside the United States of a U.S. citizen suspected of planning a terrorist attack.

In June 2007, the Court agreed to hear the case of *Lakhdar Boumediene, et al. v. George W. Bush, President of the United States*. Petitioners in this case are non-citizens seized overseas in the War on Terror and classified as enemy combatants. Legal experts expect the ruling in this case (expected by June 2008) to finally address whether or not Guantánamo detainees have Constitutional rights and whether or not the right to habeas corpus was rightfully suspended.

This chapter begins with a brief review of public attitudes toward civil liberties during World War II, the Vietnam War, and the Cold War. It then provides a brief overview of the scholarly literature on public opinion regarding civil liberties. The body of the chapter shows how the events of September 11, 2001, dramatically raised the level of salience regarding national security and in doing so altered the landscape of opinion regarding civil liberties. Since then, public opinion regarding civil liberties has increasingly polarized along partisan lines.

Support for Civil Liberties during Earlier Wars

The earliest public opinion polling on the issue of wartime restrictions on civil liberties dates from the 1940s (see Table 13.1). During World War II, a majority of respondents polled were willing to accept limitations on civil liberties for groups of citizens that they perceived as potential threats to the national interest, even if they believed that only a small percentage of the group posed

Table 13.1

Before the War on Terror: Attitudes on Civil Liberties During World War II

Do you think the Japanese who were moved inland from the Pacific coast should be allowed to return to the Pacific coast when the war is over?

Yes	36%
No	48%
No opinion	16%

(Asked of those answering "no" to previous question) What should be done with them (the Japanese who were moved inland from the Pacific coast)?

Send them back to Japan/Put them out of this country	63%
Leave where they are/keep away from coast	14%
Kill them/get rid of them/destroy them	7%
Other/no answer	16%

Source: Gallup Poll, 1942.

a threat. For example, in a 1942 Gallup poll, 48% of Americans agreed that individuals of Japanese descent who had been forced to leave their homes on the Pacific coast and were held in inland internment camps should not be allowed to return to the coast after the war. Of those opposing allowing Japanese-Americans to return to their homes, 63% said they should be deported.[1] In 1946, 50% of respondents to a poll conducted by the National Opinion Research Center (NORC) agreed that the average person of Japanese descent living in the United States was loyal to the American government, but 66% in the same survey agreed that during the war, some Japanese living in the United States had spied for the Japanese government (NORC, May 1946).

During the Vietnam War, surveys asked about the civil liberties of antiwar protesters. Soon after the Democratic Convention in 1968, a majority of Americans felt that the antiwar demonstrators' right to protest had not been unlawfully denied, and most supported the tactics used by the police (Louis Harris & Associates, September 1968). In 1971, 76% of a national sample believed that the mass arrests of antiwar demonstrators in Washington, D.C., were justified (Opinion Research Corporation, May 1971). The public was split on the release of the Pentagon Papers, the Defense Department's classified history of U.S. involvement in Vietnam, by the *New York Times* and the *Washington Post*. While a plurality (43%) of Americans agreed with the Supreme Court ruling that the publication of the Pentagon Papers was legal (*The New York Times Co. vs. United States*), 70% also agreed that if, in a hypothetical future case, there was any doubt about publication being a threat to national security, documents should not be published (Louis Harris & Associates, July 1971). As in the case of opinions about Japanese Americans during World War II, how questions were worded significantly influenced the pattern of responses.

In their major study of public opinion toward civil liberties, McClosky and Brill (1983) surveyed both the mass public and groups of opinion leaders. Conducted in 1978 and 1979, their study asked a large number of questions regarding due process and tolerance for unpopular speech and political activity. Conducted in 1978, after urban violence and antiwar protests had subsided, most of their questions dealt with crime and political dissent rather than terrorism or military threats to national security. A few items, though, are relevant here. Among the general public, 51% believed that books advocating the overthrow of the government should be banned from the library, and 54% said that a group wanting to buy space in a newspaper to advocate war against another country should be turned down by the newspaper (McClosky & Brill 1983, 71). Large majorities of the public also said a local community should not allow its civic auditorium to be used by a wide range of groups, including student protesters calling for a sit-in against the city, "patriotic groups advocating war against another country," and the Palestine Liberation Organization calling for the destruction of Israel (McClosky & Brill 1983, 124, 125). On other issues relating to current weapons in the war on terrorism, 61% agreed that the police should be able to "bug the meeting place of leaders of organized crime," and 73% felt that tapping telephones with a legal warrant was justified when used against known criminals suspected of planning new crimes. At the same time, 79% of the public said that they rated as "extremely important" the right to privacy in their own correspondence and phone conversations (McClosky & Brill 1983, 188).

More generally, Americans are willing to limit the freedom of speech and association of groups deemed to be a threat to public safety and prevailing morality (Stouffer 1955; McClosky & Brill 1983, Sullivan et al. 1981). The main targets of intolerance have varied over time from Communists and atheists during earlier surveys to racists, radicals, and homosexuals in more recent ones. Political and legal elites are more likely to respect the civil liberties of unpopular groups (McClosky & Brill 1983); age, education, political ideology, and intense patriotism consistently are correlated with attitudes toward the civil liberties of dissenting or unpopular groups. The better educated and politically informed, younger citizens, and liberals consistently are more politically tolerant.

Increasingly, scholars recognize that support for civil liberties expressed in survey responses also reflects affective and cognitive processes, as well as media frames and the political context presented by current events (Marcus et al. 2005; Nelson, Clawson, & Oxley 1997; Gibson & Gouws 2001). In a series of findings highly relevant to the response to terrorism, researchers have found that feelings of threat and anxiety levels are key elements of tolerance judgments (Sniderman et al. 1991). In particular, scholars have found that threat—actual or perceived—activates authoritarian predispositions, leading those who are more authoritarian to express less tolerance for minority groups and civil liberties (Feldman & Stenner 1997; Stenner 2005). Threat also motivates individuals to become informed about politics (Marcus & MacKuen 1993) and it appears to lead them to value policy options that escalate rather than defuse conflict (Gordon & Arian 2001). In research conducted since the September 11 attacks, Gadarian (2007) finds that citizens with higher levels of threat perception prefer more aggressive types of foreign policy and that exposure to media coverage of terrorism moderates this relationship. Information is thus a key to judgments about how to balance political tolerance and security needs in high-stress situations—and therefore media frames play a central role in how individuals tilt the balance between preserving civil liberties and maintaining order. For example, in one experiment, respondents who saw a local news story describing a Ku Klux Klan rally as a free speech issue expressed more tolerant attitudes than respondents who saw the story framed as a public order issue (Nelson, Clawson, & Oxley 1997).

The Terrorist Threat, Civil Liberties, and Public Opinion

The scarcity of research and survey data prior to 2001 concerning public attitudes toward different means to combat a terrorist threat makes analysis of long-term trends difficult. Even if the terrorism-related Supreme Court decisions described here were salient to the mass public (they were not), the data are simply unavailable to assess responses to similar surveys before and after the decisions. However, we can make some inferences about the effect of the September 11th attacks on respondents' attitudes toward the civil liberties–national security trade-off. It is unsurprising that in the immediate aftermath of September 11th, there was pervasive support for giving the government extensive powers to combat the threat of terrorism. As time passed and the 2001 attack receded somewhat in the public's mind, however, respondents became more politically polarized in their attitudes. The level of concern about another attack and the nature of specific policy proposals influence how people make the trade-off between protecting civil liberties and combating potential threats to public safety. At the elite level, the Iraq war initiated a highly partisan debate about solutions to terrorism, the validity of increased surveillance of private and public activities, and the proper way to hold and try suspected terrorists. The division in public opinion gradually came to reflect these elite partisan conflicts.

Before September 11

Americans were no strangers to terrorism before September 2001: according to the FBI, there were 327 incidents of terrorism in the United States between 1980 and 1999, and domestic actors caused well over half (239) of these attacks.[2] In all of those attacks combined, 205 people were killed, and before September 11th the largest number of casualties from a terrorist attack was the 168 people killed in the 1995 Oklahoma City bombing. Although the events of September 11th overshadowed all that preceded them and reshaped the national agenda, by some measures public perception of threat from terrorist

Table 13.2
Fear of Terrorist Attacks, 1986–1996

	NBC/WSJ* 5/86	NBC/WSJ* 1/89	Princeton University Survey** 7/93	Hart Research** 6/95	ABC News* 8/96
Very concerned	63	51	48	44	31
Somewhat concerned	28	34	43	46	43
Not very concerned	8	13	9	10	18
Not sure	1	2	0	1	8
N	1,599	2,025	725	1,008	1,514

Data reported in Kuzma (2000).

Question wording:
*How concerned are you that there will be violence from international terrorists in the United States?
**How concerned are you that terrorists will commit acts of violence in the United States?

activity was high long before 2001 (see Table 13.2). In 1977, 90% of Americans said terrorism was a very serious problem in the world, and 60% said it was a serious problem in the United States (Louis Harris & Associates 1977). Kuzma (2000) reports that a May 1986 NBC/WSJ poll showed that 63% of Americans were very concerned about international terrorist violence within the United States. Although that level of concern diminished somewhat in subsequent years, a majority of Americans remained very or somewhat concerned about the threat of an international terrorist attack at home throughout the 1990s.

Before 1995, no publicly available polling indicates whether Americans believed domestic or international terrorists were the greater threat. After the 1995 Oklahoma City bombing, the salience of that event led a plurality of Americans (40% in 1995 and an average of 48% in two polls taken in 1996 and 1997) to agree that the greater threat to America from terrorism came from people inside the country (Kuzma 2000). Subsequent surveys, taken before September 2001, suggest a growing public concern about attacks by foreign terrorists (Global Strategy Group 1998, General Social Survey 2000, Pew Research Center for the Council on Foreign Relations 2001).[3]

Pollsters also asked Americans about the trade-off between the fight against terrorism and civil liberties well before 2001. In 1978, 59% of Americans said it is frequently or sometimes justifiable to limit civil liberties in order to fight terrorism (Gallup/Chicago Council on Foreign Relations). More specific survey questions about civil liberties and terrorism appeared in the mid-1990s (Kuzma 2000). As shown in Figure 13.1, immediately after the Oklahoma City bombing in 1995, slightly more Americans agreed than disagreed that it would be necessary for "ordinary Americans" to give up some civil liberties to curb terrorism. At that time, 76% of respondents told CBS

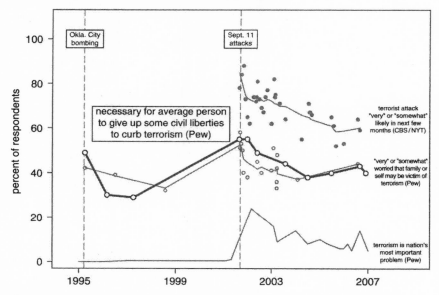

Figure 13.1. Salience of Terrorist Threat and Support for Restrictions on Civil Liberties, 1995–2006.

Question wording: Give up civil liberties: In order to curb terrorism in this country, do you think it will be necessary for the average person to give up some civil liberties, or not? (source: Pew Research Center; except for 1995 data, which is from Los Angeles Times poll).

Likelihood of terrorist attack: How likely do you think it is that there will be another terrorist attack in the United States within the next few months—very likely, somewhat likely, not very likely, or not at all likely? (source: CBS News/New York Times).

Victim of terrorism: All in all, how worried are you that you or someone in your family might become a victim of a terrorist attack? (sources: Gallup; Pew Research Center).

Most important problem: What do you think is the most important problem facing the country today? (source: Pew Research Center).

News that the federal government should have more authority to investigate and plant undercover agents in possible terrorist groups. Just one year later, attitudes had changed dramatically: only 30% of respondents in April 1996 said it was necessary for average Americans to sacrifice some civil liberties to fight terrorism.

Perceived Terrorist Threat and Support for Restrictions on Civil Liberties after September 11

After the terrorist attacks of September 2001, pollsters began more systematic measurement of Americans' perceptions of the terrorist threat and their attitudes to new domestic security measures, such as the surveillance of phone records, increased screening at airports, and the monitoring of bank records. Scholars, with Davis and Silver (2004) in the forefront, are now investigating the determinants of these beliefs and focusing on whether the structure of opinion formation relating to political tolerance and due process for criminals still applies.

As we would expect from the literature on the relationship between threat and civil liberties judgments, previous research has shown that Americans are more willing to trade off civil liberties for security in the immediate aftermath of a terrorist attack. They also are more willing to restrict liberties when the subject of the restrictions is a suspected terrorist, and when specific restrictions rather than civil liberties in the abstract are mentioned (Chong 1993; Gould 2002; Huddy, Khatib, & Capelos 2002; Davis & Silver 2004; Lewis 2005). Americans tend to support civil liberties when they are presented generally, to oppose policies that might affect their own rights, and to oppose limits on civil liberties as the time since an attack passes. Two of the nation's most extensive antiterror policy measures passed in the days immediately following the Oklahoma City bombing and the September 11th attacks. It is unclear whether the public would have supported these measures and accepted the limitations they impose on civil liberties in the absence of these dramatic events (Gould 2002: Lewis 2005). In the same vein, Huddy, Khatib, and Capelos (2002) found that support for government surveillance policies was high in September 2001 but that that support had diminished significantly by December 2001.

Figure 13.1 shows both the unprecedented extent to which September 11th focused the nation's attention on the threat of terrorism and how this was accompanied by a rise in the proportion of Americans willing to forgo civil liberties. In the immediate aftermath of the attacks, the percentage of respondents who told Gallup that they were "very" or "somewhat" worried that they or their families would be victims of terrorism jumped by 26 percentage points to 58% (from 32% when the question had last been asked in 1998). Similarly, the proportion of Americans stating that terrorism was the nation's most important problem rose from nearly zero to 24%, and more than 80% of Americans feared that the nation would face another terrorist attack within months.[4] As shown in Figure 13.1, Americans' support for curtailing civil liberties rose dramatically at the same time: in mid-September 2001, the Pew Research Center found that 55% of respondents agreed that it was necessary for "the average person to give up some civil liberties" in order to fight terrorism. Only 29% had agreed with this statement in April 1997, the previous time Pew had posed this question.

However, after September 2001, the strong support for restrictions on civil liberties faded in close parallel with a decline in salience of the terrorist threat. Figure 13.1 indicates that Americans' perceptions of such a threat dropped considerably—but remained high—between 2001 and 2006. At the same time, the proportion of Americans willing to forgo civil liberties in order to curb terrorism fell below 50%.

These findings parallel the in-depth analysis of Davis and Silver (2004), who use results from a survey conducted between November 2001 and January 2002 to show that perceived threat of a terrorist attack had a significant effect on support for civil liberties in the months immediately following September 11th. However, this relationship was moderated by the extent to which respondents expressed trust in the federal government. High-threat, low-trust respondents were less likely to support curtailing civil liberties than high-threat, high-trust respondents, but the relationship between trust and support for civil liberties was reversed among low-threat respondents.[5] Davis and Silver note that African Americans, 18- to 24-year-olds, urban residents, and college graduates showed especially high levels of support for civil liberties, and respondents over the age of 60 showed less support.[6]

Americans' stated willingness to curtail civil liberties can vary dramatically with the way survey questions are worded. Since 2001, pluralities of Americans have expressed more concern that the government will "excessively restrict the average person's civil liberties" than that it will "fail to enact strong new anti-terrorism laws" (Bowman 2007, 104). Americans seem more likely to worry that the government will go too far in restricting civil liberties when they make prospective judgments than they are to say the government went too far in their retrospective evaluations. In August 2006, the Pew Research Center asked Americans whether they were more concerned that government antiterrorism policies have "not gone far enough to adequately protect the country" or that the policies have "gone too far in restricting the average person's civil liberties." The former option was chosen by 55% of respondents, and the later was chosen by just 26%—consistent with the pattern of responses since the question was first asked in July 2004 (Pew Research Center 2004, 2005, 2006).

Support for Specific Measures Curtailing Civil Liberties after September 11

Surveillance and Searches by Police

Since September 2001, support for specific measures regarding surveillance and police activity has varied roughly by their level of intrusiveness into the private lives of Americans. Figure 13.2 indicates that strong majorities of Americans support issuing a national identity card that must be shown to police officers upon request. But less than 50% of Americans favor allowing the government to monitor their credit card purchases or their personal communications. Support for all three of these tactics has declined substantially since 2001.[7] Figure 13.3 shows how Americans are much more comfortable with liberty restrictions that are targeted at suspected wrongdoers than at the public at large. Support for monitoring the phone calls and emails of "Americans that the government is suspicious of" typically exceeds support for the monitoring of "ordinary Americans on a regular basis" by nearly 40 percentage points. (Unfortunately, these questions do not indicate whether respondents believe that the government must obtain a search warrant to

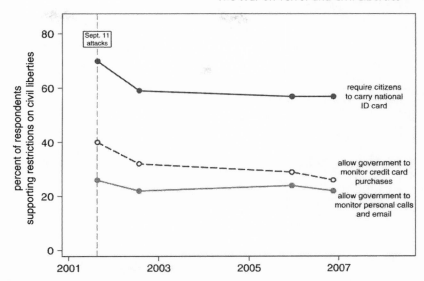

Figure 13.2. Support for Government Actions Taken against Terrorism, 2001–2006. Question wording: Would you favor or oppose the following measures to curb terrorism:…requiring that all citizens carry a national identity card to show to a police officer upon request?…allowing the U.S. government to monitor your credit card purchases?…allowing the U.S. government to monitor your personal telephone calls and emails? Source: Pew Research Center.

engage in such monitoring, an issue that has been at the center of many debates regarding surveillance of suspected terrorists.) What constitutes "suspicion" for Americans appears to depend on context and stereotypes: since 2002, consistent majorities (57% in 2006) have approved of allowing airport personnel to do "extra checks on passengers who appear to be of Middle Eastern descent" (Pew Research Center, 2002, 2006).

Americans appear quite willing to accept some government surveillance in public places. Eighty-five percent of respondents told *USA Today* in the wake of the Oklahoma City bombing in April 1995 that they would support security checkpoints in most office buildings. In October 2001, 91% of Americans said they would favor increased security checkpoints at public events and in public places, even if that meant a lengthy wait (CBS News/New York Times). Several years after the September 11th attacks, nearly 60% of Americans reported they would favor increased camera surveillance on the streets and in public places to curb terrorism (Harris Poll September 2002, March 2004).

The Patriot Act
Enacted in October 2001 and reauthorized in 2006, the Uniting and Strengthening America by Providing Appropriate Tools Required to Intercept and

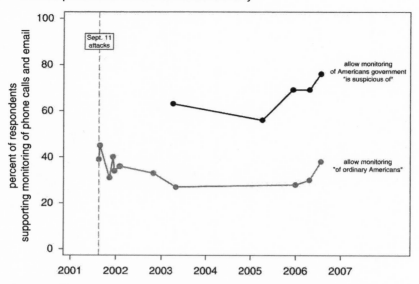

Figure 13.3. Support for Monitoring of Personal Communications by Type of Target, 2001–2006. Question wording: In order to reduce the threat of terrorism, would you be willing or not willing to allow government agencies to monitor the telephone calls and email of...Americans that the government is suspicious of?... ordinary Americans on a regular basis? Source: CBS News/New York Times poll.

Obstruct Terrorism Act of 2001—more commonly known as the Patriot Act—is probably the most publicly recognized legislation in the debate over the proper balance between civil liberties and national security in the wake of September 11th. Although the law granted federal authorities important new law enforcement powers, Americans know very little about the Patriot Act. In August 2003, half of all respondents in a USA Today/CNN/Gallup Poll said they were not too or not at all familiar with the Patriot Act. Nearly a quarter of Americans (24%) remained mostly unfamiliar with the legislation in the midst of congressional action to reauthorize the law in January 2006.

Americans have expressed mixed attitudes toward specific provisions within the Patriot Act. In March 2004, a strong majority (71%) told Gallup that they disapproved of the provision allowing federal agents to secretly search a U.S. citizen's home without informing the person of that search for an unspecified period of time. In that same poll, 51% of respondents said they disapproved of the Patriot Act provision that requires businesses, including libraries, hospitals, and bookstores, to turn over records in terrorism investigations without revealing it to clients. In contrast, a majority of respondents (51%) said they approved of the provision that allows federal agents in money-laundering or terrorism investigations, without a judge's approval, to learn whether specific individuals have accounts with financial institutions.

Table 13.3
Attitudes Regarding the Patriot Act and Civil Liberties, 2003–2005

		August 2003	November 2003	February 2004	December 2005
In restricting civil liberties, the Patriot Act…	goes too far	22	24	26	34
	is about right	48	45	43	44
	doesn't go far enough	21	20	21	18
	no opinion/don't know	9	10	10	4

Question wording: As you may know, shortly after the terrorist attacks on September 11, 2001 (on the World Trade Center and the Pentagon), a law called the Patriot Act was passed. That law deals with the ways the federal government can obtain private information on people living in the U.S. (United States) who are suspected of having ties with terrorists. Based on what you have read or heard, do you think the Patriot Act—goes too far, is about right, or does not go far enough—in restricting people's civil liberties in order to investigate suspected terrorism?
Source: Gallup.

A plurality of Americans have consistently stated that the Patriot Act is "about right" to the extent that it restricts people's civil liberties in order to investigate suspected terrorism. But support for the Patriot Act has diminished in concert with the decline in approval for other counterterrorism measures that curtail civil liberties (see Table 13.3). In 2003, 22% of Americans said the legislation goes too far, while 21% said it doesn't go far enough. By 2005, 34% of Americans agreed the legislation goes too far and only 18% said it doesn't go far enough. Despite their limited knowledge of the legislation, nearly all Americans agree the Patriot Act should be revised or eliminated altogether. Only 13% say all of the provisions of the legislation should be kept, 74% said the legislation needs minor or major changes, and 7% say it should be eliminated altogether (USA Today/CNN/Gallup Poll, January 2006).

Suspected Terrorists and Prisoners
While Americans tend to agree with the Bush administration's handling of suspected terrorists, they tend to disapprove of extreme measures in the abstract. In November 2001 and January 2002, a majority of respondents (59% and 60%, respectively) agreed non-U.S. citizens charged with terrorism should be tried in special military tribunals and not in the regular U.S. court system (ABC News/Washington Post). Americans were just as likely to agree that a U.S. citizen charged with planning an Al Qaeda attack should be held by the U.S. military as a wartime prisoner, without being put on trial or given access to a lawyer (54% agreed) (ABC News, June 2002).

A majority of respondents in February 2002 (59%) agreed that prisoners at Guantánamo Bay, Cuba, should not be considered prisoners of war and therefore held under the standards of the Geneva Convention (Los Angeles Times). Sixty-one percent of Americans in June 2005 said they were confident that the United States was adequately protecting the rights of the terror suspects at Guantánamo Bay (ABC News). Public support for the administration's handling of the Guantánamo Bay prisoners slipped over the following year, however. Only 44% of Americans told the Pew Research Center they support holding terror suspects at Guantánamo Bay without a formal trial or charges being filed, and 43% disagreed (Pew Research Center, March 2006). While 57% of Americans said they support holding suspected terrorists without a trial at Guantánamo Bay in June 2006, 71% of respondents also agreed those prisoners should be given prisoner-of-war rights or charged with a crime so they can defend themselves at trial (ABC News, June 22–25, 2006).

The question of the use of torture to gain information from terrorist suspects gained salience after revelations in April 2004 that U.S.-run prisons in Iraq and Guantánamo Bay were engaging in tactics against their prisoners that many considered torture. When asked by Gallup whether they are "willing" to have the U.S. government "torture known terrorists if they know details about future terrorist attacks on the U.S.," Americans have consistently said no. In a poll conducted just one month after the September 11th attacks, 52% of respondents were unwilling to endorse this tactic; 45% were willing to do so. Using the same question four years later, Gallup found that 56% disapproved of torture, and just 38% approved. These findings are echoed by responses to a question posed by the Pew Research Center, which has asked Americans whether torturing suspected terrorists to gain "important information" can "often," "sometimes," "rarely," or "never" be justified. Pluralities of respondents have generally stated that torture is either "rarely" or "never" justified, but the margin is slim: in December 2006, 54% of respondents fell into these two categories; 43% said torture was either "often" or "sometimes" justified.

The Structure of Public Opinion Regarding the Terrorist Threat and Civil Liberties

In this section, we describe how different demographic, social, and political groups in the population evaluate the trade-off between responding to the threat of terrorism and support for civil liberties. All the data presented here have been collected by the Pew Research Center, which since 1997 has been asking respondents: "In order to curb terrorism in this country, do you think it will be necessary for the average person to give up some civil liberties, or not?" (Over-time change in responses to this question has already been addressed in our discussion of Figure 13.1.)

Table 13.4 shows the proportion of respondents from various subgroups who are willing to give up some civil liberties. The table indicates that support for curtailing civil liberties has been consistently strong among older, better educated, and higher income respondents. In addition, the table shows that a deep divide has opened up between Democrats and Republicans regarding this question—a trend shown graphically in Figure 13.4. Whereas there was virtually no distinction between partisans on this topic

Table 13.4
Support for Giving Up Civil Liberties to Curb Terrorism, 1997–2006

	July 1997	Sept. 2001	Jan. 2002	July 2004	Sept. 2006
Overall	33.5	62.5	58.7	43.1	46.0
Gender					
Men	35.8	59.4	58.3	44.7	48.8
Women	31.2	65.2	64.0	41.6	43.1
Race					
White	32.3	63.0	59.7	42.1	49.7
Black	33.2	56.1	48.8	36.3	35.2
Hispanic	27.3	55.9	56.1	41.5	34.9
Age					
18–24	24.1	36.6	46.7	28.7	25.3
24–34	32.4	56.5	58.2	33.8	44.1
35–44	35.6	69.3	60.6	42.6	46.4
45–54	33.8	61.6	60.9	42.0	51.3
55–64	35.5	63.3	65.2	47.5	47.4
65 and older	36.1	67.8	59.0	46.0	55.3
Urban	29.8	N/A	57.5	37.6	N/A
Region					
Northeast	34.8	N/A	63.6	43.0	53.1
Midwest	34.9	N/A	60.3	43.3	45.4
South	32.3	N/A	60.2	45.2	46.4
West	31.6	N/A	61.7	40.0	39.8
Education					
High school or less	30.0	60.3	51.7	36.7	40.1
Some college	29.5	54.5	63.5	46.8	47.8
College educated	38.4	68.6	66.2	44.2	52.1
Postgrad	44.7	68.8	65.8	47.2	54.8
Income					
<$10,000–49,999	32.6	59.6	54.1	36.7	39.7
$50,000–99,999	39.9	64.1	68.9	46.2	54.8
$100,000+	38.0	59.1	61.9	52.9	52.9
Party					
Democrat	35.3	N/A	54.8	32.7	37.8
Independent	27.1	N/A	54.9	34.4	42.2
Republican	32.6	N/A	63.6	57.2	57.5
Worry about another terror attack					
Very worried	N/A	N/A	66.0	37.2	N/A
Somewhat worried	N/A	N/A	64.7	44.5	N/A
Not too worried	N/A	N/A	51.6	36.2	N/A
Not at all worried	N/A	N/A	55.0	39.6	N/A

Question wording: see text.

Source: Pew Research Center.

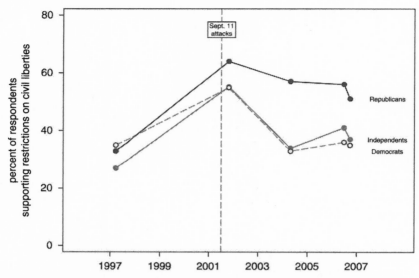

Figure 13.4. Support for Restrictions on Civil Liberties by Party Identification, 1997–2006. Question wording: See wording for "give up civil liberties" in Figure 13.1. Source: Pew Research Center.

in 1997 and very little difference after the September 2001 attacks, recent surveys have found a gap of roughly 20 percentage points between Democrats and Republicans.

The table also contains some unexpected results. As Davis and Silver (2004) find, African Americans are the least supportive racial group regarding giving up civil liberties. But Hispanics are nearly as supportive of trading off civil liberties as are whites. Urban residents—who presumably have most to fear from a subsequent terrorist attack—are less likely than the rest of the nation to support cutting back on civil liberties. And women—who are typically more liberal than men with regard to social issues—have at times been more supportive of giving up civil liberties than men. There is a bivariate relationship between fear of another terrorist attack and support for giving up civil liberties, but it is weaker than we might expect.

To understand the structure of opinion on civil liberties in the face of terrorism, it is necessary to go beyond these bivariate results. We undertook two multivariate analyses to examine the effects of particular demographic characteristics that are present when the effects of other variables are held constant. Because much of the research on civil liberties has focused on the effects of perceived threat, we first analyze a model designed to identify the individual characteristics particularly associated with fear about terrorist attacks. We then turn to a model that incorporates this fear to predict support for curtailing civil liberties. At this writing, only two Pew data sets (from surveys conducted in January 2002 and July 2004) were available that included questions about both perceived threat and willingness to forgo civil liberties. The analyses presented here pool the data from these two survey administrations.

Table 13.5 presents the multivariate analyses. Model I is an analysis estimating the strength of the association between fear of terrorism and various demographic, social, and political characteristics. We perform an ordered probit analysis, as the dependent variable—the degree to which respondents worry that there will be soon be another terrorist attack—takes on four values in ascending order ("not at all," "not too," "somewhat," and "very" worried). As shown in Model I, holding all other variables constant, women, the less educated, those who are parents of children under 18, those who follow the news more closely, and those living in the New York metropolitan area were significantly more likely to report being worried about a terror attack. In addition, the negative coefficient on the "dummy variable" for 2004 indicates that holding all other factors constant, those in the 2004 survey were less worried about an attack than those in the 2002 survey. It is remarkable that perception of threat is bipartisan: as shown by the insignificant coefficients on "Democrat" and "Republican," the threat levels of Democrats, Independents, and Republicans are statistically indistinguishable after controlling for other variables. The same is true for liberals and conservatives, as shown by the zero coefficient on ideology. Finally, we note the low value of the pseudo-R-squared statistic (.02), which indicates that the model does a poor job in explaining variation in the dependent variable. This result may mean that fear of terrorism is better accounted for by other variables (perhaps those that have more to do with individual predispositions and personality characteristics). It also suggests that fear of terrorism may be distributed throughout the population in a more random fashion than many other attitudes regarding politics and public affairs. Another conclusion that may be drawn is that Americans evaluate the terrorist threat "sociotropically"—focusing on the threat to the nation at large rather than to themselves individually—in a way similar to how they evaluate economic concerns (Kinder & Kiewiet 1981).

Model II allows us to examine the factors associated with support for curtailing civil liberties in the fight against terrorism. It is a probit model in which support for restrictions on civil liberties is scored 1 and opposition is scored 0. It includes all of the variables from Model I, plus respondents' fear of a subsequent terror attack, as predictors. In addition, following Zaller (1992), we hypothesized that attention to news and its accompanying information effects would moderate the effects of two important predictors of opinion regarding civil liberties: education and ideology. Prior (2005) notes that Americans' news consumption skyrocketed after the 2001 attacks, and finds that the typical American's political informedness—on matters both related to terrorism and not—increased as a result. We therefore included terms that interacted news interest with these two variables.

The statistically significant coefficients in Model II indicate that those who are older, have higher incomes, or are Republicans are more likely to support curtailing civil liberties, holding all other variables constant. Respondents who say they are registered voters (which we take to be a proxy for civic engagement) are significantly more likely to oppose curtailment of

Table 13.5
Fear of Terrorism and Support for Restrictions on Civil Liberties, 2002 and 2004

Variable	Model I Worry that there will soon be another terrorist attack (ordered probit)	Model II Support for restrictions on civil liberties to curb terrorism (probit)
Female	.293***	.044
	(.049)	(.079)
Black	−.047	.150
	(.083)	(.144)
Hispanic	−.044	.232
	(.092)	(.151)
Age	.002	.008**
	(.002)	(.003)
Education	−.071***	.154**
	(.017)	(.049)
Income	.017	.070**
	(.013)	(.022)
Parent of child under 18 in household	.133*	−.086
	(.054)	(.086)
Born-again Christian	−.052	−.089
	(.054)	(.088)
Live in large city	.010	−.089
	(.060)	(.098)
Interest in news	.005***	.013*
	(.001)	(.006)
Registered voter	−.079	−.176+
	(.063)	(.101)
Democrat	−.102	−.040
	(.091)	(.153)
Republican	−.072	.382*
	(.093)	(.156)
Ideology	.000	.002
	(.028)	(.086)
Live in New York metro area	.242**	−.049
	(.087)	(.135)
Live in Washington, D.C., metro area	.122	−.098
	(.105)	(.175)
2004 dummy	−.191**	−.618***
	(.063)	(.087)
Worry regarding terrorist attack		.118**
		(.045)
Education × news interest		−.001
		(.001)
Ideology × news interest		−.003+
		(.001)

Table 13.5
(*continued*)

Variable	Model I Worry that there will soon be another terrorist attack (ordered probit)	Model II Support for restrictions on civil liberties to curb terrorism (probit)
Thresholds	−1.163***	
	(.175)	
	−.233	
	(.173)	
	1.061***	
	(.174)	
Intercept		−1.232+
		(.410)
N	2,051	1,162
Pseudo-R²	.02	.10
Log likelihood statistic	2,549.49	−728.42

Coefficients significantly different from zero at +$p < .10$, *$p < .05$, **$p < .01$, ***$p < .001$ (two-tailed test). Standard errors in parentheses.

Question wording: See Figure 13.1.
Variable coding:
Worry regarding terror attack: coded 1 (not at all worried) to 4 (very worried)
Education: coded 1 (8th grade or less) to 7 (postgraduate degree)
Income: coded 1 (less than $10,000 per year) to 8 ($100,000 per year or more)
Ideology: coded 1 (very conservative) to 5 (very liberal)
Interest in news: coded by percentile of news interest in year of survey (0 to 100) on an index of items asking how closely respondents were following various stories in the news. The items varied, depending on the year of survey administration and the survey form to which respondents were assigned. Wordings for these items are available from the authors upon request.
All other variables coded 0-1. Residents of Connecticut, New Jersey, and New York are coded as living in the New York metro area. Residents of the District of Columbia, Maryland, and Virginia are coding as living in the Washington, D.C., metro area.
Source: Pew Research Center.

civil liberties. Those interviewed in 2004 were also significantly more opposed to restricting civil liberties. Notably, most of the predictors of fear of a terror attack—including gender, parenthood, and residence in the New York metropolitan area—are not predictors of support for curtailing civil liberties.[8]

To interpret the effects of the interaction terms in the model, we follow Brambor, Clark, and Golder (2006) and focus on the marginal effects of ideology and education conditioned on level of news interest. The top panel of Figure 13.5 depicts the effect of a shift from the minimum to maximum

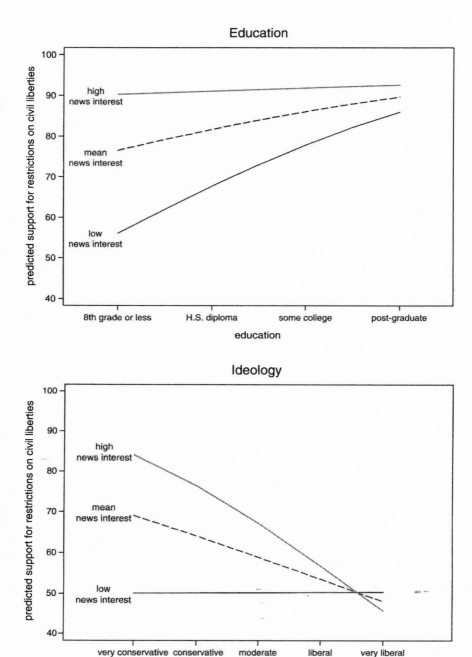

Figure 13.5. The Effects of Education and Ideology on Support for Restricting Civil Liberties, Conditional on Interest in the News. Question wording: See wording for "give up civil liberties" in Figure 13.1. Source: Pew Research Center.

level of education on support for curtailing civil liberties at low, mean, and high levels of interest in the news, holding all other variables in the model at their means. As shown in the figure, education affects attitudes on civil liberties only among those with lower levels of news interest. Education has no significant effect among those with high levels of interest in the news. In the bottom panel of Figure 13.5, we plot the effect of a shift from very conservative to very liberal views on opinion regarding civil liberties at varying levels of news interest, again holding all other variables constant at their means. This figure shows that ideology affects opinion regarding civil liberties only at higher levels of news interest.[9]

In sum, Americans who follow the news closely are polarized along ideological lines regarding the trade-off between preventing terrorist acts and protecting civil liberties. In addition, exposure to the news leads less-educated Americans to support restrictions on civil liberties at levels comparable to those with higher levels of education. We note here how different these conclusions are from those reached by the political tolerance literature, which stresses the sympathy of educated, informed elites for the civil liberties of marginalized groups. In an era dominated by the U.S. government's response to terrorism and overshadowed by the fear of subsequent attacks, it is possible that education and exposure to the news lead many Americans to decide that the times require that some civil liberties be curtailed.

Conclusion

The argument over how to preserve Americans' civil liberties while safeguarding national security is as old as our nation itself. But the events of September 2001—in which more lives were lost on American soil than in any military attack since the Civil War—has changed this debate in ways we are just beginning to understand. We hope this chapter will serve as a useful starting point for other research as new data become available and as America's response to terrorism inevitably evolves.

In previous national security crises, Americans have shown a willingness to limit the liberties of political minorities, even when they recognize that only a minority of that group actually poses a threat. (We note here one additional poll result: 29% of participants in a Pew Research Center survey conducted days after the September 11 attacks favored "allowing the U.S. government to take legal immigrants from unfriendly countries to internment camps during times of tension or crisis.") In some ways, the present controversy bears similarity to aspects of the concerns about domestic security during World War II. As our nation does battle abroad, an enemy—identified with relative ease by language, looks, and culture—is feared to lurk within our borders among their brethren, who are predominantly upstanding Americans. In other ways, the response to terrorism incorporates themes similar to those of the Red Scare: the enemy is believed to harbor an ideological (rather than a national) agenda, and it is thought to be organized in a relatively decentralized, secretive fashion.

Of course, many features of the current debate over civil liberties are unprecedented. September 11th awakened Americans to the possibility that just a handful of people could perpetrate destruction on a massive scale and demonstrated how such events could be experienced with heartbreaking vividness by a nation connected with sophisticated, round-the-clock information technologies. In addition, the 2001 attacks took place in the middle of an intensely partisan period in American politics, and the nation has come to see the controversy over civil liberties through a partisan lens. Finally, America's reaction to the attacks has in some ways been tempered in comparison with the country's response to crises past—due in some part to our experience with multiculturalism and globalization, and due as well to a distrust of authority that is much greater than in those previous eras.

In this light, the American response to the current threat to national security appears at turns nuanced and erratic. A majority of the public tends to say average Americans should not have to give up any civil liberties to fight terrorism. But majorities also support specific antiterror policies, especially when those policies apply to suspected terrorists, are not particularly intrusive, or seem to improve public safety. A plurality of Americans declare themselves comfortable with the Patriot Act, the government's signature law-enforcement response to the terror attacks. But majorities say they want to see the legislation revised or repealed—and majorities are also uncomfortable with several of the law's specific provisions. Unlike in previous eras, the nation's elites—as demarcated by characteristics such as education, income, and interest in public affairs—are generally more likely to support giving up civil liberties than are their fellow citizens.

A question that remains is the extent to which the Supreme Court will evaluate the constitutionality of the government's counterterrorism activities and if so, lead public opinion on the proper balance between national security and civil liberties—a topic on which it would seem uniquely appropriate for the public to follow the Court's cue. Thus far, the Court has yet to issue rulings regarding terrorism and civil liberties that have far-reaching, easily graspable implications, which makes an assessment of its persuasive powers in this area impossible.

We close by reiterating that support for restrictions on civil liberties has risen and declined with Americans' perceptions of an imminent terrorist threat. Remarkably, whether any individual experiences such a threat appears to be somewhat unpredictable with the usual variables that shape attitudes about public affairs. The few factors associated with threat perception are for the most part distinct from those leading Americans to be willing to give up civil liberties. What this means is that opinion in the near future regarding the trade-off between security and liberty may rest largely on whether additional attacks occur and how the country's elites respond. Their reaction will determine the extent to which the national debate emphasizes protecting the nation or specific freedoms like privacy and speech—a debate that will in turn shape Americans' choice between the timeless values of security and liberty.

Notes

1. Data for this poll and others cited in this section were provided by the Roper Center for Public Opinion Research, University of Connecticut.

2. FBI, "Terrorism in the United States: 1999."

3. Pew Research Center, "America's Place in the World III," August 21–September 5, 2001. For a differing view on American public opinion after the Oklahoma City bombing, see Lewis (2000).

4. Researchers have found that direct self-interest seems to have little effect on how individuals evaluate the state of the nation in the wake of terrorism. Soon after the September 2001 attacks, respondents in a national survey based their evaluations of the overall terrorist threat on their general concerns about a future attack in the United States and not on their concerns about being personally harmed (Huddy, Khatib, & Capelos 2002).

5. Unfortunately, the data sets used to construct Figure 13.1 do not include comparable measures of trust in government, which prohibits us from undertaking a similar analysis here.

6. Davis and Silver measured respondents' personal sense of threat through a series of questions about potential sources of threat. They measured fears about the threat to the nation through respondents' level of concern about another attack. To measure trust, they asked questions about trust in law enforcement and trust in the government in Washington, D.C.

7. Similarly, in 2005, strong majorities of Americans opposed allowing police to stop people randomly on the street for searches (70% opposed) or allowing police to enter a person's home at any time without a search warrant (93% opposed) as efforts to fight terrorism (Gallup July 2005).

8. This held true in a model we estimated without the fear of terrorist attack variable. It also held true in an instrumental variables model that used results from Model I to generate a predicted "fear of terrorism" variable and excluded the New York and Washington, D.C., metro areas variables from the second-stage estimation. The estimates derived from these two models (not shown here) were broadly similar to the estimates in Model II.

9. The statistical significance of these effects can be described as follows: the effect of a shift from the minimum to maximum value of education on civil liberties attitudes is significantly different from zero ($p < .05$) for respondents with the lowest level of news interest, as well as those with the mean level of news interest. It is not significant for those with the highest level of news interest. Similarly, the effect of ideology is significant at the mean and highest levels of news interest, but not the lowest level of news interest.

References

Bowman, Karlyn. 2007. "AEI Studies in Public Opinion: America and the War on Terrorism." Available online at http://aei.org/publications/pubID.22819,filter.all/pub_detail.asp. Accessed August 18, 2007.

Brambor, Thomas, William Roberts Clark, and Matt Golder. 2006. "Understanding Interaction Models: Improving Empirical Analyses." *Political Analysis* 14: 63–82.

Chong, Dennis. 1993. "How People Think, Reason, and Feel about Rights and Liberties." *American Journal of Political Science* 37(3): 867–99.

Davis, Darren W., and Brian D. Silver. 2004. "Civil Liberties vs. Security: Public Opinion in the Context of the Terrorist Attacks on America." *American Journal of Political Science* 48(1): 28–46.

Federal Bureau of Investigation. 1999. "Terrorism in the United States: 1999." Available from http://www.fbi.gov/publications/terror/terror99.pdf. Retrieved July 30, 2006.

Feldman, Stanley and Karen Stenner. 1997. "Perceived Threat and Authoritarianism." *Political Psychology* 18(4): 741–770.

Gadarian, Shana Kushner. 2007. "The Politics of Threat: Terrorism, Media and Foreign Policy Opinion." Princeton University. Typescript.

Gibson, James L., and Amanda Gouws. 2001. "Making Tolerance Judgments: The Effects of Context, Local and National." *Journal of Politics.* 63(4): 1067–90.

Gordon, Carol, and Asher Arian. 2001. "Threat and Decision-making." *Journal of Conflict Resolution* 45(2): 196–215.

Gould, Jan B. 2002. "Playing with Fire: The Civil Liberties Implications of September 11th." *Public Administration Review* 62: 74–79.

Huddy, Leonie, Nadia Khatib, and Theresa Capelos. 2002. "Trends: Reactions to the Terrorist Attacks of September 11, 2001." *Public Opinion Quarterly* 66: 418–40.

Kinder, Donald R., and D. Roderick Kiewiet. 1981. "Sociotropic Politics: The American Case." *British Journal of Political Science* 11(2): 129–61.

Kuzma, Lynn M. 2000. "Trends: Terrorism in the United States." *Public Opinion Quarterly* 64(1): 90–105.

Lewis, Carol W. 2000. "The Terror That Failed: Public Opinion in the Aftermath of the Bombing in Oklahoma City." *Public Administration Review* 60(3): 201–10.

Lewis, Carol W. 2005. "The Clash between Security and Liberty in the U.S. Response to Terror." *Public Administration Review* 65(1): 18–30.

Marcus, George E. and Michael B. MacKuen. 1993. "Anxiety, Enthusiasm, and the Vote: The Emotional Underpinnings of Learning and Involvement During Presidential Campaigns." *American Political Science Review* 87(3): 672–85.

Marcus, George E., John L. Sullivan, Elizabeth Theiss-Morse, and Daniel Stevens. 2005. "The Emotional Foundation of Political Cognition: The Impact of Extrinsic Anxiety on the Formation of Political Tolerance Judgments." *Political Psychology* 26(6): 949–63.

McClosky, Herbert, and Alida Brill. 1983. *Dimensions of Tolerance: What Americans Believe about Civil Liberties.* New York: Russell Sage Foundation.

Nelson, Thomas E., Rosalee A. Clawson, and Zoe M. Oxley. 1997. "Media Framing of a Civil Liberties Conflict and Its Effect on Tolerance." *American Political Science Review* 91(3): 567–83.

Prior, Markus. 2002. "Political Knowledge after September 11." *PS: Political Science and Politics* 35(3): 523–29.

Sniderman, Paul M., Joseph F. Fletcher, Peter H. Russell, Philip E. Tetlock, and Brian J. Gaines. 1991. "The Fallacy of Democratic Elitism: Elite Competition and Commitment to Civil Liberties." *British Journal of Political Science* 21: 349–70.

Stenner, Karen. 2005. *The Authoritarian Dynamic.* New York: Cambridge University Press.

Stouffer, Samuel A. 1955. *Communism, Conformity, and Civil Liberties.* New York: John Wiley & Sons.

Sullivan, John L., George E. Marcus, Stanley Feldman, and James E. Pierson. 1981. "The Sources of Political Tolerance: A Multivariate Analysis." *American Political Science Review* 75(1): 92–106.

Zaller, John, 1992. *The Nature and Origins of Mass Opinion.* Cambridge: Cambridge University Press.

14

The 2000 Presidential Election Controversy

Manoj Mate and Matthew Wright

The Supreme Court's decision in *Bush v. Gore* (2000) may have decided the disputed 2000 presidential election, but in its immediate aftermath, the controversy lived on in the divisions the case caused in public opinion toward the Court itself. This chapter of the book is unique in that it evaluates the effect of a particular Supreme Court decision on public opinion toward the Court, rather than its impact on opinions about a particular legal or policy issue. It therefore follows in a long line of scholarship that measures the public's trust, confidence, and support for the Court in the wake of controversial decisions (e.g., Gibson, Caldeira & Spence 2003a, 2003b). Those scholars generally find that the Court's strong "reservoir of goodwill" allows it to weather controversies that might otherwise threaten its legitimacy in the public mind. The Court's legitimacy is stable and secure, as it is generally unaffected by public reaction to particular decisions, even controversial ones.

This chapter tests these more global propositions in the context of what might be described as the Court's most controversial decision in recent memory. We analyze data from the 2000 and 2004 National Annenberg Election Studies, which provide various measures of support for the Supreme Court both immediately before and after *Bush v. Gore*. The findings of short-term polarization immediately following *Bush v. Gore*, which recedes completely four years later, attests to the resiliency of popular attitudes toward the Court even in the face of its most "legitimacy-threatening" decisions.

Legitimacy and Confidence in the Court

To measure public support for the Supreme Court, the General Social Survey (GSS) asks: "How much confidence do you have in the people running the Supreme Court—a great deal of confidence, some confidence or not much confidence?" The GSS asks the same question about confidence in the executive branch, Congress, and the military. Over the past thirty years, respondents have expressed more confidence in the Court than in the executive and legislative branches (see Figure 14.1), but in most years less than 50% of respondents expressed a "great deal" of confidence in the Court (Marshall 1989). According to Caldeira (1986), confidence in the Court declined in the late 1960s because of the Court's unpopular decisions in areas such as criminal rights and its invalidation of certain federal statutes. At times, confidence rose and fell because of factors completely outside the Court's control: high levels of inflation may have dampened confidence in the Court, whereas the early popularity of the Johnson administration and the Watergate scandal were associated with periods of rising confidence (Caldeira 1986; see Tanenhaus & Murphy 1981). Since 1973, however, confidence levels have remained fairly stable. The Court has fared well in relative terms vis-à-vis other institutions,

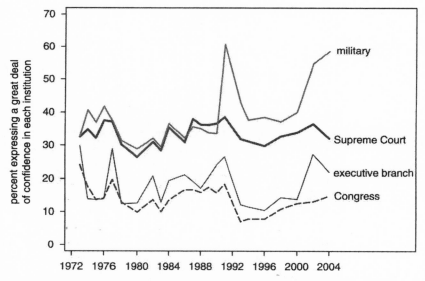

Figure 14.1. Confidence in Institutions of American Government, 1973–2004. Question wording: I am going to name some institutions in this country. As far as the people running these institutions are concerned, would you say you have a great deal of confidence, only some confidence, or hardly any confidence at all in them?...The military...The U.S. Supreme Court....The executive branch of the federal government...Congress. Source: General Social Survey.

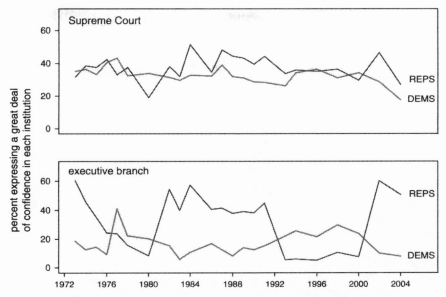

Figure 14.2. Confidence in the Supreme Court and the Executive Branch by Party Identification, 1973–2004. Question wording: see Figure 14.1. Source: General Social Survey.

and confidence in the Court has closely tracked confidence in the military, which has traditionally registered the highest levels of confidence among GSS respondents. Only at two points has the confidence in the military far surpassed that of the Court: during the first Persian Gulf War and after the September 11th terrorist attacks (see Figure 14.1).

Most striking are two periods of partisan polarization, one that began in the early 1980s and persisted into Bill Clinton's first term, and a second that occurred in the wake of *Bush v. Gore* and continued into 2004 (see Figure 14.2). It is worth noting, however, that Americans view the Court through a much less partisan lens than they view the executive branch (see Figure 14.2).

Scholarship on public opinion and the Court has offered competing approaches for understanding the effect of controversial decisions on the Court's legitimacy. One approach is exemplified by Grosskopf and Mondak (1998), who studied two controversial decisions, *Webster v. Reproductive Health Services* (1989) and *Texas v. Johnson* (1989), and Mondak and Smithey (1997). Grosskopf and Mondak concluded that individual decisions of the Court can strongly affect confidence in the Court and that unpopular decisions can undermine institutional support. They also found that the overall pattern of effects reflected a negativity bias:[1] disagreement with one or both of the decisions reduced confidence in the Court quite substantially, but agreement with the two decisions brought about only marginal gains in confidence. Observing that "democratic values facilitate regeneration of institutional support," Mondak and Smithey (1997, 1124) argue that individual decisions may also bolster confidence in the Court and advance a dynamic model in which the Court can gradually "regenerate" public support over time through judicial decisions that reaffirm the link between the Court and basic democratic values.

On the other hand, Gibson, Caldeira, and Spence (2003a, 2003b) contend that the Court's legitimacy is more stable and functions as a "reservoir of goodwill," and they posit that unpopular decisions do not so easily erode that goodwill or institutional loyalty. Following Easton (1965, 1975), Gibson and colleagues distinguish between *specific support*, which denotes "approval of policy outputs in the short term," and *diffuse support*, which refers to "fundamental loyalty to an institution over the long term." They suggest that the latter is the more appropriate metric of legitimacy because it captures "support not contingent upon satisfaction with the immediate outputs of the institution" (2003b, 537). Gibson and his colleagues therefore suggest a different set of measures to assess legitimacy or diffuse support, arguing that confidence is "typically not institution specific" and captures "general attitudes toward institutions," and that confidence, like specific support, is "heavily dependent upon the immediate performance of the institution" (2003a, 355).

In analyzing the effect of *Bush v. Gore* on public opinion, Gibson and his colleagues found that diffuse support for the Court did not decline among Democrats, but it increased among Republicans and independents. The authors suggest that their findings are consistent with the "positivity frames" hypotheses, which posit that exposure to courts and the "symbolic trappings of judicial power" can enhance judicial legitimacy, even among those who are extremely unhappy with a particular decision (2003b, 553; Scheb & Lyons 2000). Gibson and his colleagues contend that the powerful effect of these legitimizing symbols of law may explain how institutional loyalty "inoculates against an unwelcome policy decision," even among partisans (2003b, 554).[2]

However, data from another study suggests that the *Bush v. Gore* decision had a polarizing effect. In a study of individual-level data, Kritzer (2001) attempted to measure the decision's impact on the public's general evaluation of the Court and knowledge of the Court and found that the decision polarized public opinion along partisan lines. However, as Gibson and his colleagues note, Kritzer's study examined general evaluations of the Court's performance and not diffuse support for the institution. The question Kritzer asked was: "On a scale of 1 to 10, where 1 means very poor and 10 means excellent, how would you rate the job the Supreme Court is doing?"

Kritzer found that although the effect of the decision on public evaluation of the Court was effectively zero (with increases in negative evaluations offset by increases in positive evaluations), the decision restructured public evaluation of the Court along party lines (see Franklin & Kosaki 1989). Before the decision was announced, party identification (partisanship) was not related to respondents' evaluation of the Court; after the decision, however, there was a clear relationship between party and evaluation, and that relationship was mediated by the level of approval or disapproval of the decision itself. Thus, Kritzer's model for the postdecision time frame shows that when disposition toward the decision is included, it replaces party identification as a significant predictor of Kritzer's measure of confidence.

This chapter contributes to this debate by examining the determinants of both specific and diffuse support for the Court in the context of *Bush v. Gore*. At the most basic level, that case was a story of winners and losers. The losers included the Gore-Lieberman ticket, Democratic partisans who voted for that ticket, and other stable constituencies of the Democratic party, such as ideological liberals and blacks. Among the winners were Republican identifiers and ideological conservatives more generally.

Data and Methodology

The 2000 and 2004 National Annenberg Election Survey (NAES) are part of the largest series of studies of American public opinion and voting behavior in individual presidential elections. The 2000 NAES is particularly useful because of the number of interviews and reinterviews conducted in the weeks after the 2000 presidential election.[3] Also, the NAES includes items that approximate both diffuse support and specific support, and these items appear continuously on the interview schedule from November 28, 2000, through January 19, 2001. The NAES data thus allow us to focus on the effect of the December 12 decision because a large sample is available both before and after the date of the decision.

Unfortunately, the NAES does not attempt to reliably ascertain the respondent's political information (a key variable in Kritzer's 2000 analysis) by means of factual questions both before and after the decision. Here, we must rely on the interviewer's judgment of the respondent's political sophistication. Nor does the NAES include measures of allegiance to "democratic values" and other attitudinal variables employed by Gibson, Caldeira, and their colleagues. All in all, however, the advantages of the NAES data set far outweigh these analytic shortcomings. Among the many questions that the NAES 2000 asked about the Court and the *Bush v. Gore* decision, only one on specific support and one on diffuse support were asked both before and after the decision:

> [Specific support] How much confidence do you have in the US Supreme Court to deal fairly with the situation surrounding the results of the election for president? A great deal, a fair amount, not too much or none at all? [After the decision was announced, the first part of this question was reworded: How much confidence do you have that the US Supreme Court dealt fairly....]

> [Diffuse support] Please tell me how much confidence you have in the Judicial Branch of the federal government—this includes the US

Supreme Court. Do you have a great deal, a fair amount, not too much or none at all?

Unlike the measure of confidence used by the GSS, which captures elements of both specific and diffuse support, these two NAES measures are less affected by the flaws described by Gibson, Caldeira, and Spence (2003a).[4] The first question focuses the respondent's attention on a salient, high-visibility current event and the Court's role in that event. In contrast, the second question asks about confidence in the federal judiciary as an institution.

The conceptual difference between the two questions seems to be, at least on the surface, empirically sustainable; responses to both correlate at roughly .50, and this correlation is quite stable over different subperiods of the NAES. In other words, although the two variables are strongly related to one another (as we would expect), there is enough of a distinction between them that they can be fairly said not to be different measures of the same concept. One could thus reasonably expect some positive correlation between specific and diffuse support. It is worth noting that these two variables closely mirror or approximate two variables used by Gibson, Caldeira, and Spence (2003b, 547–549, Table 5), "Perceived fairness of *Bush v. Gore*," and the diffuse support measure, "Loyalty to the Supreme Court," roughly approximate measures of specific and diffuse support, respectively.

Our third measure captures the difference between a respondent's specific support and diffuse support, and we call this "residual support." For each respondent, we subtracted the specific support response from the diffuse support response, producing a variable that ranges from −3 (highest level of specific support relative to the lowest level of diffuse support) to 3 (highest level of diffuse support relative to the lowest level of specific support).

Our independent variables included age, education level, gender, religious attendance, and Southern residence. We also included a dichotomous measure of race because of the perceived discrimination against blacks in Florida during the election (for general treatments of race and Court legitimacy, see Caldeira & Gibson 1992; Jaros & Roper 1980; for specific analyses with respect to *Bush v. Gore*, see Kritzer 2001; Gibson et al. 2003b). Kritzer's measures of political interest and knowledge played a significant role in his analysis, and we captured these concepts with a fairly standard measure of political interest and an interviewer rating of the respondent's political intelligence.

To control for the overall level of goodwill the respondent has toward the political system, we created a variable composed of the factor score of the respondent's overall confidence in the executive branch, Congress, and the military (scored from 0 = least institutional confidence to 1 = most institutional confidence). Partisan identification and self-rated political ideology also enter into our analysis.

We expected the highly political nature of the election controversy and the Court's role in it to have a significant effect on both specific and diffuse support, with the former effect likely to be much stronger. We also expected the residual support (the difference between diffuse and specific support) to polarize along partisan lines as a result of the decision.

Analysis

Given that *Bush v. Gore* is basically a story of political winners and losers, it is worth noting that prior to the decision, the public was confident that the Supreme Court would deal with the election controversy fairly. When asked whether they would accept a Supreme Court ruling if both candidates did, 83.3% of respondents said they would be either very likely or somewhat likely to support the decision.[5] Significantly, this percentage did not vary by party identification or ideology, and blacks were only slightly less confident than whites. When asked—again prior to the decision—how likely it would be that both candidates would accept the decision regardless of what it was, 66.3% of respondents answered either "very likely" or "somewhat likely."[6] These percentages did not vary by partisan identification or ideology.

The response patterns changed after the decision was rendered. When asked whether they felt that the Supreme Court justices had been influenced by their personal political views, respondents were almost exactly split: 47.3% felt that the justices had been, and 47.1% felt that they had not. The differences among partisans are stark: 29.3% of Republicans and 39.2% of self-reported strong conservatives felt the justices had acted on their own political views, compared with 63.3% of Democrats and 66.2% of strong liberals (see Figure 14.3). After the decision, the level of specific support for the Court among Democrats decreased, and specific support among Republicans increased—exactly what one would expect, given the outcome.

We also found strong and persistent polarization among liberals and conservatives after the decision was rendered. The level of distrust among liberals was markedly higher after December 12, and the level among conservatives remained fairly constant (see Figure 14.3).

In comparing the responses of whites and blacks, we found a high level of polarization, both in specific support and diffuse support (see bottom panels of Figures 14.3 and 14.4). These findings seem to be partially at odds with those of Gibson and his colleagues (2003b, 543), who found "no indication of an overall diminution of loyalty towards the Court between 1987 and 2001" among blacks.[7] These findings thus appear to confirm that the decision did have a pronounced negative impact on blacks' specific support of the Supreme Court. Although these findings are noteworthy, we acknowledge the quite small sample size of blacks on a day-to-day basis, which almost certainly accounts for some of the random fluctuations in both Figures 14.3 and 14.4.

The relationships between other personal characteristics and specific support for the Court's decision in *Bush v. Gore* are shown in Table 14.1. As expected, institutional confidence, measured by confidence in the other

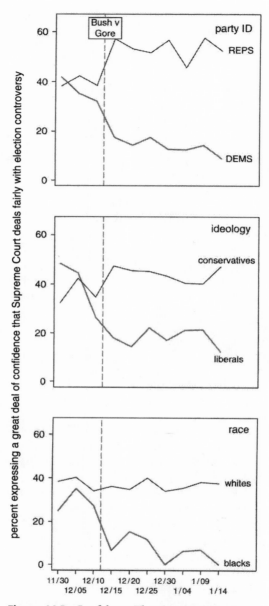

Figure 14.3. Confidence That Supreme Court
Fairly Adjudicates 2000 Election Controversy,
November 2000–January 2001. Question wording:
see text. Source: National Annenberg Election
Survey.

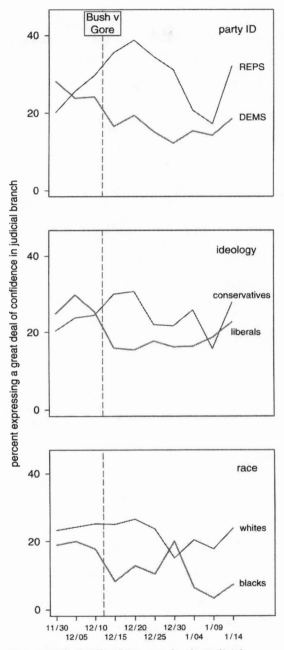

Figure 14.4. "Diffuse" Support for the Judicial
Branch, Including the U.S. Supreme Court,
November 2000–January 2001. Question wording:
see text. Source: National Annenberg Election Survey.

Table 14.1

Predictors of Confidence that Supreme Court Fairly Adjudicates 2000 Election Controversy, November 2000–January 2001

Variable	before Bush v. Gore	after Bush v. Gore
Female	−.01	−.14***
	(.05)	(.04)
Black	−.22*	−.60***
	(.09)	(.06)
Age: 25–34	.03	.06
	(.10)	(.07)
Age: 35–54	.06	.00
	(.09)	(.07)
Age: 55 and older	.05	−.09
	(.09)	(.07)
Attendance at religious services	.01	.05
	(.07)	(.06)
Education: high school diploma	−.15	.12
	(.09)	(.08)
Education: some college	−.06	.19*
	(.09)	(.08)
Education: college	−.04	.25**
	(.09)	(.08)
Education: graduate degree	.04	.09
	(.10)	(.08)
South	−.04	.11**
	(.05)	(.04)
Political knowledge	.10	.03
	(.11)	(.09)
Interest in politics	.15	−.11
	(.08)	(.07)
Party identification	−.12	−.97***
	(.07)	(.06)
Political ideology	.03	−.47***
	(.11)	(.09)
General confidence in institutions	1.11***	.85***
	(.11)	(.09)
Constant	2.46***	3.11***
	(.16)	(.13)
R² statistic	.12	.31
N	1,071	2,190
SEE	.74	.84

Cell entries are unstandardized OLS regression coefficients with their standard errors in parentheses. Dependent variable of level of confidence in Supreme Court to deal fairly with the 2000 election controversy is measured on a 4-point scale of 1 (none) to 4 (a great deal). Coefficients are significantly different from zero at * $p<.05$; ** $p<.01$; *** $p<.001$.

Source: National Annenberg Election Study.

Question wording: see text.

branches of government, affects specific support for the Court, and this specific support did not significantly change as a result of the decision.[8] But the decision did affect the association of both party identification and ideology with specific support. Prior to the decision, neither of these variables mattered, but in the period following the decision, both matter a great deal as predictors of specific confidence: the more a respondent leaned toward the Democrats or identified as liberal, the more likely the respondent was to have less specific confidence in the Court after its ruling in *Bush v. Gore*.

Whereas race matters a little as a predictor of support (a coefficient of $-.22$) prior to the Court's decision, its effect significantly increases following the decision ($-.60$), again in the expected direction. Blacks, suspicious of the Court's ability to deal fairly with the election outcome prior to the decision, were even more cynical afterward.

Our model also includes residence in a Southern state, to reflect the sharp regional polarization in the presidential vote. Southern residence is an unimportant predictor before the decision (Southerners are "indifferent" to the Court), but afterward Southerners exhibit a high level of specific support for the Court. The overall fit of this model increases significantly after the decision, with the R-squared statistic increasing from .12 to .31.

As expected, changes in diffuse support (see Figure 14.4) are less dramatic than changes in specific support, validating the assumption that deep-seated institutional loyalty is less likely to change, even among partisan identifiers in the wake of a highly contested decision by the Court. Diffuse support among Democrats remained far below the overall mean, and diffuse support among Republicans increased significantly following the decision, despite some erratic fluctuation. These findings differ from those of Gibson and colleagues (2003b, 554), who concluded that Democrats in the aggregate did not withdraw legitimacy from the Court after the adverse ruling in *Bush v. Gore*.

The relationships between specific individual characteristics and diffuse support are shown in Table 14.2. Although education, institutional confidence, and political interest are key determinants of diffuse support prior to the decision (which comports with the work of Kritzer and of Gibson and his colleagues), after the decision their importance is wholly supplanted by political variables like party identification and ideology.[9]

As might be expected, institutional confidence is significantly more important in predicting diffuse support than in predicting specific support; one expects diffuse loyalty to be tied more closely to respondents' opinions of other institutions and less to the specific controversy at hand. In the post-decision period, race also becomes a significant predictor of diffuse support, although race was not a significant predictor before the decision. After the decision, blacks were less likely to have high levels of diffuse support than others. In sum, then, it appears that the foundations of even diffuse support for the Supreme Court were significantly altered as a result of the decision, at least in the short term.

Table 14.2

Predictors of "Diffuse" Support for the Judicial Branch, including the U.S. Supreme Court, November 2000–January 2001

Variable	before Bush v. Gore	after Bush v. Gore
Female	.02	−.02
	(.04)	(.03)
Black	−.14	−.31***
	(.08)	(.05)
Age: 25–34	−.08	−.12*
	(.09)	(.06)
Age: 35–54	−.09	−.12*
	(.08)	(.05)
Age: 55 and older	−.07	−.20***
	(.09)	(.06)
Attendance at religious services	.04	−.04
	(.07)	(.05)
Education: high school diploma	.09	−.07
	(.08)	(.06)
Education: some college	.20*	.00
	(.08)	(.06)
Education: college	.26**	.07
	(.09)	(.07)
Education: graduate degree	.33***	.11
	(.09)	(.07)
South	−.10*	.09*
	(.05)	(.03)
Political knowledge	.19	.13
	(.10)	(.08)
Interest in politics	.28***	−.01
	(.08)	(.06)
Party identification	−.04	−.24***
	(.07)	(.05)
Political ideology	.10	−.12
	(.10)	(.07)
Confidence in institutions	1.74***	1.73***
	(.10)	(.07)
Constant	1.49***	2.12***
	(.14)	(.11)
R^2 statistic	.29	.26
N	1,072	2,203
SEE	.67	.68

Cell entries are unstandardized OLS regression coefficients with their standard errors in parentheses. Dependent variable of level of confidence in the judicial system is measured on a 4-point scale of 1 (none) to 4 (a great deal). Coefficients are significantly different from zero at *$p < .05$; ** $p < .01$; *** $p < .001$.

Source: National Annenberg Election Study.

Question wording: see text.

Table 14.3
Predictors of the Difference between Americans' "Diffuse" and "Specific" Support of the Supreme Court, November 2000–January 2001

Variable	before *Bush v. Gore*	after *Bush v. Gore*
Female	.03	.11**
	(.05)	(.04)
Black	.09	.30***
	(.10)	(.07)
Age: 25–34	−.11	−.18*
	(.10)	(.07)
Age: 35–54	−.15	−.12
	(.09)	(.07)
Age: 55 and older	−.12	−.11
	(.10)	(.07)
Attendance at religious services	.04	−.09
	(.08)	(.06)
Education: high school diploma	.25**	−.17*
	(.10)	(.08)
Education: some college	.25**	−.17*
	(.10)	(.08)
Education: college	.30**	−.16
	(.10)	(.08)
Education: graduate degree	.28**	.04
	(.11)	(.09)
South	−.06	−.03
	(.05)	(.04)
Political knowledge	.09	.10
	(.12)	(.09)
Interest in politics	.13	.10
	(.09)	(.07)
Party identification	.08	.74***
	(.08)	(.06)
Political ideology	.08	.33***
	(.12)	(.09)
Confidence in institutions	.63***	.89***
	(.12)	(.09)
Constant	−.99***	−1.00***
	(.17)	(.13)
R^2 statistic	.05	.18
N	1,062	2,180
SEE	.79	.85

Cell entries are unstandardized OLS regression coefficients with their standard errors in parentheses. Dependent variable is difference between diffuse and specific support for the Supreme Court, each measured on a 4-point scale of 1 (none) to 4 (a great deal). Coefficients are significantly different from zero at *$p < .05$; ** $p < .01$; *** $p < .001$.

Source: National Annenberg Election Study.

Question wording: see text.

We also performed a regression analysis for our new variable, residual support (see Table 14.3). We subtracted each respondent's answer to the specific support question from the answer to the diffuse support question, and coded the result on a scale from −3 to +3, where −3 = very high specific support relative to diffuse support, 0 = equal diffuse and specific support, and +3 = very high diffuse support relative to specific support. We expected three coefficients to be positive and sizable—party identification, ideology, and race—because Democrats, liberals, and blacks all disliked the Supreme Court's specific decision (see Table 14.1), despite the fact that their diffuse support for the Court is typically strong (see Table 14.2). Conversely, the more conservative and Republican respondents, all else being equal, were more likely to strongly support the specific decision and the Court's handling of it, while being suspicious of the Court more generally.

These expectations were confirmed by the data. Interestingly, gender became significant after the decision, though not before, suggesting that women became more differentiated in terms of their specific and diffuse levels of support after the decision. In addition, the predictive value of educational attainment changed: among those with higher levels of education, diffuse support for the Court was quite high relative to specific support before the decision, but not after the decision. The fit of the model also improves after the decision, from an R-squared of .05 to .18.

Diffuse Support in 2004

The 2004 NAES did not include a measure of specific support comparable to the one we selected from the 2000 survey,[10] but it did include the same diffuse support item. We compared the responses in 2004 with those in 2000 to gauge whether the partisan, ideological, and racial polarization persisted (see Table 14.4).

The impact of race on diffuse support seems to have declined to its pre-*Bush v. Gore* level. Blacks still view the Court less favorably than whites do, but the extra negativity engendered by the decision seems to have disappeared. Moreover, the partisan polarization apparent in the 2000 postdecision period also seems to have largely disappeared. Indeed, the change in sign on the regression coefficient associated with party identification indicates that the effect has reversed: In 2004, diffuse support for the Court among Democrats was slightly higher than it had been before the *Bush v. Gore* decision, though the substantive significance of this finding is quite minor. Finally, the role of ideology has reversed also unexpectedly: liberals are much more supportive of the Court than they were even prior to the *Bush v. Gore* decision.

Our finding that ideology appears to play an important role as a determinant of diffuse support for the Court is different from that of Gibson (2006), who found that support for the Court was not strongly affected by the ideology of respondents in his 2005 data. Analyzing data from a 2005 survey, Gibson (2006, 15) suggests that there is "no evidence that the current political

Table 14.4

Predictors of "Diffuse" Support for the Judicial Branch, including the
U.S. Supreme Court, 2000 and 2004

	2000		2004
	before *Bush v. Gore*	After *Bush v. Gore*	
Black	−.14	−.31***	−.13***
	(.08)	(.05)	(.03)
Party identification	−.04	−.24***	.04***
	(.07)	(.05)	(.01)
Political ideology	.10	−.12	.38***
	(.10)	(.07)	(.03)
Confidence in institutions	1.74***	1.73***	1.75***
	(.10)	(.07)	(.03)
R² statistic	.05	.18	.22
N	1,062	2,180	10,674
SEE	.79	.85	.68

Cell entries are unstandardized OLS regression coefficients with their standard errors in parentheses. Dependent variable of level of confidence in the judicial system is measured on a 4-point scale of 1 (none) to 4 (a great deal). Models include controls for respondents' age, education, attendance at religious services, residence in the South, political interest, and political knowledge, plus an intercept (not shown). Coefficients are significantly different from zero at $p < .05$; ** $p < .01$; *** $p < .001$.

Question wording: see text.

Source for data: National Annenberg Election Study.

Question wording: see text.

climate has tainted the legitimacy" of the Court and that the "legitimacy of the Supreme Court has not been undermined within this most recent period of strong partisanship"; he also notes that the Court still enjoys an "extraordinarily wide and deep reservoir of goodwill" (16). Gibson finds that neither partisanship nor ideology affects diffuse support for the Court; instead, diffuse support for the Court is "grounded in broader commitments to democratic institutions and processes, and more generally in knowledge of the role of the judiciary in the American democratic system" (23).

Although *Bush v. Gore* may have had little impact on the partisan bases for diffuse support four years later, the NAES data suggest that the Court's decisions in the intervening period may have affected the ideological foundations of diffuse support. In part, this may be explained by the Rehnquist Court's key decisions on social and cultural issues during this period. As Tushnet (2005) suggests, the Rehnquist Court was not ideologically a conservative Court across all issue domains. Although the Rehnquist Court supported the agenda of economic conservatives, it did not follow the cultural conservative agenda in its decisions dealing with social or cultural issues (Tushnet 2005; see Clayton 2007).

The 2004 data might reflect approval or disapproval of the Court's land-mark decisions in *Lawrence v. Texas* (2003) (invalidating a state law banning sodomy), *Grutter v. Bollinger* (2003) (upholding the University of Michigan Law School's affirmative action program), and *McConnell v. FEC* (2003) (upholding McCain-Feingold campaign finance law regulating soft money). Arguably, the Court's decisions in these cases were more or less aligned with the liberal position on the underlying issues.

The NAES data from 2004 suggest that political ideology matters as a determinant or predictor of diffuse support for the Court. This finding may support the value-based regeneration model of Mondak and Smithey (1997) in demonstrating that the Court can indeed regenerate institutional support through decisions that reaffirm core democratic values and the Court's role "as protector of the Constitution and champion of justice and civil liberties" (Mondak & Smithey 1997, 1123). In addition, the Court's role as a countermajoritarian check on a Republican president and Congress may help explain why liberals support the Court, especially in the context of the administration's policies in the "war on terror" and their impact on civil liberties.

Alternatively, these data may show that the Court demonstrated a remark-able resiliency in restoring the ideological bases of diffuse support. In general, these findings suggest that the effects of the *Bush v. Gore* decision on the deter-minants of diffuse support have all but disappeared, and that such support is being driven by other factors altogether in 2004.

Conclusion

The Supreme Court's decision in *Bush v. Gore* altered the structure of public confidence in the Court in that after the decision, partisan identification, ide-ology, and race were more strongly associated with levels of both diffuse and specific support. In line with Mondak and Smithey's (1997) views of legiti-macy, these findings show that a specific decision that is both highly salient and highly politicized can erode even diffuse support for the Supreme Court among certain groups of people.

However, polarization was far weaker on the measure of diffuse support, and the increased partisan gap largely disappeared by 2004. Gibson (2006, 18), relying on 2005 data from his own survey, found little evidence that party identification had an impact on diffuse support or institutional loyalty and observed that support for the Court did not suffer from partisan polarization. In other words, the Court had sufficient institutional capital to weather the short-term impact of the decision.

Our finding that liberals' support for the Court was higher in 2004 than in 2000 may suggest either that the Court was able to regenerate institutional support among liberals in the intervening period or that the Court has gradu-ally developed a base of support among liberals that is relatively immune from short-term political "shocks" like *Bush v. Gore*. In a sense, liberals have become the natural constituency of the Court, which has often served as a counterma-joritarian bulwark in the areas of individual rights, criminal procedure, and civil liberties. During the Warren years, the Court defined itself as a guardian and arbiter of individual rights and civil liberties. Although the Rehnquist Court was on balance a more conservative Court, in some areas it followed the Warren Court in continuing to uphold and protect core individual rights and civil liberties. Many liberals continue to support that vision even as the Court has become more conservative in recent years.

APPENDIX: Measures

Dependent Variables

Specific Support

Question Text: "How much confidence do you have {through 12 Dec 00: in | starting 13 Dec 00: that} the US Supreme Court {to deal | dealt} fairly with the situation surrounding the results of the election for president? A great deal, a fair amount, not too much or none at all?" Coding: Scored from 1 (None at all) to 4 (A Great Deal).

Diffuse Support

Question Text: "Please tell me how much confidence you have in the Judicial Branch of the federal government—this includes the US Supreme Court. Do you have a great deal, a fair amount, not too much or none at all?"

Residual Support

This question is the mathematical difference between a respondent's diffuse support and his or her specific support. More specifically, the latter is subtracted from the former. Coding: −3 = Very high specific support relative to diffuse support; 0 = Equal diffuse and specific support; 3 = Very high diffuse support relative to specific support.

Independent Variables

Age: 4 Categories, dummy variables for 17–24, 25–34, and 55+. 35–54 is the base.

Education: 4 Categories, dummy variables for High School, Some College, College Degree, and Post-Graduate/Advanced Degree. Less than High School is the base.

Race: Dichotomous, black or white, white is the base category.

Gender: Dichotomous, male is the base category.

South: Dichotomous, non-South is the base.

Religious Attendance

Question Text: "How often do you attend religious services, apart from special events like weddings and funerals? More than once a week, once a week, once or twice a month, a few times a year or never?" Coding: Scored from 0 = Never to 1 = More Than Once a Week.

Political Interest

Question Text: "Some people seem to follow what is going on in government and public affairs most of the time, whether there is an election or not. Others are not that interested. Would you say you follow what is going on in government and public affairs most of the time, some of the time, only now and then or hardly at all?" Coding: Scored from 0 = Hardly to 1 = Most of the Time.

Political Knowledge: Based on interviewer evaluation of respondent's apparent level of political sophistication. Coding: Scored from 0 = Least to 1 = Most.

Party ID: 5 Category, coded from 0 = Strong Republican to 1 = Strong Democrat.

Ideology: Respondent ideological self-rating, 5 category, coded from 0 = Extremely Conservative to 1 = Extremely Liberal.

Institutional Confidence: Factor score of respondents' overall confidence in the Executive Branch, Congress, and the Military and scored from 0 = Least Institutional Confidence to 1 = Most Institutional Confidence).

Notes

1. In their 1997 article, Mondak and Smithey explain the concept of negativity bias as follows: "Negative reactions to Supreme Court decisions will more strongly affect subsequent evaluation of the institution than will positive reaction to decisions" (1123).

2. This work builds on Caldeira and Gibson (1992), who found that "basic democratic values, not reactions to decisions, were the strongest determinants of institutional support" (Grosskopf & Mondak 1998, 635, citing Caldeira & Gibson 1992).

3. Between late November 2000 and mid-January 2001, on average 100 interviews were conducted daily, and these were accompanied by reinterviews of 6,508 respondents interviewed before the November election to form a pre-post general election panel (NAES Codebook, i1–i5). (See Romer et al. 2006).

4. Caldeira (1986, 1224 n. 1) is also instructive on this point: "On a number of occasions during the 1970s, Gallup asked the public, 'Would you tell me how much

confidence you, yourself, have in each one [a list of institutions, of which the Court was one]—a great deal, quite a lot, some, or very little?' Gallup apparently taps a phenomenon one might label *diffuse support*." Cf. Grosskopf and Mondak (1998, 641) on the difference between the GSS measure and Caldeira and Gibson's diffuse support measure: "Reference to the 'people in charge of running the Supreme Court' likely encourages respondents to contemplate current events rather than institutional history when answering the question, and thus the item is not comparable to measures of diffuse support, such as the one developed by Caldeira and Gibson (1992)."

5. The NAES asked: "If when the Supreme Court rules on whether the Florida recount should proceed, both presidential candidates accept the ruling as the final decision on the presidential election, how likely would you be to also consider it the final decision on the election? Very likely, somewhat likely, not too likely or not at all likely?" (December 11 and 12, 2000).

6. The NAES asked: "How likely do you think strong supporters of both presidential candidates would be to consider the Supreme Court's ruling the final decision on the election? Very likely, somewhat likely, not too likely or not at all likely?" (December 11 and 12, 2000).

7. Gibson and his colleagues (2003a, 541–543, n. 28) acknowledge the weaknesses of their methodology, which employs a comparison of two cross-sectional surveys, one in 1987, and a second in 2001, to analyze individual-level change in public opinion. They admit that this method ignores the possibility that support for the Court in October 2000 may have been at much higher levels than in 1987 or 1995, and that the election controversy may have dramatically lowered this support.

8. Caldeira (1986) reports that earlier scholarship on the "presidential association" showed that opinions toward the executive branch affected attitudes toward the court (Casey 1975) and that individuals who trust in the federal government tend to exhibit greater support for the Court (Murphy et al. 1973).

9. Kritzer's model (2001), which used the general job performance approval rating of the Court as a dependent variable, generated similar results, with knowledge and political attention paid to national politics as the only statistically significant predictors of approval before the decision (education is only marginally significant at $p < .10$); after the decision, party identification and frequency of discussion of politics became significant, and attention paid to politics is replaced by interest in national politics.

10. Harris Interactive's polling in 2004 and 2005 on the conventional measure of confidence in the Court reported much lower numbers for the "great deal of confidence" category—only 29%, compared with 34%–35% from 2001 to 2004.

References

Caldeira, Gregory A. 1986. "Neither the Purse nor the Sword: Dynamics of Public Confidence in the Supreme Court." *American Political Science Review* 80(4): 1209–26.

Caldeira, Gregory A., and James L. Gibson. 1992. "The Etiology of Public Support for the Supreme Court." *American Journal of Political Science* 36(3): 635–64.

Casey, Gregory. 1975. "The Theory of Presidential Association: An Empirical Investigation." *Law & Society Review* 8:385–419.

Clayton, Cornell. 2007. "The Supreme Court and the Political Regime: The Role of the Supreme Court in American Democracy." Paper presented at the symposium Seeking a Democratic Foundation for the Judiciary: Judicial Politics and Judicial Philosophy in the U.S., Kyoto University, March 17–18, 2007.

Easton, David. 1965. *A Systems Analysis of Political Life*. New York: Wiley.

Easton, David. 1975. "A Re-Assessment of the Concept of Political Support." *British Journal of Political Science* 5: 435–57.

Franklin, Charles H., and Liane C. Kosaki. 1989. "Republican Schoolmaster: The U.S. Supreme Court, Public Opinion and Abortion." *American Political Science Review* 83: 751–71.

Gibson, James L. 2006. *The Legitimacy of the United States Supreme Court in a Polarized Polity*. Available at http://ssrn.com/abstract =909162.

Gibson, James L., Gregory A. Caldeira, and Lester Kenyatta Spence. 2003a. "Measuring Attitudes toward the United States Supreme Court." *American Journal of Political Science* 47(2): 354–67.

Gibson, James L., Gregory A. Caldeira, and Lester Kenyatta Spence. 2003b. "The Supreme Court and the Presidential Election of 2000: Wounds, Self-Inflicted or Otherwise?" *British Journal of Political Science* 33(4): 535–56.

Grosskopf, Anke, and Jeffrey J. Mondak. 1998. "Do Attitudes toward Specific Supreme Court Decisions Matter? The Impact of *Webster* and *Texas v. Johnson* on Public Confidence in the Supreme Court." *Political Research Quarterly* 51(3): 633–54.

Jaros, Dean, and Robert Roper. 1980. "The U.S. Supreme Court: Myth, Diffuse Support, Specific Support and Legitimacy." *American Politics Quarterly* 23: 85–105.

Kritzer, Herbert M. 2001. "Into the Electoral Waters: The Impact of *Bush v. Gore* on Public Perceptions and Knowledge of the Supreme Court." Presentation at 2001 annual meeting of the Law & Society Association, Budapest, Hungary, July 4–7. Available at http://www.polisci.wisc.edu/~kritzer/research/opinion/BvG_Impact.pdf. Accessed August 18, 2007.

Marshall, Thomas R. 1989. *Public Opinion and the Supreme Court*. New York: Longman.

Mondak, Jeffrey J., and Shannon Ishiyama Smithey. 1997. "The Dynamics of Public Support for the Supreme Court." *Journal of Politics* 59(4): 1114–42.

Murphy, Walter F., Joseph Tanenhaus, and Daniel Kastner. 1973. *Public Evaluations of Constitutional Courts: Alternative Explanations*. Beverly Hills: Sage Publications.

Romer, Daniel, Kate Kenski, Paul Waldman, Christopher Adasiewicz, and Kathleen Hall Jameson. 2006. *Capturing Campaign Dynamics, 2000 and 2004: The National Annenberg Election Survey*. Philadelphia: University of Pennsylvania Press.

Scheb II, John M., and William Lyons. 2000: "The Myth of Legality and Public Evaluation of the Supreme Court." *Social Science Quarterly* 81: 929–40.

Tanenhaus, Joseph, and Walter F. Murphy. 1981. "Patterns of Public Support for the Supreme Court: A Panel Study." *Journal of Politics* 43: 24.

Tushnet, Mark. 2005. *A Court Divided: The Rehnquist Court and the Future of Constitutional Law*. New York: W. W. Norton.

Index